CHILTON BOOK COMPANY

REPAIR & TUNE-UP GUIDE

MAZDA PICK-UPS 1971-86

All U.S. and Canadian models of B1600 • B1800 • B2000 •
B2000 Cab Plus • B2000 SE-5 • B2000 LX • B2200 • Rotary Pick-up

W9-CTA-254

President LAWRENCE A. FORNASIERI
Vice President and General Manager JOHN P. KUSHNERICK
Editor-in-Chief KERRY A. FREEMAN, S.A.E.
Managing Editor DEAN F. MORGANTINI, S.A.E.
Senior Editor RICHARD J. RIVELE, S.A.E.
Senior Editor W. CALVIN SETTLE, JR., S.A.E.

CHILTON BOOK COMPANY
Radnor, Pennsylvania
19089

SAFETY NOTICE

Proper service and repair procedures are vital to the safe, reliable operation of all motor vehicles, as well as the personal safety of those performing repairs. This book outlines procedures for servicing and repairing vehicles using safe, effective methods. The procedures contain many NOTES, CAUTIONS and WARNINGS which should be followed along with standard safety procedures to eliminate the possibility of personal injury or improper service which could damage the vehicle or compromise its safety.

It is important to note that repair procedures and techniques, tools and parts for servicing motor vehicles, as well as the skill and experience of the individual performing the work vary widely. It is not possible to anticipate all of the conceivable ways or conditions under which vehicles may be serviced, or to provide cautions as to all of the possible hazards that may result. Standard and accepted safety precautions and equipment should be used during cutting, grinding, chiseling, prying, or any other process that can cause material removal or projectiles.

Some procedures require the use of tools specially designed for a specific purpose. Before substituting another tool or procedure, you must be completely satisfied that neither your personal safety, nor the performance of the vehicle will be endangered.

Although the information in this guide is based on industry sources and is as complete as possible at the time of publication, the possibility exists that the manufacturer made later changes which could not be included here. While striving for total accuracy, Chilton Book Company cannot assume responsibility for any errors, changes, or omissions that may occur in the compilation of this data.

PART NUMBERS

Part numbers listed in this reference are not recommendations by Chilton for any product by brand name. They are references that can be used with interchange manuals and aftermarket supplier catalogs to locate each brand supplier's discrete part number.

SPECIAL TOOLS

Special tools are recommended by the vehicle manufacturer to perform their specific job. Use has been kept to a minimum, but where absolutely necessary, they are referred to the text by the part number of the tool manufacturer. These tools can be purchased, under the appropriate part number, from your Mazda dealer or regional distributor or an equivalent tool can be purchased locally from a tool supplier or parts outlet. Before substituting any tool for the one recommended, read the SAFETY NOTICE at the top of this page.

ACKNOWLEDGMENTS

The Chilton Book Company expresses its appreciation to the Mazda Technical Center, Inc., Irvine, California 92714; YBH Mazda, Inc., Edgemount, Pennsylvania 19028; Mazda Motors of America (East), Inc., Jacksonville, Florida; and Toyo Kogyo Co., Ltd., Hiroshima, Japan.

Copyright © 1986 by Chilton Book Company
All Rights Reserved
Published in Radnor, Pennsylvania 19089 by Chilton Book Company

Manufactured in the United States of America
    567890   54321098

Chilton's Repair & Tune-Up Guide: Mazda Pick-Ups 1971–86
ISBN 0-8019-7659-6 pbk.
Library of Congress Catalog Card No. 85-47960

CONTENTS

Quick Reference
Specifications For Your Vehicle

Fill in this chart with the most commonly used specifications for your vehicle. Specifications can be found in Chapters 1 through 3 or on the tune-up decal under the hood of the vehicle.

 ## Tune-Up

Firing Order_____

Spark Plugs:

    Type_____

    Gap (in.)_____

Torque (ft. lbs.)_____

Idle Speed (rpm)_____

Ignition Timing (°)_____

    Vacuum or Electronic Advance (Connected/Disconnected)_____

Valve Clearance (in.)

    Intake_____   **Exhaust**_____

 ## Capacities

Engine Oil Type (API Rating)_____

    With Filter Change (qts)_____

    Without Filter Change (qts)_____

Cooling System (qts)_____

Manual Transmission (pts)_____

    Type_____

Automatic Transmission (pts)_____

    Type_____

Front Differential (pts)_____

    Type_____

Rear Differential (pts)_____

    Type_____

Transfer Case (pts)_____

    Type_____

FREQUENTLY REPLACED PARTS

Use these spaces to record the part numbers of frequently replaced parts.

PCV VALVE	OIL FILTER	AIR FILTER	FUEL FILTER
Type_____	Type_____	Type_____	Type_____
Part No._____	Part No._____	Part No._____	Part No._____

General Information and Maintenance

1

HOW TO USE THIS BOOK

Chilton's Repair & Tune-Up Guide for Mazda Pick-Ups is intended to help you learn more about the inner workings of your truck and save you money on its upkeep and operation.

The first two chapters will be the most used, since they contain maintenance and tune-up information and procedures. Studies have shown that a properly tuned and maintained truck can get at least 10% better gas mileage (which translates into lower operating costs) and periodic maintenance will catch minor problems before they turn into major repair bills. The other chapters deal with the more complex systems of your truck. Operating systems from engine through brakes are covered to the extent that the average do-it-yourselfer becomes mechanically involved. This book will not explain such things as rebuilding the differential for the simple reason that the expertise required and the investment in special tools make this task uneconomical. It will give you the detailed instructions to help you change your own brake pads and shoes, tune-up the engine, replace spark plugs and filters, and do many more jobs that will save you money, give you personal satisfaction and help you avoid expensive problems.

A secondary purpose of this book is a reference guide for owners who want to understand their truck and/or their mechanics better. In this case, no tools at all are required. Knowing just what a particular repair job requires in parts and labor time will allow you to evaluate whether or not you're getting a fair price quote and help decipher itemized bills from a repair shop.

Before attempting any repairs or service on your truck, read through the entire procedure outlined in the appropriate chapter. This will give you the overall view of what tools and supplies will be required. There is nothing more frustrating than having to walk to the bus stop on Monday morning because you were short one gasket on Sunday afternoon. So read ahead and plan ahead. Each operation should be approached logically and all procedures thoroughly understood before attempting any work. Some special tools that may be required can often be rented from local automotive jobbers or places specializing in renting tools and equipment. Check the yellow pages of your phone book.

All chapters contain adjustments, maintenance, removal and installation procedures, and overhaul procedures. When overhaul is not considered practical, we tell you how to remove the failed part and then how to install the new or rebuilt replacement. In this way, you at least save the labor costs. Backyard overhaul of some components (such as the alternator or water pump) is just not practical, but the removal and installation procedure is often simple and well within the capabilities of the average truck owner.

Two basic mechanic's rules should be mentioned here. First, whenever the LEFT side of the truck or engine is referred to, it is meant to specify the DRIVER'S side of the truck. Conversely, the RIGHT side of the truck means the PASSENGER'S side. Second, all screws and bolts are removed by turning counterclockwise, and tightened by turning clockwise.

Safety is always the most important rule. Constantly be aware of the dangers involved in working on or around an automobile and take proper precautions to avoid the risk of personal injury or damage to the vehicle. See the section in this chapter "Servicing Your Vehicle Safely" and the SAFETY NOTICE on the acknowledgment page before attempting any service procedures and pay attention to the instructions provided. There are 3 common mistakes in mechanical work:

1. Incorrect order of assembly, disassembly

or adjustment. When taking something apart or putting it together, doing things in the wrong order usually just costs you extra time; however it CAN break something. Read the entire procedure before beginning disassembly. Do everything in the order in which the instructions say you should do it, even if you can't immediately see a reason for it. When you're taking apart something that is very intricate (for example a carburetor), you might want to draw a picture of how it looks when assembled at one point in order to make sure you get everything back in its proper position. We will supply exploded views whenever possible, but sometimes the job requires more attention to detail than an illustration provides. When making adjustments (especially tune-up adjustments), do them in order. One adjustment often affects another and you cannot expect satisfactory results unless each adjustment is made only when it cannot be changed by any other.

2. Overtorquing (or undertorquing) nuts and bolts. While it is more common for overtorquing to cause damage, undertorquing can cause a fastener to vibrate loose and cause serious damage, especially when dealing with aluminum parts. Pay attention to torque specifications and utilize a torque wrench in assembly. If a torque figure is not available remember that, if you are using the right tool to do the job, you will probably not have to strain yourself to get a fastener tight enough. The pitch of most threads is so slight that the tension you put on the wrench will be multiplied many times in actual force on what you are tightening. A good example of how critical torque is can be seen in the case of spark plug installation, especially where you are putting the plug into an aluminum cylinder head. Too little torque can fail to crush the gasket, causing leakage of combustion gases and consequent overheating of the plug and engine parts. Too much torque can damage the threads or distort the plug, which changes the spark gap at the electrode. Since more and more manufacturers are using aluminum in their engine and chassis parts to save weight, a torque wrench should be in any serious do-it-yourselfer's tool box.

There are many commercial chemical products available for ensuring that fasteners won't come loose, even if they are not torqued just right (a very common brand is Loctite®). If you're worried about getting something together tight enough to hold, but loose enough to avoid mechanical damage during assembly, one of these products might offer substantial insurance. Read the label on the package and make sure the product is compatible with the materials, fluids, etc. involved before choosing one.

3. Crossthreading. This occurs when a part such as a bolt is screwed into a nut or casting at the wrong angle and forced, causing the threads to become damaged. Crossthreading is more likely to occur if access is difficult. It helps to clean and lubricate fasteners, and to start threading with the part to be installed going straight in, using your fingers. If you encounter resistance, unscrew the part and start over again at a different angle until it can be inserted and turned several times without much effort. Keep in mind that many parts, especially spark plugs, use tapered threads so that gentle turning will automatically bring the part you're threading to the proper angle if you don't force it or resist a change in angle. Don't put a wrench on the part until it's been turned in a couple of times by hand. If you suddenly encounter resistance and the part has not seated fully, don't force it. Pull it back out and make sure it's clean and threading properly.

Always take your time and be patient; once you have some experience, working on your truck will become an enjoyable hobby.

TOOLS AND EQUIPMENT

Naturally, without the proper tools and equipment it is impossible to properly service your vehicle. It would be impossible to catalog each tool that you would need to perform each or every operation in this book. It would also be unwise for the amateur to rush out and buy an expensive set of tools on the theory that he may need one or more of them at sometime.

The best approach is to proceed slowly, gathering together a good quality set of those tools that are used most frequently. Don't be misled by the low cost of bargain tools. It is far better to spend a little more for better quality. Forged wrenches, 10 or 12 point sockets and fine tooth ratchets are by far preferable to their less expensive counterparts. As any good mechanic can tell you, there are few worse experiences than trying to work on a truck with bad tools. Your monetary savings will be far outweighed by frustration and mangled knuckles.

Begin accumulating those tools that are used most frequently; those associated with routine maintenance and tune-up.

In addition to the normal assortment of screwdrivers and pliers you should have the following tools for routine maintenance jobs (your Mazda, depending on the model year, uses both SAE and metric fasteners):

1. SAE/Metric wrenches, sockets and combination open end/box end wrenches in sizes from 1/8 in. (3mm) to 3/4 in. (19mm); and a spark plug socket (13/16 in.)

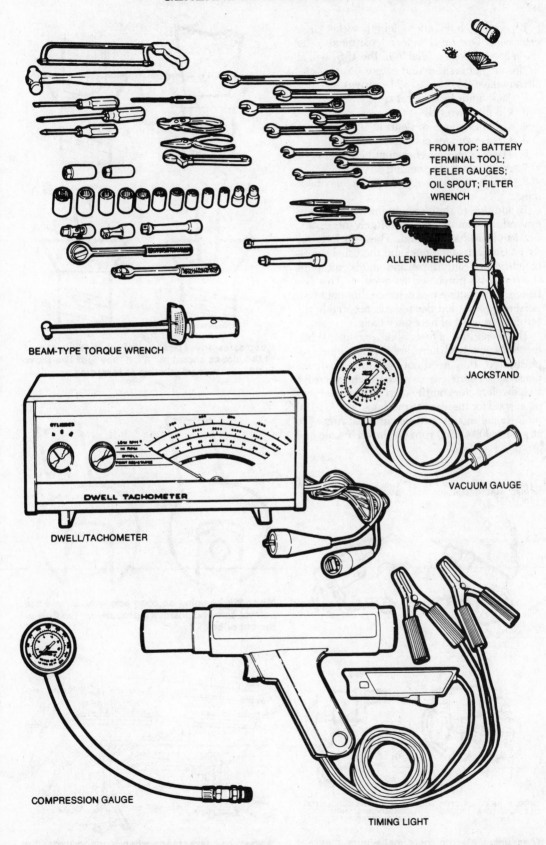

FROM TOP: BATTERY TERMINAL TOOL; FEELER GAUGES; OIL SPOUT; FILTER WRENCH

ALLEN WRENCHES

BEAM-TYPE TORQUE WRENCH

JACKSTAND

DWELL TACHOMETER

DWELL/TACHOMETER

VACUUM GAUGE

COMPRESSION GAUGE

TIMING LIGHT

You need only a basic assortment of hand tools and test instruments for most maintenance and repair jobs

If possible, buy various length socket drive extensions. One break in this department is that the metric sockets available in the U.S. will all fit the ratchet handles and extensions you may already have (¼, ⅜, and ½ in. drive).

2. Jackstands for support
3. Oil filter wrench
4. Oil filter spout for pouring oil
5. Grease gun for chassis lubrication
6. Hydrometer for checking the battery
7. A container for draining oil
8. Many rags for wiping up the inevitable mess.

In addition to the above items there are several others that are not absolutely necessary, but handy to have around. These include oil-dry, a transmission funnel and the usual supply of lubricants, antifreeze and fluids, although these can be purchased as needed. This is a basic list for routine maintenance, but only your personal needs and desires can accurately determine your list of necessary tools.

The second list of tools is for tune-ups. While the tools involved here are slightly more sophisticated, they need not be outrageously expensive. There are several inexpensive tach/dwell meters on the market that are every bit as good for the average mechanic as a $100.00 professional model. Just be sure that it goes to at least 1,200–1,500 rpm on the tach scale and

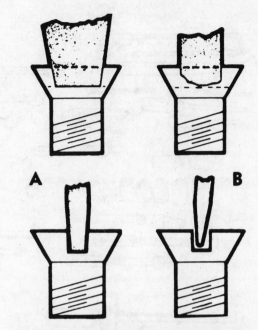

A   B

Keep screwdriver tips in good shape. They should fit the slot as shown in "A". If they look like those in "B", they need grinding or replacing

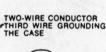

TWO-WIRE CONDUCTOR THIRD WIRE GROUNDING THE CASE

THREE-WIRE CONDUCTOR GROUNDING THRU A CIRCUIT

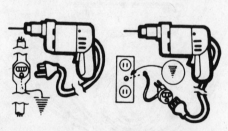

THREE-WIRE CONDUCTOR ONE WIRE TO A GROUND

THREE-WIRE CONDUCTOR GROUNDING THRU AN ADAPTER PLUG

When using electric tools make sure they properly grounded

When you're using an open end wrench, use the correct size and position it properly on the flats of the nut or bolt

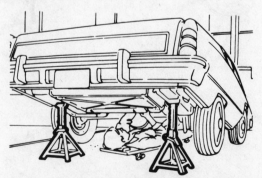

Always use jackstands when working under the truck

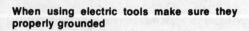

that it works on 4, 6 and 8 cylinder engines. A basic list of tune-up equipment could include:

1. Tach-dwell meter
2. Spark plug wrench
3. Timing light (a DC light that works from the truck's battery is best, although an AC light that plugs into 110V house current will suffice at some sacrifice in brightness)
4. Wire spark plug gauge/adjusting tools
5. Set of feeler blades.

Here again, be guided by your own needs. A feeler blade will set the point gap as easily as dwell meter will read dwell, but slightly less accurately. And since you will need a tachometer anyway . . . well, make your own decision.

In addition to these basic tools, there are several other tools and gauges you may find useful. These include:

1. A compression gauge. The screw-in type is slower to use, but eliminates the possibility of a faulty reading due to escaping pressure
2. A manifold vacuum gauge
3. A test light
4. An induction meter. This is used for determining whether or not there is current in a wire. These are handy for use if a wire is broken somewhere in a wiring harness.

As a final note, you will probably find a torque wrench necessary for all but the most basic work. The beam type models are perfectly adequate, although the newer click (breakaway) type are more precise, and you don't have to crane your neck to see a torque reading in awkward situations. The breakaway torque wrenches are more expensive and should be recalibrated periodically.

Torque specification for each fastener will be given in the procedure in any case that a specific torque value is required. If no torque specifications are given, use the following values as a guide, based upon fastener size:

Bolts marked 6T
- 6mm bolt/nut — 5–7 ft.lb.
- 8mm bolt/nut — 12–17 ft.lb.
- 10mm bolt/nut — 23–34 ft.lb.
- 12mm bolt/nut — 41–59 ft.lb.
- 14mm bolt/nut — 56–76 ft.lb.

Bolts marked 8T
- 6mm bolt/nut — 6–9 ft.lb.
- 8mm bolt/nut — 13–20 ft.lb.
- 10mm bolt/nut — 27–40 ft.lb.
- 12mm bolt/nut — 46–69 ft.lb.
- 14mm bolt/nut — 75–101 ft.lb.

Special Tools

Normally, the use of special factory tools is avoided for repair procedures, since these are not readily available for the do-it-yourself mechanic. When it is possible to perform the job with more commonly available tools, it will be pointed out, but occasionally, a special tool was designed to perform a specific function and should be used. Before substituting another tool, you should be convinced that neither your safety nor the performance of the vehicle will be compromised.

Some special tools are available commercially from major tool manufacturers. Others can be purchased through your Mazda dealer.

SERVICING YOUR VEHICLE SAFELY

It is virtually impossible to anticipate all of the hazards involved with automotive maintenance and service, but care and common sense will prevent most accidents.

The rules of safety for mechanics range from "don't smoke around gasoline," to "use the proper tool for the job." The trick to avoiding injuries is to develop safe work habits and take every possible precaution.

Do's

- Do keep a fire extinguisher and first aid kit within easy reach.
- Do wear safety glasses or goggles when cutting, drilling or prying, even if you have 20–20 vision. If you wear glasses for the sake of vision, they should be made of hardened glass that can also serve as safety glasses, or wear safety goggles over your regular glasses.
- Do shield your eyes whenever you work around the battery. Batteries contain sulphuric acid; in case of contact with the eyes or skin, flush the area with water or a mixture of water and baking soda and get medical attention immediately.
- Do use safety stands for any undertruck service. Jacks are for raising vehicles; safety stands are for making sure the vehicle stays raised until you want it to come down. Whenever the vehicle is raised, block the wheels remaining on the ground and set the parking brake.
- Do use adequate ventilation when working with any chemicals. Like carbon monoxide, the asbestos dust resulting from brake lining wear can be poisonous in sufficient quantities.
- Do disconnect the negative battery cable when working on the electrical system. The primary ignition system can contain up to 40,000 volts.
- Do follow manufacturer's directions whenever working with potentially hazardous mate-

rials. Both brake fluid and antifreeze are poisonous if taken internally.

• Do properly maintain your tools. Loose hammerheads, mushroomed punches and chisels, frayed or poorly grounded electrical cords, excessively worn screwdrivers, spread wrenches (open end), cracked sockets, slipping ratchets, or faulty droplight sockets can cause accidents.

• Do use the proper size and type of tool for the job being done.

• Do when possible, pull on a wrench handle rather than push on it, and adjust your stance to prevent a fall.

• Do be sure that adjustable wrenches are tightly adjusted on the nut or bolt and pulled so that the face is on the side of the fixed jaw.

• Do select a wrench or socket that fits the nut or bolt. The wrench or socket should sit straight, not cocked.

• Do strike squarely with a hammer—avoid glancing blows.

• Do set the parking brake and block the drive wheels if the work requires that the engine be running.

Don'ts

• Don't run an engine in a garage or anywhere else without proper ventilation—EVER! Carbon monoxide is poisonous; it takes a long time to leave the human body and you can build up a deadly supply of it in your system by simply breathing in a little every day. You may not realize you are slowly poisoning yourself. Always use power vents, windows, fans or open the garage doors.

• Don't work around moving parts while wearing a necktie or other loose clothing. Short sleeves are much safer than long, loose sleeves and hard-toed shoes with neoprene soles protect your toes and give a better grip on slippery surfaces. Jewelry such as watches, fancy belt buckles, beads or body adornment of any kind is not safe working around a truck. Long hair should be hidden under a hat or cap.

• Don't use pockets for toolboxes. A fall or bump can drive a screwdriver deep into your body. Even a wiping cloth hanging from the back pocket can wrap around a spinning shaft or fan.

• Don't smoke when working around gasoline, cleaning solvent or other flammable material.

• Don't smoke when working around the battery. When the battery is being charged, it gives off explosive hydrogen gas.

• Don't use gasoline to wash your hands; there are excellent soaps available. Gasoline may contain lead, and lead can enter the body through a cut, accumulating in the body until you are very ill. Gasoline also removes all the natural oils from the skin so that bone dry hands will suck up oil and grease.

• Don't service the air conditioning system unless you are equipped with the necessary tools and training. The refrigerant, R-12, is extremely cold and when exposed to the air, will instantly freeze any surface it comes in contact with, including your eyes. Although the refrigerant is normally non-toxic, R-12 becomes a deadly poisonous gas in the presence of an open flame. One good whiff of the vapors from burning refrigerant can be fatal.

HISTORY

Toyo Kogyo Co., Ltd., Mazda's parent company, began manufacturing cork products over fifty years ago. In 1927, the company expanded into the machinery and tool business; by 1930 they were producing motorcycles under the Mazda name.

The first three-wheeled trucks appeared in 1931. The first automobile prototype was built in 1940, but is was not until twenty years later that a production car, the Mazda R-360 coupe was sold.

In the interim, Toyo Kogyo produced light three-wheeled trucks, reaching, in 1957, a peak annual production of 20,000 units.

Shortly after automobile production began in 1960, Toyo Kogyo obtained a license from NSU-Wankel to develop and produce the rotary engine.

The first prototype car powered by this engine was the Mazda 110S, a two passenger sports car which appeared in August 1963. The car did not go on sale until it had been thoroughly tested. The first units were offered for sale in May 1967. The 110S was soon joined by a smaller, cheaper model which put the rotary engine within the reach of the average consumer. Various models powered by the rotary engine were produced for the Japanese home market.

In 1970, Toyo Kogyo began importing Mazda cars (both rotary engined and and conventional) into the United States. At first they were available only in the Pacific Northwest, but they have rapidly expanded their market to include almost all of the U.S.

Inspired by the success of the rotary engined cars in this country, Mazda was moved to expand their horizons into the light truck market. The first Mazda pickups arrived in the United States in December of 1972. These were titled as 1972 vehicles and approximately 4,800 were sold. The following year, which was the first full model year for the truck, approximately 14,000 B1600 piston engined trucks were sold.

In 1976 Mazda upgraded the truck with the use of a new engine, calling the it the B1800. This was followed by a styling change, with the truck becoming more sophisticated in 1979. In that year, the engine was enlarged to 1,970cc and the model renamed the B2000. In 1981, a 2,200cc diesel was offered for the first time. This engine was optional equipment through the 1984 model year.

It is important to note, at this time, that there is no 1985 model year truck. Mazda totally redesigned their truck after the 1984 model year and introduced the new truck as a 1986 model. While still called the B2000, the engine, at 1,998cc is totally different, and is, in fact, the same one used in the 626 car.

SERIAL NUMBER IDENTIFICATION

Chassis Number

The chassis number is stamped on the front of the left frame member on 1972-84 trucks, and,

Model plate

the front of the right frame member, on 1986 trucks, visible from the engine compartment.

Engine Number

The engine number of the 1,586cc, 1,796cc and 1979–84 1,970cc is stamped on a machined pad on the right, front side of the engine block. On the diesel, it is stamped on a machined pad located on the front left side of the block, just above the injection pump. On the 1986 B2000, it is located on a machined pad on the left front of the block, just behind the distributor. On the Rotary Pick-up Truck, the engine number is located on a pad at the front of the engine housing, behind the distributor.

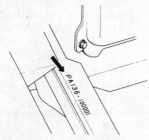

Chassis identification number location on 1972–84 trucks

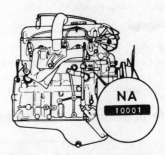

Engine number location on the 1,586cc, 1,796cc and 1,970cc engines

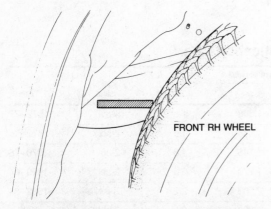

Chassis identification number location on 1986 trucks

FRONT RH WHEEL

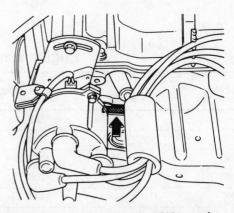

Engine number location on the 1,998cc engine

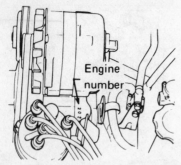

Engine number location on the rotary engine

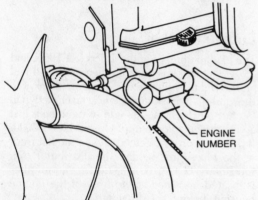

Engine number location on the diesel engine

Model Plate

The model plate, containing the truck model, engine model, engine displacement and chassis number is riveted to the right rear corner of the engine compartment on the firewall.

Motor Vehicle Safety Certification Label

This label is attached to the left door lock pillar and proclaims the fact that the truck conforms to all necessary safety regulations in effect at the time of manufacture.

Emission Control Certification Label

This label is found attached to the right hand panel of the engine compartment, and states that the truck conforms to the emission regulations for the country of destination.

ROUTINE MAINTENANCE

Routine, or preventive maintenance is exactly as it implies; maintenance that is performed at suggested intervals that keeps small problems from becoming large ones. For example, it is much easier (and cheaper in the long run) to check the engine oil regularly than to have the engine run low on oil and damage the bearings (a major overhaul job). Read this chapter carefully and follow its recommendations closely for as close to optimum performance as possible.

Air Cleaner

The air cleaner should be serviced at the recommended interval. The air cleaner uses a disposable paper element located in a housing on top of the engine. To remove the element, simply unscrew the wing nut on the top of the housing and lift off the cover plate. Lift out the element. The element can be cleaned with compressed air (if it is available) by blowing through the air cleaner from the inside out. If compressed air is not available, tap the air cleaner element lightly on a hard surface to dislodge the dirt. If a used air cleaner is reinstalled, rotate it 180° from its previous position.

NOTE: *In severe service, such as off-road use or in extremely dusty areas, the maintenance interval should be cut in half.*

Engine Identification Chart

Engine Configuration	No. of Cyl.	Displacement			Fuel System	Years
		cu. in.	cc	Liters		
2-rotor	—	79.8	1,308	1.3	4-bbl	1972–77
OHC	4	96.8	1,586	1.6	2-bbl	1972–75
OHC	4	109.6	1,796	1.8	2-bbl	1976–78
OHC	4	120.2	1,970	2.0	2-bbl	1979–84
OHC	4	134.8	2,209	2.2	Diesel	1982–84
OHC	4	121.9	1,998	2.0	2-bbl	1986

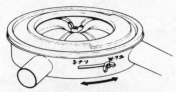

1,586cc engine air cleaner. To prevent icing, move the lever to W when temperatures drop below 50°–60°F; above 50°–60°F, move the lever to S.

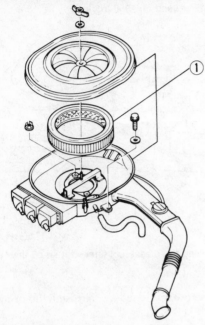

1,998cc air cleaner. 1 is the filter element

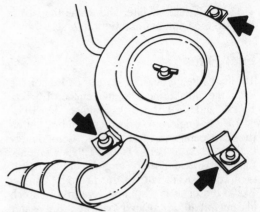

Diesel engine air cleaner. The arrows show the mounting points

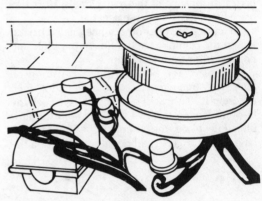

1,796cc and 1,970cc air cleaner

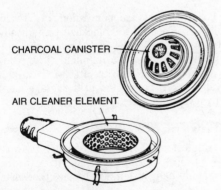

Rotary engine air cleaner

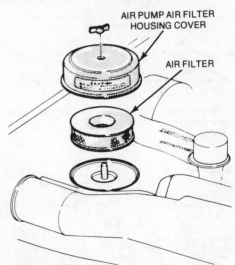

Air pump air filter

Air Pump Filter

REPLACEMENT

1972–73 California Models Only

Mazdas built to be sold in California in 1972 and 1973 have an air filter for the air pump. The air pump is used for purposes of emission control; more information on the air pump system can be found in Chapter 4. The filter must be replaced at 24,000 mile intervals.

1. Remove the wing nut holding the filter housing cover in place.

2. Remove the cover. Remove the old filter and discard it.

3. Install the new filter and install the cover. Replace the wing nut and tighten it securely.

Fuel Filter

The fuel filter is located on the center of the left frame member near the fuel tank on 1,586cc, 1,796cc and 1979-81 1,970cc engines. On 1982-84 1,970cc engines, it is located in a bracket on the front center of the fuel tank, immediately below the cargo bed. On the 1,998cc engine, the filter is located in the engine compartment, secured by a bracket, to the firewall. On the B2200 diesel, it is a spin-on type filter, much like an oil filter, located between the water separator and the injection pump. On Rotary Pick-Ups, it's under the left side of the cargo bed, just forward of the rear wheel. All trucks use a fuel filter that is replaceable.

To replace the filter on gasoline engine trucks, loosen the clamps at both ends of the filter and pop the filter from its clamp.

To replace the filter on diesels, use an oil filter type strap wrench to loosen the filter, then unscrew it. To install the new filter, coat the O-ring with clean diesel fuel and spin the new filter into place until it contacts the mounting base, then turn it ½ additional turn. Loosen the

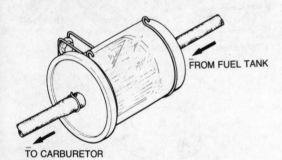

Fuel filter used on 1972–81 trucks, including Rotary engine models

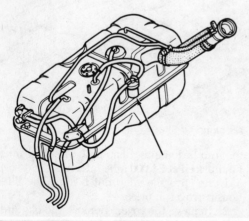

Gasoline fuel filter (arrow) location on 1982–84 trucks

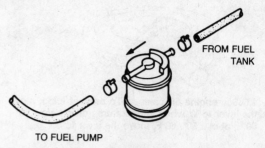

Fuel filter used on 1986 trucks

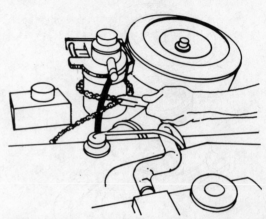

Removing the diesel fuel filter with an oil filter type wrench

vent screw and bleed any air using the priming pump.

PCV Valve

The Positive Crankcase Ventilation (PCV) valve should be inspected for blockage periodically. On trucks through 1984, it is located in a special fitting in the intake manifold, just below the carburetor. On 1986 trucks, it is located in the valve cover, connected to the intake manifold by a vacuum hose.

TESTING THE PCV VALVE

The simplest test for the PCV valve is to remove it from its fitting and shake it. A distinct rattle should be heard; if not, replace the valve.

REMOVAL AND INSTALLATION
Through 1984

1. Remove the air cleaner.
2. Disconnect the hose from the PCV valve.
3. Remove the valve from the special fitting in the intake manifold.
4. Install the valve in the intake manifold fitting and connect the hose to the valve.
5. Connect the hose to the air cleaner and install the air filter.

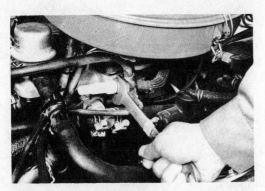

Removing the PCV valve from trucks, through 1984

6. Check for loose clamps or cracks in the PCV lines and replace the hoses if cracked.

1986

Simply pull the PCV valve from the grommet in the valve cover and remove the hose clamp. Then, pull it from the hose. Install the new valve and install the clamp.

NOTE: *If your engine exhibits lower than normal gas mileage and poor idle characteristics for no apparent reason, suspect the PCV valve. It is probably blocked and should be replaced.*

Evaporator Canister

REMOVAL AND INSTALLATION

Rotary Pick-Up

The charcoal filter for the evaporative emission control (EEC) system is located in the top of

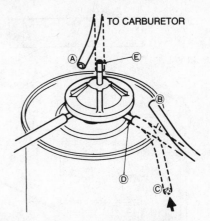

Evaporative canister used through 1984

the air cleaner housing. It should be checked as indicated.

1. Unfasten the clips and remove the top of the air cleaner case.
2. Inspect the air cleaner element and clean it as necessary.
3. Check the condition of the PCV valve as outlined above.

Piston Engine

The evaporative canister is located under the hood in the engine compartment and is designed to store fuel vapors and prevent their escaping into the atmosphere. On early models, when the engine is not running, fuel that has evaporated into the condenser tank is returned to the fuel tank as the ambient temperatures rise and the vapors are condensed. Later models

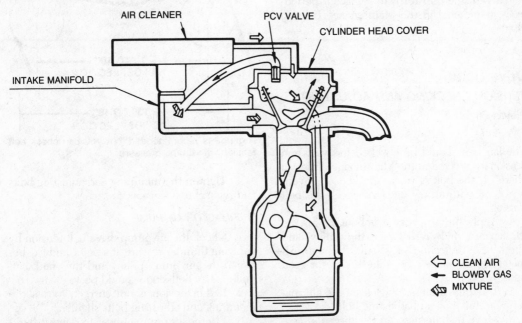

PCV system used on 1986 trucks

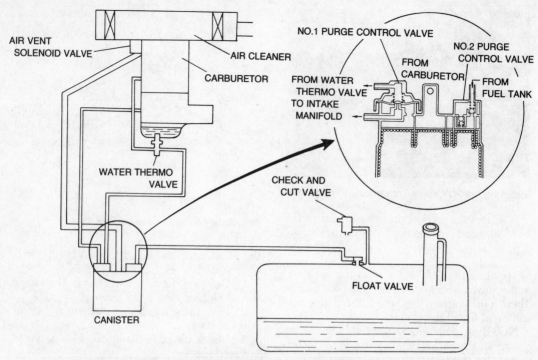

Evaporative emission system used on 1986 trucks

do not have a condenser tank. During periods when the engine is running, fuel vapor that has not condensed in the condenser tank moves to the carbon canister. The stored vapors are removed by fresh air through the bottom of the inlet hole and passed through the air cleaner to the combustion chamber. Because of the design of the system, the only maintenance associated with the canister is to replace it periodically as indicted in the Maintenance Interval charts.

Drive Belts

TENSION CHECKING AND ADJUSTING

Piston Engines

FAN BELT

The fan belt should be checked for wear and tension as indicted in the Maintenance Interval charts. If the belt is worn, cracked or frayed, replace it with a new one. To check the belt tension:

1. Apply thumb pressure (about 22 lbs.) to the fan belt midway between the pulleys and check the deflection. I should be approximately ⅜ in. for new belts and ½ in. for used belts.

2. To adjust the tension, loosen the alternator mounting bolt and adjusting bolt.

3. Move the alternator in the direction necessary to loosen or tighten the tension.

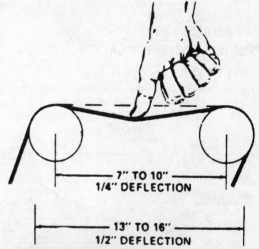

A gauge is recommended, but you can check belt tension with thumb pressure

4. Tighten the mounting and adjusting bolts and recheck the tension.

THERMACTOR AIR PUMP

1. Check the air pump drive belt tension by applying thumb pressure at a point midway between the air pump pulley and the crankshaft pulley. The deflection should be ½–⅝ in.

2. If the tension is not correct, loosen the mounting and adjusting bolts slightly.

3. Pry the air pump outward (or inward) until the proper deflection is obtained.

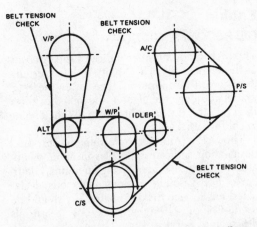

Various belt tension adjustments on the diesel engine

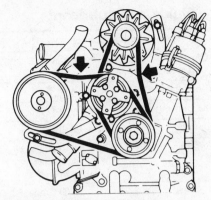

Rotary engine belt tensioning points

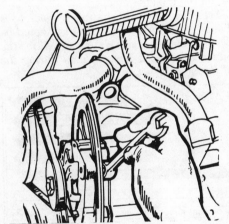

Alternator belt tension adjustment

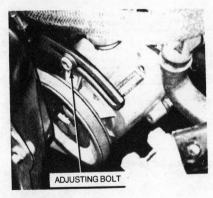

Air pump adjusting bolt

4. Tighten the adjusting and lower bolts to 22 ft.lb.

ROTARY PICK-UP
Fan Belt and Air Pump Belt

Both belts should be checked for tension and wear according to the Maintenance Interval charts. If either belt is worn, frayed, or cracked, replace it with a new belt.

To check and adjust the belt tension:

1. Apply thumb pressure (about 22 lbs.) to the belt midway between the pulleys and check the deflection. The deflection should be ⅜–½ inch.

2. To adjust the tension on the fan belt, loosen the alternator mounting and adjusting bolts. Move the alternator until the proper tension is obtained and tighten the mounting and adjusting bolts. Recheck the tension.

3. To adjust the air pump drive belt, loosen the air pump mounting and adjusting bolts. Move the air pump until the proper tension is obtained. Tighten the mounting and adjusting bolts and recheck the tension.

FLUIDS AND LUBRICANTS

Fuel Recommendations

Gasoline Engines

All gasoline engines through 1976 are designed to operate on leaded fuel of 91 research octane or higher, sold as Regular gas. All 1977 and later Mazdas sold in the U.S. use unleaded fuel of 91 research octane or higher. Regular leaded fuel may not be used in these models, because they are equipped with a catalytic converter for emission control purposes. Leaded fuel will render the converter useless, raising the emission content of the exhaust to illegal and environmentally unacceptable levels. It will also block the converter passages, increasing exhaust back pressure; in extreme cases, exhaust blockage will be raised to the point where the engine will not run. Most 1977 and later Mazdas sold in Canada are able to use regular fuel; however, converter equipped models must use unleaded fuel. In either case, fuel used in Canadian models must also have an octane rating of 91 or higher (research method).

Fluids and Lubricants

Recommended Lubricants	
Engine Oil, Gasoline Engine: SE or SF ① Diesel Engine: CC/CD	
Manual Transmission	GL-4
Automatic Transmission	Type F
Rear Axle	GL-5 ②
Wheel Bearings	NLGI Grade #2 EP Multipurpose Grease
Chassis Grease	NLGI Grade #2 Multipurpose Grease
Brake Fluid	DOT 3 or 4
Clutch Fluid	DOT 3 or 4
Manual Steering	GL-4
Power Steering	Type F ATF
Antifreeze	ethylene glycol
Hinges	engine oil

Fuels of the same octane rating have varying anti-knock qualities. Thus if your engine knocks or pings, try switching brands of gasoline before trying a more expensive higher octane fuel. If you must use unleaded fuel, this may be your only alternative.

Your engine's fuel requirements can change with time, due to carbon buildup which changes the compression ratio. If switching brands or grades of gas doesn't work, check the ignition timing. If it is necessary to retard timing from specifications, don't change it more than about four degrees. Retard timing will reduce power output and fuel mileage and increase engine temperature.

Diesel Engines

The diesel engine in your Mazda is designed to run on No.2 diesel fuel with a cetane rating of 40. For operation when the outdoor air temperature is consistently below freezing, the use of No.1 diesel fuel or the addition of a cold weather additive, is recommended.

Engine

OIL RECOMMENDATIONS

The SAE grade number indicates the viscosity of the engine oil, or its ability to lubricate under a given temperature. The lower the SAE grade number, the lighter the oil; the lower the viscosity, the easier it is to crank the engine in cold weather.

The API (American Petroleum Institute) designation indicates the classification of engine oil for use under given operating conditions. For gasoline engines, only oils designated for Service SE/SF, or just SF, should be used. For diesel engines, use only those oils designated Service CC. These oils provide maximum engine protection. Both the SAE grade number and the API designation can be found on the top of a can of oil.

NOTE: *Non-detergent or straight mineral oils should not be used. Oil viscosities should be chosen from those oils recommended for the lowest anticipated temperatures during the oil change interval.*

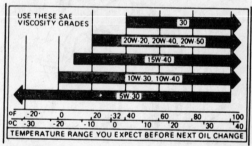

Oil viscosity chart for gasoline engines, except Rotary engines

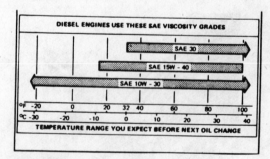

Diesel engine oil selection chart

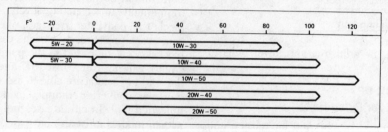

Oil viscosity chart for the Rotary engine

CHECKING ENGINE OIL

Under normal operating conditions, the Mazda rotary engine burns about one quart of oil every 1,000–1,400 miles as part of its combustion process. Therefore, the oil level should be checked frequently. The engine oil should be checked on a regular basis, ideally at each fuel stop. If the truck is used for trailer towing, or for heavy-duty use, it would be wise to check it more often.

When checking the oil level, it is best that the oil be at operating temperature, although checking the level immediately after stopping will give a false reading because all of the oil will not have drained back into the crankcase. Be sure that the truck is on a level surface, allowing time for all of the oil to drain back into the crankcase.

1. Open the hood and locate the dipstick. It is located on the right hand (passenger's side) of the engine just behind the alternator.

2. Remove the dipstick and wipe it clean with a rag.

3. Insert the dipstick fully into the tube and remove it again. Hold the dipstick horizontal and read the level on the dipstick. The level should be between the "F" (Full) and "L" (Low) marks. If the oil level is at or below the "L" mark, sufficient oil should be added to restore the level to the proper place. Oil is added through the capped opening in the top of the valve cover. See the section on "Oil and Fuel

Recommendations" for the proper viscosity and oil to use.

4. Replace the dipstick and check the level after adding oil. Be careful not to overfill the crankcase.

ENGINE OIL AND FILTER CHANGE

The engine oil and filter should always be changed together. To skip an oil filter change is to leave a quart of contaminated oil in the engine. Engine oil and filter should be changed according to the schedule in the Maintenance Intervals chart.

Under conditions such as:
- Driving in dusty conditions
- Continuous trailer pulling or RV use
- Extensive or prolonged idling
- Extensive short trip operation in freezing temperatures (when the engine is not thoroughly warmed up)
- Frequent long runs at high speeds and high ambient temperatures
- Stop-and-go service, such as delivery trucks

The oil change interval and filter replacement interval should be cut in half. Operation of the engine in severe conditions, such as a dust storm, may require an immediate oil and filter change.

To change the engine oil and filter, the truck should be parked on a level surface and the engine should be at operating temperature. This is to ensure that foreign matter will be drained away with the oil and not left behind in the

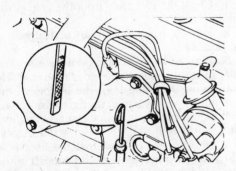

Typical engine oil dipstick on engines other than the Rotary

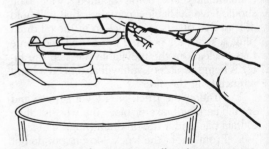

Keep an inward pressure on the plug as you unscrew it, so the oil won't escape until you pull the plug away

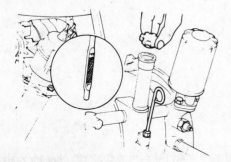

Rotary engine oil dipstick

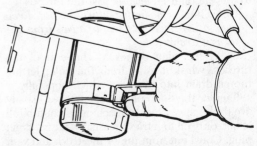

Use a strap wrench to remove the oil filter

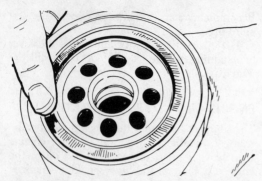

Apply a light coat of oil to the rubber gasket on the oil filter before installing it

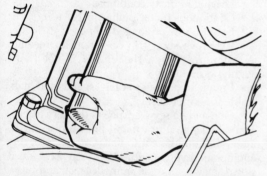

Install the new filter by hand only; DO NOT use the strap wrench

engine to form sludge, which will happen if the engine is drained cold. Oil that is slightly brownish when drained is a good sign that the contaminants are being drained away. You should have available a container that will hold at least five quarts, a wrench to fit the oil drain plug, a spout for pouring in new oil and some rags to clean up the inevitable mess. If the filter is being replaced, you will also need a band wrench to fit the filter.

1. Position the truck on a level surface and set the parking brake or block the wheels. Slide a drain pan under the oil drain plug.

2. From under the truck, loosen, but do not remove the oil drain plug. Cover your hand with a heavy rag or glove and slowly unscrew the drain plug. Push the plug against the threads to prevent oil from leaking past the threads.

CAUTION: *The engine oil will be hot. Keep your arms, face and hands away from the oil as it drains out.*

3. As the plug comes to the end of the threads, whisk it away from the hole, letting the oil drain into the pan, which hopefully is still under the drain plug. This method usually avoids the messy task of reaching into a tub full of hot, dirty oil to retrieve a usually elusive drain plug. Crawl out from under the truck and wait for the oil to drain.

4. When the oil is drained, install the drain plug. If you are replacing the filter on a Rotary Pick-Up, leave the plug out.

5. Change the engine oil filter as necessary or desired. On the 1,586cc, the filter is located at the right front of the engine, down below and behind the alternator. Loosen the filter with a band wrench and spin the filter off by hand. Be careful of the one quart of hot, dirty oil that inevitably overflows the filter. On Rotary Pick-Ups, the engine oil filter is on top of the engine, next to the dipstick. To remove it, punch a hole in the top of the filter to allow the oil in the filter to drain out through the engine. After the oil is drained from the filter, loosen it with a band wrench and remove it. When oil ceases to flow from the engine, replace the drain plug.

6. Coat the rubber gasket on a new filter with engine oil and install the filter. Screw the filter onto the mounting stud and tighten according to the directions on the filter.

7. Refill the engine with the specified amount of clean engine oil. Be sure to use the proper viscosity. Pour the oil in through the capped opening.

8. Run the engine for several minutes, checking for oil pressure and leaks. Check the level of the oil and add if necessary.

Manual Transmission
FLUID CHECK

1. Clean the dirt away from the area of the filler plug.

2. Jack the truck if necessary and support it on jackstands.

3. Remove the filler plug from the case. The filler plug is the one on the side of the case. Do not remove the plug from the bottom of the case unless you wish to drain the transmission.

4. If lubricant flows from the area of the filler plug as it is removed, the level is satisfactory. If lubricant does not flow from the filler hole when the plug is removed, add enough of the specified lubricant to bring the level to the bot-

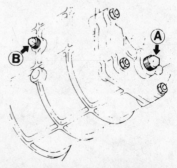

Oil pan drain (A) plug and fill (B) plug for manual transmissions, through 1984

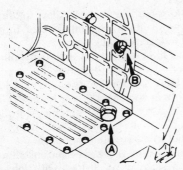

Rotary engine manual transmission drain (A) and fill (B) plugs

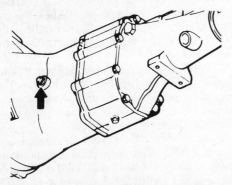

1986 manual transmission fill plug (arrow). The drain plug can be seen on the bottom of the case

tom of the filler hole with the truck in a level position.

FLUID CHANGE

The same procedure is used for both 4-speed and 5-speed transmissions, but note that 5-speed transmissions have two filler plugs and two drain plugs. Thus, to drain the 5-speed, both drain plugs must be removed, and to fill it, both filler plugs must be removed. The truck should be parked on a level surface, and the transmission should be at normal operating temperature (oil hot).

1. With the truck parked on a level surface (parking brake applied), place a pan of at least four quarts capacity under the transmission drain plug(s).

2. Remove the filler plug(s) to provide a vent; this will speed the draining process.

3. Remove the drain plug(s) and allow the old oil to drain into the pan.

4. Clean the drain plug(s) thoroughly and replace. Tighten to 15–20 ft.lb. if you have a torque wrench handy; otherwise, just snug the plug or plugs in. Overtightening will strip the aluminum threads in the case.

5. Add lubricant through the filler plug(s) until it comes right up to the edge of the filler hole. Use SAE 90 EP gear oil. It usually comes

in a squeeze bottle with a nozzle attached to the cap, but you can use a squeeze bulb or suction gun for additions.

6. Install the filler plug(s). Tightening torque is 15–20 ft.lb. Check for leaks after the truck has been driven for a few miles.

Automatic Transmission

FLUID CHECK

1. Drive the vehicle for several miles to bring the fluid level to operating temperature.

2. Park the truck on a level surface.

3. Put the automatic transmission in PARK. Leave the engine running.

4. Remove the dipstick from the tube and wipe it clean.

5. Reinsert the dipstick so that it is fully seated.

6. Remove the dipstick and note the reading. If the fluid is at or below the "Add" mark, add sufficient Type F fluid to bring the level to the "Full" mark. Do not overfill the transmission. Overfilling will lead to fluid aeration.

FLUID CHANGE

The automatic transmission fluid is a long lasting type, and Mazda does not specify that it need ever be changed. However, if you have brought the truck used, driven it in water deep enough to reach the transmission, or used the truck for trailer pulling or delivery service, you may want to change the fluid and filter. It is a

Typical automatic transmission dipstick location

Typical automatic transmission dipstick markings

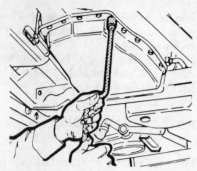

The pan must be removed to drain the automatic transmission

Install the new gasket to the pan, not the transmission flange

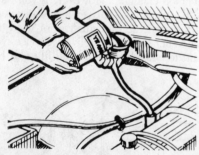

Transmission fluid is added through the dipstick tube

good idea to measure the amount of fluid drained from the transmission, and to use this as a guide when refilling. Some parts of the transmission, such as the torque converter, will not drain completely, and using the dry refill capacity listed in the Capacities chart may lead to overfilling.

1. Drive the truck until it is at normal operating temperature.

2. If a hoist is not being used, park the truck on a level surface, block the wheels, and set the parking brake. If you raise the truck on jackstands, check to see that it is reasonably level before draining the transmission.

3. There is no drain plug, so the transmission pan must be removed to drain the fluid. Carefully remove the screws from the pan and

lower the pan at the corner. Allow the fluid to drain into a suitable container. After the fluid has drained, remove the pan.

4. The filter consists of a screen bolted to the lower valve body. Remove the screen attaching bolts and remove the screen. Clean it thoroughly in solvent, allow it to air dry completely, and replace it. Tightening torque for the attaching bolts is only 2.2–2.9 ft.lb., so be careful not to overtighten them.

5. Remove the old gasket and install a new one. The pan may be cleaned with solvent, if desired. After cleaning, allow the pan to air dry thoroughly. Do not use a rag to dry it, or you risk leaving bits of lint in the pan that will clog the transmission fluid passages. When the pan is completely dry, replace it, and tighten the bolts in a circular pattern, working from the center outward. Tighten gently to 3.5–5.0 ft.lb.

6. Refill the transmission with Type F fluid. Fluid is added through the dipstick tube. This process is considerably easier if you have a funnel and a long tube to pour through. Add three quarts (2.8 liters) of fluid initially.

7. After adding fluid, start the engine and allow it to idle. Shift through all gear positions slowly to allow the fluid to fill all the hydraulic passages, and return the shift lever to Park. Do not race the engine.

8. Run the engine at fast idle to allow the fluid to reach operating temperature. Place the selector lever at "N" or "P" and check the fluid level. It should be above the "L" mark on the hot side of the dipstick. If necessary, add enough fluid to bring the level between the "L" and "F" marks. Do not overfill the transmission. Overfilling will cause foaming, fluid loss, and plate slippage.

Rear Axle
FLUID CHECK

The rear axle fluid level is checked from underneath the truck.

1. Clean the dirt and grease away from the area of the filler (top) plug.

2. Remove the filler plug. The lubricant level should be even with the bottom of the filler plug hole.

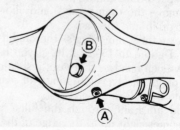

Rear axle fill (B) and drain (A) plugs

3. If lubricant is required, use only the specified type. It will probably have to be pumped in through the filler hole. Hypoid SAE 90 lubricant usually does not pour very well.

FLUID CHANGE

The Mazda uses a removable carrier axle which has a drain and fill plug.

1. Jack the rear of the vehicle and support it with jackstands.

2. Position a suitable container under the axle drain plug. Remove the fill plug to provide a vent.

3. Remove the drain plug and allow the lubricant to drain out.

NOTE: *Do not confuse the drain and fill plugs. The drain lug is magnetic to attract fine particles of metal which are inevitably present.*

4. Clean the magnetic drain plug.

5. Install the drain plug.

6. Fill the rear axle with the specified amount and type of fluid. Install the filler plug.

7. Lower the truck to the ground and drive the truck, checking for leaks after the fluid is warm.

Brake Master Cylinder

Check the level of the fluid in the brake master cylinder at the specified interval or more often. The brake master cylinder is located at the left rear corner of the engine compartment.

1. Park the truck on a level surface.

2. Clean all dirt from the area of the master cylinder reservoir cover.

3. Remove the top from the master cylinder reservoir. Be careful when doing this. Brake fluid that is dripped on painted surfaces will quickly destroy the paint.

4. The level should be maintained approximately ½ in. below the top of the reservoir.

5. If brake fluid is needed, use only a good

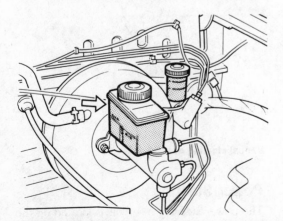

Typical brake master cylinder

quality brake fluid meeting specifications DOT-3 or DOT-4.

6. If necessary, add fluid to maintain the proper level and replace the top on the master cylinder securely.

NOTE: *If the fluid level is constantly low, it would be a good idea to look into the matter. This is a good indication of problems elsewhere in the system.*

Clutch Master Cylinder

The clutch master cylinder is located at the left rear corner of the engine compartment. Check the level in the clutch master cylinder in the same manner as the brake master cylinder. The level should be kept approximately ½ in. from the top of the cylinder. Use brake fluid in the clutch system. Be sure that the truck is on a level surface.

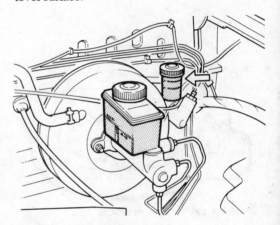

Typical clutch master cylinder

Coolant

Check the coolant level when the engine is cold. The radiator coolant level should be kept above the bottom of the filler housing elbow and below the bottom of the filler neck. When adding coolant, a mixture of permanent antifreeze and water is recommended for year around operation. It is not recommended that different brands of antifreeze be mixed, nor that any other than permanent types be used.

CAUTION: *To avoid injury when working on a hot engine, cover the radiator cap with a thick cloth and turn it slowly counterclockwise until the pressure begins to escape. After the pressure is completely removed, remove the cap. Never remove the cap until the pressure is gone. Never remove the radiator cap until the expansion tank cap is removed.*

Freeze protection should be maintained at a level for the temperatures which may occur in

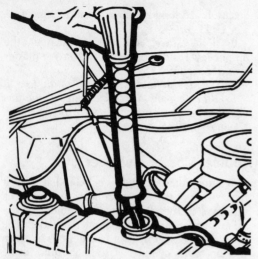

Check anti-freeze protection with an inexpensive tester

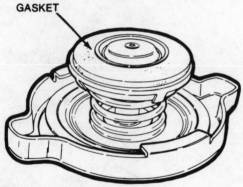

GASKET

Check the cap for wear or cracks

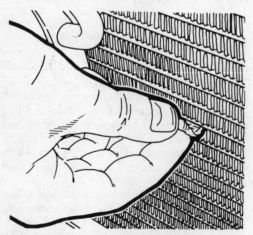

Keep the radiator fins clear of dirt and bugs for maximum cooling

the area in which the truck is to be operated. It should be maintained to at least 0°F to provide adequate corrosion and boil-over protection.

CLEANING AND FLUSHING THE COOLING SYSTEM

CAUTION: *When draining the coolant, keep in mind that cats and dogs are attracted by the ethelyne glycol antifreeze, and are quite likely to drink any that is left in an uncovered container or in puddles on the ground. This will prove fatal in sufficient quantity. Always drain the coolant into a sealable container. Coolant should be reused unless it is contaminated or several years old.*

1. Open the radiator and engine block drain cocks and drain the coolant. Remove the radiator cap.

2. Close the drain cocks and fill the system with clean water.

3. Drive the truck for about an hour, be careful not to overheat the engine.

4. Completely drain the water from the system again and flush clean water through the cooling system.

5. Close the drain cocks and add antifreeze solution or corrosion inhibitor solution according to seasonal requirements. During a complete refill of the system, always operate the engine until it reaches normal temperature to remove air from the system. Let the system cool, recheck the fluid level and refill as necessary.

Manual Steering Gear

1. Clean the area around the plug and remove the plug from the top of the gear housing.

2. The oil level should just reach the plug hole.

3. If necessary, add 80W-90 gear oil until the fluid is at the proper level.

4. Reinstall the plug.

Manual steering gear fill plug

Power Steering

The power steering reservoir is located on the left side of the engine. A dipstick is part of the

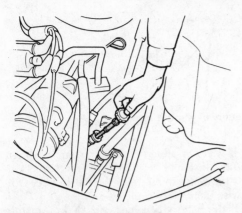

Checking the power steering fluid

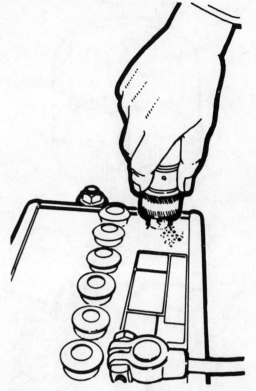

Clean the battery posts with a wire terminal cleaner

cap. With the fluid hot—10 minutes of driving—the level should be between the F and L marks. Use Type F automatic transmission fluid.

Battery

Check the battery electrolyte level at least once a month, more often in hot weather or during periods of extended vehicle operation. The electrolyte in each cell should be kept filled to the split ring. If the level is low, add only distilled water or colorless, odorless drinking water.

At least once a year check the specific gravity of the battery. It should be between 1.20–1.26 at room temperature. Clean and tighten the terminal clamps and apply a thin coating of petroleum jelly to the terminals. This will help to retard corrosion. The terminals can be cleaned with a stiff wire brush or with a terminal cleaner made for the purpose. These are inexpensive and can be purchased in most any decently equipped parts store.

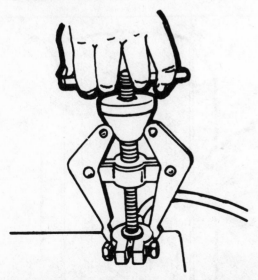

Top terminal battery cable can be removed with this inexpensive tool

Clean the cable ends with a stiff wire cleaning tool

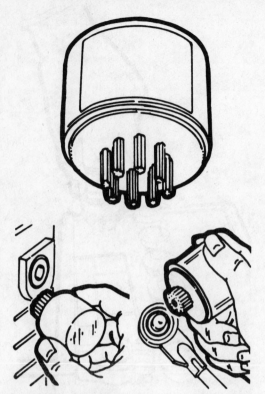

Battery electrolyte level

If water is added during freezing weather, the truck should be driven several miles to allow the water to mix with the electrolyte. Otherwise the battery could freeze.

If the battery becomes corroded, a mixture of baking soda and water will neutralize the corrosion. This should be washed off after making sure that the caps are tight and securely in place. Rinse the solution off with cold water.

If a "fast" charger is used to charge the battery while the battery is in the truck, disconnect the battery first.

NOTE: *Keep flame or sparks away from the battery; it gives off explosive hydrogen gas, while it is being charged.*

Side terminal batteries require a special wire brush for cleaning

TIRES AND WHEELS

Inspect the tire threads for cuts, bruises and other damage. Check the air valves to be sure that they are tight. Replace any missing valve caps.

The tires should be checked frequently for proper air pressure. A chart in the glove compartment or on the driver's door pillar gives the recommended inflation pressure. Pressures can increase as much as 6 psi due to heat buildup. It is a good idea to have your own

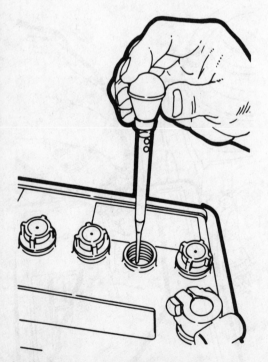

An inexpensive hydrometer will quickly test the battery's state of charge

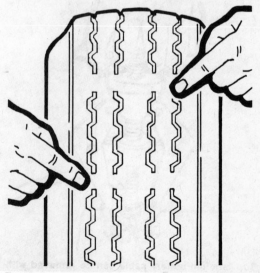

Tread wear indicators

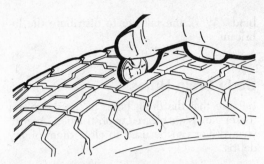

Tread depth can be checked with a penny; when the top of Lincoln's head is visible, it's time for new tires

Tread depth gauges are available for precise wear measurements

accurate gauge, and to check pressures weekly. Not all gauges on service station air pumps can be trusted.

Inspect tires for uneven wear that might indicate the need for front end alignment or tire rotation. Tires should be replaced when a tread wear indicator appears as a solid band across the tread.

When buying new tires, give some thought to the following points, especially if you are switching to larger tires or a different profile series (50, 60, 70, 78):

1. All four tires should be of the same construction type. Radial, bias, or bias-belted tires should not be mixed.

2. The wheels must be the correct width for the tire. Tire dealers have charts of tire and rim compatibility. A mismatch can cause sloppy handling and rapid tire wear. The tread width should match the rim width (inside bead to inside bead) within an inch. For radial tires, the rim width should be 80% or less of the tire (not tread) width.

3. The height (mounted diameter) of the new tires can greatly change speedometer accuracy, engine speed at a given road speed, fuel mileage, acceleration, and ground clearance. Tire manufacturers furnish full measurement specifications.

NOTE: *Dimensions of tires marked the same size may vary significantly, even among tires from the same manufacturer.*

4. The spare tire should be usable, at least for low speed operation, with the new tires.

5. There shouldn't be any body interference when loaded, on bumps, or in turning.

Tire Rotation

Tire rotation is recommended every 6,000 miles or so, to obtain maximum tire wear. The pattern you use depends on whether or not you

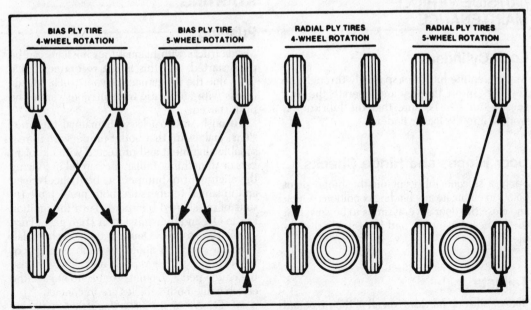

| BIAS PLY TIRE 4-WHEEL ROTATION | BIAS PLY TIRE 5-WHEEL ROTATION | RADIAL PLY TIRES 4-WHEEL ROTATION | RADIAL PLY TIRES 5-WHEEL ROTATION |

Tire rotation pattern

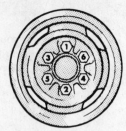

Wheel lug nut torque sequence

have a usable spare. Radial tires should not be cross-switched (from one side of the truck to the other); they last longer if their direction of rotation is not changed. Truck type tires sometimes have directional threads, indicted by arrows molded into the sidewalls; the arrow shows the direction of rotation. They will wear very rapidly if their direction of rotation is reversed.

NOTE: *Mark the wheel position or direction of rotation on radial tires or studded snow tires before removing them.*

CAUTION: *Avoid overtightening the lug nuts to prevent damage to the brake disc or drum. Alloy wheels can also be cracked by overtightening. Use of a torque wrench is highly recommended. Tighten the lug nuts in the sequence shown to 85 ft.lb.*

WHEEL BEARINGS

See Chapter 8

OUTSIDE VEHICLE MAINTENANCE

Lock Cylinders

Apply graphite lubricant sparingly through the key slot. Insert the key and operate the lock several times to be sure that the lubricant is worked into the lock cylinder.

Door Hinges and Hinge Checks

Spray a silicone lubricant on the hinge pivot points to eliminate any binding conditions. Open and close the door several times to be sure that the lubricant is evenly and thoroughly distributed.

Tailgate

Spray a silicone lubricant on all of the pivot and friction surfaces to eliminate any squeaks or

binds. Work the tailgate to distribute the lubricant.

Body Drain Holes

Be sure that the drain holes in the doors and rocker panels are cleared of obstruction. A small screwdriver can be used to clear them of any debris.

Windshield Wipers

WINDSHIELD WASHER ADJUSTMENT

The washer spray direction can be adjusted by inserting a pin into the nozzle and turning it to the desired position.

WIPER BLADE REPLACEMENT

Wiper blade replacement will vary with the amount of use, type of weather, etc. Generally, if the wiper pattern across the screen is streaked over clean glass, the blades should be replaced.

1. To remove the wiper blade, press down on the arm to unlatch the locking stud. Depress the tab on the saddle and pull the blade from the arm.

2. To install a new blade, slip the blade connector over the end of the wiper arm so that the locking stud snaps into place.

PUSHING, TOWING AND JUMP STARTING

Pushing

Mazda trucks with manual transmissions can be push started, but this is not recommended if you value the appearance of your truck. Mazda trucks with automatic transmissions cannot be push started.

To push start trucks with manual transmissions, make sure that both bumpers are in reasonable alignment and protected with old blankets or something similar. Be careful in judging the alignment of bumpers as bent sheet metal and inflamed tempers are both predictable results of misaligned bumpers. Turn the ignition key to ON and transmission in High gear. Turn off all accessories. Depress the clutch pedal. When a speed of about 10 mph is reached, lightly depress the gas pedal and slowly release the clutch pedal. Do not attempt to engage the clutch while both vehicles are in contact.

NOTE: *Never get a starting assist by having your truck towed!*

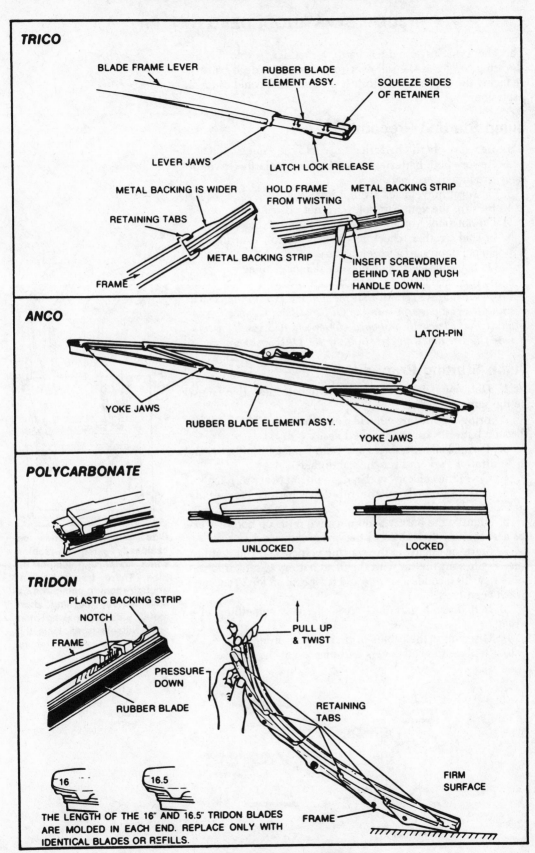

TRICO

BLADE FRAME LEVER

RUBBER BLADE ELEMENT ASSY.

SQUEEZE SIDES OF RETAINER

LEVER JAWS

LATCH LOCK RELEASE

METAL BACKING IS WIDER

HOLD FRAME FROM TWISTING

METAL BACKING STRIP

RETAINING TABS

METAL BACKING STRIP

FRAME

INSERT SCREWDRIVER BEHIND TAB AND PUSH HANDLE DOWN.

ANCO

LATCH-PIN

YOKE JAWS

RUBBER BLADE ELEMENT ASSY.

YOKE JAWS

POLYCARBONATE

UNLOCKED

LOCKED

TRIDON

PLASTIC BACKING STRIP

NOTCH

FRAME

PULL UP & TWIST

PRESSURE DOWN

RUBBER BLADE

RETAINING TABS

FIRM SURFACE

16

16.5

THE LENGTH OF THE 16" AND 16.5" TRIDON BLADES ARE MOLDED IN EACH END. REPLACE ONLY WITH IDENTICAL BLADES OR REFILLS.

FRAME

Popular styles of wiper refills

JUMP STARTING A DEAD BATTERY

The chemical reaction in a battery produces explosive hydrogen gas. This is the safe way to jump start a dead battery, reducing the chances of an accidental spark that could cause an explosion.

Jump Starting Precautions

1. Be sure both batteries are of the same voltage.
2. Be sure both batteries are of the same polarity (have the same grounded terminal).
3. Be sure the vehicles are not touching.
4. Be sure the vent cap holes are not obstructed.
5. Do not smoke or allow sparks around the battery.
6. In cold weather, check for frozen electrolyte in the battery. Do not jump start a frozen battery.
7. Do not allow electrolyte on your skin or clothing.
8. Be sure the electrolyte is not frozen.
CAUTION: *Make certain that the ignition key, in the vehicle with the dead battery, is in the OFF position. Connecting cables to vehicles with on-board computers will result in computer destruction if the key is not in the OFF position.*

Jump Starting Procedure

1. Determine voltages of the two batteries; they must be the same.
2. Bring the starting vehicle close (they must not touch) so that the batteries can be reached easily.
3. Turn off all accessories and both engines. Put both cars in Neutral or Park and set the handbrake.
4. Cover the cell caps with a rag—do not cover terminals.
5. If the terminals on the run-down battery are heavily corroded, clean them.
6. Identify the positive and negative posts on both batteries and connect the cables in the order shown.
7. Start the engine of the starting vehicle and run it at fast idle. Try to start the car with the dead battery. Crank it for no more than 10 seconds at a time and let it cool off for 20 seconds in between tries.
8. If it doesn't start in 3 tries, there is something else wrong.
9. Disconnect the cables in the reverse order.
10. Replace the cell covers and dispose of the rags.

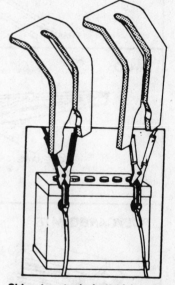

Side terminal batteries occasionally pose a problem when connecting jumper cables. There frequently isn't enough room to clamp the cables without touching sheet metal. Side terminal adaptors are available to alleviate this problem and should be removed after use.

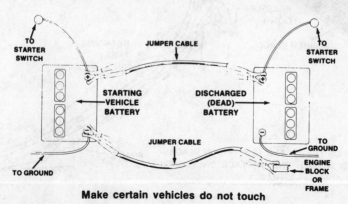

TO STARTER SWITCH   JUMPER CABLE   TO STARTER SWITCH

STARTING VEHICLE BATTERY   DISCHARGED (DEAD) BATTERY

JUMPER CABLE   TO GROUND

TO GROUND   ENGINE BLOCK OR FRAME

Make certain vehicles do not touch

This hook-up for negative ground cars only

Towing

MANUAL TRANSMISSION

If the transmission and rear axle are not damaged, the vehicle may be towed from the front. Otherwise it should be lifted and towed from the rear. Be sure that the parking brake is OFF and the transmission is in Neutral.

AUTOMATIC TRANSMISSION

With the automatic transmission, the rear wheels must be lifted off the ground or the driveshaft must be disconnected. If this is not done, the transmission may be damaged.

MANUAL OR AUTOMATIC TRANSMISSION

Do not attach chains to the bumpers or bracketing. All attachments should be made to structural members. Safety chains should also be used. If you are flat towing, remember that the power steering and power brake assists will not work with the engine OFF.

JACKING

The jack supplied with your truck was meant for changing tires. It was not meant to support the truck while you work under it. Whenever it is necessary to get under your truck to perform service operations, be sure that it is adequately supported on jackstands.

Do not lift the truck by the front bumper. Be careful when lifting the truck on a two-post hoist. Damage to the suspension may occur if care is not exercised in positioning the hoist adapters.

NOTE: *To support your Mazda with the jack supplied with the truck, refer to the accompanying illustrations.*

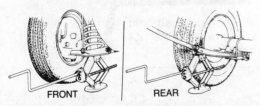

Jacking points for a scissors type jack on 1972–84 models

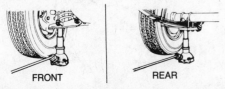

Jacking points for a hydraulic type jack on 1972–84 models

HOW TO BUY A USED TRUCK

Many people believe that a two or three year old, or older, truck is a better buy than a new one. This may be true. The new truck suffers the heaviest depreciation in the first few years, but is not old enough to present a lot of costly repairs. Whatever the age of the used truck you want to buy, this section and a little patience will help you select one that should be safe and dependable.

Shopping Tips

1. First, decide what model you want and how much you want to spend.

2. Check the used car lots and your local newspaper ads. Privately owned trucks are usually less expensive, however, you will not get a warranty that, in most cases, comes with a used truck purchased from a dealer.

3. Never shop at night. The glare of the lights makes it easy to miss defects in the paint and faults in the body caused by accident or rust repair.

4. Once you've found a truck that you're interested in, try to get the name and phone number of the previous owner. Contact that person for details about the truck. If he or she refuses information about the truck, shop elsewhere. A private seller can tell you about the truck and its maintenance history, but there are few laws requiring honesty from private citizens who are selling used vehicles. There are laws forbidding the tampering with or turning back a vehicle's odometer mileage reading. These laws apply to both a private seller as well as commercial dealers. The law also requires that the seller, or anyone transferring ownership of a vehicle, must provide the buyer with a signed statement indicating the mileage on the odometer at the time of transfer.

5. Write down the year, model and serial number of the truck before you buy it. Then, dial 1-800-424-9393, the toll-free number of the National Highway Traffic Safety Administration, and ask if the truck has ever been included on any manufacturer's recall list. If so, make sure the necessary repairs were made.

6. Use the Used Car Checklist in this section, and check all the items on the used truck that you are considering. Some items are more important than others. You've already determined how much money you can afford for repairs, and, depending on the price of the truck, you should consider doing some of the needed repairs yourself. Beware, however, of trouble in areas involving operation, safety or emissions. Problems in the Used Car Checklist are arranged as follows:

FRONT
Jack position
At the center of the
crossmember

Safety stand positions:
On both sides of the jack
point

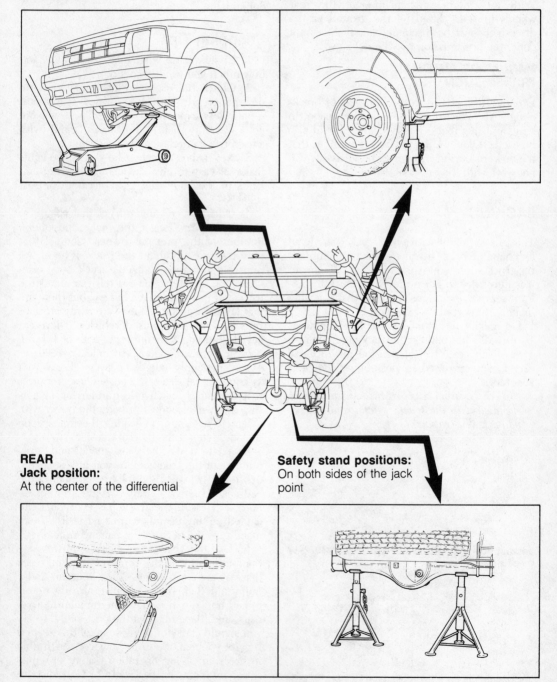

REAR
Jack position:
At the center of the differential

Safety stand positions:
On both sides of the jack
point

Jacking points for the 1986 model truck

Piston Engine Maintenance Intervals Chart

Intervals are miles or miles/months

Change engine oil and oil filter	7,500/12*
Check drive belts	15,000/12
Replace drive belts	30,000/24
Check & adjust valve clearance	15,000/12
Check and, if necessary, replace ignition points and condenser	4,000/4
Check and, if necessary, replace distributor cap and rotor	12,000/12
Check & adjust ignition timing, 1972–78	6,000/6
Check & adjust ignition timing, 1979–86	50,000/60
Check & adjust idle speed on B1600 & 1800	4,000/4
Check & adjust idle speed on B2000	15,000/12
Check & adjust throttle position system	15,000, then every 50,000
Replace fuel filter	12,000/12
Inspect fuel system for leaks	6,000/6
Replace air cleaner element	24,000/24*
Replace spark plugs, 1972–78	6,000/6
Replace spark plugs, 1979–86	30,000/24*
Replace ignition wires	24,000/24
Tighten intake and exhaust manifold bolts	8,000/12
Tighten the B1600 & 1800 cylinder head bolts	8,000/12
Check engine compression pressure	24,000/24
Replace PCV valve	24,000/24
Replace vacuum, PCV, and secondary air hoses	50,000/60
Replace fuel system hoses, fuel vapor hoses, cooling system hoses, and fuel filler cap	50,000/60
Clean PCV system	50,000/60*
Inspect evaporative system for leaks and replace canister	50,000/60
Replace oxygen sensor	50,000/60
Replace engine timing belt	60,000/60
Check coolant condition and check cooling system for leaks	15,000/12*
Change engine coolant	30,000/24*
Check A/C system and drive belt	15,000/12

*Under severe service conditions (short trips at very cold temperatures, driving in heavy dust, or towing a trailer), change the engine oil and filter every 3 months or 3,000 miles, whichever occurs first. Service the air cleaner filter, PCV system, and spark plugs at more frequent intervals. If the truck is operated in deep water, the manual transmission and rear axle fluids should be changed immediately, and the front wheel bearings should be repacked.

1–8: Two or more problems in this segment indicate a lack of maintenance. You should reconsider your selection.

9–13: Indicates a lack of proper care, however, these can usually be corrected with a tune-up or relatively simple parts replacement.

14–17: Problems in the engine or transmission can be very expensive. Walk away from any truck with problems in these areas.

7. If you are satisfied with the apparent condition of the truck, take it to an independent diagnostic center or mechanic for a complete checkout. If your state has a state inspection program, have it inspected immediately before purchase, or specify on the invoice that purchase is conditional on the truck's passing a state inspection.

8. Road test the truck. Refer to the Road Test Checklist in this section. If your original

Rotary Engine Maintenance Intervals Chart

Intervals are miles or miles/months

Change engine oil and filter	4,000/4*
Inspect accessory drive belts	4,000/4*
Inspect metering oil pump	4,000/4
Check engine compression pressure	10,000/12
Inspect starting assist system	once each winter
Check idle speed	4,000/4
Check idle mixture	12,000/12
Replace fuel filter	10,000/12*
Replace air cleaner element	10,000/12*
Check carburetor float level	14,000/12
Inspect and lubricate carburetor linkage	10,000/12*
Inspect fuel line connections	4,000/4
Inspect and replace, if needed, evap canister	12,000/12
Check ignition timing	4,000/4
Check and, if needed, replace points	4,000/4
Check and, if needed, replace distributor cap	10,000/12
Check and, if needed, replace rotor and condensers	10,000/12
Replace spark plugs	4,000/4*
Inspect spark plug wires	12,000/12
Replace spark plugs wires	24,000/24
Inspect distributor cam	10,000/10
Inspect and, if needed, replace PCV valve	24,000/24*
Inspect and, if needed, replace PCV hoses	12,000/12*
Inspect air pump	12,000/12
Inspect thermal reactor	12,000/12
Tighten exhaust pipe flange bolts	12,000/12
Inspect and, if needed, replace coolant hoses	12,000/12

*Under severe service conditions (short trips at very cold temperatures, driving in heavy dust, or towing a trailer), change the engine oil and filter every 3 months or 3,000 miles, whichever occurs first. Service the air cleaner filter, PCV system, and spark plugs at more frequent intervals. If the truck is operated in deep water, the manual transmission and rear axle fluids should be changed immediately, and the front wheel bearings should be repacked.

evaluation, and the road test agree, the rest is up to you.

Used Car Checklist

NOTE: *The numbers on the illustration correspond to the numbers in this checklist.*

1. *Mileage:* Average mileage is about 12,000 miles per year. More than average may indicate hard usage. Catalytic converter equipped models may need converter service beyond the 50,000 mile mark.

2. *Paint:* Check around the tailpipe, molding and windows for overspray, indicating that the truck has been repainted.

3. *Rust:* Check fenders, doors, rocker panels, window moldings, wheelwells, flooring and in the bed, for signs of rust. Any rust at all will be a problem. There is no way to stop the spread of rust, except to replace the part or panel.

4. *Body Appearance:* Check the moldings, bumpers, grille, vinyl roof, glass, doors, tail gate and body panels for overall condition. Check for misalignment, loose holddown clips, ripples, scratches in the glass, rips or patches in the top. Mismatched paint, welding in the bed, severe misalignment of body panels or ripples may indicate crash work.

5. *Leaks:* Get down under the truck and

Chassis Maintenance Intervals Chart

Intervals are miles or miles/months

Check brake and hydraulic clutch fluid level and check for leaks in system	15,000/12
Replace brake and hydraulic clutch fluid	60,000/48
Inspect brake front and rear brake linings and hoses	15,000/12*
Inspect ball joint, steering linkage seals	30,000/24
Lubricate front wheel bearings	30,000
Inspect power steering fluid level, hoses, and belt	15,000/12
Change automatic transmission fluid	30,000*
Check manual transmission level	12 months*
Check drive axle fluid	12 months*
Change drive axle fluid	50,000/60
Check all exhaust system connections and inspect for excessive corrosion	15,000/12

*Under severe service conditions (short trips at very cold temperatures, driving in heavy dust, or towing a trailer), change the engine oil and filter every 3 months or 3,000 miles, whichever occurs first. Service the air cleaner filter, PCV system, and spark plugs at more frequent intervals. If the truck is operated in deep water, the manual transmission and rear axle fluids should be changed immediately, and the front wheel bearings should be repacked.

Capacities Chart

Year	Engine (cc)	Crankcase Includes Filter (qt)	Transmission (pts)			Drive Axle (pts)	Fuel Tank (gal)	Cooling System (qt)	
			4-sp	5-sp	Auto			w/AC	wo/AC
1972–75	1,586	4.8	3.2	—	—	2.7	11.7	—	6.8
1972–77	1,308	6.8	3.6	—	13.2	2.7	21.1	—	10.2
1976–78	1,796	4.8	2.9	3.6	—	2.7	①	—	7.6
1979–84	1,970	5.0	3.2	3.6	13.2	2.8	①	7.5	7.5
1982–84	2,209	5.3	—	3.6	—	2.8	①	—	11.1
1986	1,998	4.5	3.0	2.6	—	2.8	②	7.9	7.9

① Short bed: 15.0
   Long bed: 17.5
② Short bed: 14.6
   Long bed: 15.6

take a good look. There are no "normal" leaks, other than water from the air conditioning condenser drain tube.

6. *Tires:* Check the tire air pressure. A common trick is to pump the tires up hard to make the truck roll more easily. Check the tread wear and the spare tire condition. Uneven wear is a sign that the front end is, or was, out of alignment. See the Troubleshooting Chapter for indications of treadwear.

7. *Shock Absorbers:* Check the shocks by forcing downward sharply on each corner of the truck. Good shocks will not allow the truck to rebound more than twice after you let go.

8. *Interior:* Check the entire interior. You're looking for an interior condition that agrees with the overall condition of the truck. Reasonable wear can be expected, but be suspicious of new seatcovers on sagging seats, new pedal pads, and worn armrests. These indicate an attempt to cover up hard usage. Pull back the carpets and/or mats and look for signs of water leaks or flooding. Look for missing hardware, door handles, control knobs, etc. Check lights and signal operations. Make sure that all accessories, such as air conditioner, heater, radio, etc., work. Air conditioning, especially automatic temperature control units, can be very expensive to repair. Check the operation of the windshield wipers.

9. *Belts and Hoses:* Open the hood and check all belts and hoses for wear, cracks, or weak spots. Check around hose connections for stains, indicating leaks.

10. *Battery:* Low electrolyte level, corroded terminals and/or a cracked battery case, indicate a lack of maintenance.

11. *Radiator:* Look for corrosion or rust in the coolant, indicating a lack of maintenance.

12. *Air Filter:* A dirty air filter element indicates a lack of maintenance.

13. *Spark Plug Wires:* Check the wires for cracks, burned spots or wear. Worn wires will have to be replaced.

14. *Oil Level:* If the level is low, chances are that the engine either uses an excessive amount of oil, or leaks. If the oil on the dipstick appears foamy or tan in color, a leakage of coolant into the oil is indicated. Stop here, and go elsewhere for your truck. If the oil appears thin or has the smell of gasoline, stop here and go elsewhere for your truck.

15. *Automatic Transmission:* Pull the transmission dipstick out when the engine is running in PARK. If the fluid is hot, the dipstick should read FULL. If the fluid is cold, the level will show about one pint low. The fluid itself should be bright red and translucent, with no burned odor. Fluid that is brown or black and has a burned odor is a sign that the transmission needs major repairs.

16. *Exhaust:* Check the color of the exhaust smoke. Blue smoke indicates excessive oil usage, usually due to major internal engine problems. Black smoke can indicate burned valves or carburetor problems. Check the exhaust system for leaks. A leaky system is dangerous and expensive to replace.

17. *Spark Plugs:* Remove one of the spark plugs. An engine in good condition will have spark plugs with a light tan or gray deposit on the electrodes. See the color Tune-Up section for a complete analysis of spark plug condition.

Road Test Check List

1. *Engine Performance:* The truck should have good accelerator response, whether cold or warm, with adequate power and smooth acceleration through the gears.

2. *Brakes:* Brakes should provide quick, firm stops, with no squealing, pulling or fade.

3. *Steering:* Sure control with no binding, harshness or looseness, and no shimmy in the wheel should be encountered. Noise or vibration from the steering wheel means trouble.

4. *Clutch:* Clutch action should be quick and smooth with easy engagement of the transmission.

5. *Manual Transmission:* The transmission should shift smoothly and crisply with easy change of gears. No clashing and grinding should be evident. The transmission should not stick in gear, nor should there be any gear whine evident at road speed.

6. *Automatic Transmission:* The transmission should shift rapidly and smoothly, with no noise, hesitation or slipping. The transmission should not shift back and forth, but should stay in gear until an upshift or downshift is needed.

7. *Differential:* No noise or thumps should

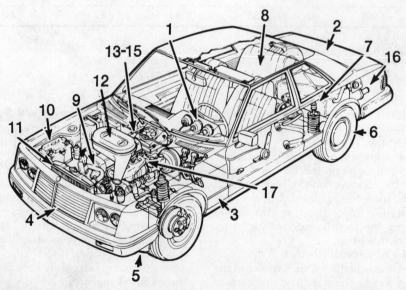

You should check these points when buying a used car. The "Used Car Checklist" gives an explanation of the numbered items

be present. No external leakage should be present.

8. *Driveshaft, Universal Joints:* Vibration and noise could mean driveshaft problems. Clicking at low speed or coast conditions means worn U-joints.

9. *Suspension:* Try hitting bumps at different speeds. A truck that bounces has weak shock absorbers. Clunks mean worn bushings or ball joints.

10. *Frame:* Wet the tires and drive in a straight line. Tracks should show two straight lines, not four. Four tire tracks indicates a frame bent by collision damage. If the tires can't be wet for this purpose, have a friend drive along behind you and see if the car appears to be traveling in a straight line.

Tune-Up and Performance Maintenance

2

TUNE-UP PROCEDURES

Neither tune-up nor troubleshooting can be considered independently since each has direct bearing on the other.

NOTE: *The procedures contained in this section are specific procedures applicable to your Mazda. More general procedures that would apply to almost any vehicle are contained in the Tune-up and Troubleshooting section at the end of this chapter.*

An engine tune-up is a service designed to restore the maximum capability of power, performance, economy and reliability in an engine, and, at the same time, assure the owner of a complete check and more lasting results in efficiency and trouble-free performance. Engine tune-up becomes increasingly important each year, to ensure that pollutant levels are in compliance with federal emissions standards.

It is advisable to follow a definite and thorough tune-up procedure. Tune-up consists of three separate steps: Analysis, the process of determining whether normal wear is responsible for performance loss, and whether parts require replacement or service; Parts Replacement or Service; and Adjustment, where engine adjustments are returned to the original factory specifications.

The extent of an engine tune-up is usually determined by the length of time since the previous service, although the type of driving and the general mechanical condition of the engine must be considered. Specific maintenance should also be performed at regular intervals, depending on operating conditions.

Troubleshooting is a logical sequence of procedures designed to lead the owner or service man to the particular cause of trouble. The troubleshooting section of this manual is general in nature, yet specific enough to locate the problem. Service usually comprises two areas; diagnosis and repair. While the apparent cause of trouble, in many cases, is worn or damaged parts, performance problems are less obvious. The first job is to locate the problem and cause. Once the problem has been isolated, refer to the appropriate section for repair, removal or adjustment procedures.

It is advisable to read the entire chapter before beginning a tune-up, although those who are more familiar with tune-up procedures may wish to go directly to the instructions.

Spark Plugs

The function of a spark plug is to ignite the air/fuel mixture in the cylinder as the mixture is compressed by the piston. The expansion of the ignited mixture forces the piston down, which turns the crankshaft and supplies power to the drive train.

Spark plugs should be checked frequently (approximately 5,000 miles) depending on use. All the recommendations are based on the am-

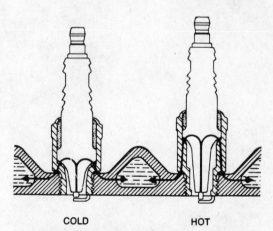

COLD   HOT

The plug with the higher heat range is on the right; it has a longer heat flow path and thus operates at a higher tip temperature. It should be used for slower driving and light load conditions which promote carbon accumulation

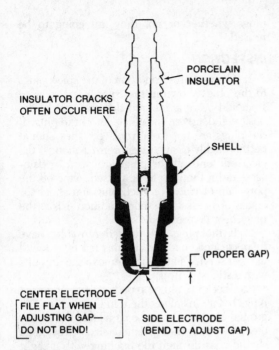

PORCELAIN INSULATOR

INSULATOR CRACKS OFTEN OCCUR HERE

SHELL

(PROPER GAP)

CENTER ELECTRODE
[FILE FLAT WHEN ADJUSTING GAP— DO NOT BEND!]

SIDE ELECTRODE (BEND TO ADJUST GAP)

Spark plug cutaway

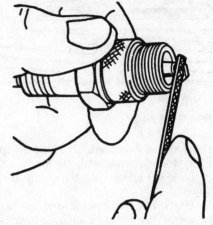

Plugs still in good condition can be filed and reused

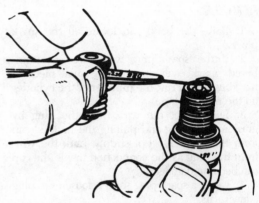

Always use a wire gauge to check the electrode gap

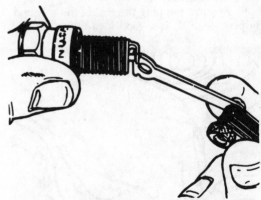

Adjust the electrode gap by bending the side electrode

bient conditions as well as driving conditions. If you drive at high speeds constantly, the plugs will probably not need as much attention as those used for constant stop-and-start driving.

The electrode end of the plug (the end with the threads) is a good indicator of the internal condition of your engine. If a spark plug has fouled and caused the engine to misfire, the problem will have to be found and corrected. Often, reading the spark plugs will lead you to the cause of the problem. Spark plug conditions and probable causes are shown in the color insert section of this chapter. It is a good idea to pull the plugs once in a while just to get an idea of the internal condition of your engine.

NOTE: *A small amount of light tan colored deposits on the electrode end of the spark plug is quite normal. These plugs need not be replaced unless they are severely worn.*

Heat range is a term used to describe the cooling characteristics of spark plugs. Plugs with longer nosed insulators take a longer time to dissipate heat effectively, and are termed "hot" plugs. The reverse is also true, shorter nosed plugs dissipate heat rapidly, and are thus called "cold" plugs. It is generally advisable to use the factory specified spark plugs. However, in conditions of extreme hard usage (e.g., driving cross country in August), going to the next cooler heat range is all right. The same is true if most driving is done in the city or over short distances, go to the next hotter range spark plug to eliminate spark plug fouling. If in doubt concerning spark plug substitution, consult a Mazda dealer.

Spark plugs should be gapped when installed new and when they are checked periodically. To gap the spark plugs, remove each one in turn and measure the gap with a round feeler gauge of the appropriate thickness. The round feeler gauge is inserted between the center and

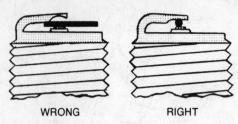

WRONG   RIGHT

Gapping spark plugs

side electrode, as illustrated. To adjust the gap, bend the side electrode with the tool on the end of the feeler gauge until the specified gap is obtained.

CAUTION: *The spark plugs used on the rotary engine are not adjustable. Attempting to adjust the air gap will damage the porcelain.*

REMOVAL

1. Raise the hood and locate all the spark plugs.

2. If the spark plug wires are not numbered, mark each one with a small piece of masking tape. Print the number of the cylinder on the piece of tape.

3. Disconnect the wire from the plug by grasping, twisting and pulling the molded cap from the plug. Do not simply yank the wire from the plug as the connection inside the cap can become damaged.

4. Using a spark plug socket, loosen the plug a few turns.

5. If compressed air is available, blow out the area around the base of the spark plug to remove foreign matter.

6. Remove the plug the rest of the way and inspect them. It is a good idea to inspect the

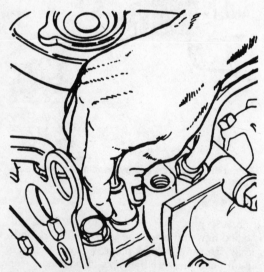

Twist and pull on the rubber boot to remove the spark plug wires; never pull on the wire itself

plugs whether or not they are going to be reused.

INSPECTION

1. Compare the condition of the spark plugs to the plugs shown in the color insert section. It should be remembered that any type of deposit will decrease the efficiency of the plug. If the plugs are not to be replaced, they should be thoroughly cleaned before installation. If the electrode ends of the plugs are worn or damaged and if they are to be reused, wipe off the porcelain insulator on each plug and check for cracks or breaks. If either condition exists, the plug must be replaced.

2. If the plugs are judged reusable, have them cleaned on a plug cleaning machine (found in most service stations) or remove the deposits with a stiff wire brush.

3. Check the plug gap on both new and used plugs before installing them in the engine. The ground electrode must be parallel to the center electrode and the specified size wire gauge should pass through the opening with a slight drag. If the center or ground electrode has worn unevenly, level them off with a file. If the air gap between the two electrodes is not correct, open or close the ground electrode, with the proper tool, to bring it to specifications. Such a tool is usually provided with a gap gauge.

INSTALLATION

1. Coat the threads of new plugs with an anti-seize compound. Insert the plugs into the engine and tighten them finger tightly.

2. Be sure that the plugs are not cross-threaded. If the plugs use metal gaskets, new gaskets should be installed each time the plugs are removed and installed.

3. Tighten the spark plugs to 9–13 ft.lb. (Rotary Pick-Up) or 11–15 ft.lb. (piston engine).

4. Install the spark plug wires on their respective plugs. Be sure that each wire is firmly connected.

5. While you are checking the spark plugs, the spark plug wires should also be checked. Any wires that are cracked or brittle should be replaced.

FIRING ORDERS

The firing order of the Rotary Pick-Up engine is alternate (1–2). The distributor cap terminals should be identified by T_1, L_1, T_2 and L_2 (Trailing no. 1 cylinder, Leading no. 1 cylinder, etc.). The top plug of each cylinder is the trailing plug and the bottom of the leading. The rotors are numbered from front to rear.

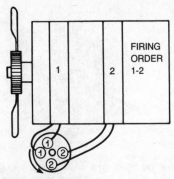

Rotary engine firing order
Firing order: 1, 2

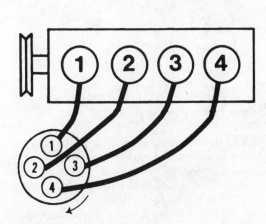

Firing order for the 1,998cc engine
Firing order: 1, 3, 4, 2

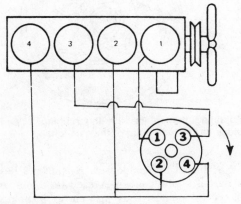

Firing order for the 1,586cc, 1,796cc and 1,970cc engines
Firing order: 1, 3, 4, 2

Breaker Points and Condenser
OPERATIONS

NOTE: *Point type ignition was used through the 1978 model year. The following information applies only to these model years. Beginning in 1979, electronic ignition became standard equipment. Testing and adjustments on 1979 and later models is given a little later in this chapter.*

When the breaker points are closed, current flows from the battery through the ignition switch and ballast type resistor to the primary windings in the coil, then to ground through the closed breaker points. When the points

Tune-Up Specifications

Years	Engine (cc)	Spark Plugs Type	Spark Plugs Gap (in.)	Distributor Point Gap (in.)	Distributor Dwell (deg.)	Ignition Timing (deg.) Man. Trans.	Ignition Timing (deg.) Auto. Trans.	Valve * Clearance In.	Valve * Clearance Exh.	Idle Speed Man. Trans.	Idle Speed Auto. Trans.
1972–77	1,308	B-7EM	0.026	0.026	58	①	①	—	—	800	750
1972–75	1,586	BP-6ES	0.031	0.020	52	5B	—	0.012	0.012	825	—
1976–78	1,796	BP-6ES	0.031	0.020	52	8B	—	0.012	0.012	700	—
1979–84	1,970	BPR-6ES	0.031	Electronic		8B	8B	0.012	0.012	650	650
1982–84	2,209	—	—	Diesel		2A**	—	0.012	0.012	700	—
1986	1,998	BPR-5ES	0.031	Electronic		6B	—	0.012	0.012	850	—

TDC: Top Dead Center
B: Before TDC
A: After TDC
* Valve side; engine hot
** Diesel injection static timing
① Leading: TDC
　Trailing: 15A

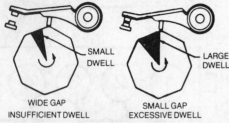

WIDE GAP
INSUFFICIENT DWELL — SMALL DWELL

SMALL GAP
EXCESSIVE DWELL — LARGE DWELL

Dwell as a function of point gap

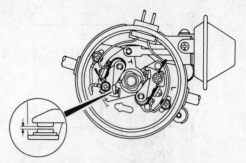

Adjusting the point gap on the rotary engine. The arrows indicate the lockscrews to be loosened

open, the magnetic field built up in the primary windings of the coil, moves through the secondary windings of the coil, producing high voltage. The high voltage flows through the coil high tension lead to the distributor cap, where the rotor distributes it to the spark plug terminals. This procedure is repeated for every power stroke of the engine.

REMOVAL AND INSTALLATION

All Models

NOTE: *Because of engine design, the rotary engine uses 2 sets of points in the distributor. Removal and installation is basically the same as for a single set of points.*

1. Raise the hood and locate the distributor. It is on the front of the engine.
2. Scribe an alignment mark on the distributor cap and the distributor body. This way you will get the cap on the right way.
3. Remove the distributor cap and rotor. The rotor goes on the shaft only one way.
4. Disconnect the primary and condenser wires from the breaker point terminal. Note the position of the wires before removing them from the terminal.
5. Remove the screws attaching the breaker points to the base plate. If possible, it is best to use a magnetic screwdriver to do this. The screws are very small and can be dropped easily.
6. Lift the breaker point(s) assemblies from the distributor. Remove the condenser.
7. Place the breaker point(s) assemblies on the base plate. Install the attaching screws, again using a magnetic screwdriver, if you have one.

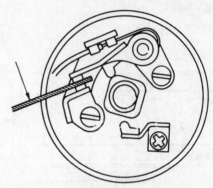

Adjusting the points with the rubbing block on the high point of the cam lobe

8. Install the condenser. It is always best to install a new condenser each time you replace the points. It is just cheap insurance against condenser failure.
9. Connect the primary and condenser wires to the point(s) terminal and tighten the connection.
10. Be sure that the points are aligned.
11. Set the point gap or dwell angle and install the rotor and distributor cap. Use the alignment marks made previously to get the cap on correctly.

Dwell Angle

When setting ignition contact points, it is advisable to observe the following general rules:

1. If the points are used, they should not be adjusted using a feeler gauge. The gauge will not give an accurate reading on a pitted surface.
2. Never file the points. This removes their protective coating and results in rapid pitting.
3. When using a feeler gauge to set new points, be certain that the points are fully open. The fiber rubbing block must rest on the highest point of the cam lobe.
4. Always make sure that a feeler gauge is free of oil or grease before setting the points.
5. Make sure that the points are properly

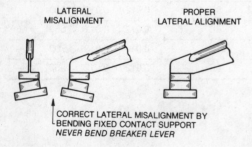

LATERAL MISALIGNMENT

PROPER LATERAL ALIGNMENT

CORRECT LATERAL MISALIGNMENT BY BENDING FIXED CONTACT SUPPORT
NEVER BEND BREAKER LEVER

Breaker point alignment

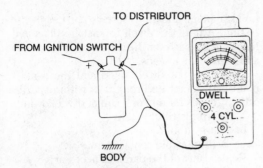

TO DISTRIBUTOR

FROM IGNITION SWITCH

DWELL

4 CYL.

BODY

Dwell meter connections

aligned and that the feeler gauge is not tilted. If points are misaligned, bend the fixed contact support only, never the movable breakable arm. A dwell meter virtually eliminates errors in point gap caused by the distributor cam lobes being unequally worn, or human error. In any case, point dwell should be checked as soon as possible after setting with a feeler gauge because it is a far more accurate check of point operation under normal operating conditions. The dwell meter is also capable of detecting high point resistance (oxidation) or poor connections within the distributor.

The dwell meter, actually a modified voltmeter, depends on the nature of contact point operation for its usefulness. In this electro-mechanical system, a fiber block slides under tension, over a cam. The angle that the block traverses on the cam, during which time current is made available to the coil primary winding, is an inverse function of point gap. In other words, the wider the gap, the smaller the dwell (expressed in degrees); the closer the gap, the greater the dwell.

Because the fiber block wears down gradually in service, it is a good practice to set the dwell on the low side of any dwell range (smaller number of degrees) given in specifications. As the block wears, the dwell becomes greater (toward the center of the range) and point life is increased between adjustments.

To connect the dwell meter, switch the meter to the appropriate cylinder range, as the case may be, and connect one lead to ground. The other lead should be connected to the coil distributor terminal (the one having the wire going to contact points). Follow the manufacturer's instructions if they differ from those listed. Zero the meter, start the engine and gradually allow it to assume normal idle speed. See Tune-Up Specifications. The meter should agree with the specifications. Any excessive variation in dwell indicates a worn distributor shaft or bushings, or perhaps a worn distributor cam or breaker plate.

It is obvious from the above procedure that

some means of measuring engine rpm must also be employed when checking dwell. An external tachometer should be employed. Hook-up is the same as for the dwell meter and both can be used in conjunction. Most commercial dwell meters have a tachometer scale built in and switching between them is possible.

ADJUSTMENT

Single Point Distributors

There are two methods to adjust the breaker point gap. By far the more accurate is the method of measuring dwell angle electronically.

FEELER BLADE METHOD

1. Check and adjust the breaker point alignment. Bend the fixed contact support only.
2. Crank the engine in short bursts until the rubbing block rests on a peak of a cam lobe.
3. Insert a feeler blade of the specified thickness between the breaker points. Adjust the gap until the feeler blade will slide through the gap with a slight drag, by loosening the adjustment screw and moving the point base. When the correct gap is obtained, tighten the adjustment screw.
4. Clean the breaker cam and apply a thin coating of distributor cam lubricant to the cam. Do not use engine oil.
5. After setting the breaker point gap, set the ignition timing.
6. Install the distributor rotor and cap.

DWELL METER METHOD

1. Connect a dwell meter and tachometer or a dwell/tach to the engine following the manufacturer's instructions.
2. Remove the distributor cap and rotor.
3. Crank the engine and note the dwell reading.
4. If the dwell angle is not as specified, adjust the point gap. Crank the engine again and note the dwell reading. Repeat this process until the dwell is within specifications.
5. Lock the points in position.
6. Install the rotor and distributor cap. Disconnect the instrument and adjust the ignition timing.

Dual Point Distributors

There are two methods to adjust the points. By far the most accurate and preferable, on used points, is the dwell meter method.

FEELER BLADE METHOD

1. Remove the distributor high tension lead and the distributor cap and rotor.
2. Check the breaker point alignment. If

necessary, align the points by bending the stationary contact. Never bend the movable contact.

3. Crank the engine in short bursts until the rubbing block on the breaker arm rests on the high point of the cam lobe. This is the maximum point opening.

4. Insert a feeler blade of the specified thickness between each set of breaker points in turn.

5. If adjustment is required, loosen the setscrews and move the stationary contact and base until the correct gap is obtained.

6. Tighten the setscrews and recheck the gap.

7. Install the rotor and distributor cap. Reconnect the high tension lead.

DWELL METER METHOD

1. Disconnect the vacuum line from the distributor and plug it with a pencil or a golf tee.

2. Connect the dwell meter in accordance with the manufacturer's instructions.

3. Run the engine at idle, after it has warmed up.

4. Observe the dwell meter reading. It should be according to specifications.

5. If it is not within specifications, adjust the dwell.

NOTE: *If dwell angle is above the specified amount, the point gap is too small; if it is below, the gap is too large.*

6. Remove the high tension leads and ground them. Remove the distributor cap. Loosen the

breaker point attaching screws and crank the engine. Adjust the dwell to specifications and tighten the setscrews. Install the distributor cap and high tension leads.

7. If both the dwell angle and the contact point gap cannot be brought to within specifications, check for one or more of the following:

   a. Worn distributor cam

   b. Worn rubber block

   c. Bent movable contact arm.

Replace any of the parts, as necessary.

8. When the dwell angle check is completed, disconnect the meter and reconnect the vacuum line.

Electronic Ignition

NOTE: *Electronic ignition was first used on the 1979 B2000.*

INSPECTION

1. The distributor cap is held on by two screws. Unscrew them and lift the cap straight up with the wires still attached. Inspect the cap for cracks, carbon tracking and worn contacts. Replace it, if necessary, transferring the wires one at a time to avoid miswiring.

2. On 1979 models, pull the rotor straight up to remove it. On 1980 and later models, the rotor is held in place by two screws. Use a magnetic screwdriver to remove them and lift off the rotor. Replace the rotor if it appears worn, burned or pitted.

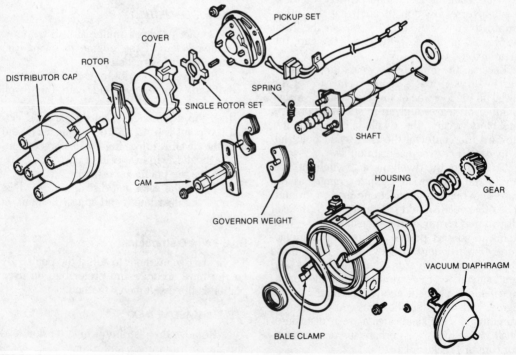

Exploded view of the 1979 electronic distributor

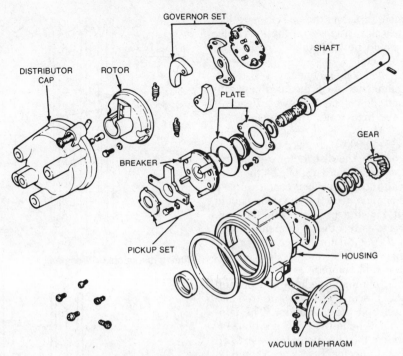

Exploded view of the 1980–84 electronic distributor

3. Inspect the wires for cracks or brittleness. Replace them, one at a time, if they appear at all suspect. Avoid bending the wires sharply, or kinking them, as the carbon cores are subject to such damage.

TROUBLESHOOTING

You will need an accurate ohmmeter, a jumper wire and a 3.4 watt test light. Before proceeding with troubleshooting, make sure that all connections are tight and all wiring is intact.

1. Check for spark at the coil high tension lead by removing the lead from the distributor cap and holding it about ¼ inch from the engine block or other good ground. Use a heavy rubber glove or non-conductive clamp, such as a fuse puller or clothes pin, to hold the wire. Crank the engine and check for spark. If a good spark is noted, check the cap and rotor; if the spark is weak or nonexistent, replace the high tension lead, clean and tighten the connections and retest. If a weak spark is still noted, proceed to step 2.

2. Check the coil primary resistance. Con-

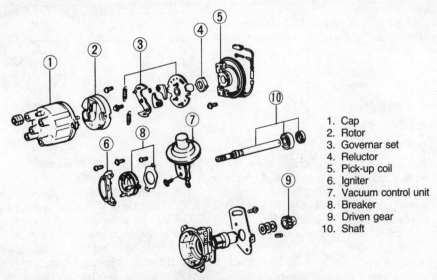

1. Cap
2. Rotor
3. Governar set
4. Reluctor
5. Pick-up coil
6. Igniter
7. Vacuum control unit
8. Breaker
9. Driven gear
10. Shaft

Exploded view of the 1986 electronic distributor

nect an ohmmeter across the coil primary terminals and check resistance on the low scale. Resistance should be 0.81–0.98Ω @ 70°F. If not, replace the coil.

3. Check the coil secondary resistance. Connect an ohmmeter across the distributor side of the coil and the coil center tower. Read resistance on the high scale. Resistance should be 6,800–9,200Ω @ 70°F. If resistance is much higher (30,000–40,000Ω), replace the coil.

4. Next, remove the distributor cap and rotor. Crank the engine until a spoke on the rotor is aligned with the pick-up coil contact. Use a flat feeler gauge to check the gap. Gap should be 0.008–0.024 in. If not, gently bend the pick-up coil contact to correct the adjustment on 1979 models. On 1980 and later models, the gap is not adjustable. On these models, gap is corrected by parts replacement.

5. Using an ohmmeter, check the pick-up coil resistance. Disconnect the 2-wire (red and green) connector at the distributor. The ignition switch should be in the OFF position. Insert the probes of the ohmmeter in the pick-up coil side of the connector. Resistance should be 760–840Ω for 1979 models, or 1,050Ω ± 10% for 1980 and later models. If not, replace the pick-up coil.

6. Finally, test the ignition module. On 1979 models, connect the test light between the positive and negative terminal of the ignition coil. Connect a jumper wire between the positive coil terminal and the red wire of the pick-up coil, at the connector that you unplugged in the previous test. Be sure that you are attaching the wire to the pick-up coil side of the connector. Turn the ignition switch ON. The test light should light. Disconnect the jumper wire from the connector. The light should go out. If not, replace the module.

On 1980 and later models, the only way to test the module is to substitute a known good module in its place.

Ignition Timing
ADJUSTMENT
Piston Engines

1. Raise the hood and clean and mark the timing marks. Chalk or fluorescent paint makes a good, visible mark.

2. Disconnect the vacuum line to the distributor and plug the disconnected line. Disconnect the line at the vacuum source, not at the distributor.

3. Connect a timing light to the front (no. 1) cylinder, a power source and ground. Follow the manufacturer's instructions.

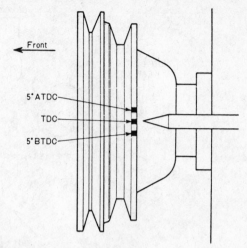

Timing marks on 1972 engines

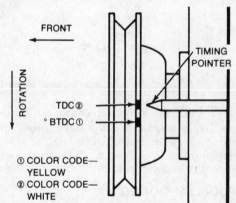

Timing marks 1973–78. Although the number of degrees indicated by the BTDC mark changes from year to year, the general set-up of the marks remains the same.

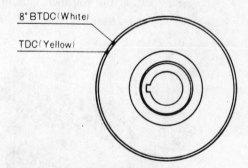

Timing marks for 1979–84 engines

4. Connect a tachometer to the engine.

5. Start the engine and reduce the idle to 700–750 rpm to be sure that the centrifugal advance mechanism is not working.

6. With the engine running, shine the timing light at the timing pointer and observe the position of the pointer in relation to the timing mark on the crankshaft pulley. 1972 49

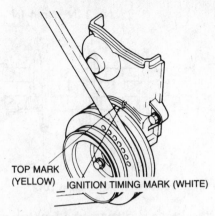

Timing marks for 1986 engines

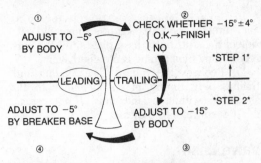

Schematic diagram of timing procedures for the rotary engine

states/Canada models have three notches on the pulley; all others have two. Looking straight down on the marks, the one on the left is ATDC, the one in the center is TDC, the one on the right is BTDC, the mark you want. On 1973 and later models, the one on the left is TDC, the one on the right is BTDC.

7. If the timing is not as specified, adjust the timing by loosening the distributor hold-down bolt and rotating the distributor in the proper direction. When the proper ignition timing is obtained, tighten the holddown bolt on the distributor.

8. Check the centrifugal advance mechanism by accelerating the engine to about 2,000 rpm. If the ignition timing advances, the mechanism is working properly.

9. Stop the engine and remove the timing light.

10. Reset the idle to specifications.

11. Remove the tachometer.

Rotary Pick-Up

1. Connect a tachometer to the engine.

2. Disconnect and plug the vacuum tube on the distributor.

3. Connect a timing light to the wire from the leading (lower) plug of the front rotor housing.

4. Start the engine and run it at idle speed.

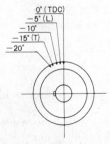

Rotary engine timing marks. Numbers preceded by a minus sign (−), are degrees ATDC

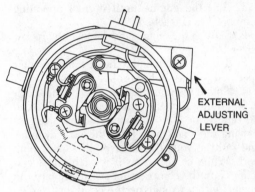

The external adjusting lever on rotary engine distributors

5. Shine the timing light on the indicator pin located on the front cover.

6. If the leading timing mark is not correctly aligned with the pointer, stop the engine.

7. Loosen the distributor locknut and rotate the distributor housing (with the engine running) until the timing marks align. Stop the engine and tighten the distributor locknut.

8. Recheck the timing.

9. Change the connection of the timing light to the wire from the trailing (top) plug in the front rotor housing.

10. Start the engine and shine the timing light at the indicator pin. If the trailing timing falls within the specifications, no further adjustments are necessary.

11. If the trailing timing is not within specifications, proceed with the rest of the procedure.

12. If the trailing timing is not within specifications, adjust the trailing and leading timing as follows:

13. Adjust the trailing timing to specification by rotating the distributor body, as in Step 7.

14. Check the leading timing again and record how much it differs from specification.

15. Remove the distributor cap and rotor.

16. Loosen the breaker base setscrews (the ones directly opposite each other near the outside of the distributor base plate until the correct leading plug timing is obtained again.

17. Recheck the timing. The leading and trailing plug timing marks should both be aligned (or within specifications). If not, repeat the procedure until they are.

Valve Lash

ADJUSTMENT

All Piston Engines

1. Run the engine until normal operating temperature is reached.

2. Shut off the engine and remove the rocker cover.

3. Torque the cylinder head bolts to their specified torque, in the proper sequence.

4. Rotate the crankshaft so that the no.1 cylinder (front) is in the firing position. This can be determined, on gasoline engines, by removing the spark plug from the no.1 cylinder and putting your thumb over the spark plug port. When compression is felt, the no.1 cylinder is on the compression stroke. Rotate the engine with a wrench on the crankshaft pulley and stop it at TDC of the compression stroke on the no.1 cylinder, as confirmed by the alignment of the TDC mark in the crankshaft pulley and the timing pointer. On the diesel, no.1 TDC can be determined by loosening the no.1 injection pipe at the injection pump. Whe the engine is slowly cranked, fuel will squirt

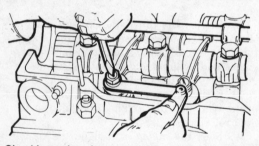

Checking valve clearance at the valve

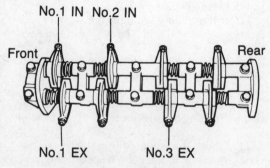

Adjust these valves with #1 piston at TDC

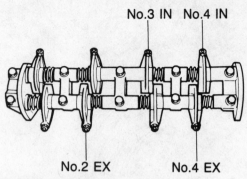

Adjust these valves with #4 piston at TDC

from the loosened fitting as no.1 piston approaches TDC. Confirm TDC by the timing mark alignment.

5. Check the valve clearances by inserting a flat feeler gauge between the end of the valve stem and the rocker arm. The clearance can be checked for no.1 and no.2 intake valves and no.1 and no.3 exhaust valves.

6. If the valve clearance is incorrect, loosen the adjusting screw locknut and adjust the clearance by turning the adjusting screw with the feeler blade inserted. Hold the adjusting screw in the correct position and tighten the locknut.

7. Rotate the crankshaft (in the normal direction of rotation), until no.4 piston is at TDC compression. Adjust no.3 and no.4 intake valves and no.2 and no.4 exhaust valves.

8. Install the rocker arm cover and torque the nuts to 18 in.lb.

Rotary Pick-Up

Because of its unique design, there are no valves to adjust on the rotary engine.

Carburetor

IDLE SPEED AND MIXTURE ADJUSTMENT

Gasoline Piston Engines

1. Thoroughly warm the engine to normal operating temperature. The water temperature gauge will tell you when normal operating temperature is reached.

2. Make sure that the choke valve is fully open. On 1978 and later models, run the engine at 2,000 rpm for 3 minutes. Disconnect the canister purge hose at the canister.

3. Connect a tachometer according to the manufacturer's instructions.

4. Adjust the idle speed screw to specifications.

5. The mixture should be checked by, at least, a CO meter. On 1986 models, the mixture should not have to be adjusted, and, must be adjusted by a qualified technician. The car-

1. Mixture adjust screw   2. Speed adjust screw

Idle speed adjustment points for the 1,586cc engine

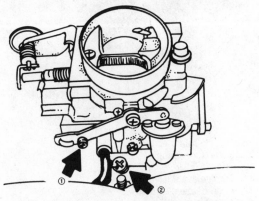

1. Throttle adjust screw   2. Mixture adjust screw

Idle speed adjustment points for the 1,796cc and 1970cc engines. 1970cc engines have a limiter cap over the mixture screw which must be removed with a hacksaw for adjustment

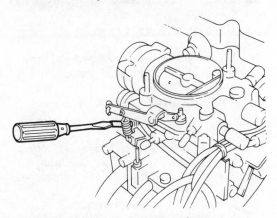

Idle adjustment screw on 1986 engines

Rotary Pick-Up

1. Warm the engine to normal operating temperature.

2. Be sure that the secondary throttle valve is fully returned.

3. Set the parking brake and block the front wheel.

4. Connect a tachometer according to the manufacturer's instructions.

5. Adjust the idle speed to specifications. The idle speed should ONLY be adjusted with the idle air screw. Never use the idle fuel jet screw to adjust the idle. This screw is preset at the factory and should not be moved.

6. After idle speed adjustment, you should also have the mixture checked with a CO analyzer.

Diesel Engine

1. Make sure that the throttle cable deflection, at the pump, is 1.0mm–3.0mm. Adjust it with the adjusting nut, if it is not.

2. Loosen the locknut on the idle speed adjusting bolt. Turn the bolt to the right to increase the idle; to the left to decrease it.

3. Race the engine two or three times and let it return to idle. Check the idle speed and readjust if necessary. Idle speed should be 700 rpm.

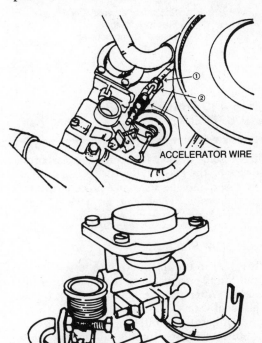

ACCELERATOR WIRE

bon monoxide percentage at idle should be as specified on the underhood sticker.

6. Disconnect the tachometer. Connect the purge hose on 1978 and later models.

Diesel idle speed adjustment points. No. 1 is the accelerator cable locknut, no. 2 is the accelerator cable adjusting nut, no. 3 is the idle adjusting bolt locknut, no. 4 is the idle adjusting bolt

1. Primary stage
2. Secondary stage
3. Primary air vent
4. Secondary air vent
5. Fuel inlet fitting
6. Bimetal spring housing
7. Vacuum diaphragm
8. Throttle return spring
9. Sub-return spring
10. Throttle lever
11. Throttle adjust screw
12. Mixture adjust screw
13. Air adjust screw
14. Accelerating pump connecting rod

Rotary engine carburetor

IDLE AND THROTTLE SCREW ADJUSTMENT

Gasoline Engine

If for some reason (tampering or carburetor overhaul) the idle and throttle screws need adjustment, use the following procedures. Two procedures are given; one for a HC/CO analyzer and one for a fuel flow meter.

FUEL FLOW METER

It is best to use this procedure to set the idle and throttle screws after they have been disturbed. After you are finished, check the adjustment with a HC/CO analyzer.

1. Adjust the throttle angle opening to specifications with the throttle adjustment screw. The adjustment should be made from the fully closed position. Tighten the locknut after the adjustment is complete.

2. Connect a fuel flow meter.

3. Start the engine and set the approximate idle speed with the idle air screw.

4. Adjust the idle fuel flow to specifications with the idle fuel screw.

5. Use the idle air screw to set the idle speed again.

6. Repeat this procedure (Steps 4 and 5) until both the idle fuel flow and the idle speed are within specifications.

7. Disconnect the fuel flow meter.

HC/CO ANALYZER

1. If you have not already done so, adjust the throttle angle opening to specifications. Make the adjustment from the fully closed position.

2. Lock the nut after adjustment.

3. Start the engine and adjust the idle speed with the idle air screw.

4. Using the gas analyzer, check the HC (hydrocarbon) and CO (carbon monoxide) readings. If the HC is less than 200 ppm (parts per million) and the CO is between 0.1–2.0%, no further adjustment is needed.

5. If the HC and CO are not within specifi-

cations, adjust the CO reading to as close to 0.1% as possible, keeping the HC reading below 200 ppm. Use the idle fuel screw to make this adjustment.

6. Recheck the idle speed and adjust if necessary, using the idle air screw.

7. Recheck the HC and CO readings to be sure that they are within limits. Repeat Steps 5 and 6 until the CH, CO and idle speed are all within specifications.

Engine and Engine Overhaul

3

ENGINE ELECTRICAL

Electronic Ignition

Used for the first time on the 1979 models, this system replaces the points and condenser in the distributor. It is almost maintenance free. The most commonly replaced parts are the rotor and cap, which are still routine maintenance items. Other items, such as the pick-up coil and signal rotor, are replaced when they fail. An air gap adjustment is possible only on the 1979 models. Adjustments are not possible on later models.

NOTE: *This book contains simple testing procedures for the electronic ignition. More comprehensive testing on this system and other electronic control systems on your truck can be found in CHILTON'S GUIDE TO ELECTRONIC ENGINE CONTROLS, book part number 7535, available at most book stores and auto parts stores, or available directly from Chilton Co.*

AIR GAP ADJUSTMENT

1979 MODELS ONLY

1. Using a wrench on the crankshaft pulley nut, turn the distributor shaft until one of the high points on the pick-up coil is aligned with the signal rotor face.
2. Loosen the set screws and move the pick-up coil until the gap between it and the signal rotor is 0.008–0.024 in., measured with a brass or plastic feeler gauge.
3. Tighten the set screws and recheck the gap.

TESTING

Pick-Up Coil Resistance

Unplug the primary ignition wire connector and connect an ohmmeter across the two prongs of the pick-up coil connector. Resistance, at 68°F

(20°C), should be 800Ω ± 80Ω for 1979 models, 1,050Ω ± 105Ω for 1980 and later models.

Ignition Wires

TESTING

Ignition wires are those which carry electricity between the center tower of the distributor cap and the center tower of the coil, and those that carry electricity between the distributor cap and the spark plugs.

These may be tested visually by gently bending them and inspecting the bends for signs of cracking. If cracks are found, replace the wires. It's a good idea to replace the wires in sets, rather than individually.

The wires should also be tested for resistance with an ohmmeter. Resistance should be 16KΩ per meter (39.37 inches).

Ignition Coil

TESTING

Piston Engine

Measure the primary resistance by connecting an ohmmeter across the positive (+) and negative (−) terminals of the coil. Primary resistance, at 68°F (20°C), should be 6–30KΩ.

Measure the secondary resistance by connecting an ohmmeter across the center tower connector and the positive (+) terminal. Resistance, at 68°F (20°C), should be 6–30KΩ

If a megaohm tester is available, connect it between the negative (−) terminal and the outside of the coil casing. This will test the coil insulation and show if there is an internal short. Resistance, at 68°F (20°C), should be >10MΩ.

Rotary Engine

Two coils, leading and trailing, are used. The leading coil is type HP5-13J; the trailing, type HP5-13E.

Measure the primary resistance by connecting an ohmmeter across the positive (+) and negative (−) terminals of the coil. Primary resistance, at 68°F (20°C), should be 1.35Ω on the leading coil; 1.46Ω on the trailing coil.

Measure the secondary resistance by connecting an ohmmeter across the center tower connector and the positive (+) terminal. Resistance, at 68°F (20°C), should be 8.7KΩ on the leading coil; 9.5KΩ on the trailing coil.

Check across the external resistor on each coil. Resistance, at 68°F (20°C), should be 1.4Ω on the leading coil; 1.6Ω on the trailing coil.

Distributor

REMOVAL AND INSTALLATION

Rotary Engine

The distributor is located on the right front side of the engine. In contrast to earlier rotary engines from Mazda, this uses only one distributor, not two.

1. Open the hood and locate the distributor.
2. Remove the distributor cap.
3. Disconnect the vacuum tube from the advance unit.
4. Disconnect the primary wires from the distributor.
5. Matchmark the distributor body in relation to the engine front housing.
6. Remove the distributor holddown bolt.
7. Pull the distributor from the front cover.
8. Turn the eccentric shaft until the TDC mark on the drive pulley aligns with the indicator pin on the front cover.
9. Align the matchmarks on the distributor housing and drive gear.
10. Install the distributor so that the distributor lockbolt is located in the center of the slot. Engage the gears.
11. Rotate the distributor clockwise until the

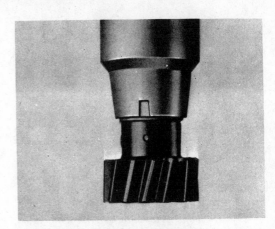

Rotary engine distributor matchmarks

leading contact point set starts to separate, and tighten the distributor lockbolt.

12. Install the distributor cap and connect the primary wires.
13. Set the ignition timing.
14. Connect the vacuum tube to the vacuum unit on the distributor.

Piston Engine

1. Matchmark the distributor cap and the body of the distributor. Remove the distributor cap.
2. Disconnect the vacuum hose from the diaphragm.
3. Scribe matchmarks on the distributor body and the cylinder block to indicate the relative positions.
4. Scribe another mark on the distributor body indicating the position of the rotor.
5. Disconnect the primary wires from the distributor.
6. Remove the distributor holddown nut, lockwasher and flat washer.
7. Remove the distributor from the engine.

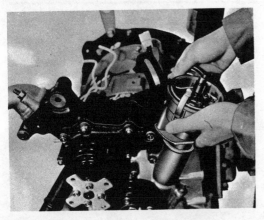

Pull the distributor from the rotary engine

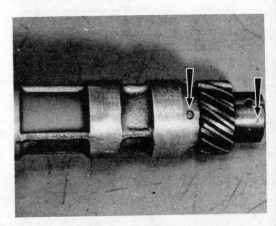

Typical piston engine distributor matchmarks

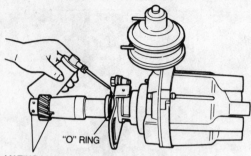

"O" RING

MATING MARK

Lubricating O-ring

NOTE: *Do not crank the engine while the distributor is removed.*

8. Align the matchmarks on the distributor gear and body.

9. If the engine was cranked while the distributor was removed, turn the crankshaft until the no. 1 cylinder is at the top of the compression stroke. This can be determined by feeling compression with your thumb over the spark plug port. The 5° BTDC mark on the crankshaft pulley should also be aligned with the timing pointer. Slide the distributor into the engine with the rotor pointing to the no. 1 cylinder firing position (see Firing Order).

10. Lubricate the O-ring with clean engine oil. If the engine has not been cranked while the distributor was removed, slide the distributor (with the O-ring) into the engine, aligning the matchmarks made during removal.

11. Install the flat washer, lockwasher and holddown nut, but do not tighten the nut.

12. Install the distributor cap and connect the primary wires.

13. Set the ignition timing, and tighten the holddown nut.

14. Connect the vacuum line.

Alternator

ALTERNATOR PRECAUTIONS

Some precautions should be taken when working on this, or any other, AC charging system.

1. Never switch battery polarity.

2. When installing a battery, always connect the grounded terminal first.

3. Never disconnect the battery while the engine is running.

4. If the molded connector is disconnected from the alternator, never ground the hot wire.

5. Never run the alternator with the main output cable disconnected.

6. Never electric weld around the truck without disconnecting the alternator.

7. Never apply any voltage in excess of battery voltage while testing.

8. Never jump a battery for starting purposes with more than 12v.

REMOVAL AND INSTALLATION

Piston Engine

1. Open the hood and remove the battery. Disconnect the negative (ground) cable first.

2. Remove the nut holding the alternator wire to the terminal at the rear of the alternator.

3. Pull the multiple connector from the rear of the alternator.

4. Remove the alternator adjusting arm bolt. Swing the alternator in and disengage the fan belt.

5. On the 1,586cc and 1,796cc, remove the distributor cap and rotor from the distributor.

6. Remove the alternator pivot bolt and remove the alternator from the truck.

7. Installation is the reverse of the removal. Be sure to adjust the drive belt tension and to connect the battery properly.

Alternator and Regulator Specifications

Engine (cc)	Years	Alternator Field Current @ 12v (amps)	Output (amps)	Regulated Volts @ 75°F	Regulator Air Gap (in.)	Point Gap (in.)	Back Gap (in.)
1,308	1972–77	40	50	14.5	0.040	0.035	0.040
1,586	1972	28	45	14.5	0.040	0.035	0.035
1,586	1973–75	28	45	14.5	0.045	0.015	0.043
1,796	1976–78	30	45	14–15	0.040	0.015	0.043
1,970	1979–81	30	45	14–15	0.040	0.015	0.040
	1982–84	23	45	13.5	—	—	—
1,998	1986	21	55	14.7	—	—	—
2,209	1982–84	28	80	13.5	—	—	—

Rotary Engine

1. Disconnect the battery ground cable at the negative (–) terminal.

2. Disconnect all of the leads from the alternator.

3. Remove the alternator adjusting link bolt. Do not remove the adjusting link.

4. Remove the alternator securing nuts and bolts. Withdraw the drive belt and remove the alternator.

5. Installation is performed in the reverse order of removal. Adjust the drive belt tension as detailed below.

BELT TENSION ADJUSTMENT

1. Check the drive belt tension by applying about 22 lbs. of thumb pressure to the belt, midway between the eccentric shaft and alternator pulleys.

2. If belt deflection is not within specifications, loosen, but do not remove, the bolt on the adjusting link.

3. Push the alternator in the direction required to obtain proper belt deflection.

CAUTION: *Do not pry or pound on the alternator housing.*

4. Tighten the adjusting link bolt to 20 ft.lb.

Regulator

NOTE: *1982 and later trucks use an integral regulator, built into the alternator. No adjustments are possible.*

REMOVAL AND INSTALLATION

Piston Engine

1. Raise the hood and disconnect the negative battery cable.

2. Disconnect the regulator wires at the multiple connector.

3. Remove the two regulator attaching screws and remove the regulator from the splash shield.

4. Position the regulator on the fender splash shield and install the two attaching screws.

5. Connect the regulator wires at the multiple connector.

6. Connect the negative battery cable.

7. Start the engine and be sure that the charging system indicator light goes out.

Rotary Engine

1. Disconnect the battery ground cable at the negative (–) battery terminal.

2. Disconnect the wiring from the regulator.

3. Remove the regulator mounting screws.

4. Remove the regulator.

5. Installation is performed in the reverse order of removal.

REGULATOR TEST

The alternator regulator is composed of two control units: a constant voltage relay and a pilot lamp relay.

Checking The Constant Voltage Relay

1. Use an almost fully charged battery and connect a voltmeter between the A and E terminals of the regulator.

2. Run the engine at 2,000 rpm and read the voltmeter. It should read from 14–15v.

3. If not, adjust the voltage relay.

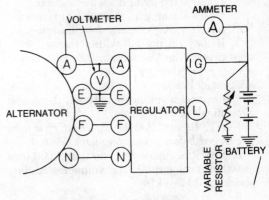

Checking the constant voltage relay

Checking The Pilot Lamp Relay

1. Using a voltmeter and variable resistor, construct a circuit as shown.

2. Light the pilot lamp.

3. Slide the knob of the variable resistor so that the voltage gradually increases.

4. Read the voltage between the N and E terminals of the regulator. If the voltage is 3.7–5.7v, it is operating properly.

5. Slide the knob of the variable resistor to decrease the voltage. Note the point on the voltmeter where the light will light again. If the reading is less than 3.5v, the unit is working properly.

6. Disconnect the test instruments.

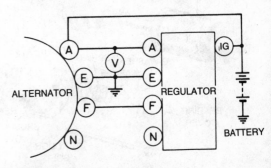

Checking the pilot lamp relay

ADJUSTING THE REGULATOR

Piston Engine

1. Check the air gap, back gap and point gap with a wire gauge. If they are not within specifications, adjust the gap by bending the stationary bracket.

2. After the gaps are correctly set, adjust the voltage setting. Bend the upper plate down to increase the voltage setting, or bend it up to increase the voltage setting.

Rotary Engine

1. Remove the cover from the regulator.

2. Check the air gap, the point gap, and the back gap with a feeler gauge (see illustration).

3. If they do not fall within the specifications given in the Alternator and Regulator chart above, adjust the gaps by bending the stationary contact bracket.

4. Connect a voltmeter between the A and E terminals of the regulator.

NOTE: *Be sure that the car's battery is fully charged before proceeding with this test.*

5. Start the engine and run it at 2,000 rpm (4,000 alternator rpm). The voltmeter reading should be 13.5–14.5v.

6. Stop the engine.

7. Bend the upper plate down to decrease the voltage setting, or up to increase the setting as required.

8. If the regulator cannot be brought within specifications, replace it.

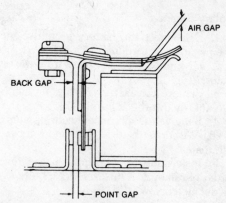

Regulator mechanical adjustments

9. When the test is completed, disconnect the voltmeter and replace the regulator cover.

Starter

The Mazda starter is a 4-brush, 4-field, 4-pole wound unit. Engine cranking occurs when the starter solenoid (mounted on the starter) in energized through the ignition switch. The solenoid shifts the starter pinion into mesh with the flywheel ring gear. At the same time, the main contacts of the solenoid are closed and the battery current is directed to the starter causing the armature to rotate. After the engine starts, the starter is disengaged when the ignition switch is returned to the RUN position. This opens the circuit to the starter sole-

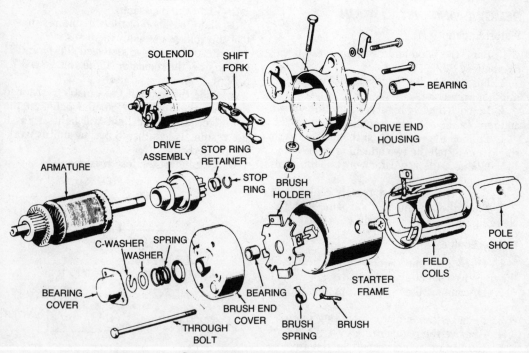

Starter used on 1972–76 engines

Starter Specifications

Engine (cc)	Year	Lock Test			No-Load Test			Brush * Spring Tension (oz.)
		Amps	Volts	Torque (ft. lb.)	Amps	Volts	RPM	
1,308	1972–77	①	5.0	②	③	11.5	④	49–63
1,586	1972	<560	7.5	>9.4	<60	11.5	>6,000	35–46
1,586	1973–75	<400	6.0	6.7	<53	10.5	>5,000	49–63
1,796	1976–78	<310	5.0	5.4	<53	11.5	>6,800	49–63
1,970	1979–84	310	5.0	5.4	<53	11.5	>6,800	49–63
1,998	1986	<430	5.0	7.2	<60	11.5	>6,500	50–60
2,209	1982–84	1,050	2.0	21.6	180	11.0	3,800	49–63

① standard starter: 780
   high torque starter: 1,100
② standard starter: 8.0
   high torque starter: 17.4
③ standard starter: <75
   high torque starter: <100
④ standard starter: >4,900
   high torque starter: >7,800

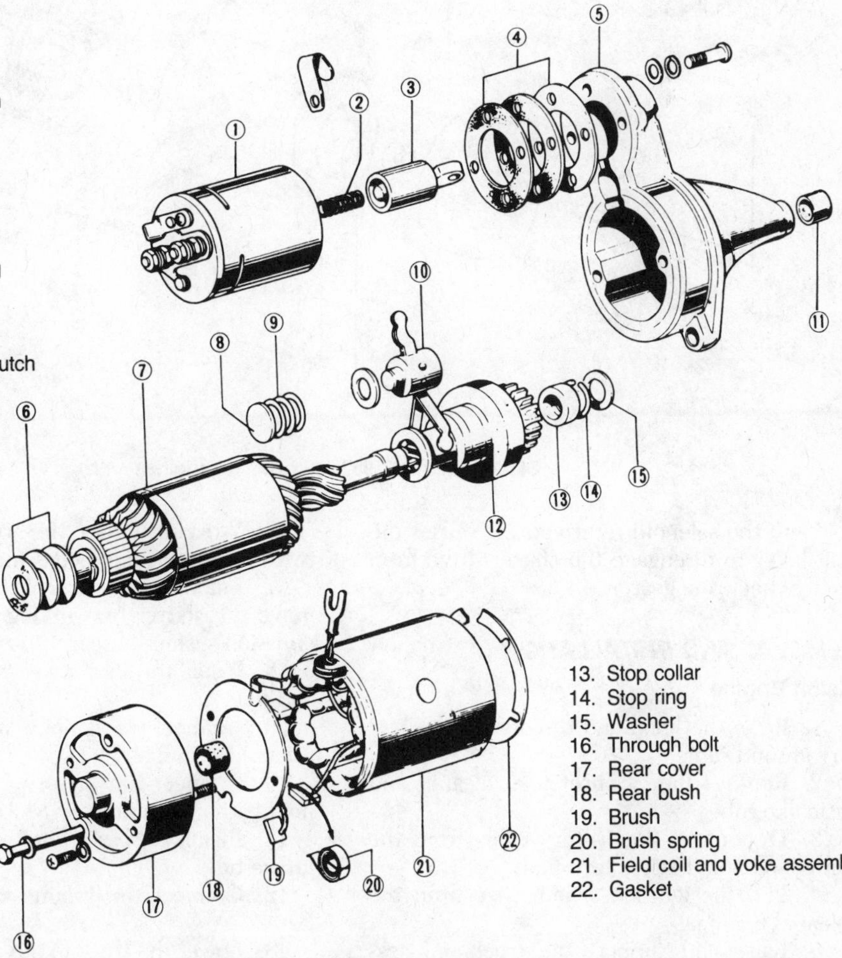

1. Magnetic switch
2. Spring
3. Plunger
4. Washer
5. Driving housing
6. Washer
7. Armature
8. Rubber packing
9. Spring
10. Driving lever
11. Front bush
12. Over-running clutch

13. Stop collar
14. Stop ring
15. Washer
16. Through bolt
17. Rear cover
18. Rear bush
19. Brush
20. Brush spring
21. Field coil and yoke assembly
22. Gasket

Starter used on 1979–81 engines

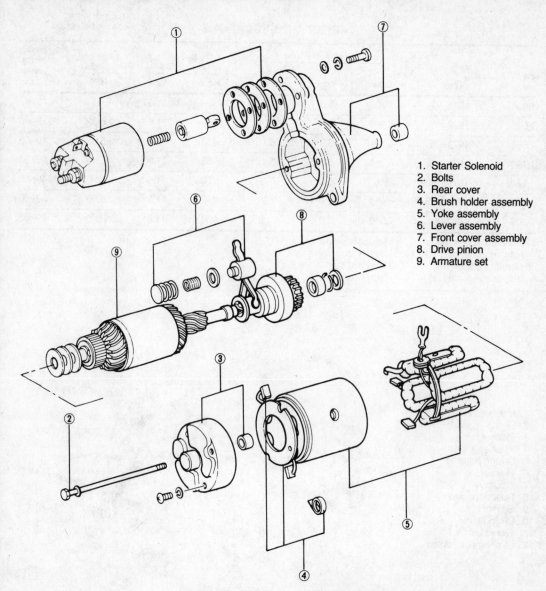

1. Starter Solenoid
2. Bolts
3. Rear cover
4. Brush holder assembly
5. Yoke assembly
6. Lever assembly
7. Front cover assembly
8. Drive pinion
9. Armature set

Starter used on 1982–86 gasoline engines

noid and the solenoid return spring causes the shift lever to disengage the starter drive from the flywheel ring gear.

REMOVAL AND INSTALLATION

Piston Engine

1. Raise the hood and disconnect the battery ground cable.

2. Remove the carburetor air cleaner and air intake tube.

3. Disconnect the battery cable from the starter solenoid battery terminal.

4. Pull the ignition switch wire from the solenoid terminal.

5. Raise and support the truck on jackstands.

6. Working under the truck, remove the two starter attaching bolts, washers and nuts.

7. Tilt the drive end of the starter and remove the starter by working it out below the emission system hoses.

8. Install the starter and two bolts, washers and nuts.

9. Connect the ignition switch wire to the solenoid terminal.

10. Connect the battery cable to the solenoid battery terminal.

11. Install the carburetor air cleaner and air intake tube.

12. Connect the ground cable to the battery.

13. Lower the truck to the ground and check the operation of the starter.

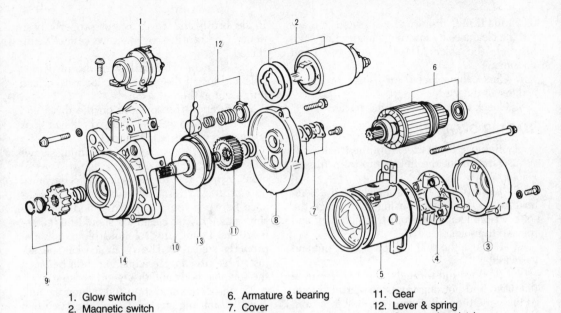

1. Glow switch
2. Magnetic switch
3. Rear bracket
4. Brush holder assembly
5. Yoke assembly
6. Armature & bearing
7. Cover
8. Center bracket
9. Drive pinion
10. Pinion shaft
11. Gear
12. Lever & spring
13. Over running clutch
14. Front bracket assembly

Starter used on 1982–84 diesel engines

Rotary Engine

NOTE: *There are two possible locations for the starter motor; one is the lower right hand side of the engine and the other is on the upper right hand side.*

1. Remove the ground cable from the negative (–) battery terminal.

2. If the car is equipped with the lower mounted starter, remove the gravel shield from underneath the engine.

CAUTION: *Be extremely careful not to contact the hot exhaust pipe, while working underneath the car.*

3. Remove the battery cable from the starter terminal.

4. Disconnect the solenoid leads from the solenoid terminals.

5. Remove the starter securing bolts and withdraw the starter assembly.

6. Installation is the reverse of the above steps.

BRUSH REPLACEMENT

1. Remove the starter. Remove the two screws attaching the brush end bearing cover and remove the bearing cover.

2. Remove the through-bolts.

3. Remove the C-washer, washer and spring from the brush end of the armature shaft.

4. Pull the brush end cover from the starter frame.

5. Unsolder the two brushes from the field terminals and slide the brush holder from the armature shaft.

6. Cut the two brush wires at the brush holder and solder two new brushes to the brush holder.

7. Install the brush holder on the armature shaft and install the brushes in the brush holder.

8. Install the brush end cover on the starter frame and be sure that the ear tabs of the brush holder are aligned with the through-bolt holes.

9. Install the through-bolts.

10. Install the rubber gasket, spring, washer and C-washer on the armature shaft.

11. Install the brush end bearing cover on the brush end cover and install the two screws. If the brush holder tabs are not aligned with the through-bolts, the bearing cover screws cannot be installed.

SOLENOID REPLACEMENT

1. Remove the starter from the truck.

2. Disconnect the field strap from the solenoid terminal.

3. Remove the two solenoid attaching screws.

4. Disengage the solenoid plunger from the shift fork and remove the solenoid.

5. Install the solenoid on the drive end housing, making sure that the solenoid plunger hook is engaged with the shift fork.

6. Apply 12v to the solenoid S terminal and measure the clearance between the starter drive and the stop-ring retainer. It should be 0.080–

0.020 in. If not, remove the solenoid and adjust the clearance by inserting an adjusting shim between the solenoid body and drive end housing.

7. Check the solenoid for proper operation and install the starter.

8. Check the operation of the starter.

STARTER OVERHAUL

1. Remove the starter from the truck.

2. Disconnect the field strap from the solenoid.

3. Remove the screws attaching the solenoid to the drive end housing. Disengage the solenoid plunger hook from the shift fork and remove the solenoid.

4. Remove the shift fork pivot bolt, nut and lockwasher.

5. Remove the through-bolts and separate the drive end housing from the starter frame. At the same time, disengage the shift fork from the drive assembly.

6. Remove the two screws attaching the brush end bearing cover to the brush end cover.

7. Remove the C-washer, washer and spring from the brush end of the armature shaft.

8. Pull the brush end cover from the starter frame.

9. Slide the armature from the starter frame and brushes.

10. Slide the drive stop-ring retainer toward the armature and remove the stop-ring. Slide the retainer and drive assembly off the armature shaft.

11. Remove the field brushes from the brush holder and separate the brush holder from the starter frame.

12. Position the drive assembly on the armature shaft.

13. Position the drive stop-ring retainer on the armature shaft and install the drive stop-ring. Slide the stop-ring retainer over the stop-ring to secure the stop-ring on the shaft.

14. Position the armature in the starter frame. Install the brush holder on the armature and starter frame. Install the brushes in the brush holder.

15. Install the drive end housing on the armature shaft and starter housing. Engage the shift fork with the starter drive assembly as you move the drive end housing toward the starter frame.

16. Install the brush end cover on the starter frame making sure that the rear tabs of the brush holder are aligned with the through-bolt holes.

17. Install the through-bolts.

18. Install the rubber washer, spring, washer and C-washer on the armature shaft at the brush end. Install the brush end bearing cover on the brush end cover and install the attaching screws.

If the brush end cover is not properly positioned, the bearing cover screws cannot be installed.

19. Align the shift fork with the pivot bolt hole and install the pivot bolt, lockwasher and nut. Tighten the nut securely.

20. Position the solenoid on the drive end housing. Be sure that the solenoid plunger hook is engaged with the shift fork.

21. Install the two solenoid retaining screws and washers.

22. Apply 12v to the solenoid S terminal (ground the M terminal) and check the clearance between the starter drive and the stop-ring retainer. The clearance should be 0.080–0.020 in. If not, the solenoid plunger is not properly adjusted. The clearance can be adjusted by inserting an adjusting shim between the solenoid body and drive end housing.

23. Install the field strap and tighten the nut.

24. Install the starter. Check the operation of the starter.

Battery
REMOVAL AND INSTALLATION
Piston Engine

The battery is located under the hood at the front corner of the engine compartment, on the passenger's side. It can be removed by disconnecting the two battery cables and removing the holddown clamps. Installation is the reverse of removal.

Rotary Engine

The battery is located in a compartment on the right side of the cargo bed just in front of the rear wheel.

1. Open the door and hold it open with the rubber snubber provided.

2. Pull the latch handle (on the outside of the battery box) upward to release the latch.

3. Swing the outside of the battery box downward and push the top strap upward.

4. Grab the metal tab at the bottom edge of the battery box and pull it outward, sliding the battery into the open.

5. Installation is the reverse of removal.

PISTON ENGINE SERVICE

Design

Mazda piston engines are 1,586cc (96.8 cu. in.), used from 1972–75; 1,796cc (109.6 cu.in.) used from 1976–78; 1,970cc (120.2 cu.in.) used from 1979–84; a 2,209cc (134.8 cu.in.) diesel, used from 1981–84; a 1,998cc gasoline engine first used in the 1986 models.

General Engine Specifications

Year	Engine (cc)	Fuel System Type	SAE net Horsepower @ rpm	SAE net Torque ft. lb. @ rpm	Bore x Stroke	Comp. Ratio	Oil Press. (psi.) @ 2000 rpm
1972–77	1,308	4-bbl	90 @ 6000	96 @ 4000	—	9.2:1	70
1972–75	1,586	2-bbl	70 @ 5000	82 @ 3400	3.071 x 3.267	8.6:1	50–64
1976–78	1,796	2-bbl	75 @ 4800	93 @ 3000	3.071 x 3.700	8.6:1	50–64
1979–84	1,970	2-bbl	77 @ 4300	109 @ 2400	3.150 x 3.860	8.6:1	50–64
1982–84	2,209	Diesel	58 @ 4000	88 @ 2500	3.500 x 3.500	21.0:1	55–60
1986	1,998	2-bbl	80 @ 4500	110 @ 2500	3.390 x 3.390	8.6:1	55–60

All are single overhead camshaft, four cylinder engines. Water cools the thin cast iron block and case aluminum alloy cylinder head with multispherical type combustion chambers. The diesel engine utilizes replaceable cylinder liners.

Engine Overhaul

Most engine overhaul procedures are fairly standard. In addition to specific parts replacement procedures and complete specifications for your individual engine, this chapter also is a guide to acceptable rebuilding procedures. Examples of standard rebuilding practice are shown and should be used along with specific details concerning your particular engine.

Competent and accurate machine shop services will ensure maximum performance, reliability and engine life.

In most instances it is more profitable for the do-it-yourself mechanic to remove, clean and inspect the component, buy the necessary parts and deliver these to a shop for actual machine work.

On the other hand, much of the rebuilding work (crankshaft, block, bearings, piston rods, and other components) is well within the scope of the do-it-yourself mechanic.

TOOLS

The tools required for an engine overhaul or parts replacement will depend on the depth of your involvement. With a few exceptions, they will be the tools found in a mechanic's tool kit (see Chapter 1). More in-depth work will require any or all of the following:
 • a dial indicator (reading in thousandths) mounted on a universal base
 • micrometers and telescope gauges
 • jaw and screw-type pullers
 • scraper
 • valve spring compressor
 • ring groove cleaner
 • piston ring expander and compressor
 • ridge reamer
 • cylinder hone or glaze breaker
 • Plastigage®
 • engine stand

Use of most of these tools is illustrated in this chapter. Many can be rented for a one-time use from a local parts jobber or tool supply house specializing in automotive work.

Occasionally, the use of special tools is called for. See the information on Special Tools and Safety Notice in the front of this book before substituting another tool.

INSPECTION TECHNIQUES

Procedures and specifications are given in this chapter for inspecting, cleaning and assessing the wear limits of most major components. Other procedures such as Magnaflux® and Zyglo® can be used to locate material flaws and stress cracks. Magnaflux® is a magnetic process applicable only to ferrous materials. The Zyglo® process coats the material with a fluorescent dye penetrant and can be used on any material. Check for suspected surface cracks can be more readily made using spot check dye. The dye is sprayed onto the suspected area, wiped off and the area sprayed with a developer. Cracks will show up brightly.

OVERHAUL TIPS

Aluminum has become extremely popular for use in engines, due to its low weight. Observe the following precautions when handling aluminum parts:
 • Never hot tank aluminum parts (the caustic hot tank solution will eat the aluminum.
 • Remove all aluminum parts (identification tag, etc.) from engine parts prior to the tanking.
 • Always coat threads lightly with engine oil or anti-seize compounds before installation, to prevent seizure.
 • Never over-torque bolts or spark plugs especially in aluminum threads.

Stripped threads in any component can be repaired using any of several commercial repair kits (Heli-Coil®, Microdot®, Keenserts®, etc.).

When assembling the engine, any parts that will be frictional contact must be prelubed to provide lubrication at initial start-up. Any product specifically formulated for this purpose can be used, but engine oil is not recommended as a prelube.

When semi-permanent (locked, but removable) installation of bolts or nuts is desired, threads should be cleaned and coated with Loctite® or other similar, commercial non-hardening sealant.

REPAIRING DAMAGED THREADS

Several methods of repairing damaged threads are available. Heli-Coil® (shown here), Keenserts® and Microdot® are among the most widely used. All involve basically the same principle—drilling out stripped threads, tapping the hole and installing a prewound insert—making welding, plugging and oversize fasteners unnecessary.

Two types of thread repair inserts are usually supplied—a standard type for most Inch Coarse, Inch Fine, Metric Course and Metric Fine thread sizes and a spark lug type to fit most spark plug port sizes. Consult the individual manufacturer's catalog to determine exact applications. Typical thread repair kits will contain a selection of prewound threaded in-

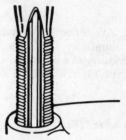

Drill out the damaged threads with specified drill. Drill completely through the hole or to the bottom of a blind hole

With the tap supplied, tap the hole to receive the thread insert. Keep the tap well oiled and back it out frequently to avoid clogging the threads

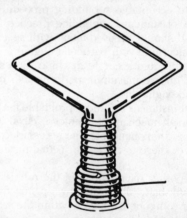

Screw the threaded insert onto the installation tool until the tang engages the slot. Screw the insert into the tapped hole until it is ¼–½ turn below the top surface. After installation break off the tang with a hammer and punch

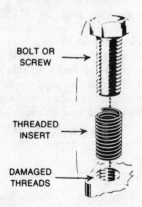

BOLT OR SCREW

THREADED INSERT

DAMAGED THREADS

Damaged bolt holes can be repaired with thread repair inserts

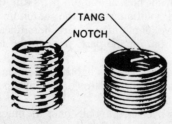

TANG

NOTCH

Standard thread repair insert (left) and spark plug thread insert (right)

serts, a tap (corresponding to the outside diameter threads of the insert) and an installation tool. Spark plug inserts usually differ because they require a tap equipped with pilot threads and a combined reamer/tap section. Most manufacturers also supply blister-packed thread repair inserts separately in addition to a master kit containing a variety of taps and inserts plus installation tools.

Before effecting a repair to a threaded hole, remove any snapped, broken or damaged bolts or studs. Penetrating oil can be used to free frozen threads; the offending item can be removed with locking pliers or with a screw or stud extractor. After the hole is clear, the thread can be repaired, as follows:

Checking Engine Compression

A noticeable lack of engine power, excessive oil consumption and/or poor fuel mileage measured over an extended period are all indicators of internal engine war. Worn piston rings, scored or worn cylinder bores, blown head gaskets, sticking or burnt valves and worn valve seats are all possible culprits here. A check of each cylinder's compression will help you locate the problems.

As mentioned in the Tools and Equipment section of Chapter 1, a screw-in type compression gauge is more accurate than the type you simply hold against the spark plug hole, although it takes slightly longer to use. It's worth it to obtain a more accurate reading. Follow the procedures below for gasoline and diesel engined trucks.

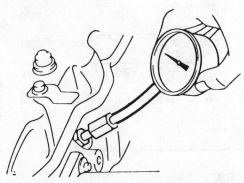

The screw-in type compression gauge is more accurate

Gasoline Engines

1. Warm up the engine to normal operating temperature.

2. Remove all spark plugs.

3. Disconnect the high tension lead from the ignition coil.

4. On fully open the throttle either by operating the carburetor throttle linkage by hand or by having an assistant floor the accelerator pedal.

5. Screw the compression gauge into the no. 1 spark plug hole until the fitting is snug.

NOTE: *Be careful not to crossthread the plug hole. On aluminum cylinder heads use extra care, as the threads in these heads are easily ruined.*

6. Ask an assistant to depress the accelera-

tor pedal fully on both carbureted and fuel injected trucks. Then, while you read the compression gauge, ask the assistant to crank the engine two or three times in short bursts using the ignition switch.

7. Read the compression gauge at the end of each series of cranks, and record the highest of these readings. Repeat this procedure for each of the engine's cylinders. Compare the highest reading of each cylinder to the compression pressure specification in the Tune-Up Specifications chart in Chapter 2. The specs in this chart are maximum values.

A cylinder's compression pressure is usually acceptable if it is not less than 80% of maximum. The difference between each cylinder should be no more than 12–14 pounds.

8. If a cylinder is unusually low, pour a tablespoon of clean engine oil into the cylinder through the spark plug hole and repeat the compression test. If the compression comes up after adding the oil, it appears that the cylinder's piston rings or bore are damaged or worn. If the pressure remains low, the valves may not be seating properly (a valve job is needed), or the head gasket may be blown near that cylinder. If compression in any two adjacent cylinders is low, and if the addition of oil doesn't help the compression, there is leakage past the head gasket. Oil and coolant water in the combustion chamber can result from this problem. There may be evidence of water droplets on the engine dipstick when a head gasket has blown.

Diesel Engines

Checking cylinder compression on diesel engines is basically the same procedure as on gasoline engines except for the following:

1. A special compression gauge adaptor suitable for diesel engines (because these engines have much greater compression pressures) must be used.

2. Remove the injector tubes and remove the injectors from each cylinder.

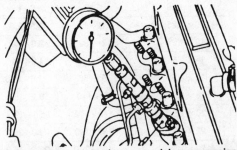

Diesel engines require a special compression gauge adaptor

Standard Torque Specifications and Fastener Markings

In the absence of specific torques, the following chart can be used as a guide to the maximum safe torque of a particular size/grade of fastener.

- There is no torque difference for fine or coarse threads.
- Torque values are based on clean, dry threads. Reduce the value by 10% if threads are oiled prior to assembly.
- The torque required for aluminum components or fasteners is considerably less.

U.S. Bolts

SAE Grade Number	1 or 2			5			6 or 7		
Number of lines always 2 less than the grade number.									
Bolt Size (Inches)—(Thread)	Maximum Torque			Maximum Torque			Maximum Torque		
	Ft./Lbs.	Kgm	Nm	Ft./Lbs.	Kgm	Nm	Ft./Lbs.	Kgm	Nm
1/4 — 20	5	0.7	6.8	8	1.1	10.8	10	1.4	13.5
— 28	6	0.8	8.1	10	1.4	13.6			
5/16 — 18	11	1.5	14.9	17	2.3	23.0	19	2.6	25.8
— 24	13	1.8	17.6	19	2.6	25.7			
3/8 — 16	18	2.5	24.4	31	4.3	42.0	34	4.7	46.0
— 24	20	2.75	27.1	35	4.8	47.5			
7/16 — 14	28	3.8	37.0	49	6.8	66.4	55	7.6	74.5
— 20	30	4.2	40.7	55	7.6	74.5			
1/2 — 13	39	5.4	52.8	75	10.4	101.7	85	11.75	115.2
— 20	41	5.7	55.6	85	11.7	115.2			
9/16 — 12	51	7.0	69.2	110	15.2	149.1	120	16.6	162.7
— 18	55	7.6	74.5	120	16.6	162.7			
5/8 — 11	83	11.5	112.5	150	20.7	203.3	167	23.0	226.5
— 18	95	13.1	128.8	170	23.5	230.5			
3/4 — 10	105	14.5	142.3	270	37.3	366.0	280	38.7	379.6
— 16	115	15.9	155.9	295	40.8	400.0			
7/8 — 9	160	22.1	216.9	395	54.6	535.5	440	60.9	596.5
— 14	175	24.2	237.2	435	60.1	589.7			
1 — 8	236	32.5	318.6	590	81.6	799.9	660	91.3	894.8
— 14	250	34.6	338.9	660	91.3	849.8			

Metric Bolts

Relative Strength Marking	4.6, 4.8			8.8		
Bolt Markings						
Bolt Size Thread Size x Pitch (mm)	Maximum Torque			Maximum Torque		
	Ft./Lbs.	Kgm	Nm	Ft./Lbs.	Kgm	Nm
6 x 1.0	2–3	.2–.4	3–4	3–6	.4–.8	5–8
8 x 1.25	6–8	.8–1	8–12	9–14	1.2–1.9	13–19
10 x 1.25	12–17	1.5–2.3	16–23	20–29	2.7–4.0	27–39
12 x 1.25	21–32	2.9–4.4	29–43	35–53	4.8–7.3	47–72
14 x 1.5	35–52	4.8–7.1	48–70	57–85	7.8–11.7	77–110
16 x 1.5	51–77	7.0–10.6	67–100	90–120	12.4–16.5	130–160
18 x 1.5	74–110	10.2–15.1	100–150	130–170	17.9–23.4	180–230
20 x 1.5	110–140	15.1–19.3	150–190	190–240	26.2–46.9	160–320
22 x 1.5	150–190	22.0–26.2	200–260	250–320	34.5–44.1	340–430
24 x 1.5	190–240	26.2–46.9	260–320	310–410	42.7–56.5	420–550

NOTE: *Don't forget to remove the washer underneath each injector; otherwise, it may get lost when the engine is cranked.*

3. When fitting the compression gauge adaptor to the cylinder head, make sure the bleeder of the gauge (if equipped) is closed.

4. When reinstalling the injector assemblies, install new washers underneath each injector.

Engine

REMOVAL AND INSTALLATION

1,586cc

1. Scribe the locations of the hood hinges and remove the hood.

2. Remove the engine splash shield.

3. Drain the coolant.

CAUTION: *When draining the coolant, keep in mind that cats and dogs are attracted by the ethelyne glycol antifreeze, and are quite likely to drink any that is left in an uncovered container or in puddles on the ground. This will prove fatal in sufficient quantity. Always drain the coolant into a sealable container. Coolant should be reused unless it is contaminated or several years old.*

4. Drain the engine oil.

5. Disconnect the battery cables and remove the battery.

6. Disconnect the primary wire and coil wire from the distributor.

7. Disconnect the wire at the B terminal of the alternator and disconnect the plug from the rear of the alternator.

8. Disconnect the wire from the oil pressure switch.

9. Disconnect the engine ground wire.

10. Remove the air cleaner and heat insulator.

11. Disconnect the breather hose from the rocker cover.

12. Disconnect the water temperature gauge wire and solenoid valve wire.

13. Disconnect the starter wires.

14. Remove the upper and lower radiator hoses.

15. Remove the bolts attaching the radiator cowling. The cowling can only be removed after the radiator has been removed.

16. Unbolt and remove the radiator and cowling.

17. Disconnect the heater hoses from the intake manifold.

18. Disconnect the throttle cable from the carburetor and remove the throttle linkage from the rocker cover attaching point.

19. Disconnect the choke cable from the carburetor.

20. Disconnect the fuel ventilation hose from the oil separator.

21. Disconnect the fuel line at the carburetor and plug the fuel line.

22. Remove the starter.

23. Disconnect the exhaust pipe from the manifold.

24. Remove the clutch cover plate.

25. Support the transmission with a jack and remove the bolts attaching the engine to the transmission.

26. Unbolt the right and left engine mounts.

27. Attach a lifting sling to the engine and pull the engine forward until it clears the clutch shaft.

28. Lift the engine from the truck.

29. Installation is the reverse of removal. Be sure to check all fluid levels.

1,796cc, 1979–84 1,970cc

1. Scribe the locations of the hood hinges and remove the hood.

2. Remove the engine splash shield.

3. Drain the coolant.

CAUTION: *When draining the coolant, keep in mind that cats and dogs are attracted by the ethelyne glycol antifreeze, and are quite likely to drink any that is left in an uncovered container or in puddles on the ground. This will prove fatal in sufficient quantity. Always drain the coolant into a sealable container. Coolant should be reused unless it is contaminated or several years old.*

4. Drain the engine oil.

5. Disconnect the battery cables and remove the battery.

6. Disconnect the primary wire and coil wire from the distributor.

7. Disconnect the wires at the alternator and disconnect the plug from the rear of the alternator. Remove the drive belts from the alternator, thermactor and air conditioning compressor. Remove each of these items from their mounting brackets and position them out of the way. It is not necessary to disconnect any refrigerant lines.

8. Disconnect the wire from the oil pressure switch.

9. Disconnect the engine ground wire.

10. Remove the air cleaner and heat insulator.

11. Disconnect the breather hose from the rocker cover.

12. Disconnect the water temperature gauge wire and solenoid valve wire.

13. Disconnect the starter wires.

14. Remove the upper and lower radiator hoses. On models with automatic transmission, disconnect the cooling lines at the radiator tank.

15. Remove the bolts attaching the radiator

cowling. The cowling can only be removed after the radiator has been removed.

16. Unbolt and remove the radiator and cowling.

17. Disconnect the heater hoses from the intake manifold.

18. Disconnect the throttle cable from the carburetor and remove the throttle linkage from the rocker cover attaching point or the intake manifold clamps, on later models.

19. Disconnect the choke cable from the carburetor.

20. Disconnect the fuel ventilation hose from the oil separator.

21. Disconnect the fuel line at the carburetor and plug the fuel line.

22. Raise and support the truck on jackstands. Remove the starter.

23. Disconnect the exhaust pipe from the manifold.

24. Remove the engine skid plate. Remove the clutch cover plate. On trucks with automatic transmission, disconnect the vacuum line at the modulator. Remove the torque converter access cover, matchmark the converter and drive plate and remove the four converter-to-drive plate bolts.

25. Support the transmission with a jack and remove the bolts attaching the engine to the transmission.

26. Unbolt the right and left engine mounts.

27. Attach a lifting sling to the engine and pull the engine forward until it clears the clutch shaft.

28. Lift the engine from the truck.

29. Installation is the reverse of removal. Be sure to check all fluid levels. Observe the following torques:
　　Converter-to-drive plate: 25–35 ft.lb.
　　Transmission-to-engine: 25–35 ft.lb.

1986 1,998cc

1. Scribe the locations of the hood hinges and remove the hood.

2. Remove the engine splash shield.

3. Drain the coolant.

CAUTION: *When draining the coolant, keep in mind that cats and dogs are attracted by the ethelyne glycol antifreeze, and are quite likely to drink any that is left in an uncovered container or in puddles on the ground. This will prove fatal in sufficient quantity. Always drain the coolant into a sealable container. Coolant should be reused unless it is contaminated or several years old.*

4. Drain the engine oil.

5. Disconnect the battery cables and remove the battery.

6. Remove the air cleaner and the oil dipstick.

7. Remove the radiator shroud and the engine fan. Place the fan in an upright position to avoid fluid loss from the fan clutch.

8. Disconnect and tag all wires, hoses, cables, pipes and linkage from the engine.

9. Remove the 3-way solenoid valves, but don't disconnect the vacuum tubes.

10. Remove the duty solenoid valves, but don't disconnect the vacuum tubes.

11. Remove the emissions canister.

12. Remove the radiator.

13. Disconnect the exhaust pipe at the manifold and remove the exhaust manifold.

14. Dismount the air conditioning compressor and position it out of the way. Don't disconnect any refrigerant lines.

15. Dismount the power steering pump and position it out of the way without disconnecting any hoses.

16. Raise and support the truck on jackstands.

17. Remove the starter.

18. Attach a lifting sling and shop crane to the engine lifting eyes and take up the weight of the engine.

19. Support the transmission with a floor jack and remove the transmission-to-engine bolts.

20. Remove the engine support plates and mounting nuts, push the engine forward to clear the transmission and lift it out of the truck.

21. Installation is the reverse of removal. Torque the exhaust manifold-to-engine nuts to 16–21 ft.lb.

2,209cc Diesel

1. Scribe the locations of the hood hinges and remove the hood.

2. Remove the engine splash shield.

3. Drain the coolant.

CAUTION: *When draining the coolant, keep in mind that cats and dogs are attracted by the ethelyne glycol antifreeze, and are quite likely to drink any that is left in an uncovered container or in puddles on the ground. This will prove fatal in sufficient quantity. Always drain the coolant into a sealable container. Coolant should be reused unless it is contaminated or several years old.*

4. Drain the engine oil.

5. Disconnect the battery cables and remove the battery.

6. Remove the air cleaner and the oil dipstick.

7. Remove the radiator shroud and the engine fan. Place the fan in an upright position to avoid fluid loss from the fan clutch.

8. Disconnect and tag all wires, hoses, cables, pipes and linkage from the engine.

9. Remove the clutch release cylinder.

10. Remove the oil cooler.

11. Remove the radiator.

12. Disconnect the exhaust pipe at the manifold and remove the exhaust manifold.

13. Dismount the air conditioning compressor and position it out of the way. Don't disconnect any refrigerant lines.

14. Dismount the power steering pump and position it out of the way without disconnecting any hoses.

15. Raise and support the truck on jackstands.

16. Attach a lifting sling and shop crane to the engine lifting eyes and take up the weight of the engine.

17. Support the transmission with a floor jack and remove the transmission-to-engine bolts.

18. Remove the engine support plates and mounting nuts, push the engine forward to clear the transmission and lift it out of the truck.

19. Installation is the reverse of removal.

Rocker Shafts

REMOVAL AND INSTALLATION

1,586cc, 1,796cc, 1979-84 1,970cc

This operation should only be performed on a cold engine; the bolts which hold the rocker shafts in place also hold the cylinder head to the block.

1. Raise the hood and cover the fenders.

2. Disconnect the choke cable, if so equipped.

3. If equipped, disconnect the air by-pass valve cable.

4. Disconnect the spark plug wires. Remove the wires from the spark plug wire clips on the rocker covers and position them out of the way.

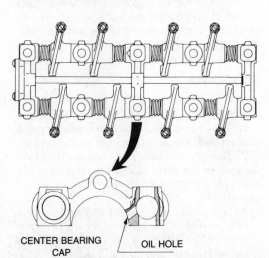

Rocker arm assembly used on the 1,586cc, 1,796cc and 1,970cc engines

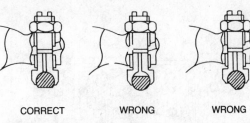

Proper positioning of the rocker arm adjusting screw ball

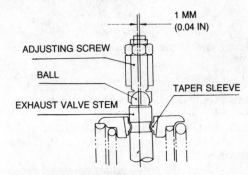

Offset of the exhaust rocker arm

5. Remove the rocker cover and discard the gasket.

6. Remove the rocker arm shaft attaching bolts evenly and remove the rocker arm shafts.

7. Install the rocker arm assemblies on the cylinder head. Install the balls on each rocker arm as shown. Temporarily tighten the cylinder head bolts to specifications and offset each rocker arm support 0.04 in. from the valve stem center. Torque the bolts to specifications.

8. Adjust the valves cold.

9. Clean the mating surfaces of the cylinder head and rocker cover.

10. Install the rocker cover with a new gasket. Torque the bolts to 24–36 in.lb.

11. Install the spark plug wire on the plugs. Place the wires in the clips on the rocker cover. Connect the choke and air by-pass valve cable.

12. Start the engine and check for leaks.

13. Allow the engine to reach operating temperature, torque the head bolts to specifications and adjust the valves hot.

1986 1,998cc

1. Raise the hood and cover the fenders.

2. Disconnect the accelerator cable, if necessary.

3. If equipped, disconnect the air by-pass valve cable.

4. Disconnect the spark plug wires. Remove the wires from the spark plug wire clips on the rocker covers and position them out of the way.

5. Remove the rocker cover and discard the gasket.

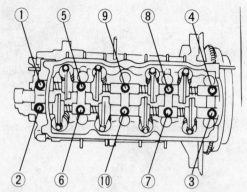

Rocker arm torque sequence for the 1,998cc engine

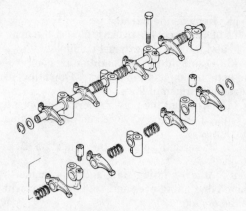

Diesel rocker arm parts

6. Remove the rocker arm shaft attaching bolts evenly, in the order shown, and remove the rocker arm shafts.

7. Install the rocker arm assemblies on the cylinder head. Torque the bolts, in the order shown, to 13–20 ft.lb.

8. Check the valve adjustment and reset, if necessary.

9. Clean the mating surfaces of the cylinder head and rocker cover.

10. Install the rocker cover with a new gasket. Torque the bolts to 24–36 in.lb.

11. Install the spark plug wire on the plugs. Place the wires in the clips on the rocker cover. Connect the choke and air by-pass valve cable.

12. Start the engine and check for leaks.

13. Allow the engine to reach operating temperature, torque the head bolts to specifications and adjust the valves hot.

2,209cc Diesel

This operation should only be performed on a cold engine; the bolts which hold the rocker shafts in place also hold the cylinder head to the block.

1. Raise the hood and cover the fenders.

2. Disconnect the accelerator cable, if necessary.

3. Remove the rocker cover and discard the gasket.

4. Remove the rocker arm shaft attaching bolts evenly and remove the rocker arm shafts. Lift out the pushrods, keeping them in order for proper installation. When installing the pushrods, make sure they are seated in the depressed bottom section of the tappets.

5. Install the rocker arm assemblies on the cylinder head. Torque the bolts to specifications.

6. Adjust the valves cold.

7. Clean the mating surfaces of the cylinder head and rocker cover.

8. Install the rocker cover with a new gasket. Torque the bolts to 24–36 in.lb.

9. Install the spark plug wire on the plugs. Place the wires in the clips on the rocker cover. Connect the choke and air by-pass valve cable.

10. Start the engine and check for leaks.

11. Allow the engine to reach operating temperature, torque the head bolts to specifications and adjust the valves hot.

DISASSEMBLY

All Except the Diesel

NOTE: *Don't mix up the parts! Keep them identified!*

1. Lay out a clean piece of heavy paper marked with a location for each component.

2. Remove the end caps and slide each piece from the shafts, placing it on its identifying mark on the paper.

NOTE: *Don't hammer off any piece. If any piece is difficult to remove, soak it in Liquid Wrench®, WD-40® or similar solution. Hammering on any part will distort it!*

3. Check each component for wear, damage, heat scoring or cracks. Replace any suspect part. Clean all parts in a safe solvent. Make sure that all oil holes are clear.

4. Assembly is the reverse of disassembly.

Diesel Engine

NOTE: *Don't mix up the parts! Keep them identified!*

1. Lay out a clean piece of heavy paper marked with a location for each component.

2. Remove the snap rings and washers from the ends of the shaft. Slide each piece from the shaft, placing it on its identifying mark on the paper.

NOTE: *Don't hammer off any piece. If any piece is difficult to remove, soak it in Liquid Wrench®, WD-40® or similar solution. Hammering on any part will distort it!*

3. Check each component for wear, damage, heat scoring or cracks. Replace any sus-

pect part. Clean all parts in a safe solvent. Make sure that all oil holes are clear.

4. Assembly is the reverse of disassembly.

Intake Manifold
REMOVAL AND INSTALLATION
Gasoline Engine

1. Drain the cooling system.

CAUTION: *When draining the coolant, keep in mind that cats and dogs are attracted by the ethelyne glycol antifreeze, and are quite likely to drink any that is left in an uncovered container or in puddles on the ground. This will prove fatal in sufficient quantity. Always drain the coolant into a sealable container. Coolant should be reused unless it is contaminated or several years old.*

2. Remove the air cleaner.
3. Remove the accelerator linkage.
4. Disconnect the choke cable and fuel line. Plug the fuel line.
5. Disconnect the PCV valve hose.
6. Disconnect the heater return hose and by-pass hose.
7. Remove the intake manifold-to-cylinder head attaching nuts.
8. Remove the manifold and carburetor as an assembly.
9. Clean the gasket mating surfaces.
10. Install a new gasket and the manifold on the studs. Torque the attaching nuts to specification, working from the center outward.
11. Connect the PCV valve hose to the manifold.
12. Connect the by-pass and heater return hoses.
13. Install the accelerator linkage.
14. Connect the fuel line and choke cable.
15. Replace the air cleaner.
16. Fill the cooling system. Run the engine and check for leaks.

Diesel Engine

1. Remove the air inlet tube.
2. Remove the vacuum sensing line.
3. Bleed the fuel system and remove the injection lines. Cap the lines to prevent the entrance of dirt.
4. Disconnect the accelerator linkage and any other hose or wire connected to the manifold.
5. Remove the fuel return line.
6. Unbolt and remove the manifold.
7. Discard the gasket and thoroughly clean the gasket surfaces of the head and manifold.
8. Installation is the reverse of removal. Always use a new gasket. Torque the manifold bolts to 11–17 ft.lb.

Exhaust Manifold
REMOVAL AND INSTALLATION

1. Raise and support the truck.
2. Remove the two attaching nuts from the exhaust pipe at the manifold. On the 1986 1,998cc, remove the exhaust manifold heat shield.
3. Remove the manifold attaching nuts.
4. Remove the manifold.
5. Apply a light film of graphite grease to the exhaust manifold mating surfaces before installation.
6. Install the manifold on the studs and install the attaching nuts. Torque the attaching nuts to specifications.
7. Install a new exhaust pipe gasket. Connect the exhaust pipe gasket. Connect the exhaust pipe and torque the nuts to specifications.

Thermostat
REMOVAL AND INSTALLATION

1. Drain enough coolant to bring the coolant level down below the thermostat housing. the thermostat housing is located on the left front side of the cylinder block. Disconnect the temperature sending unit wire.

CAUTION: *When draining the coolant, keep in mind that cats and dogs are attracted by the ethelyne glycol antifreeze, and are quite likely to drink any that is left in an uncovered container or in puddles on the ground. This will prove fatal in sufficient quantity. Always drain the coolant into a sealable container. Coolant should be reused unless it is contaminated or several years old.*

2. Remove the coolant outlet elbow. If so equipped, position the vacuum control valve out of the way. The vacuum control valve is not used on California trucks.

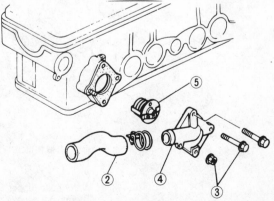

Thermostat used on the 1,586cc, 1,796cc and 1,970cc engines. Remove the parts in the order shown

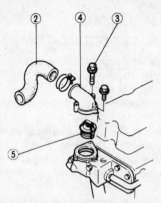

Thermostat used on the diesel engine. Remove the parts in the order shown

3. Disconnect the coolant by-pass hose from the thermostat housing.

4. Remove the thermostat and housing from the engine.

5. Note the position of the jiggle pin and remove the thermostat from the housing.

6. Remove all gasket material from the parts.

7. Position the thermostat in the housing with the jiggle pin up. Coat a new gasket with sealer and install it on the thermostat housing.

8. Install the thermostat housing using a new gasket with water resistant sealer. Torque the bolts to 20 ft.lb.

9. Install the coolant outlet elbow and vacuum control valve (if equipped).

10. Connect the by-pass and radiator hoses.

11. Connect the temperature sending unit wire.

12. Fill the cooling system with the proper coolant. Operate the engine and check the coolant lever. Check for leaks.

Cylinder Head

REMOVAL AND INSTALLATION

1,586cc, 1,796cc, and 1979–84 1,970cc

NOTE: *The engine must be cold before proceeding.*

1. Drain the cooling system.

CAUTION: *When draining the coolant, keep in mind that cats and dogs are attracted by the ethelyne glycol antifreeze, and are quite likely to drink any that is left in an uncovered container or in puddles on the ground. This will prove fatal in sufficient quantity. Always drain the coolant into a sealable container. Coolant should be reused unless it is contaminated or several years old.*

2. Scribe alignment marks around the hood hinges and remove the hood.

3. Remove the air cleaner.

4. Disconnect the coil wire and vacuum line from the distributor.

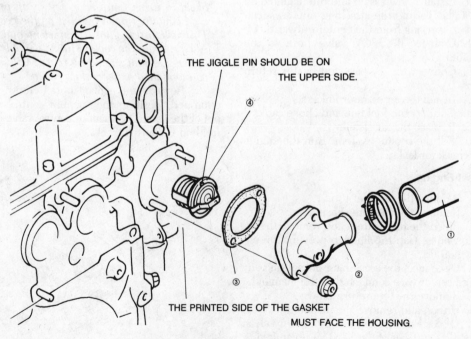

THE JIGGLE PIN SHOULD BE ON THE UPPER SIDE.

THE PRINTED SIDE OF THE GASKET MUST FACE THE HOUSING.

1. Water hose, upper
2. Thermostat cover
3. Gasket
4. Thermostat

Thermostat used on the 1,998cc engine. Remove the parts in the order shown

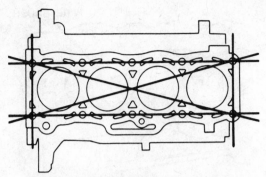

Check the block deck for distortion by running a straightedge along both sides, both ends, and diagonally, as shown

5. Rotate the crankshaft to put the no.1 cylinder at TDC on the compression stroke.

6. Remove the plug wires and distributor cap as a unit.

7. Remove the distributor.

8. Remove the rocker arm cover.

9. Raise and support the truck. Disconnect the exhaust pipe from the manifold.

10. Remove the accelerator linkage. Disconnect and tag all wiring, cable and hoses from the engine.

11. Remove the water pump. Remove the nut, washer and the distributor gear from the camshaft.

12. Remove the nut, washer and camshaft gear. Support the timing chain from falling into the timing chain case. Do not remove the cam gear from the timing chain. The relationship between the chain and gear teeth should not be disturbed.

13. Remove the cylinder head bolts, and cylinder head-to-front cover bolt.

14. Remove the rocker arm assembly.

15. Remove the camshaft and camshaft gear.

16. Lift off the cylinder head.

17. Remove all tension from the timing chain.

18. Clean the rocker cover gasket surface at the head and the cover. Clean the head gasket surface at the head and the block. Clean the

water pump gasket surface at the head and the block. Clean the water pump gasket surface at the head gasket surface and the front cover.

19. Check the cylinder head flatness with a straightedge and feeler blades. It should not exceed 0.003 in. in any six in. span or 0.006 in. overall. If necessary, the cylinder head can be milled, not to exceed 0.008 in.

20. Clean the cylinder head bolt holes of oil and dirt.

21. Position a new head gasket on the cylinder block.

22. Install the cylinder head on the block using the guides at either end of the block.

23. Install the camshaft on the head and camshaft gear.

24. Install the rocker arm assembly.

25. Install the head bolts. Torque the bolts to specification, in the order shown.

26. Install the camshaft gear washer and nut.

27. Install the distributor gear, washer and nut.

28. Time the engine. Follow the instructions under Timing Chain Tensioner Adjustment.

29. Adjust the timing chain tension. See Timing Chain Tensioner Adjustment.

30. Connect the exhaust pipe to the exhaust manifold. Lower the truck.

31. Install the distributor, distributor cap and plug wires.

32. Install the lower intake bracket bolt.

33. Install the accelerator linkage.

34. Connect the vacuum line and coil wire.

35. Adjust the valve clearance cold.

36. Install the rocker arm cover. Torque the bolts to 24–36 in.lb. Fill the cooling system.

37. Run the engine until normal operating temperature is reached, and check for leaks. Adjust the valve clearance hot.

38. Adjust the carburetor and ignition timing. Install the air cleaner and install the hood.

1986 1,998cc

NOTE: *The engine must be cold before proceeding.*

1. Drain the cooling system.

CAUTION: *When draining the coolant, keep in mind that cats and dogs are attracted by the ethelyne glycol antifreeze, and are quite likely to drink any that is left in an uncovered container or in puddles on the ground. This will prove fatal in sufficient quantity. Always drain the coolant into a sealable container. Coolant should be reused unless it is contaminated or several years old.*

2. Scribe alignment marks around the hood hinges and remove the hood.

3. Remove the air cleaner.

4. Disconnect, and tag, all wires, hoses,

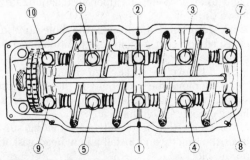

Rocker shaft/head bolt torque sequence for the 1,586cc, 1,796cc and 1970cc engines

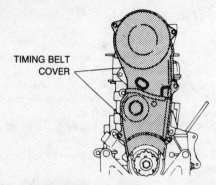

TIMING BELT COVER

1,998cc engine timing belt covers

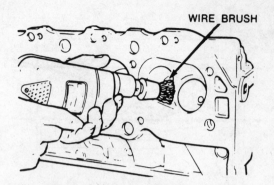

WIRE BRUSH

Remove the carbon from the cylinder head with a wire brush and electric drill

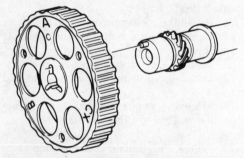

Camshaft pin/mark alignment on the 1,998cc engine

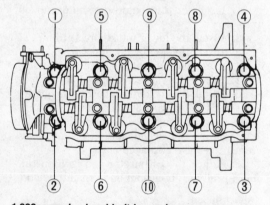

1,998cc engine head bolt loosening sequence

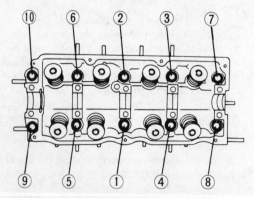

1,998cc engine head bolt tightening sequence

cables, pipes and linkage from the cylinder head.

5. Remove the 3-way solenoid valves, but don't disconnect the vacuum tubes.

6. Remove the duty solenoid valves, but don't disconnect the vacuum tubes.

7. Remove the emissions canister.

8. Remove the distributor cap. Matchmark the rotor position and distributor body, and the body-to-head position. Remove the distributor. Remove the spark plugs.

9. Remove the intake manifold and carburetor as an assembly.

10. Remove the exhaust manifold.

11. Remove the alternator.

12. Disconnect the air injection pipes.

13. Remove the fan pulley, hub and bracket.

14. If so equipped, remove the air conditioning compressor drive belt.

15. If so equipped, remove the power steering pump drive belt.

17. Remove the crankshaft pulley and baffle plate.

18. Remove the upper, then the lower, belt covers.

19. Turn the crankshaft so that the A mark on the camshaft pulley is at the top, aligned with the notch in the front housing.

20. Loosen the tensioner lock bolt and remove the tensioner spring.

21. Mark the forward rotation of the belt with paint to avoid confusion upon installation. Remove the belt.

22. Insert a bar through the hole in the camshaft sprocket to hold it in position and remove the sprocket bolt.

23. Remove the rocker arm cover.

24. Remove the head bolts in the sequence shown, and, with the aid of an assistant or a lifting device, lift off the head.

25. Clean the head and block mating surfaces thoroughly and install a new head gasket on the block.

26. Install the head and tighten the head bolts, in the order shown, to 60–64 ft.lb. If new

head bolts are being used, make sure you use the new, surface treated plain washers.

27. Install the camshaft pulley with the dowel pin on the camshaft engaging the pulley slot just below the A mark on the pulley. Tighten the bolt to 40–48 ft.lb. The timing mark on the front housing and the A mark must be aligned.

28. Lubricate the distributor O-ring with clean engine oil, align all the matchmarks and install the distributor.

29. Replace the belt if it has been contaminated by oil or grease, or shows any sign of damage, wear, cracks or peeling.

30. Make sure that the timing mark on the camshaft is aligned as described above, and that the timing mark (notch) on the crankshaft sprocket is aligned with the triangular shaped mark on the front housing.

31. Install the tensioner and spring, positioning the tensioner all the way to the intake manifold side and temporarily secure it there with the lock bolt.

32. Install the belt onto the sprockets from YOUR right side. If you are reusing the original belt, make sure you follow the directional mark previously made.

33. Loosen the lock bolt so that the tensioner applies tension to the belt.

34. Turn the crankshaft two full revolutions in the direction of normal rotation. This will apply equal tension to all points of the belt.

35. Make sure that the timing marks are still aligned. If not, repeat the belt installation procedure.

36. Tighten the tensioner lock bolt to 30–35 ft.lb.

37. Measure the timing belt tension by pressing on the belt at the midpoint of the longest straight run. Belt deflection should be 11–13mm. If not, repeat the belt adjustment procedure, above.

38. Installation of all other parts is the reverse of removal. Observe the following torques:
- Belt covers: 80 in.lb.
- Fan bracket: 40 ft.lb.
- Exhaust manifold: 16–21 ft.lb.
- Intake manifold: 14–19 ft.lb.
- Spark plugs: 11–17 ft.lb.
- Rocker arm cover: 24–36 in.lb.

39. When installing the drive belts on the various accessories, check the belt deflection as follows:
- Alternator: New, 0.28–0.32 in.
  Used, 0.31–0.36 in.
- Power steering pump:
  New, 0.31–0.49 in.
  Used, 0.43–0.51 in.
- Air conditioning compressor:
  New, 0.39–0.47 in.
  Used, 0.47–0.55 in.

2,209cc Diesel

NOTE: *The engine must be cold before proceeding.*

1. Drain the cooling system.

CAUTION: *When draining the coolant, keep in mind that cats and dogs are attracted by the ethelyne glycol antifreeze, and are quite likely to drink any that is left in an uncovered container or in puddles on the ground. This will prove fatal in sufficient quantity. Always drain the coolant into a sealable container. Coolant should be reused unless it is contaminated or several years old.*

2. Scribe alignment marks around the hood hinges and remove the hood.

3. Remove the air cleaner.

4. Disconnect, and tag, all wires, hoses, cables, pipes and linkage from the cylinder head.

5. Remove the injection lines and injectors. See chapter 4.

6. Remove the intake and exhaust manifolds.

7. Dismount the alternator and move it out of the way.

8. Remove the rocker arm cover. Remove the rocker arm assembly and lift out the pushrods, keeping them in order for proper installation.

9. Remove the cylinder head bolts and, with the aid of an assistant, lift off the head.

10. Installation is the reverse of removal. Make sure that the mating surfaces of the head and block are absolutely clean. Use a new head gasket. When inserting the pushrods, make certain that they bottom in the depressed part of the tappet. Tighten the head bolts, in the order shown, to 80–85 ft.lb., in three equal steps. Torque the rocker cover bolts to 24–36 in.lb.

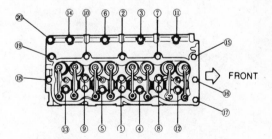

Diesel engine head bolt tightening sequence

Valves and Valve Spring
REMOVAL AND INSTALLATION

1. Remove the cylinder head. On the diesel and the 1986 1,998cc, remove the rocker shaft assembly. On the 1986 1,998cc, lift out the camshaft.

Valve Specifications

Engine (cc)	Seat Angle (deg)	Face Angle (deg)	Spring Test Pressure (lbs. @ in.)	Spring Installed Height (in.)	Stem to Guide Clearance (in.)		Stem Diameter (in.)	
					Intake	Exhaust	Intake	Exhaust
1,586	45	45	①	②	0.0007–0.0021	0.0007–0.0023	0.3150	0.3150
1,796	45	45	①	②	0.0007–0.0021	0.0007–0.0023	0.3150	0.3150
1,970	45	45	①	②	0.0007–0.0021	0.0007–0.0023	0.3150	0.3150
1,998	45	45	③	④	0.0010–0.0024	0.0010–0.0024	0.3177–0.3185	0.3159–0.3165
2,209	⑤	45	⑥	⑦	0.0015–0.0046	0.0020–0.0051	0.3150	0.3150

① Inner: 20.9 @ 1.26
   Outer: 31.4 @ 1.34
② 1972–81 Inner: 1.260
          Outer: 1.339
   1982–84 Inner: 1.306
           Outer: 1.385
③ Outer: 96.3 @ 2.007
   Inner: 95.8 @ 1.722

④ Outer: 2.007
   Inner: 1.722
⑤ Inner: 45
   Exhaust: 30
⑥ Inner: 28 @ 1.488
   Outer: 39.6 @ 1.587
⑦ Inner: 1.488
   Outer: 1.587

2. Remove the deposits from the combustion chambers with a stiff wire brush and scraper before removing the valves. Do not scratch the cylinder head surface.

3. Compress the valve springs with a valve spring compressor. Remove the valve spring retainer locks and release the springs.

4. Fabricate a valve arrangement board to use when you remove the valves, which will indicate the port in which each valve was originally installed. Also note that the valve keys, caps, etc. should be arranged in a manner which

FOR DIMENSIONS, REFER TO SPECIFICATIONS

CHECK FOR BENT STEM

DIAMETER

VALVE FACE ANGLE

1/32" MINIMUM

THIS LINE PARALLEL WITH VALVE HEAD

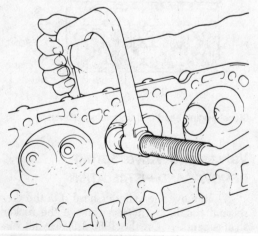

Compressing valve spring—typical

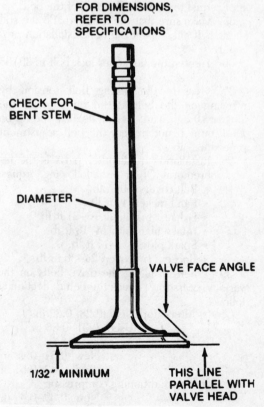

Critical valve dimensions

will allow you to install them on the valve on which they were originally used.

5. Remove and discard the valve seals. On models using the umbrella type seals, note the location of the large and small seals for assembly purposes.

6. Thoroughly clean the valves on the wire wheel of a bench grinder, then clean the cylinder head mating surface with a soft wire wheel, a soft wire brush, or a wooden scraper. Avoid using a metallic scraper, since this can cause damage to the cylinder head mating surface, especially on models with aluminum heads.

7. Using a valve guide cleaner chucked into a drill, clean all of the valve guides.

8. Install each valve into its respective port (guide) of the cylinder head.

9. Mount a dial indicator so that the stem is at 90° to the valve stem, as close to the valve guide as possible.

10. Move the valve off its seat, and measure the valve guide-to-stem clearance by rocking the stem back and forth to actuate the dial indicator.

11. Measure the valve stems using a micrometer, and compare to specifications, to determine whether stem or guide wear is responsible for excessive clearance.

NOTE: *Consult the Specifications tables earlier in this chapter.*

12. Check the cylinder head flatness as described under Cylinder Head Removal and Installation.

REFACING

Using a valve grinder, resurface the valves according to specifications in this chapter.

NOTE: *All machine work should be performed by a competent, professional machine shop.*

Home made valve lapping tool

Lapping the valves by hand

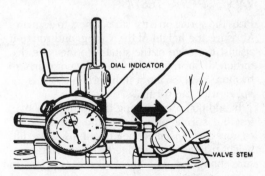

Check the valve stem-to-guide clearance

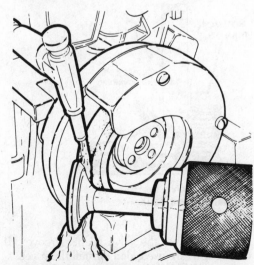

Valve grinding by machine

CAUTION: *Valve face angle is not always identical to valve seat angle.*

A minimum margin of $\frac{1}{32}$ in. should remain after grinding the valve. The valve stem top should also be squared and resurfaced, by placing the stem in the V-block of the grinder, and turning it while pressing lightly against the grinding wheel. Be sure to chamfer the edge

of the tip so that the squared edges don't dig
into the rocker arm.

LAPPING

This procedure should be performed after the
valves and seats have been machined, to insure
that each valve mates to each seat precisely.

1. Invert the cylinder head, lightly lubricate
the valve stems, and install the valves in the
head as numbered.

2. Coat valve seats with fine grinding compound, and attach the lapping tool suction cup
to a valve head.

NOTE: *Moisten the suction cup.*

3. Rotate the tool between your palms,
changing position and lifting the tool often to
prevent grooving.

4. Lap the valve until a smooth, polished seat
is evident.

5. Remove the valve and tool, and rinse away
all traces of grinding compound.

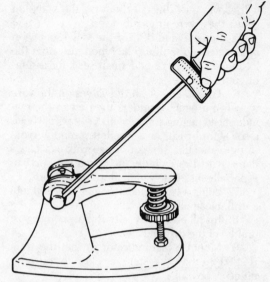

Have the valve spring test pressure checked
professionally

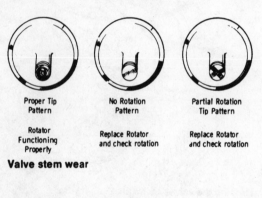

Valve stem wear

VALVE SPRING TESTING

Place the spring on a flat surface next to a square.
Measure the height of the spring, and rotate it
against the edge of the square to measure distortion. If spring height varies (by comparison)
by more than 1/16 in. or if distortion exceeds 1/16
in., replace the spring.

In addition to evaluating the spring as above,
test the spring pressure at the installed and
compressed (installed height minus valve lift)
height using a valve spring tester. Spring pressure should be ± 1 lb. of all other springs in
either position.

VALVE AND SPRING INSTALLATION

NOTE: *Be sure that all traces of lapping
compound have been cleaned off before the
valves are installed.*

1. Lubricate all of the valve stems with a light
coating of engine oil, then install the valves into
the proper ports/guides.

2. If umbrella-type valve seals are used, install them at this time. Be sure to use a seal
protector to prevent damage to the seals as they

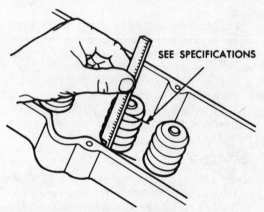

Check valve spring installed height

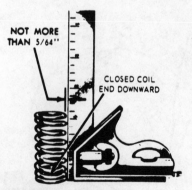

Check the valve spring
free length and square-
ness

are pushed over the valve keeper grooves. If
O-ring seals are used, don't install them yet.

3. Install the valve springs and the spring

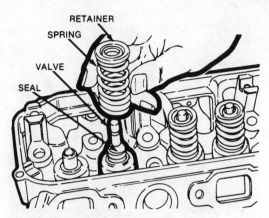

Install valve stem seals

proper driver. On the 1,586cc, 1,796cc, and 1979-84 1,970cc, press the guide in until the ring on the guide just touches the head. On the diesel and the 1986 1,998cc, check the protru-

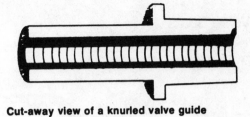

Cut-away view of a knurled valve guide

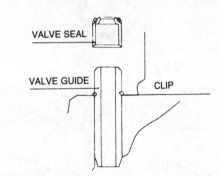

Valve seal

retainers, and using the valve compressing tool, compress the springs.

4. If umbrella-type seals are used, just install the valve keepers (white grease may be used to hold them in place) and release the pressure on the compressing tool. If O-ring type seals are used, carefully work the seals into the second groove of the valve (closest to the head), install the valve keepers and release the pressure on the tool.

NOTE: *If the O-ring seals are installed BEFORE the springs and retainers are compressed, the seal will be destroyed.*

5. After all of the valves are installed and retained, tap each valve spring retainer with a rubber mallet to seat the keepers in the retainer.

Valve Guides

REMOVAL AND INSTALLATION

Valve guides are driven out of the head from the combustion chamber side. Use a driver meant for this purpose. New guides are driven into place from the top of the head, using the

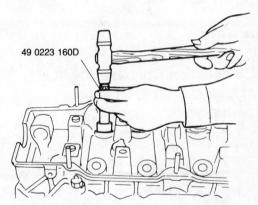

Valve guide driver

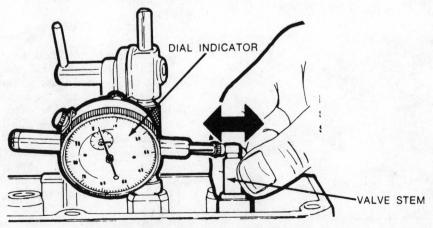

Measuring valve stem-to-guide clearance

sion of the valve guide above the head surface, measuring from the spring seat upward. Protrusion on the diesel should be 16.5mm; on the 1986 1,998cc, 19.1–19.6mm.

Valve Seats

The valve seats are integral with the head. They are not replaceable.

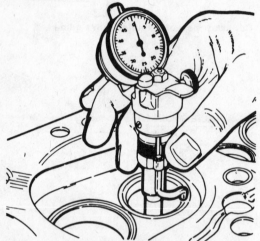

Have the valve seat concentricity checked at a machine shop

Combustion Chamber Inserts

REMOVAL AND INSTALLATION

Diesel Engine

1. Remove the cylinder head from the engine.
2. Remove the rocker arm assembly.
3. Remove the glow plugs.
4. From the top of the head, insert a driver through the glow plug hole and drive out the insert. Discard the welch washer.
5. Position a new insert, aligning it with the

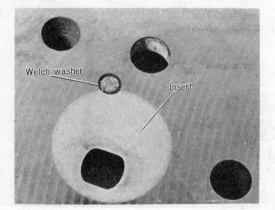

Combustion chamber insert

Driving out the inserts

welch washer hole. Drive the new welch washer into position, with the projected side out. Mark the washer by lightly striking its center with a punch.

Front Cover

REMOVAL AND INSTALLATION

1,586cc, 1,796cc, 1979–84 1,970cc

1. Scribe alignment marks on the hood hinges and remove the hood.
2. Drain the cooling system.
CAUTION: *When draining the coolant, keep in mind that cats and dogs are attracted by the ethylene glycol antifreeze, and are quite likely to drink any that is left in an uncovered container or in puddles on the ground. This will prove fatal in sufficient quantity. Always drain the coolant into a sealable container. Coolant should be reused unless it is contaminated or several years old.*
3. Disconnect the upper and lower radiator hose. Remove the radiator.
4. Remove the accessory drive belts.
5. Remove the crankshaft pulley and the water pump.
6. Remove the cylinder head-to-front cover bolt.
7. Raise and support the truck.
8. Remove the engine skid plate.
9. Disconnect the emission line from the oil pan. Drain the oil from the engine.
10. Remove the oil pan.
11. Remove the alternator and bracket and lay the alternator aside.
12. Remove the steel tube from the front of the engine.
13. Unbolt and remove the front cover.
14. Clean all the gasket mating surfaces.
15. Clean the crankshaft pulley.
16. Use contact cement to cement a new front cover gasket on the block.

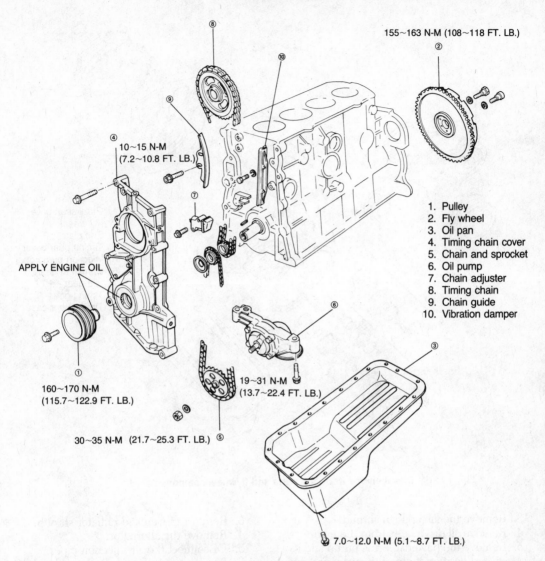

155~163 N-M (108~118 FT. LB.)

10~15 N-M
(7.2~10.8 FT. LB.)

APPLY ENGINE OIL

1. Pulley
2. Fly wheel
3. Oil pan
4. Timing chain cover
5. Chain and sprocket
6. Oil pump
7. Chain adjuster
8. Timing chain
9. Chain guide
10. Vibration damper

160~170 N-M
(115.7~122.9 FT. LB.)

19~31 N-M
(13.7~22.4 FT. LB.)

30~35 N-M (21.7~25.3 FT. LB.)

7.0~12.0 N-M (5.1~8.7 FT. LB.)

Front end parts of the 1,586cc, 1,796cc and 1,970cc engines

17. Install the front cover and torque the attaching bolts to specifications.

18. Install the air pump (if equipped).

19. Install the alternator and bracket.

20. Install the water pump and a new gasket. Torque the bolts to specifications.

21. Connect the by-pass hose and heater hose to the water pump.

22. Install the crankshaft pulley and attaching bolt. Torque the bolt to specifications.

23. Install the alternator belts, and the water pump pulley.

24. Install the fan. Adjust the tension of the belt(s).

25. Install the radiator and the upper and lower hoses.

26. Install the air cleaner.

27. Install the oil pan and the emission line.

28. Install the engine skid plate.

29. Lower the truck to the ground.

30. Fill the engine with oil and fill the cooling system. Run the engine and check for leaks.

31. Install the hood.

2,209cc Diesel

1. Disconnect the battery ground.

2. Drain the cooling system.

CAUTION: *When draining the coolant, keep in mind that cats and dogs are attracted by the ethelyne glycol antifreeze, and are quite likely to drink any that is left in an uncovered container or in puddles on the ground. This will prove fatal in sufficient quantity. Always drain the coolant into a sealable container. Coolant should be reused unless it is contaminated or several years old.*

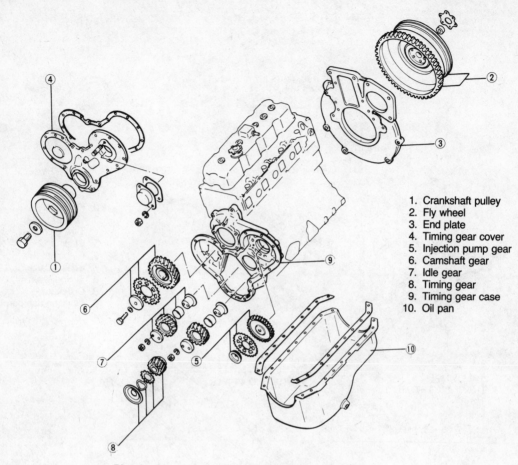

1. Crankshaft pulley
2. Fly wheel
3. End plate
4. Timing gear cover
5. Injection pump gear
6. Camshaft gear
7. Idle gear
8. Timing gear
9. Timing gear case
10. Oil pan

Diesel engine front end parts and flywheel components

3. Remove the fan and fan shroud.

4. Remove all drive belts from the engine.

5. Remove the power steering pump and its bracket, and position it out of the way, without disconnecting the hoses.

6. Remove the water pump.

7. Remove the crankshaft pulley bolt and, using a puller, remove the pulley. Unbolt and remove the timing gear cover. Discard the gasket. The front cover seal may be replaced at this time. Coat the outer circumference of the new seal with sealer, and the sealing surface with clean engine oil.

8. Installation is the reverse of removal. Make sure that the gasket mating surfaces are clean. Use a new gasket coated with sealer. Tighten the timing gear cover bolts to 12–17 ft.lb.; the crankshaft pulley bolts to 150–180 ft.lb.

Timing Belt Covers
REMOVAL AND INSTALLATION
1986 1,998cc

1. Disconnect the battery ground.
2. Remove the distributor.

3. Remove the fan and radiator shroud.

4. Remove the alternator.

5. Disconnect the air injection pipes.

6. Remove the fan pulley, hub and bracket.

7. If so equipped, remove the air conditioning compressor drive belt.

8. If so equipped, remove the power steering pump drive belt.

9. Remove the crankshaft pulley and baffle plate.

10. Remove the upper, then the lower, belt covers.

11. Installation is the reverse of removal.

Front Cover Oil Seal
REMOVAL AND INSTALLATION
All except Diesel and 1986 1,998cc

The front cover oil seal can be removed and a new one installed without removing the front cover.

1. Scribe alignment marks on the hood hinges and remove the hood.

2. Drain the cooling system.

CAUTION: *When draining the coolant, keep*

in mind that cats and dogs are attracted by the ethelyne glycol antifreeze, and are quite likely to drink any that is left in an uncovered container or in puddles on the ground. This will prove fatal in sufficient quantity. Always drain the coolant into a sealable container. Coolant should be reused unless it is contaminated or several years old.

3. Disconnect the upper and lower radiator hoses and remove the radiator.

4. Remove the drive belt(s).

5. Remove the crankshaft pulley.

6. Pry the front oil seal from the front cover.

7. Clean the pulley and seal area.

8. Press a new front seal into position (flush).

9. Install the crankshaft pulley and torque the bolt to specifications.

10. Install the drive belt(s) and adjust the tension.

11. Install the radiator and connect the upper and lower hoses. Fill the cooling system.

12. Start the engine and check for leaks.

13. Install the hood.

2,209cc Diesel

See the procedure for front cover removal, above.

Front Housing and Camshaft Oil Seal

REMOVAL AND INSTALLATION

1986 1,998cc

1. Disconnect the battery ground.

2. Drain the cooling system.

CAUTION: *When draining the coolant, keep in mind that cats and dogs are attracted by the ethelyne glycol antifreeze, and are quite likely to drink any that is left in an uncovered container or in puddles on the ground. This will prove fatal in sufficient quantity. Always drain the coolant into a sealable container. Coolant should be reused unless it is contaminated or several years old.*

3. Remove the distributor.

4. Remove the fan shroud and fan.

5. Remove the alternator.

6. Disconnect the air injection pipes.

7. Remove the fan pulley, hub and bracket.

8. If so equipped, remove the air conditioning compressor drive belt.

9. If so equipped, remove the power steering pump drive belt.

10. Remove the crankshaft pulley and baffle plate.

11. Remove the upper, then the lower, belt covers.

12. Turn the crankshaft so that the A mark on the camshaft pulley is at the top, aligned with the notch in the front housing.

13. Loosen the tensioner lock bolt and remove the tensioner spring.

14. Mark the forward rotation of the belt with paint to avoid confusion upon installation. Remove the belt.

15. Unbolt and remove the front housing.

16. Carefully, drive the camshaft seal from the housing.

17. Coat the outside of a new seal with clean engine oil and press it into place in the front housing.

18. Coat the seal lip with clean engine oil. Install the front housing, using a new gasket. Torque the bolts to 14–19 ft.lb.

19. Replace the timing belt if it has been contaminated by oil or grease, or shows any sign of damage, wear, cracks or peeling.

20. To ease installation of the belt, remove all the spark plugs.

21. Make sure that the timing mark on the camshaft is aligned as described above, and that the timing mark (notch) on the crankshaft sprocket is aligned with the triangular shaped mark on the front housing.

22. Install the tensioner and spring, positioning the tensioner all the way to the intake manifold side and temporarily secure it there with the lock bolt.

23. Install the belt onto the sprockets from YOUR right side. If you are reusing the original belt, make sure you follow the directional mark previously made.

24. Loosen the lock bolt so that the tensioner applies tension to the belt.

25. Turn the crankshaft two full revolutions in the direction of normal rotation. This will apply equal tension to all points of the belt.

26. Make sure that the timing marks are still aligned. If not, repeat the belt installation procedure.

27. Tighten the tensioner lock bolt to 30–35 ft.lb.

28. Measure the timing belt tension by pressing on the belt at the midpoint of the longest straight run. Belt deflection should be 11–13mm. If not, repeat the belt adjustment procedure, above.

29. Installation of all other parts is the reverse of removal. Torque the belt cover bolts to 80 in.lb.; the fan bracket bolts to 40 ft.lb. When installing the drive belts on the various accessories, check the belt deflection as follows:

• Alternator: New, 0.28–0.32 in.
        Used, 0.31–0.36in.

• Power steering pump: New, 0.31–0.49 in.
        Used, 0.43–0.51 in.

• Air conditioning compressor:
        New, 0.39–0.47 in.
        Used, 0.47–0.55 in.

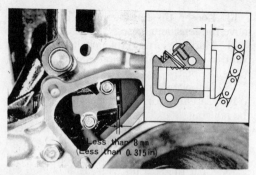

Checking the 1,586cc and 1,796cc engine timing chain for stretch

Installing the timing chain on the 1,586cc and 1,796cc engines

Timing Chain and Tensioner

REMOVAL AND INSTALLATION

1,586cc, 1,796cc

1. Remove the cylinder head and front cover. It is not necessary that the intake and exhaust manifolds be removed from the head.

2. Remove the oil pump and chain.

3. Remove the timing chain tensioner.

4. Loosen the timing chain guide strip screws.

5. Remove the oil slinger.

6. Remove the oil pump gear and chain as an assembly.

7. Remove the timing chain, crankshaft gear and camshaft gears from the engine.

8. Position the crankshaft gear in the timing chain.

9. Position the oil pump chain and gear on the crankshaft and oil pump. Check the oil pump drive chain slack. It should be 0.15 in. Adjusting the shims (between the oil pump body and cylinder block) are available in thickness of 0.006 in.

10. Install the oil slinger.

Timing chain tension adjusting shim used on the 1,586cc and 1,796cc engines

11. Install the oil pump washer and nut. Bend the washer over the nut.

12. Install the timing chain tensioner. Fully compress the snubber spring and wedge a screwdriver into the tensioner release mechanism. Without removing the screwdriver, install the tensioner.

13. Install the cylinder head and camshaft. Be sure that the valve timing is as illustrated. It must be exact. You may have to move the cam gear one or two teeth to obtain the correct alignment.

14. Install the rocker arm shafts and cam bearing caps.

15. Install and torque the cylinder head bolts.

16. Adjust the timing chain tension. Press in on the chain guide strip. Tighten the guide strip attaching screws. Remove the screwdriver from the tensioner, allowing the snubber to take up the chain slack.

17. Replace the front cover.

18. Adjust the valve clearance cold.

Checking the oil pump chain for slack on the 1,586cc and 1,796cc engines

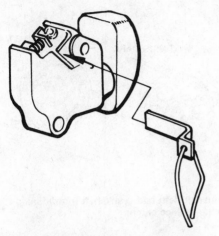

Inserting the plate in the timing chain tensioner on 1,586cc and 1,796cc engines

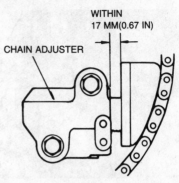

Checking timing chain stretch on 1,970cc engines

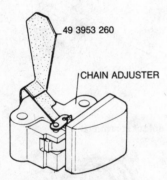

Timing chain tension adjusting guide for the 1,970cc engine

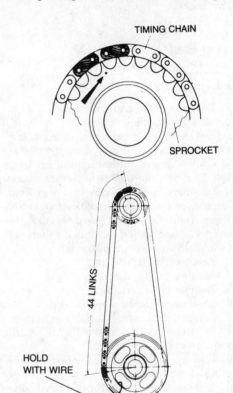

Timing chain installation on the 1,970cc engine

1979–84 1,970cc

NOTE: *Chain adjuster guide, 49 3953 260, is necessary for this procedure.*

1. Remove the cylinder head and front cover. It is not necessary that the intake and exhaust manifolds be removed from the head.

2. Remove the oil pan, oil pump and pump drive chain.

3. Install the chain adjuster guide mentioned above.

4. Loosen the chain guide strip adjusting screws. Slightly rotate the timing chain in the direction of normal engine rotation. Press the top of the chain guide strip with a prybar and tighten the guide strip adjusting screws. Check the protrusion of the chain adjuster head, as shown. If protrusion exceeds 17mm, replace the chain.

5. Remove the timing chain tensioner.

6. Remove the timing chain from the gears.

7. When installing the chain, make sure that the gears and chain are aligned as shown. The alignment marks on the gears must appear on the left, and fall between the nickel plated links.

8. Check the slack in the oil pump drive chain, after installation. Press on the chain, midway between the gears. If slack exceeds 4.0mm, install adjusting shims between the block and oil pump body. Shims are available in thicknesses of 0.15mm. Tighten the oil pump sprocket bolt to 25 ft.lb.

9. Follow step 4, above, and adjust the timing chain. Remove the guide tool.

10. Install the oil pan, using a new gasket and sealer.

11. Install all other parts in reverse order of removal.

Installing timing chain tension adjusting shims on the 1,970cc engine

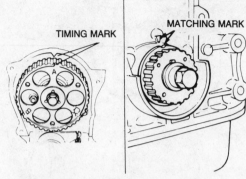

Camshaft (left) and crankshaft (right) timing marks on the 1,998cc engine

Timing Belt

REMOVAL AND INSTALLATION

1986 1,998cc

1. Disconnect the battery ground.
2. Drain the cooling system.

CAUTION: *When draining the coolant, keep in mind that cats and dogs are attracted by the ethelyne glycol antifreeze, and are quite likely to drink any that is left in an uncovered container or in puddles on the ground. This will prove fatal in sufficient quantity. Always drain the coolant into a sealable container. Coolant should be reused unless it is contaminated or several years old.*

3. Remove the distributor.
4. Remove the fan shroud and fan.
5. Remove the alternator.
6. Disconnect the air injection pipes.
7. Remove the fan pulley, hub and bracket.
8. If so equipped, remove the air conditioning compressor drive belt.
9. If so equipped, remove the power steering pump drive belt.
10. Remove the crankshaft pulley and baffle plate.
11. Remove the upper, then the lower, belt covers.
12. Turn the crankshaft so that the A mark on the camshaft pulley is at the top, aligned with the notch in the front housing.
13. Loosen the tensioner lock bolt and remove the tensioner spring.
14. Mark the forward rotation of the belt with paint to avoid confusion upon installation. Remove the belt.
15. Replace the belt if it has been contaminated by oil or grease, or shows any sign of damage, wear, cracks or peeling.
16. To ease installation of the belt, remove all the spark plugs.
17. Make sure that the timing mark on the camshaft is aligned as described above, and that

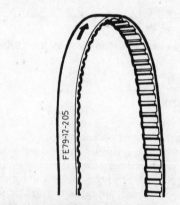

Camshaft sprocket removal

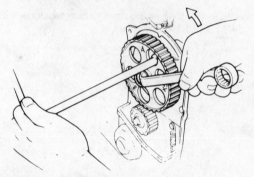

Marking the 1,998cc timing belt for forward rotation

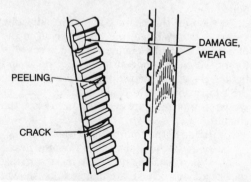

Checking timing belt damage

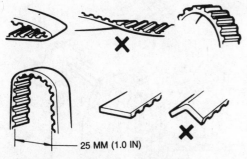

Checking timing belt wear and stretch

25 MM (1.0 IN)

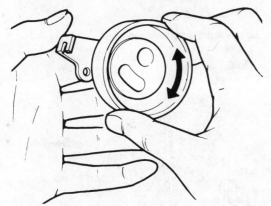

Checking timing belt tensioner rotation

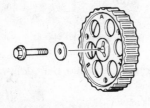

Camshaft and crankshaft sprockets on the 1,998cc engine

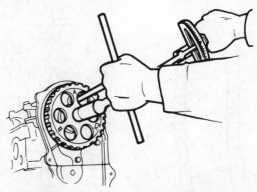

MATING MARK

Aligning the crankshaft sprocket timing marks on the 1,998cc engine

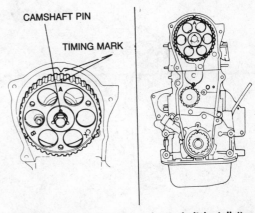

Camshaft sprocket installation on the 1,998cc engine

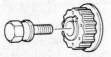

CAMSHAFT PIN

TIMING MARK

Aligning all timing marks, prior to belt installation, on the 1,998cc engine

the timing mark (notch) on the crankshaft sprocket is aligned with the triangular shaped mark on the front housing.

18. Install the tensioner and spring, positioning the tensioner all the way to the intake manifold side and temporarily secure it there with the lock bolt.

19. Install the belt onto the sprockets from YOUR right side. If you are reusing the original belt, make sure you follow the directional mark previously made.

20. Loosen the lock bolt so that the tensioner applies tension to the belt.

21. Turn the crankshaft two full revolutions in the direction of normal rotation. This will apply equal tension to all points of the belt.

22. Make sure that the timing marks are still aligned. If not, repeat the belt installation procedure.

23. Tighten the tensioner lock bolt to 30–35 ft.lb.

24. Measure the timing belt tension by

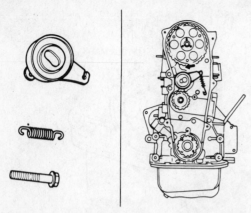

Timing belt tensioner installation on the 1,998cc engine

Loosening the tensioner lockbolt

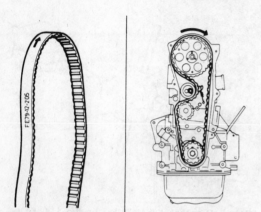

Timing belt installation on the 1,998cc engine

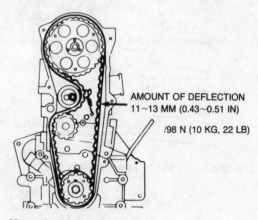

AMOUNT OF DEFLECTION
11~13 MM (0.43~0.51 IN)

/98 N (10 KG, 22 LB)

Measuring timing belt deflection

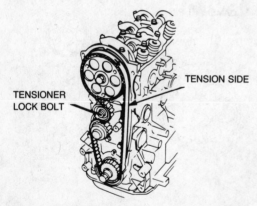

TENSION SIDE

TENSIONER LOCK BOLT

Timing belt tensioner lockbolt on the 1,998cc engine

pressing on the belt at the midpoint of the longest straight run. Belt deflection should be 11–13mm. If not, repeat the belt adjustment procedure, above.

25. Installation of all other parts is the reverse of removal. Torque the belt cover bolts to 80 in.lb.; the fan bracket bolts to 40 ft.lb. When installing the drive belts on the various accessories, check the belt deflection as follows:

- Alternator: New, 0.28–0.32 in.
  Used, 0.31–0.36in.
- Power steering pump: New, 0.31–0.49 in.
  Used, 0.43–0.51 in.
- Air conditioning compressor:
  New, 0.39–0.47 in.
  Used, 0.47–0.55 in.

Timing Gears and Gear Case
REMOVAL AND INSTALLATION
Diesel Engine

1. Rotate the engine so that no.1 piston is on TDC of its firing stroke.
2. Disconnect the battery ground.
3. Drain the cooling system.

CAUTION: *When draining the coolant, keep in mind that cats and dogs are attracted by the ethelyne glycol antifreeze, and are quite likely to drink any that is left in an uncovered container or in puddles on the ground. This will prove fatal in sufficient quantity. Always drain the coolant into a sealable con-*

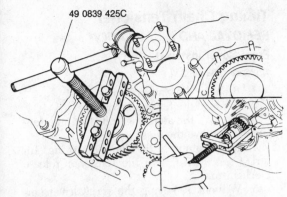

49 0839 425C

Removing timing gear from the diesel engine

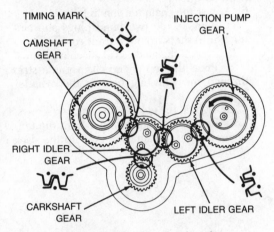

TIMING MARK

INJECTION PUMP GEAR

CAMSHAFT GEAR

RIGHT IDLER GEAR

CARKSHAFT GEAR

LEFT IDLER GEAR

Timing gear alignment on the diesel engine

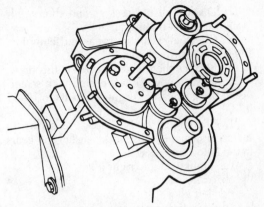

Removing the camshaft gear from the diesel engine

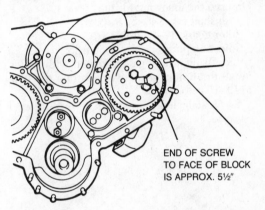

END OF SCREW TO FACE OF BLOCK IS APPROX. 5½"

Removing the injection pump gear from the diesel engine

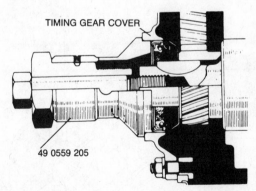

TIMING GEAR COVER

49 0559 205

Timing gear cover seal installation on the diesel engine

tainer. Coolant should be reused unless it is contaminated or several years old.

4. Remove the fan and fan shroud.

5. Remove all drive belts from the engine.

6. Remove the power steering pump and its bracket, and position it out of the way, without disconnecting the hoses.

7. Remove the water pump.

8. Remove the crankshaft pulley bolt and, using a puller, remove the pulley. Unbolt and remove the timing gear cover, discard the gasket. The front cover seal may be replaced at this time. Coat the outer circumference of the new seal with sealer, and the sealing surface with clean engine oil.

9. Remove the oil pan.

10. Make sure that all timing marks are aligned as illustrated. If not, rotate the engine to align them.

11. Remove the bolts from the camshaft gear, and remove the washer and friction gear.

12. Remove the bolts from the injection pump gear, and remove the washer and friction gear.

13. Using a puller, remove the camshaft, crankshaft and injection pump gears.

14. Matchmark the idler gears for installation reference and remove the nuts and gears.

15. Support the injection pump and remove the nuts attaching it to the timing gear case. Support the pump in this position for the rest of the procedure.

16. Remove the bolts attaching the gear case to the block and remove the case.

17. Discard all old gaskets and thoroughly clean the gasket mating surfaces.

18. Check all gears for wear and chipping. Replace any suspect parts.

19. Replace the front cover seal at this time.

20. Using a new gasket, coated with sealer, install the gear case. Torque the bolts to 12–17 ft.lb.

21. Aligning all timing marks, as shown in the accompanying illustration, install the gears in the following order:

  a. crankshaft and right idler
  b. camshaft
  c. left idler
  d. injection pump
  e. all friction gears and washers

22. Install all the nuts and bolts on the gears. Observe the following torques:

Camshaft gear, 45–50 ft.lb.
Idler gears, 17–23 ft.lb.
Injection pump gear, 40–50 ft.lb.

23. Using a new gasket coated with sealer, install the timing gear cover. Torque the bolts to 12–17 ft.lb.

24. Install all other parts in reverse order of removal.

Timing Chain Tensioner
REMOVAL AND INSTALLATION
Front Cover Installed
1,586cc, 1,796cc ONLY

1. Remove the water pump.
2. Remove the tensioner cover.
3. Remove the attaching bolts from the tensioner. Remove the tensioner.
4. Fully compress the snubber spring. Insert a screwdriver into the tensioner release mechanism.
5. Without removing the screwdriver, insert the tensioner and align the bolt holes. Install the torque and bolts.
6. Adjust the chain tension as follows:

  a. Remove the two blind plugs and aluminum washers from the front cover.
  b. Loosen the guide strip attaching screws.
  c. Press the top of the chain guide strip through the adjusting hole in the cylinder head.
  d. Tighten the guide strip attaching screws.
  e. Remove the screwdriver from the tensioner and let the snubber take up the slack in the chain.

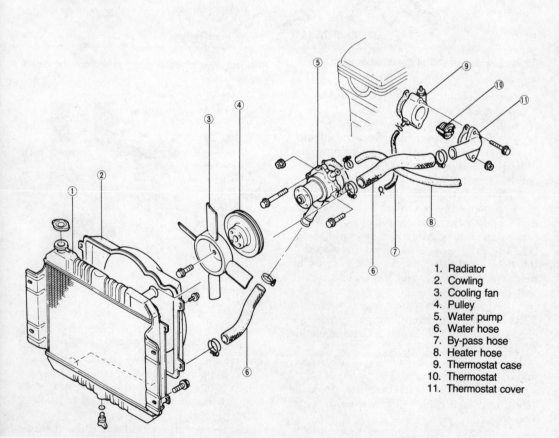

1. Radiator
2. Cowling
3. Cooling fan
4. Pulley
5. Water pump
6. Water hose
7. By-pass hose
8. Heater hose
9. Thermostat case
10. Thermostat
11. Thermostat cover

Cooling system components used on the 1,596cc, 1,796cc and 1,970cc engines

f. Install the blind plugs and aluminum washers.

g. Install the tensioner cover and gasket.

h. Install a new gasket and water pump. Install the crankshaft pulley and drive belt and adjust the tension. Check the cooling system level.

TIMING CHAIN TENSIONER ADJUSTMENT

Perform Steps 1 and 4 through 6h of the preceding procedure.

Water Pump

REMOVAL AND INSTALLATION

1,586cc, 1,796cc and 1979–84 1,970cc

1. Drain the cooling system.

CAUTION: *When draining the coolant, keep in mind that cats and dogs are attracted by the ethelyne glycol antifreeze, and are quite likely to drink any that is left in an uncovered container or in puddles on the ground. This will prove fatal in sufficient quantity. Always drain the coolant into a sealable container. Coolant should be reused unless it is contaminated or several years old.*

2. Remove the lower hose from the water pump.

3. Disconnect the upper radiator hose from the engine and the lower radiator hose at the radiator.

4. Remove the radiator.

5. Remove the drive belts.

6. Remove the fan and pulley.

7. Remove the two small hoses from the water pump.

8. Unbolt and remove the water pump.

9. Clean the gasket surfaces of the water pump and cylinder block.

10. Install the water pump and new gasket on the block.

11. Install the lower hose on the water pump.

12. Install the fan and pulley. Install the crankshaft pulley.

13. Install the drive belts and adjust the tension.

14. Install the radiator.

15. Refill the cooling system with the specified amount and type of coolant. Install the radiator cap and start the engine. Check for leaks.

16. Install the hood.

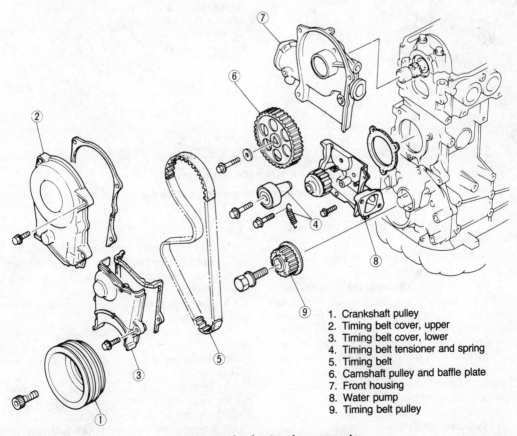

1. Crankshaft pulley
2. Timing belt cover, upper
3. Timing belt cover, lower
4. Timing belt tensioner and spring
5. Timing belt
6. Camshaft pulley and baffle plate
7. Front housing
8. Water pump
9. Timing belt pulley

1,998cc engine front end components

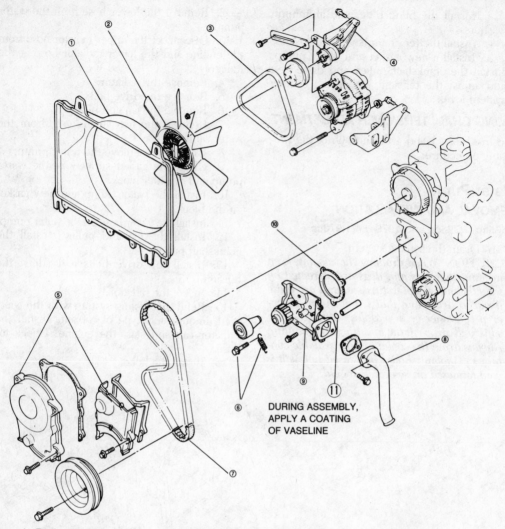

1. Radiator cowling
2. Cooling fan and pulley
3. Alternator drive belt
4. Cooling fan bracket
5. Timing belt cover, upper and lower
6. Timing belt tensioner and spring
7. Timing belt
8. Coolant inlet pipe and gasket
9. Water pump
10. Gasket
11. O-ring

DURING ASSEMBLY, APPLY A COATING OF VASELINE

Cooling system components used on the 1,998cc engine

1986 1,998cc

1. Disconnect the battery ground.

2. Drain the cooling system.

CAUTION: *When draining the coolant, keep in mind that cats and dogs are attracted by the ethelyne glycol antifreeze, and are quite likely to drink any that is left in an uncovered container or in puddles on the ground. This will prove fatal in sufficient quantity. Always drain the coolant into a sealable container. Coolant should be reused unless it is contaminated or several years old.*

3. Remove the distributor.

4. Remove the fan shroud and fan.

5. Remove the alternator.

6. Disconnect the air injection pipes.

7. Remove the fan pulley, hub and bracket.

8. If so equipped, remove the air conditioning compressor drive belt.

9. If so equipped, remove the power steering pump drive belt.

10. Remove the crankshaft pulley and baffle plate.

11. Remove the upper, then the lower, belt covers.

12. Turn the crankshaft so that the A mark on the camshaft pulley is at the top, aligned with the notch in the front housing.

13. Loosen the tensioner lock bolt and remove the tensioner spring.

14. Mark the forward rotation of the belt with paint to avoid confusion upon installation. Remove the belt.

15. Remove the coolant inlet pipe and gasket from the pump.

16. Unbolt and remove the pump. Discard the gasket and O-ring.

17. Install the pump, using a new O-ring coated with clean coolant and a new gasket coated with sealer. Torque the bolts to 14–19 ft.lb.

18. Install the coolant inlet pipe, using a new gasket coated with sealer.

19. Replace the timing belt if it has been contaminated by oil or grease, or shows any sign of damage, wear, cracks or peeling.

20. To ease installation of the belt, remove all the spark plugs.

21. Make sure that the timing mark on the camshaft is aligned as described above, and that the timing mark (notch) on the crankshaft sprocket is aligned with the triangular shaped mark on the front housing.

22. Install the tensioner and spring, positioning the tensioner all the way to the intake manifold side and temporarily secure it there with the lock bolt.

23. Install the belt onto the sprockets from

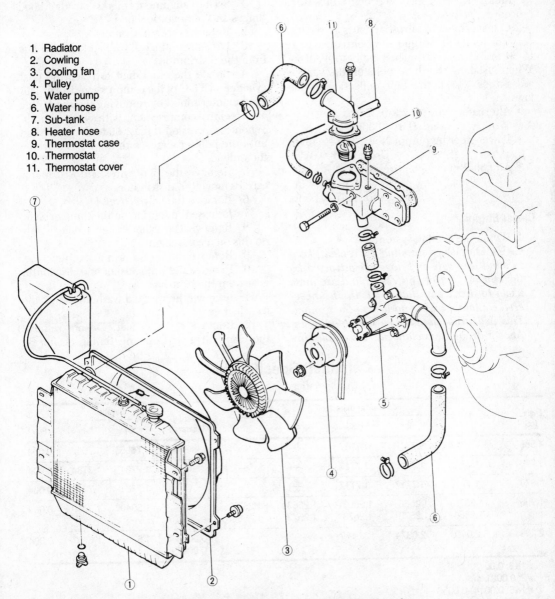

1. Radiator
2. Cowling
3. Cooling fan
4. Pulley
5. Water pump
6. Water hose
7. Sub-tank
8. Heater hose
9. Thermostat case
10. Thermostat
11. Thermostat cover

Cooling system components used on the diesel engine

YOUR right side. If you are reusing the original belt, make sure you follow the directional mark previously made.

24. Loosen the lock bolt so that the tensioner applies tension to the belt.

25. Turn the crankshaft two full revolutions in the direction of normal rotation. This will apply equal tension to all points of the belt.

26. Make sure that the timing marks are still aligned. If not, repeat the belt installation procedure.

27. Tighten the tensioner lock bolt to 30–35 ft.lb.

28. Measure the timing belt tension by pressing on the belt at the midpoint of the longest straight run. Belt deflection should be 11–13mm. If not, repeat the belt adjustment procedure, above.

29. Installation of all other parts is the reverse of removal. Torque the belt cover bolts to 80 in.lb.; the fan bracket bolts to 40 ft.lb. When installing the drive belts on the various accessories, check the belt deflection as follows:

- Alternator: New, 0.28–0.32 in.
  Used, 0.31–0.36in.
- Power steering pump: New, 0.31–0.49 in.
  Used, 0.43–0.51 in.
- Air conditioning compressor:
  New, 0.39–0.47 in.
  Used, 0.47–0.55 in.

Diesel Engine

1. Drain the cooling system.
CAUTION: *When draining the coolant, keep in mind that cats and dogs are attracted by the ethelyne glycol antifreeze, and are quite likely to drink any that is left in an uncovered container or in puddles on the ground. This will prove fatal in sufficient quantity. Always drain the coolant into a sealable container. Coolant should be reused unless it is contaminated or several years old.*

2. Remove the fan shroud.

3. Remove the fan, fan belt and pulley.

4. Disconnect the lower hose from the pump.

5. Remove the pump and discard the gasket.

6. Installation is the reverse of removal. Use a new water pump gasket coated with sealer.

Camshaft

REMOVAL AND INSTALLATION

1,586cc, 1,796cc, and 1979–84 1,970cc

Perform this operation on a cold engine only.

1. Scribe alignment marks on the hood hinges and remove the hood.

2. Remove the water pump.

3. Disconnect the coil wire and vacuum line from the distributor.

4. Rotate the crankshaft to place the no.1 cylinder on TDC of the compression stroke. This can be determined by removing the spark plug and feeling compression with your thumb. When compression is felt, rotate the crankshaft until the pointer aligns with the TDC mark on the pulley.

5. Remove the plug wires and distributor cap. Remove the distributor.

6. Remove the valve cover.

7. Release the tension on the timing chain.

8. Remove the cylinder head bolts. Only do this on a cold engine.

9. Remove the rocker arm assembly.

10. Remove the nut, washer and distributor gear from the camshaft.

11. Remove the nut and washer holding the camshaft gear.

12. Remove the camshaft. Do not remove the camshaft gear from the timing chain. Be

Camshaft Specifications

(All specifications in inches)

Engine (cc)	Journal Diameter					Bearing Clearance	Elevation		End Play
	1	2	3	4	5		Int.	Exh.	
1,586	1.7717	1.7717	1.7717	—	—	①	1.7605	1.7592	0.004
1,796	1.7717	1.7717	1.7717	—	—	①	1.7731	1.7784	0.004
1,970	1.7717	1.7717	1.7717	—	—	①	1.7731	1.7718	0.004
1,998	1.2575–1.2584	1.2563–1.2573	1.2563–1.2573	1.2563–1.2573	1.2575–1.2584	②	1.5040	1.5040	0.004
2,209	2.0473	2.0374	2.0177	—	—	0.0024–0.0047	1.6767	1.6767	0.004

① #1&3: 0.0017
  #2: 0.0021
② #1&5: 0.0014–0.0033
  #2,3,4: 0.0026–0.0045

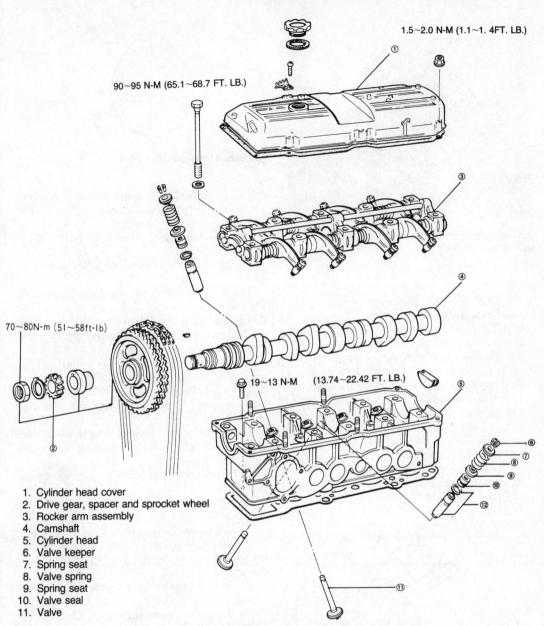

1.5~2.0 N-M (1.1~1. 4FT. LB.)

90~95 N-M (65.1~68.7 FT. LB.)

70~80N-m (51~58ft-1b)

19~13 N-M (13.74~22.42 FT. LB.)

1. Cylinder head cover
2. Drive gear, spacer and sprocket wheel
3. Rocker arm assembly
4. Camshaft
5. Cylinder head
6. Valve keeper
7. Spring seat
8. Valve spring
9. Spring seat
10. Valve seal
11. Valve

1,586cc, 1,796cc and 1,970cc engine cylinder head components

sure that the gear teeth and chain relationship is not disturbed. Wire the chain and cam gear to a place so that they will not fall into the front cover.

13. Clean all the gasket surfaces.

14. Clean the cylinder head bolt holes.

15. Install the camshaft on the head and install the camshaft gear.

16. Check the valve timing.

17. Install the rocker arm assembly.

18. Install and torque the head bolts.

19. Install the cam gear washer an nut.

20. Install the distributor gear, washer and nut.

21. Adjust the timing chain tension.

22. Check the camshaft endplay. It should be 0.001–0.007 in. If it exceeds 0.008 in., replace the thrust plate with a new one.

23. Install the distributor, distributor cap and plug wires.

24. Connect the vacuum line and coil wire.

25. Adjust the valve clearance cold. Install the valve cover and fill the cooling system.

26. Run the engine and check for leaks. When normal operating temperature is reached, adjust the hot valve clearance.

27. Adjust the carburetor and ignition.

28. Install the air cleaner and hood.

Checking camshaft endplay on the 1,586cc, 1,796cc and 1,970cc engines

1,998cc

1. Disconnect the battery ground.
2. Drain the cooling system.
CAUTION: *When draining the coolant, keep in mind that cats and dogs are attracted by the ethelyne glycol antifreeze, and are quite likely to drink any that is left in an uncovered container or in puddles on the ground. This will prove fatal in sufficient quantity. Always drain the coolant into a sealable container. Coolant should be reused unless it is contaminated or several years old.*
3. Remove the distributor.
4. Remove the fan shroud and fan.
5. Remove the alternator.
6. Disconnect the air injection pipes.

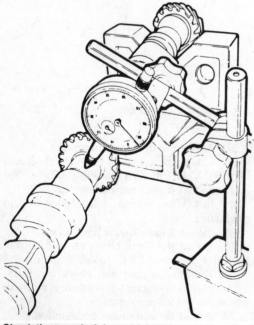

Check the camshaft for straightness

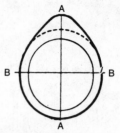

Camshaft lobe measurement

7. Remove the fan pulley, hub and bracket.
8. If so equipped, remove the air conditioning compressor drive belt.
9. If so equipped, remove the power steering pump drive belt.
10. Remove the crankshaft pulley and baffle plate.
11. Remove the upper, then the lower, belt covers.
12. Turn the crankshaft so that the A mark on the camshaft pulley is at the top, aligned with the notch in the front housing.
13. Loosen the tensioner lock bolt and remove the tensioner spring.
14. Mark the forward rotation of the belt with paint to avoid confusion upon installation. Remove the belt.
15. Insert a bar through the hole in the camshaft sprocket to hold it in position and remove the sprocket bolt.
16. Disconnect the accelerator cable, if necessary.
17. If equipped, disconnect the air by-pass valve cable.
18. Disconnect the spark plug wires. Remove the wires from the spark plug wire clips on the rocker covers and position them out of the way.
19. Remove the rocker cover and discard the gasket.
20. Remove the rocker arm shaft attaching bolts evenly in the order shown, and remove the rocker arm shafts.
21. Remove the camshaft rear seal cap.
22. Lift out the camshaft.
23. Inspect the camshaft for wear, heat scoring or obvious damage. Replace it if necessary. Check the lobes and journals for wear according to the specifications in the Camshaft Specification Chart.
24. Coat the camshaft with clean engine oil and install it in position, making sure that the lug on the nose of the shaft is at the 12:00 o'clock position.
25. Apply a thin coat of sealant to the areas shown, and install the rocker shaft assembly. Torque the bolts evenly, and in the order shown, to 15–20 ft.lb. Install the camshaft sprocket.

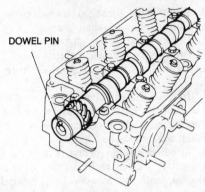

Installing the 1,998cc engine camshaft with the locating dowel in the 12:00 o'clock position

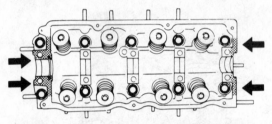

Sealant application areas on the 1,998cc cylinder head

Torque the camshaft sprocket bolt to 40–45 ft.lb.

26. Replace the belt if it has been contaminated by oil or grease, or shows any sign of damage, wear, cracks or peeling.

27. To ease installation of the belt, remove all the spark plugs.

28. Make sure that the timing mark on the camshaft is aligned as described above, and that the timing mark (notch) on the crankshaft sprocket is aligned with the triangular shaped mark on the front housing.

29. Install the tensioner and spring, positioning the tensioner all the way to the intake manifold side and temporarily secure it there with the lock bolt.

30. Install the belt onto the sprockets from YOUR right side. If you are reusing the original belt, make sure you follow the directional mark previously made.

31. Loosen the lock bolt so that the tensioner applies tension to the belt.

32. Turn the crankshaft two full revolutions in the direction of normal rotation. This will apply equal tension to all points of the belt.

33. Make sure that the timing marks are still aligned. If not, repeat the belt installation procedure.

34. Tighten the tensioner lock bolt to 30–35 ft.lb.

35. Measure the timing belt tension by pressing on the belt at the midpoint of the longest straight run. Belt deflection should be 11–13mm. If not, repeat the belt adjustment procedure, above.

36. Check the valve adjustment and reset, if necessary.

37. Clean the mating surfaces of the cylinder head and rocker cover.

38. Install the rocker cover with a new gasket. Torque the bolts to 24–36 in.lb.

39. Install the spark plug wire on the plugs. Place the wires in the clips on the rocker cover. Connect the choke and air by-pass valve cable.

40. Installation of all other parts is the reverse of removal. Torque the belt cover bolts to 80 in.lb.; the fan bracket bolts to 40 ft.lb. When installing the drive belts on the various accessories, check the belt deflection as follows:
- Alternator: New, 0.28–0.32 in. Used, 0.31–0.36 in.
- Power steering pump: New, 0.31–0.49 in. Used, 0.43–0.51 in.
- Air conditioning compressor: New, 0.39–0.47 in. Used, 0.47–0.55 in.

41. Install all other parts is reverse of removal. See related procedures in this chapter.

Diesel Engine

1. Scribe the locations of the hood hinges and remove the hood.

2. Remove the engine splash shield.

3. Drain the coolant.

CAUTION: *When draining the coolant, keep in mind that cats and dogs are attracted by the Ethylene glycol antifreeze, and are quite likely to drink any that is left in an uncovered container or in puddles on the ground. This will prove fatal in sufficient quantity. Always drain the coolant into a sealable container. Coolant should be reused unless it is contaminated or several years old.*

4. Drain the engine oil.

5. Disconnect the battery cables and remove the battery.

6. Remove the air cleaner and the oil dipstick.

7. Remove the radiator shroud and the engine fan. Place the fan in an upright position to avoid fluid loss from the fan clutch.

8. Disconnect and tag all wires, hoses, cables, pipes and linkage from the engine.

9. Remove the clutch release cylinder.

10. Remove the oil cooler.

11. Remove the radiator.

12. Disconnect the exhaust pipe at the manifold and remove the exhaust manifold.

13. Dismount the air conditioning compressor and position it out of the way. Don't disconnect any refrigerant lines.

14. Dismount the power steering pump and

position it out of the way without disconnecting any hoses.

15. Raise and support the truck on jackstands.

16. Attach a lifting sling and shop crane to the engine lifting eyes and take up the weight of the engine.

17. Support the transmission with a floor jack and remove the transmission-to-engine bolts.

18. Remove the engine support plates and mounting nuts, push the engine forward to clear the transmission and lift it out of the truck.

19. Remove the rocker arm cover, rocker arm assemblies and pushrods, making sure you keep the pushrods in order of their removal. Remove the lifters, marking them also, for installation.

20. Remove the timing gear case cover.

21. Remove the camshaft gear.

22. Remove the oil pan and oil pump.

23. Remove the camshaft thrust plate.

24. Carefully slide the camshaft from the block.

25. Inspect the camshaft for wear, damage or heat scoring. Check the dimensions of the shaft according to the specifications given in the Camshaft Specifications Chart.

26. Installation is the reverse of removal. Coat the camshaft journal and bearings with clean engine oil, and the lobes with polyethelene grease, prior to installation. See the appropriate related procedures in this chapter.

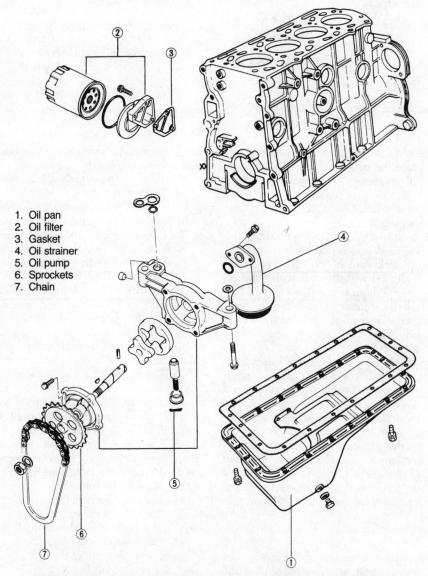

1. Oil pan
2. Oil filter
3. Gasket
4. Oil strainer
5. Oil pump
6. Sprockets
7. Chain

Lubricating system components for the 1,586cc, 1,796cc and 1,970cc engines

Oil Pan

REMOVAL AND INSTALLATION

1,586cc, 1,796cc and 1979–84 1,970cc

1. Raise and support the truck.
2. Remove the engine skid plate.
3. Drain the engine oil.
4. Remove the clutch release cylinder attaching nuts. Let the cylinder hang.
5. Remove the clutch cover plate.
6. Remove the oil pan nuts and bolts and let the oil pan rest on the crossmember.
7. Remove the oil pump pickup tube from the pump.
8. Remove the oil pan.
9. Clean all the gasket surfaces.
10. Clean the oil pan, oil pump pickup tube and oil pump screen.
11. Install a new oil pan gasket with oil resistant sealer.
12. Install the oil pump pickup tube and screen.
13. Install the oil pan on the block. Torque the nuts and bolts to specifications.
14. Connect the emission line to the oil pan.
15. Attach the rear engine bracket. Torque the bolts to specifications.
16. Reinstall the clutch release cylinder. Torque the nuts to 5–7 ft.lb. (60–72 in.lb.)
17. Replace the engine skid plate.
18. Lower the truck. Fill the crankcase, and run the engine. Check for leaks and oil pressure.

1986 1,998cc

1. Disconnect the battery ground cable.
2. Raise and support the truck on jackstands. Drain the oil.
3. Remove the skid plate.
4. Place a floor jack under the front of the engine at the crankshaft pulley and take up the weight of the engine. Or use a shop crane to support the engine.
5. Remove the crossmember.

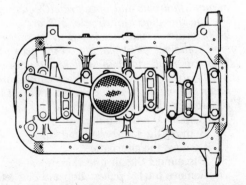

RTV sealer application points when using a gasket on the 1,998cc engine oil pan

RTV sealer application on the 1,998cc engine oil pan when not using a gasket

6. Remove the cotter pin and nut and, with a puller, disconnect the idler arm from the center link.
7. Remove the engine mount gusset plates from the sides of the engine.
8. Remove the bell housing front cover.
9. Unbolt and remove the oil pan. A flat tipped screwdriver may be used to break the seal between the pan and block.
10. Clean all the gasket surfaces. Straighten any portion of the pan rim that is bent.
11. Clean the oil pan, oil pump pickup tube and oil pump screen.
12. If you are using a gasket, install a new oil pan gasket coated with oil resistant sealer. Place RTV silicone sealer at the points shown in the accompanying illustration. If you are using RTV silicone gasket material in place of a conventional gasket, run a ⅛ inch bead around the rim of the pan, going inboard of each bolt hole. Tighten the pan bolts within 30 minutes of application. Tighten the pan bolts to 5–9 ft.lb.
13. Install all other parts in reverse order of removal. Torque the idler arm nut to 25–30 ft.lb.; the bell housing cover to 15–20 ft.lb.

Diesel Engine

1. Raise and support the truck on jackstands.
2. Remove the skid plate.
3. Drain the oil.
4. Unbolt and remove the oil pan.
5. Clean all the gasket surfaces. Straighten any portion of the pan rim that is bent.
6. Clean the oil pan, oil pump pickup tube and oil pump screen.
7. Install the pan, using a new gasket coated with sealer. Torque the bolts to 5–9 ft.lb.

Oil Pump

REMOVAL AND INSTALLATION

1,586cc, 1,796cc, 1979–84 1,970cc

1. Remove the oil pan.
2. Remove the oil pump gear attaching nut.

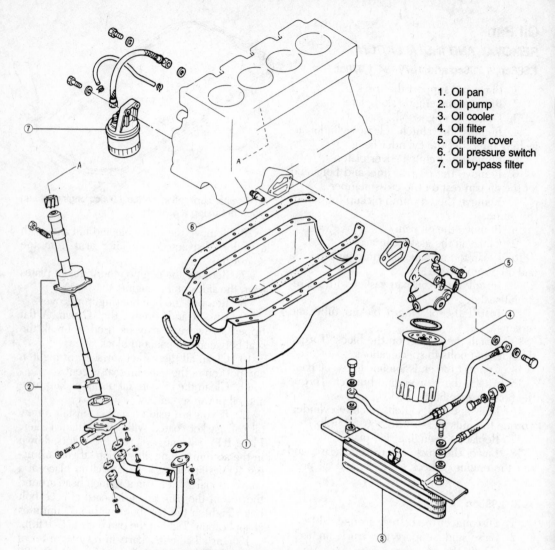

1. Oil pan
2. Oil pump
3. Oil cooler
4. Oil filter
5. Oil filter cover
6. Oil pressure switch
7. Oil by-pass filter

Lubricating system components used on the diesel engine

3. Remove the bolts attaching the oil pump to the block. Loosen the gear on the pump.

4. Remove the oil pump and gear.

5. Install the oil pump gear in the chain.

6. Prime the oil pump and install it on the cylinder block. Install the bolts and tighten them securely.

7. Install the washer, gear and nut. Bend the locktab on the washer.

8. Install the oil pan. Fill the engine with oil. Start the engine and check for oil pressure. Check for leaks.

Diesel Engine

1. Remove the oil pan.
2. Remove the oil pump set screw.
3. Remove the oil pipe attaching bolts.
4. Remove the oil pump.
5. Installation is the reverse of removal. Torque the pump and pipe bolts to 8 ft.lb.

1986 1,998cc

1. Disconnect the battery ground.
2. Drain the cooling system.

CAUTION: *When draining the coolant, keep in mind that cats and dogs are attracted by the ethelyne glycol antifreeze, and are quite likely to drink any that is left in an uncovered container or in puddles on the ground. This will prove fatal in sufficient quantity. Always drain the coolant into a sealable container. Coolant should be reused unless it is contaminated or several years old.*

3. Remove the distributor.
4. Remove the fan shroud and fan.
5. Remove the alternator.
6. Disconnect the air injection pipes.
7. Remove the fan pulley, hub and bracket.
8. If so equipped, remove the air conditioning compressor drive belt.

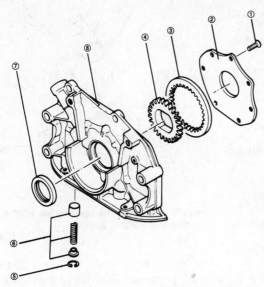

DURING ASSEMBLY, COAT THE
THREADS OF THE BOLTS WITH A
LOCKING AGENT

1. Bolt
2. Pump cover
3. Outer gear
4. Inner gear
5. Snap ring
6. Plunger assembly
7. Oil seal
8. Pump body

1,998cc oil pump

9. If so equipped, remove the power steering pump drive belt.

10. Remove the crankshaft pulley and baffle plate.

11. Remove the upper, then the lower, belt covers.

12. Turn the crankshaft so that the A mark on the camshaft pulley is at the top, aligned with the notch in the front housing.

13. Loosen the tensioner lock bolt and remove the tensioner spring.

14. Mark the forward rotation of the belt with paint to avoid confusion upon installation. Remove the belt.

15. Unbolt and remove the crankshaft sprocket.

16. Drain the oil.

17. Remove the skid plate.

18. Place a floor jack under the front of the engine at the crankshaft pulley and take up the weight of the engine. Or use a shop crane to support the engine.

19. Remove the crossmember.

20. Remove the cotter pin and nut and, with a puller, disconnect the idler arm from the center link.

21. Remove the engine mount gusset plates from the sides of the engine.

22. Remove the bell housing front cover.

23. Unbolt and remove the oil pan. A flat tipped screwdriver may be used to break the seal between the pan and block.

24. Remove the oil pick-up tube.

25. Unbolt and remove the oil pump.

26. Apply a thin coating of grease to the O-ring and install it in its recess in the pump body.

27. Apply a thin bead of RTV silicone sealer to the pump mounting surface.

28. Coat the oil seal lip with clean engine oil and install the pump. Torque the bolts to 14–19 ft.lb.

29. Clean all the gasket surfaces. Straighten any portion of the pan rim that is bent.

30. Clean the oil pan, oil pump pickup tube and oil pump screen.

31. If you are using a gasket, install a new oil pan gasket coated with oil resistant sealer. Place RTV silicone sealer at the points shown in the accompanying illustration. If you are using RTV silicone gasket material in place of a conventional gasket, run a 1/8 inch bead around the rim of the pan, going inboard of each bolt hole. Tighten the pan bolts within 30 minutes of application. Tighten the pan bolts to 5–9 ft.lb.

32. Install all other parts in reverse order of removal. Torque the idler arm nut to 25–30 ft.lb.; the bell housing cover to 15–20 ft.lb.

33. Replace the timing belt if it has been contaminated by oil or grease, or shows any sign of damage, wear, cracks or peeling.

34. To ease installation of the belt, remove all the spark plugs.

35. Make sure that the timing mark on the camshaft is aligned as described above, and that the timing mark (notch) on the crankshaft sprocket is aligned with the triangular shaped mark on the front housing.

36. Install the tensioner and spring, positioning the tensioner all the way to the intake manifold side and temporarily secure it there with the lock bolt.

37. Install the belt onto the sprockets from YOUR right side. If you are reusing the origi-

nal belt, make sure you follow the directional mark previously made.

38. Loosen the lock bolt so that the tensioner applies tension to the belt.

39. Turn the crankshaft two full revolutions in the direction of normal rotation. This will apply equal tension to all points of the belt.

40. Make sure that the timing marks are still aligned. If not, repeat the belt installation procedure.

41. Tighten the tensioner lock bolt to 30–35 ft.lb.

42. Measure the timing belt tension by pressing on the belt at the midpoint of the longest straight run. Belt deflection should be 11–13mm. If not, repeat the belt adjustment procedure, above.

43. Installation of all other parts is the reverse of removal. Torque the belt cover bolts to 80 in.lb.; the fan bracket bolts to 40 ft.lb. When installing the drive belts on the various accessories, check the belt deflection as follows:

- Alternator: New, 0.28–0.32 in.
                           Used, 0.31–0.36 in.
- Power steering pump: New, 0.31–0.49 in.
                           Used, 0.43–0.51 in.
- Air conditioning compressor:
                           New, 0.39–0.47 in.
                           Used, 0.47–0.55 in.

INSPECTION

1,586cc, 1,796cc, 2,209cc and 1979–84 1,970cc

PUMP BODY TO SHAFT CLEARANCE

Make this check using a dial indicator mounted on a magnet base. Bear the indicator on the drive gear. Clearance should not exceed 0.0039 in. (0.10mm). If it does, replace the pump.

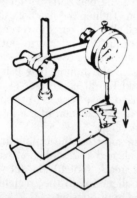

Oil pump body-to-shaft clearance for the 1,586cc, 1,796cc, 1,970cc and 2,209cc engine

INNER TO OUTER ROTOR CLEARANCE

Using a feeler gauge, check between the lobes of the rotors. Standard clearance should be

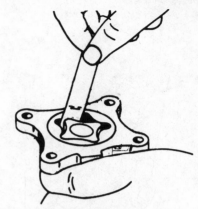

Inner-to-outer rotor clearance for the 1,586cc, 1,796cc, 1,970cc and 2,209cc engine

0.002–0.006 in. (0.04–0.15mm). If the clearance is greater than 0.010 in. (0.25mm), replace both rotors.

OUTER ROTOR TO PUMP BODY CLEARANCE

Insert a feeler gauge between the outer rotor and the pump body. Standard clearance is 0.006–0.010 in. (0.14–0.25mm). If clearance exceeds 0.012 in. (0.30mm), replace the rotor or body.

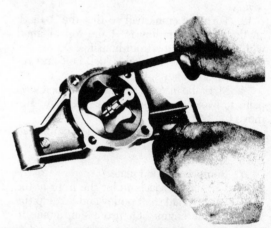

Outer rotor-to-body clearance for the 1,586cc, 1,796cc, 1,970cc and 2,209cc engine

ROTOR END FLOAT

Place a straightedge across the pump body and measure the clearance between the rotor and the straightedge with a feeler gauge. Then, place the straightedge across the pump cover and, with a feeler gauge, measure between the straightedge and the cover center. If the total of these two measurements exceeds 0.006 in. (0.15mm), the condition may be corrected by grinding the cover or replacing the cover or pump body.

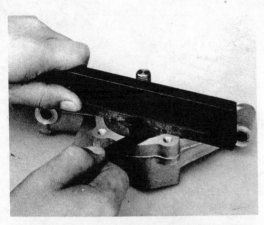

Measuring between the rotor and straightedge. This is part 1 of the rotor end float computation

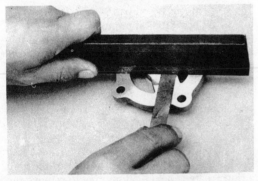

Measuring between the pump cover and straightedge. This is part 2 of the rotor end float computation

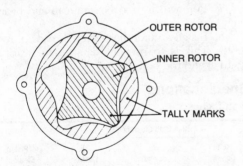

Inner-to-outer rotor tally marks used for alignment when assembling the oil pump

1986 1,998cc

NOTE: *The crescent referred to in these procedures is the crescent-shaped slinger between the inner and outer pump gears.*

OUTER GEAR TOOTH TIP TO CRESCENT CLEARANCE

Check this clearance with a feeler gauge. If the clearance exceeds 0.013 in. (0.35mm), replace the gear.

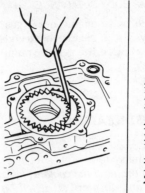
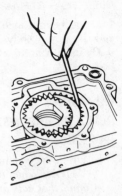

Inner (left), and outer (right) gear tooth tip-to-crescent clearance measurements on the 1,998cc engine oil pump

INNER GEAR TOOTH TIP TO CRESCENT CLEARANCE

Check this clearance with a feeler gauge. If the clearance exceeds 0.016 in. (0.40mm), replace the gear.

SIDE CLEARANCE

Lay a straightedge across the pump body and, using a feeler gauge, measure between the gear faces and straightedge. If the clearance exceeds 0.004 in. (0.10mm), replace the pump.

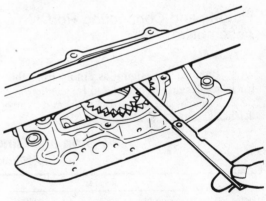

1,998cc engine oil pump side clearance measurement

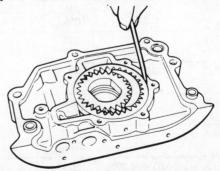

Outer gear-to-pump body clearance measurement

OUTER GEAR TO PUMP BODY CLEARANCE

Insert a feeler gauge between the outer gear and the pump body. If the clearance exceeds 0.008 in. (0.20mm), replace the gear or pump body.

Oil Cooler

REMOVAL AND INSTALLATION

1986 1,998cc

1. Drain the cooling system.
CAUTION: *When draining the coolant, keep in mind that cats and dogs are attracted by the ethelyne glycol antifreeze, and are quite likely to drink any that is left in an uncovered container or in puddles on the ground. This will prove fatal in sufficient quantity. Always drain the coolant into a sealable container. Coolant should be reused unless it is contaminated or several years old.*
2. Disconnect the coolant hoses at the oil cooler.
3. Remove the oil filter.
4. Remove the nut securing the cooler to the oil filter mounting stud.
5. Remove the cooler.
6. Installation is the reverse of removal. Coat the O-rings on the filter and cooler with clean engine oil prior to installation.

Pistons and Connecting Rod Assemblies

REMOVAL

1. Remove the engine assembly from the truck, see Engine Removal and Installation.
2. Remove the intake manifold and cylinder head.

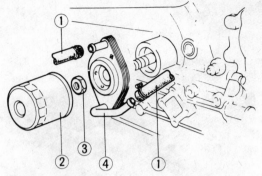

1. Water hoses
2. Oil filter
3. Nut
4. Oil cooler

1,998cc engine oil cooler

3. Remove the oil pan.
4. Remove the oil pump assembly.
5. Stamp the cylinder number on the machine surfaces of the bolt bosses of the connecting rod and cap for identification when reinstalling. If the pistons are to be removed from the connecting rod, mark the cylinder number on the piston with a silver pencil or quick drying paint for proper cylinder identification and cap-to-rod location.
6. Examine the cylinder bore above the ring travel. If a ridge exists, remove the ridge with a ridge reamer before attempting to remove the piston and rod assembly. Never cut into the ring travel area in excess of 1/32 in. when removing the ridges.
7. Remove the rod bearing cap and bearing.
8. Install a guide hose over threads of rod bolts. This is to prevent damage to bearing journal and rod bolt threads.

Piston and Ring Specifications
(All specifications in inches)

Engine (cc)	Ring Gap			Ring Side Clearance			Piston Clearance
	#1 Compr.	#2 Compr.	Oil Control	#1 Compr.	#2 Compr.	Oil Control	
1,586	0.0080–0.0160	0.0080–0.0160	0.0120–0.0350	0.0014–0.0028	0.0012–0.0025	0.0012–0.0025	0.0022–0.0028
1,796	0.0080–0.0160	0.0080–0.0160	0.0120–0.0350	0.0014–0.0028	0.0012–0.0025	snug	0.0022–0.0028
1,970	0.0080–0.0160	0.0080–0.0160	0.0120–0.0350	0.0012–0.0028	0.0012–0.0025	snug	①
1,998	0.0080–0.0120	0.0060–0.0120	0.0120–0.0350	0.0012–0.0028	0.0012–0.0028	snug	0.0014–0.0030
2,209	0.0157–0.0217	0.0118–0.0157	0.0138–0.0217	0.0020–0.0035	0.0016–0.0031	0.0012–0.0028	0.0021–0.0031

① 1979–81: 0.0014–0.0030
1982–84: 0.0019–0.0025

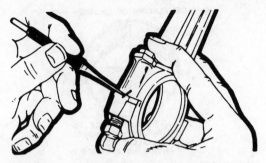

Match the connecting rods to their caps with a scribe mark

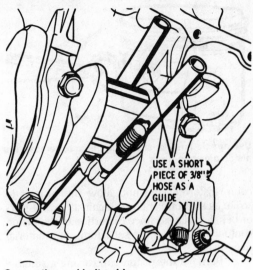

USE A SHORT PIECE OF 3/8" HOSE AS A GUIDE

Connecting rod bolt guide

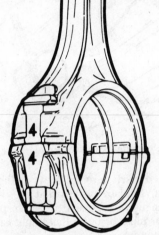

Match the connecting rods to their cylinders with a number stamp

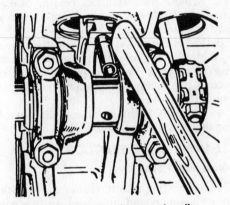

Push the piston out with a hammer handle

RIDGE CAUSED BY CYLINDER WEAR

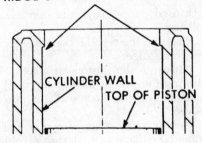

CYLINDER WALL
TOP OF PISTON

Cylinder bore ridge

9. Remove the rod and piston assembly through the top of the cylinder bore.

10. Remove the other rod and piston assemblies in the same manner.

PISTON PIN REMOVAL AND INSTALLATION

Use care at all times when handling and servicing connecting rods and pistons. To prevent possible damage to these units, do not clamp the rod or piston in a vise since they may be-

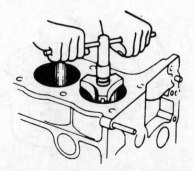

Removing the ridge with a ridge reamer

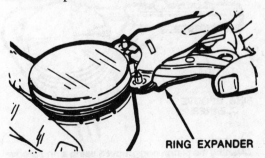

RING EXPANDER

Removing the piston rings

Use needle-nose or snap-ring pliers to remove the piston pin snap-rings

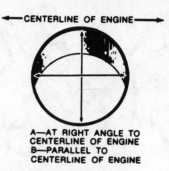

Cylinder bore measuring points

come distorted. Do not allow the pistons to strike against one another, against hard objects or bench surfaces, since distortion of the piston contour or nicks in the soft aluminum material may result.

1. Remove the piston rings using a suitable piston ring remover.

2. Remove the piston pin lockring, if used. Install the guide bushing of the piston pin removing and installing tool.

3. Install the piston and connecting rod assembly on a support, and place the assembly in an arbor press. Press the pin out of the connecting rod, using the appropriate piston pin tool.

4. Assembly is the reverse of disassembly. Use new lockrings where needed.

CLEANING AND INSPECTION

Connecting Rods

Wash connecting rods in cleaning solvent and dry with compressed air. Check for twisted or bent rods and inspect for nicks or cracks. Replace connecting rods that are damaged.

Pistons

Clean varnish from piston skirts and pins with a cleaning solvent. DO NOT WIRE BRUSH ANY PART OF THE PISTON. Clean the ring grooves with a groove cleaner and make sure oil ring holes and slots are clean.

Inspect the piston for cracked ring lands, skirts or pin bosses, wavy or worn ring lands, scuffed

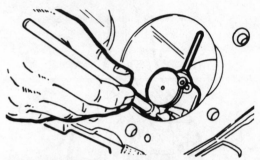

Measuring cylinder bore with a dial gauge

or damaged skirts, eroded areas at the top of the piston. Replace pistons that are damaged or show signs of excessive wear. Inspect the grooves for nicks or burrs that might cause the rings to hang up.

Measure piston skirt (across center line of piston pin) and check piston clearance.

MEASURING THE OLD PISTONS

Check used piston-to-cylinder bore clearance as follows:

1. Measure the cylinder bore diameter with a telescope gauge.

2. Measure the piston diameter. When measuring the pistons for size or taper, measurements must be made with the piston pin removed.

3. Subtract the piston diameter from the cylinder bore diameter to determine piston-to-bore clearance.

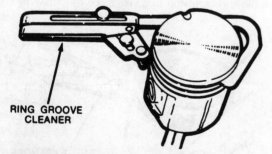

RING GROOVE CLEANER

Cleaning the piston ring grooves using a ring groove cleaner

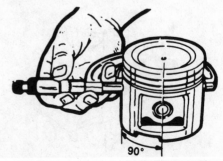

90°

Measuring the piston prior to fitting

4. Compare the piston-to-bore clearances obtained with those clearances recommended. Determine if the piston-to-bore clearance is in the acceptable range.

5. When measuring taper, the largest reading must be at the bottom of the skirt.

SELECTING NEW PISTONS

1. If the used piston is not acceptable, check the service piston size and determine if a new piston can be selected. Service pistons are available in standard, and oversizes of 0.254mm (0.010 in.) and 0.508mm (0.020 in.).

2. If the cylinder bore must be reconditioned, measure the new piston diameter, then hone the cylinder bore to obtain the preferred clearance.

3. Select a new piston and mark the piston to identify the cylinder for which it was fitted.

CYLINDER HONING

1. When cylinders are being honed, follow the manufacturer's recommendations for the use of the hone.

2. Occasionally during the honing operation, the cylinder bore should be thoroughly cleaned and the selected piston checked for correct fit.

3. When finish-honing a cylinder bore, the hone should be moved up and down at a sufficient speed to obtain a very fine uniform surface finish in a cross-hatch pattern of approximately 45–65 degrees included angle. The finish marks should be clean but not sharp, free from imbedded particles and torn or folded metal.

4. Permanently mark the piston for the cylinder to which it has been fitted and proceed to hone the remaining cylinders.

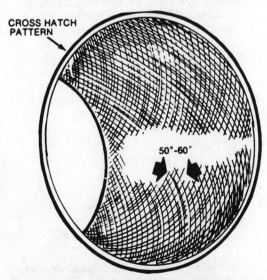

CROSS HATCH PATTERN

50°-60°

Cylinder bore cross-hatching after honing

NOTE: *Handle pistons with care. Do not attempt to force pistons through cylinders until the cylinders have been honed to correct size. Pistons can be distorted through careless handling.*

5. Thoroughly clean the bores with hot water and detergent. Scrub well with a stiff bristle brush and rinse thoroughly with hot water. It is extremely essential that a good cleaning operation be performed. If any of the abrasive material is allowed to remain in the cylinder bores, it will rapidly wear the new rings and cylinder bores. The bores should be swabbed several times with light engine oil and a clean cloth and then wiped with a clean dry cloth. CYLINDERS SHOULD NOT BE CLEANED WITH KEROSENE OR GASOLINE. Clean the remainder of the cylinder block to remove the excess material spread during the honing operation.

CHECKING CYLINDER BORE

Cylinder bore size can be measured with inside micrometers or a cylinder gauge. The most wear will occur at the top of the ring travel.

Reconditioned cylinder bores should be held to not more than 0.025mm (0.001 in.) taper.

If the cylinder bores are smooth, the cylinder walls should not be deglazed. If the cylinder walls are scored, the walls may have to be honed before installing new rings. It is important that reconditioned cylinder bores be thoroughly washed with a soap and water solution to remove all traces of abrasive material to eliminate premature wear.

Piston Rings

The pistons have three rings (two compression rings and one oil ring). The oil ring consists of two rails and an expander.

RING TOLERANCES

When installing new rings, ring gap and side clearance should be checked as follows:

Piston Ring and Rail Gap

Each ring and rail gap must be measured with the ring or rail positioned squarely and at the bottom of the ring-travel area of the bore.

Side Clearance

Each ring must be checked for side clearance in its respective piston groove by inserting a feeler gauge between the ring and its upper land. The piston grooves must be cleaned before checking the ring for side clearance specifications. To check oil ring side clearance, the oil rings must be installed on the piston.

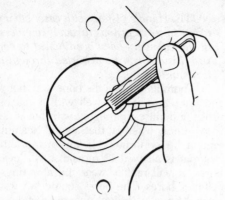

Check the piston ring end gap

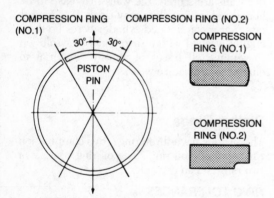

Check the piston ring side clearance

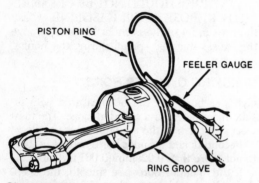

Compression ring installation

RING INSTALLATION

For service ring specifications and detailed installation productions, refer to the instructions furnished with the parts package.

Connecting Rod Bearings

If you have already removed the connecting rod and piston assemblies from the engine, follow only Steps 3–7 of the following procedure.

REMOVAL, INSPECTION, INSTALLATION

The connecting rod bearings are designed to have a slight projection above the rod and cap

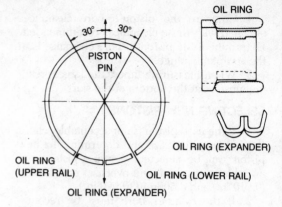

Oil ring installation

faces to insure a positive contact. The bearings can be replaced without removing the rod and piston assemblies from the engine.

1. Remove the oil pan. See the Oil Pan procedures, below.

2. With the the connecting rod journal at the bottom, stamp the cylinder number on the machined surfaces of the connecting rod and cap for identification when installing, then remove the caps.

3. Inspect journals for roughness and wear. Slight roughness may be removed with a fine grit polishing cloth saturated with engine oil. Burrs may be removed with a fine oil stone by moving the stone on the journal circumference. Do not move the stone back and forth across the journal. If the journals are scored or ridged, the crankshaft must be replaced.

4. The connecting rod journals should be checked for out-of-round and correct size with a micrometer.

NOTE: *Crankshaft rod journals will normally be standard size. If any undersized bearings are used, all will be 0.254mm undersize and 0.254mm will be stamped on the number 4 counterweight.*

If plastic gauging material is to be used:

5. Clean oil from the journal bearing cap, connecting rod and outer and inner surfaces of the bearing inserts. Position the insert so that the tang is properly aligned with the notch in the rod and cap.

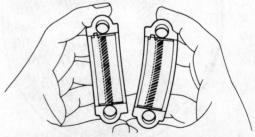

Inspect the rod bearings for scuffing and other wear; also check the crankshaft journal

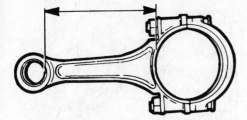

Check the connecting rod length (arrow)

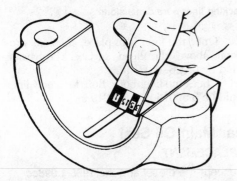

Measuring the connecting rod bearing oil clearance with a strip of Plastigage® material

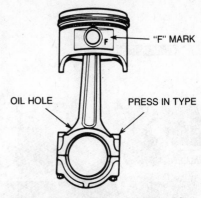

Typical piston-to-connecting rod relationship

RING COMPRESSOR

Using a wooden hammer handle, tap the piston down through the ring compressor and into the cylinder

6. Place a piece of plastic gauging material in the center of lower bearing shell.

7. Remove the bearing cap and determine the bearing clearances by comparing the width of the flattened plastic gauging material at its widest point with the graduation on the container. The number within the graduation on the envelope indicates the clearance in thousandths of an inch or millimeters. If this clearance is excessive, replace the bearing and re-check the clearance with the plastic gauging material. Undersized bearings are available in sizes of 0.254mm (0.010 in.), 0.508mm (0.020 in.) and 0.750mm (0.295 in.). Lubricate the bearing with engine oil before installation. Repeat Steps 2–7 on the remaining connecting rod bearings. All rods must be connected to their journals when rotating the crankshaft, to prevent engine damage.

Piston and Connecting Rod

INSTALLATION

1. Install some lengths of rubber tubing over the connecting rod bolts to prevent damage to the journals.

2. Apply engine oil to the rings and piston, then install a piston ring compressing tool on the piston.

3. Install the assembly in its respective cylinder bore.

4. Lubricate the crankshaft journal with engine oil and install the connecting rod bearing and cap, with the bearing index tang in rod and cap on same side.

NOTE: *When more than one rod and piston assembly is being installed, the connecting rod cap attaching nuts should be tightened only enough to keep each rod in position until all have been installed. This will aid installation of the remaining piston assemblies.*

5. Torque the rod bolt nuts to specification. Using a feeler gauge and small prybar, check connecting rod side clearance.

6. Install all other parts in reverse order of removal.

7. Install the engine in the truck. See Engine Removal and Installation.

Cylinder Liners

REMOVAL AND INSTALLATION

Diesel Only

A hydraulic press and adapters are necessary for this procedure.

1. Remove the engine.

2. Remove the head.

3. Remove the pistons and connecting rods.

4. Remove the crankshaft and bearings.

5. Remove the camshaft.

6. Mount the block in the holding fixture under the press ram, bottom side up.

Removing the diesel cylinder liners

Installing the diesel cylinder liners

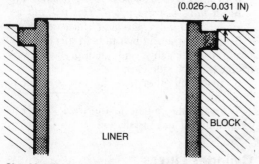

Checking liner protrusion

7. Drive the liners from the block.

8. Check the block bore for scratches. Remove them with an oil-soaked fine emery paper.

9. Invert the block and press the new liners in from the top.

NOTE: *Normal pressing pressure is 2,200–6,600 lb. Press pressure higher than 6,600 lb. will distort the liner; pressures lower than 2,200 lb. will result in a loose fit.*

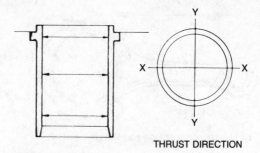

Checking liner bore dimensions

10. Once the liner is in place, check its protrusion above the head surface. Protrusion should be 0.026–0.031 in.

11. Check the liner bore. Bore for a new liner should be 3.5001 in. + 0.0019 in.

Rear Main Oil Seal
REPLACEMENT
All except the diesel and the 1986 1,998cc

If the rear main oil seal is being replaced independently of any other parts, it can be done with the engine in place. If the rear main oil seal and the rear main bearing are being replaced, together, the engine must be removed from the truck.

1. Remove the transmission.

2. On trucks with a manual transmission, remove the clutch disc, pressure plate and flywheel. On trucks with an automatic transmission, remove the drive plate.

3. Using an awl, punch two holes in the crankshaft rear oil seal. They should be punched on opposite sides of the crankshaft, just above the bearing cap-to-cylinder block split line.

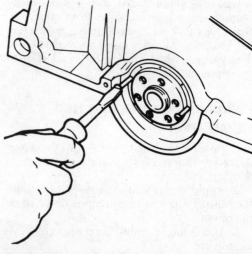

Removing the rear main seal from the 1,586cc, 1,796cc and 1,970cc engines

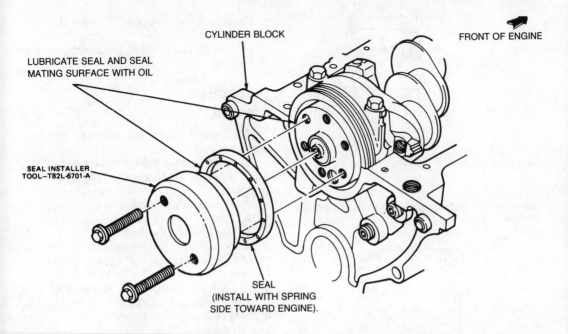

CYLINDER BLOCK

FRONT OF ENGINE

LUBRICATE SEAL AND SEAL
MATING SURFACE WITH OIL

SEAL INSTALLER
TOOL—T82L-6701-A

SEAL
(INSTALL WITH SPRING
SIDE TOWARD ENGINE).

NOTE: REAR FACE OF SEAL MUST BE WITHIN 0.127mm (0.005-INCH) OF THE REAR FACE OF THE BLOCK.

Installing the rear main seal from the 1,586cc, 1,796cc and 1,970cc engines

4. Install a sheet metal screw in each hole. Pry against both screws at the same time to remove the oil seal. Do not scratch the oil seal surface on the crankshaft.

5. Clean the oil recess in the cylinder block and bearing cap. Clean the oil seal surface on the crankshaft.

6. Coat the oil seal surfaces with oil. Coat the oil surface and the seal surface on the crankshaft with Lubriplate®. Install the oil seal and be sure that it is not cocked. Be sure that the seal surface was not damaged.

7. Install the flywheel. Coat the threads of the flywheel or drive plate attaching bolts with oil resistant sealer. Torque the bolts to specifications in sequence across from each other.

- Flywheel: Gasoline engine, 115–120 ft.lb.
  Diesel engine, 100–140 ft.lb.
- Drive plate: 60–69 ft.lb.

8. Install the clutch, pressure plate and transmission.

Diesel Engine

1. Remove the transmission.
2. Remove the clutch assembly.
3. Remove the flywheel.
4. Remove the rear main seal housing.
5. Drive the old seal from the housing.
6. Clean the housing bore thoroughly.
7. Coat the outer edge of the new seal with gasket sealer.
8. Drive the new seal into the housing until it bottoms.

Diesel engine rear main seal and housing

9. Coat the seal lip with clean engine oil and install the housing onto the engine. Torque the bolts, in a criss-cross pattern, to 10–14 ft.lb.

10. Install all other parts in reverse of removal.

1986 1,998cc

1. Remove the transmission.
2. Remove the clutch assembly.
3. Remove the flywheel.
4. Remove the end plate.
5. The seal is located in the rear cover. Remove the rear cover. Discard the gasket.
6. Drive the old seal from the rear cover.
7. Apply clean engine oil to the outer rim

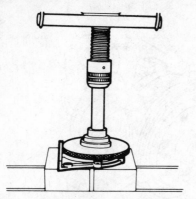

Installing the 1,998cc engine rear main seal into the housing

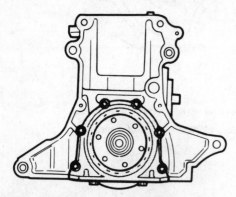

1,998cc engine rear cover installation

of the new seal and the seal bore in the rear cover. Press the new seal into place.

8. Coat the seal lip with clean engine oil. Install the rear cover and new gasket. Torque the bolts to 72–102 in.lb. (6–8.5 ft.lb.).

9. Using a sharp knife, cut away the part of the gasket that projects below the rear cover.

10. Install the end plate. Torque the bolts to 14–22 ft.lb.

11. Installation of other parts is the reverse of removal.

Crankshaft

REMOVAL

1. Remove the engine assembly as previously outlined.

2. Remove the engine front cover.

3. Remove the timing chain/belt/gears and sprockets.

4. Remove the oil pan.

5. Remove the oil pump.

6. Remove the flywheel.

7. Stamp the cylinder number on the machined surfaces of the bolt bosses of the connecting rods and caps for identification when installing. If the pistons are to be removed from the connecting rod, mark the cylinder number on each piston with an indelible marker, silver pencil or quick drying paint for proper cylinder identification and cap to rod location.

8. Remove the connecting rod caps and store them so that they can be installed in their original positions.

9. Remove all the main bearing caps.

10. Note the position of the keyway in the crankshaft so it can be installed in the same position.

11. Lift the crankshaft out of the block. The rods will pivot to the center of the engine when the crankshaft is removed.

12. Remove the rear main oil seal.

INSPECTION AND INSTALLATION

1. Using a dial indicator, check the crankshaft journal runout. Measure the crankshaft

Crankshaft and Connecting Rod Specifications
(All specifications in inches)

| | Crankshaft | | | | Connecting Rod | | |
Engine (cc)	Main Bearing Journal Dia.	Main Bearing Oil Clearance	Shaft End Play	Thrust on No.	Journal Dia.	Oil Clearance	Side Clearance
1,586	2.4804	0.0012–0.0024	0.0030–0.0090	3	2.0866	0.0011–0.0030	0.0040–0.0080
1,796	2.4804	0.0012–0.0020	0.0030–0.0090	3	2.0866	0.0011–0.0030	0.0040–0.0080
1,970	2.4804	0.0012–0.0020	0.0030–0.0090	3	2.0866	0.0011–0.0030	0.0040–0.0080
1,998	2.3597–2.3604	0.0012–0.0019	0.0030–0.0070	3	2.0050–2.0060	0.0010–0.0026	0.0040–0.0100
2,209	2.5591	0.0016–0.0036	0.0055–0.0154	3	2.0866	0.0014–0.0030	0.0094–0.0134

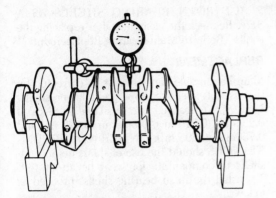

Checking crankshaft journal runout

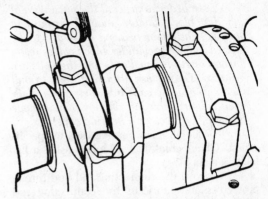

Use a feeler gauge to check the crankshaft end play during assembly

journals with a micrometer to determine the correct size rod and main bearings to be used. Whenever a new or reconditioned crankshaft is installed, new connecting rod bearings and main bearings should be installed. See Main Bearings and Rod Bearings.

2. Clean all oil passages in the block (and crankshaft if it is being reused).

NOTE: *A new rear main seal should be installed anytime the crankshaft is removed or replaced.*

3. Install sufficient oil pan bolts in the block to align with the connecting rod bolts. Use rubber bands between the bolts to position the connecting rods as required. Connecting rod position can be adjusted by increasing the tension on the rubber bands with additional turns around the pan bolts or thread protectors.

4. Position the upper half of main bearings in the block and lubricate them with engine oil.

5. Position crankshaft keyway in the same position as removed and lower it into block. The connecting rods will follow the crank pins into the correct position as the crankshaft is lowered.

6. Lubricate the thrust flanges with rebuilding oil. Install caps with the lower half of the bearings lubricated with engine oil. Lubricate the cap bolts with engine oil and install, but do not tighten.

7. With a block of wood, bump the shaft in

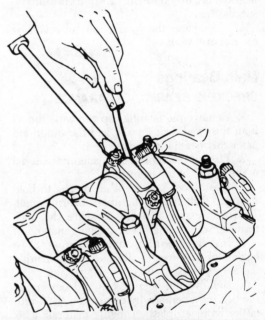

Check the connecting rod side clearance with a feeler gauge. Use a small pry bar to carefully spread the rods to specified clearance

each direction to align the thrust flanges of the main bearing. After bumping the shaft in each direction, wedge the shaft to the front and hold it while torquing the thrust bearing cap bolts.

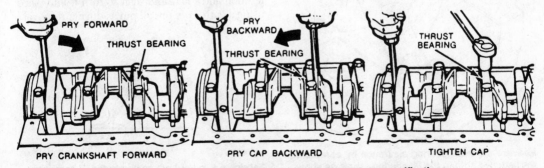

Align the thrust bearing as illustrated. Torque the caps to specifications

NOTE: *In order to prevent the possibility of cylinder block and/or main bearing cap damage, the main bearing caps are to be tapped into their cylinder block cavity using a wood or rubber mallet before the bolts are installed. Do not use attaching bolts to pull the main bearing caps into their seats. Failure to observe this information may damage the cylinder block or a bearing cap.*

8. Torque all main bearing caps to specification. Check crankshaft endplay, using a flat feeler gauge.

9. Remove the connecting rod bolt thread protectors and lubricate the connecting rod bearings with engine oil.

10. Install the connecting rod bearing caps in their original position. Torque the nuts to specification.

11. Complete the installation by reversing the removal steps.

Main Bearings

CHECKING BEARING CLEARANCE

1. Remove the bearing cap and wipe the oil from the crankshaft journal and the outer and inner surfaces of the bearing shell.

2. Place a piece of plastic gauging material in the center of the bearing.

3. Use a floor jack or other means to hold the crankshaft against the upper bearing shell. This is necessary to obtain accurate clearance readings when using plastic gauging material.

4. Install the bearing cap and bearing. Place engine oil on the cap bolts and install. Torque the bolts to specification.

5. Remove the bearing cap and determine the bearing clearance by comparing the width of the flattened plastic gauging material at its widest point with the graduations on the gauging material container. The number within the graduation on the envelope indicates the clearance in millimeters or thousandths of an inch. If the clearance is greater than allowed, RE-

PLACE BOTH BEARING SHELLS AS A SET. Recheck the clearance after replacing the shells. (Refer to Main Bearing Replacement).

REPLACEMENT

Main bearing clearances must be corrected by the use of selective upper and lower shells. Undersized bearings are available in sizes of 0.254mm (0.010 in.), 0.508mm (0.020 in.) and 0.750mm (0.295 in.). UNDER NO CIRCUMSTANCES should the use of shims behind the shells to compensate for wear be attempted. To install the main bearing shells, proceed as follows:

1. Remove the oil pan as outlined below. On some models, the oil pump may also have to be removed.

2. Loosen all main bearing caps.

3. Remove the bearing cap and remove the lower shell.

4. Insert a flattened cotter pin or roll pin in the oil passage hole in the crankshaft, then rotate the crankshaft in the direction opposite from cranking rotation. The pin will contact the upper shell and roll it out.

5. The main bearing journals should be checked for roughness and wear. Slight roughness may be removed with a fine grit polishing cloth saturated with engine oil. Burrs may be removed with a fine oil stone. If the journals are scored or ridged, the crankshaft must be replaced.

The journals can be measured for out-of-round with the crankshaft installed by using a crankshaft caliper and inside micrometer or a main bearing micrometer. The upper bearing shell must be removed when measuring the crankshaft journals. Maximum out-of-round of the crankshaft journals must not exceed 0.050mm (0.0020 in.).

6. Clean the crankshaft journals and bearing caps thoroughly for installing new main bearings.

7. Apply clean engine oil or rebuilding oil, to the thrust flanges of bearing shells.

8. Place a new upper shell on the crankshaft journal with locating tang in the correct position and rotate the shaft to turn it into place using a cotter pin or roll pin as during removal.

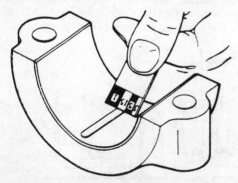

Measure the main bearing clearance by comparing the flattened strip to the Plasticgage scale as shown

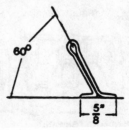

Fabricate a roll-out pin as illustrated, if necessary

Torque Specifications
Piston Engines
(All specifications in ft. lb.)

Engine (cc)	Cyl. Head	Conn. Rod	Main Bearing	Crankshaft Damper	Flywheel	Manifold	
						Intake	Exhaust
1,586	①	36–40	61–65	101–108	112–118	14–19	12–17 ②
1,796	①	36–40	61–65	101–108	112–118	14–19	16–21
1,970	①	30–33	61–65	101–108	112–118	14–19	16–21
1,998	59–64	37–41	61–65	9–12	71–76	14–19	16–21
2,209	80–85	50–54	80–85	145–181	95–137	11–17	11–17

① 1979–81 Torque cold to 59–64 ft. lb.; then retorque hot to 69–72 ft. lb.
  1982–84 Torque cold to 65–69 ft. lb.; then retorque hot to 69–72 ft. lb.
② 1973–75: 16–21 ft. lb.

9. Place a new bearing shell in the bearing cap.

10. Install a new oil seal in the rear main bearing cap and block.

11. Lubricate the main bearings with engine oil. Lubricate the thrust surface with lubricant rebuilding oil.

12. Lubricate the main bearing cap bolts with engine oil.

NOTE: *In order to prevent the possibility of cylinder block and/or main bearing cap damage, the main bearing caps are to be tapped into their cylinder block cavity using a wood or rubber mallet before the attaching bolts are installed. Do not use attaching bolts to pull the main bearing caps into their seats. Failure to observe this information may damage the cylinder block or a bearing cap.*

13. Torque the main bearing cap bolts as specified.

Radiator
REMOVAL AND INSTALLATION

1. Drain the cooling system.

CAUTION: *When draining the coolant, keep in mind that cats and dogs are attracted by the ethylene glycol antifreeze, and are quite likely to drink any that is left in an uncovered container or in puddles on the ground. This will prove fatal in sufficient quantity. Always drain the coolant into a sealable container. Coolant should be reused unless it is contaminated or several years old.*

2. If equipped, remove the fan shroud.

3. Remove the fan. Don't lay the fan, if equipped with a fan clutch, on its side. Fluid will be lost and the fan clutch will have to be replaced.

4. Disconnect the upper and lower radiator hoses.

5. Unbolt and remove the radiator.

6. Install the radiator against the supports and tighten the mounting bolts.

7. Install the hoses on the radiator. Tighten the clamps.

8. Install the fan.

9. If equipped, install the fan shroud.

10. Refill the cooling system with the specified amount and type of coolant. Run the engine and check for leaks.

ROTARY ENGINE SERVICE

Design

The Mazda rotary engine replaces conventional pistons with three-cornered rotors which have rounded sides. The rotors are mounted on a shaft which has eccentrics rather than crank throws.

The chamber in which the rotor travels is roughly oval shaped, but with the sides of the oval bowed in slightly. The technical name for this shape is a two lobe epitrochoid.

As the rotor travels its path in the chamber, it performs the same four functions as the piston in a regular four cycle engine:

1. Intake
2. Compression
3. Ignition
4. Exhaust

But all four functions in a rotary engine are happening concurrently, rather than in four separate stages.

Ignition of the compressed fuel/air mixture occurs each time a side of the rotor passes the spark plugs. Since the rotor has three sides there are three complete power impulses for each complete revolution of the rotor. As it moves, the rotor experts pressure on the cam of the eccentric shaft, causing the shaft to turn.

Because there are three power pulses for every revolution of the rotor, the eccentric shaft

E
FUEL/AIR MISTURE IS
DRAWN INTO COMBUSTION
CHAMBER BY REVOLVING
ROTOR THROUGH INTAKE
PORT (UPPER LEFT). NO
VALVES OR VALVE-
OPERATING MECHANISM
NEEDED.

2.COMPRESSION.
AS ROTOR CONTINUES
REVOLVING, IT REDUCES
SPACE IN CHAMBER
CONTAINING FUEL AND AIR
THIS COMPRESSES
MIXTURE.

3.IGNITION.
FUEL/AIR MIXTURE NOW
FULLY COMPRESSED.
LEADING SPARKPLUG
FIRES. A SPLIT-SECOND
LATER, FOLLOWING PLUG
FIRES TO ASSURE COMPLETE
COMBUSTION.

4.EXHAUST.
EXPLODING MIXTURE
DRIVES ROTOR, PROVIDING
POWER. ROTOR THEN
EXPELS GASES THROUGH
EXHAUST PORT.

The rotary engine combustion cycle

must make three complete revolutions for every one revolution of the rotor. To maintain this ratio, the rotor has an internal gear that meshes with a fixed gear in a three-to-one ratio. If it was not for this gear arrangement, the rotor would spin freely and timing would be lost.

The Mazda rotary engine has two rotors mounted 60 degrees out of phase. This produces six power impulses for each complete revolution of both rotors and two power impulses for each revolution of the eccentric shaft.

Because of the number of power impulses for each revolution of the rotor and because all four functions are concurrent, the rotary engine is able to produce a much greater amount of power for its size and weight than a comparable reciprocating piston engine.

Instead of using valves to control the intake and exhaust operations, the rotor uncovers and covers ports on the wall of the chambers, as it turns. Thus, a complex valve train is unnecessary. The resulting elimination of parts further reduces the size and weight of the engine, as well as eliminating a major source of mechanical problems.

Spring loaded carbon seals are used to prevent loss of compression around the rotor apexes and cast iron seals are used to prevent loss of compression around the side faces of the rotor. These seals are equivalent to compression rings on a conventional piston, but must be more durable because of the high rotor rpm to which they are exposed.

Oil is controlled by means of circular seals

mounted in two grooves on the side face of the rotor. These oil seals function to keep oil out of the combustion chamber and gasoline out of the crankcase, in a similar manner to the oil control ring on a piston.

The rotor housing is made of aluminum and the surfaces of the chamber are chrome plated.

Engine
REMOVAL AND INSTALLATION

1. Scribe matchmarks on the hood and hinges. Remove the hood from the hinges.
2. Working from underneath the truck, remove the gravel shield then drain the cooling system and the engine oil.

CAUTION: *When draining the coolant, keep in mind that cats and dogs are attracted by the ethelyne glycol antifreeze, and are quite likely to drink any that is left in an uncovered container or in puddles on the ground. This will prove fatal in sufficient quantity. Always drain the coolant into a sealable container. Coolant should be reused unless it is contaminated or several years old.*

3. Disconnect the cable from the negative (–) battery terminal.
4. Remove the air cleaner, bracket, and hoses.
5. Detach the accelerator cable, choke cable, and fuel lines from the carburetor.
6. Remove the nuts which secure the thermostat housing. Disconnect the ground cable

General Engine Specifications

Year	Engine (cc)	Fuel System Type	SAE net Horsepower @ rpm	SAE net Torque ft. lb. @ rpm	Bore x Stroke	Comp. Ratio	Oil Press. (psi.) @ 2000 rpm
1972–77	1,308	4-bbl	90 @ 6000	96 @ 4000	—	9.2:1	70

from the housing and install the housing again after the cable is removed

7. Disconnect the power brake vacuum line from the intake manifold.

8. Remove the fan shroud securing bolts and then the shroud itself.

9. Remove the bolts which secure the fan clutch to the eccentric shaft pulley. Withdraw the fan and clutch as a single unit.

CAUTION: *Keep the fan clutch in an upright position so that its fluid does not leak out.*

10. Unfasten the clamps and remove both radiator hoses.

11. Note their respective positions and remove the spark plug cables. Disconnect the primary leads from the distributor and the distributor cap.

12. Detach all of the leads from the alternator, the water temperature sender, the oil pressure sender, and the starter motor.

13. Disconnect all of the wiring from the emission control system components.

14. Detach the heater hoses at the engine.

15. Detach the oil lines from the front and the rear of the engine.

16. Disconnect the battery cable from the positive (+) battery terminal and from the engine.

17. Unfasten the clutch slave cylinder retaining nuts from the clutch housing and tie the cylinder up and out of the way.

NOTE: *Do not remove the hydraulic line from the slave cylinder.*

18. Remove the exhaust pipe and the thermal reactor.

CAUTION: *Be sure that the thermal reactor has completely cooled; severe burns could result if it has not.*

19. Remove the nuts and bolts, evenly and in two or three stages, which secure the clutch housing to the engine.

20. Support the transmission with a jack.

21. Remove the nuts from each of the engine mounts.

22. Attach a lifting sling to the lifting bracket on the rear of the engine housing.

23. Use a hoist to take up the slack on the sling.

24. Pull the engine forward until it clears the transmission input shaft. Lift the engine straight up and out of the truck.

25. Remove the heat stove from the exhaust manifold.

26. Remove the thermal reactor.

27. Mount the engine on a workstand.

28. Engine installation is performed in the reverse order of removal. Remember to refill all fluids according to specifications and to adjust the ignition after installation.

ENGINE DISASSEMBLY

NOTE: *Because of the design of the rotary engine, it is not practical to attempt component removal and installation. It is best to disassemble and assemble the entire engine, or, go as far as necessary with the disassembly procedure.*

1. Mount the engine on a stand.

2. Remove the oil hose support bracket from the front housing.

3. Disconnect the vacuum hoses, air hoses and remove the decel valve.

4. Remove the air pump and drive belt. Remove the air pump adjusting bar.

5. Remove the alternator and drive belt.

6. Disconnect the metering oil pump connecting rod, oil tubes and vacuum sensing tube from the carburetor.

7. Remove the carburetor and intake manifold as an assembly.

8. Remove the intake manifold gasket and two rubber rings. Discard them.

9. Remove the thermal reactor and gaskets.

10. Remove the spark plug wires and distributor high tension leads, and remove the distributor from the front cover.

11. Remove the water pump and gasket.

12. Invert the engine on the stand.

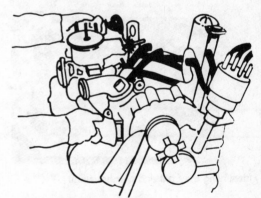

Removing the intake manifold

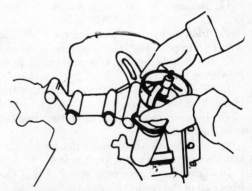

Removing the distributor

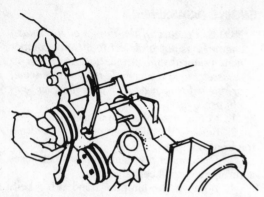

Removing the water pump

Removing the eccentric shaft pulley

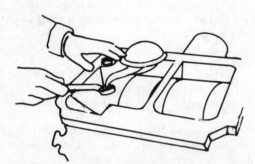

Removing the oil pump strainer

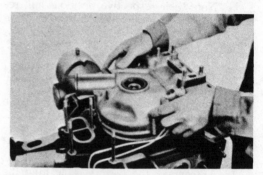

Removing the front cover

Identifying the front and rear housings

Removing the chain adjuster

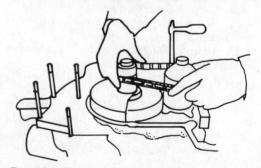

Removing the chain and sprockets

13. Remove the oil pan and gasket.

14. Remove the oil pump screen and gasket.

15. Identify the front and rear rotor housing wit a felt tip pen. These are common parts and must be identified to be reassembled in their respective locations.

16. Turn the engine on the stand so that the top of the engine is up.

17. Remove the engine mounting bracket from the front cover.

18. Hold the flywheel with a flywheel holder and remove the eccentric shaft pulley.

19. Turn the engine on a stand so that the front end of the engine is up.

20. Remove the front cover and gasket.

21. Remove the O-ring from the oil passage on the front housing.

22. Remove the oil slinger and distributor drive gear from the shaft.

23. Unbolt and remove the chain adjuster.

24. Remove the locknut and washer from the oil pump driven sprocket.

25. Slide the oil pump drive sprocket and driven sprocket together with the drive chain off the eccentric shaft and oil pump simultaneously.

26. Remove the keys from the eccentric and oil pump shafts.

27. Slide the balance weight, thrust washer and needle bearing from the shaft.

28. Unbolt the bearing housing and slide the bearing housing, needle bearing, spacer and thrust plate off the shaft.

29. Turn the engine on the stand so that the top of the engine is up.

30. If equipped with a manual transmission, remove the clutch pressure plate and clutch disc. Loosen the pressure plate bolts evenly in small stages to prevent distortion and possible injury from the pressure plate flying off. Straighten the tab of the lockwasher and remove the flywheel nut. Remove the flywheel with a puller.

31. If equipped with an automatic transmission, remove the drive plate. Straighten the tab on the lockwasher and remove the counterweight nut, while holding the flywheel with a flywheel holder. Remove the counterweight using a puller.

32. Working at the rear of the engine, loosen the tension bolts in the sequence shown, and remove the tension bolts.

NOTE: *Do not loosen the tension bolts one at a time. Loosen the bolts evenly in small stages to prevent distortion.*

33. Lift the rear housing off the shaft.

34. Remove any seals that are stuck to the rotor sliding surface of the rear housing and reinstall them in their original locations.

35. Remove all the corner seals, corner seal springs, side seal and side seal springs from the rear side of the rotor. Mazda has a special tray

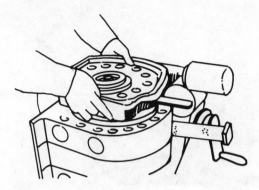
Removing the rear housing

Removing the seals

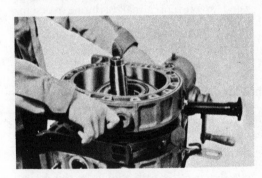
Removing the rear rotor housing

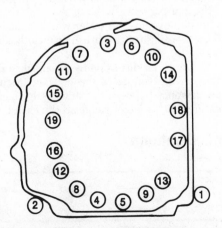
Loosen the tension bolts in the order shown

Removing the seals from the rotor

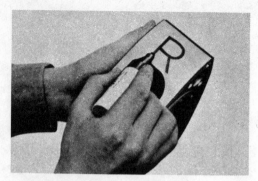

Identifying the rotors

Removing the oil seals from the rotor

which holds all the seals and keeps them segregated to prevent mistakes during reassembly. Each seal groove is marked to prevent confusion.

36. Remove the two rubber seals and two O-rings from the rear rotor housing.

37. Remove the dowels from the rear rotor housing.

38. Lift the rear rotor housing away from the rear rotor, being very careful not to drop the apex seals on the rear rotor.

39. Remove each apex seal, side piece and spring from the rear rotor and segregate them.

40. Remove the rear rotor from the eccentric shaft and place it upside down on a clean rag.

41. Remove each seal and spring from the other side of the rotor and segregate these.

42. If some of the seals fall from the rotor, be careful not to change the original position of each seal.

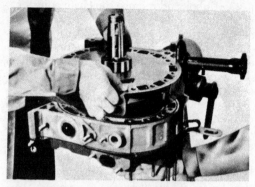

Removing the intermediate housing

43. Identify the rear rotor with a felt tip pen.

44. Remove the oil seals and the springs. Do not exert heavy pressure at only one place on the seal since it could be deformed. Replace the O-rings in the oil seal when the engine is overhauled.

45. Hold the intermediate housing down and remove the dowels from it.

46. Lift off the intermediate housing being careful not to damage the eccentric shaft. It should be removed by sliding it beyond the rear rotor journal on the eccentric shaft while holding the intermediate housing up and, at the same time, pushing the eccentric shaft up.

47. Lift out the eccentric shaft.

48. Repeat the above procedures to remove the front rotor housing and front rotor.

INSPECTION

Front Housing

1. Check the housing for signs of gas or water leakage.

2. Remove the carbon deposits from the front housing with an extra fine emery cloth.

NOTE: *If a carbon scraper must be used, be careful not to damage the mating surfaces of the housing.*

3. Remove any old sealer which is adhering to the housing using a brush or a cloth soaked in ketone.

4. Check for distortion by placing a straightedge on the surface of the housing. Measure the clearance between the straightedge and the housing with a feeler gauge. If the clearance is

Eccentric Shaft Specifications

(All specifications in inches)

Engine (cc)	Journal Diameter		Oil Clearance		Shaft End Play	Maximum Shaft Run-out
	Main Bearing	Rotor Bearing	Main Bearing	Rotor Bearing		
1,308	1.6929	2.9134	0.0016–0.0039	0.0016–0.0039	0.0026	0.0024

Rotor and Housing Specifications
(All specifications in inches)

| Engine (cc) | Rotor | | Housings | | | | | | |
| | Side Clearance | Standard Protrusion of Land | Front & Rear | | Rotor | | Intermediate | |
			Distortion Limit	Wear Limit	Width	Distortion Limit	Distortion Limit	Wear Limit
1,308	0.0039–0.0083	0.0040–0.0060	0.0016	0.0039	3.1496	0.0024	0.0016	0.0039

Seal Clearance Specifications
(All specifications in inches)

| Engine (cc) | Apex Seals | | | Side Seal | |
	To Side Housing	To Rotor Groove	Corner Seal To Rotor Groove	To Rotor Groove	To Corner Seal
1,308	0.0051–0.0018	0.0020–0.0059	0.0018–0.0019	0.0016–0.0040	0.0020–0.0059

Seal Specifications
(All specifications in inches)

| Engine (cc) | Apex Seal | | Corner Seal O.D. | Side Seal | | Oil Seal Lip Contact Width | Oil Seal Height |
	Height	Width		Thickness	Height		
1,308	0.27559	0.118	0.43307	0.03937	0.13779	0.03147	0.2205

greater than 0.002 in. at any point, replace the housing.

5. Use a dial indicator to check for wear on the rotor contact surfaces of the housing. If the wear is greater than 0.004 in., replace the housing.

NOTE: *The wear at either end of the minor axis is greater than at any other point on the housing. However, this is normal and should be no cause for concern.*

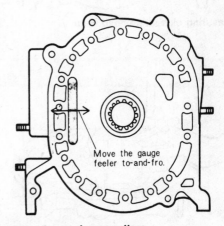

Move the gauge feeler to-and-fro.

Position of normal wear pattern

Front Stationary Gear and Main Bearing

1. Examine the teeth of the stationary gear for wear or damage.

2. Be sure that the main bearing shows no signs of excessive wear, scoring or flaking.

3. Check the main bearing-to-eccentric journal clearance by measuring the journal with

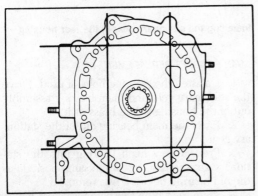

Check the housings for warpage along these lines

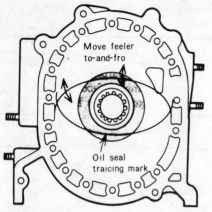

Measuring stepped wear across the middle of the housing

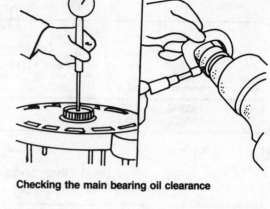

Checking the main bearing oil clearance

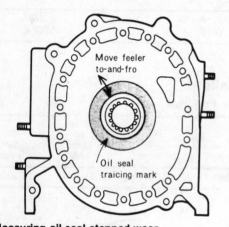

Measuring oil seal stepped wear

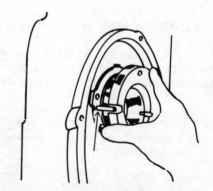

Removing the stationary gear

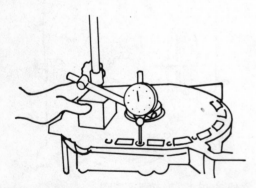

Checking the housing for wear with a dial indicator

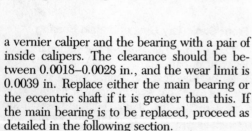

Installing the stationary gear in the rear housing

MAIN BEARING REPLACEMENT

1. Unfasten the securing bolts, if used. Drive the stationary gear and main bearing assembly out of the housing with a brass drift.

2. Press the main bearing out of the stationary gear.

3. Press a new main bearing into the stationary gear so that it is in the same position as the old bearing before it was removed.

4. Align the slot in the stationary gear flange with the dowel pin in the housing and press

a vernier caliper and the bearing with a pair of inside calipers. The clearance should be between 0.0018–0.0028 in., and the wear limit is 0.0039 in. Replace either the main bearing or the eccentric shaft if it is greater than this. If the main bearing is to be replaced, proceed as detailed in the following section.

Check the rotor housing for distortion along the lines shown

the gear into place. Install the securing bolts, if required.

NOTE: *To aid in stationary gear and main bearing removal and installation, Mazda supplies a special tool, part number 49 0813 235.*

Intermediate and Rear Housings

Inspection of the intermediate and rear housings is carried out in the same manner as detailed for the front housing above. Replacement of the rear main bearing and stationary gear (mounted on the rear housing) is given below.

Rear Stationary Gear and Main Bearing

Inspect the rear stationary gear and main bearing in a similar manner to the front. In addition, examine the O-ring which is located in the stationary gear, for signs of wear or damage. Replace the O-ring, if necessary. If required, replace the stationary gear in the following manner:

1. Remove the rear stationary gear securing bolts.
2. Drive the stationary gear out of the rear housing with a brass drift.
3. Apply a light coating of grease on a new O-ring and fit it into the groove on the stationary gear.
4. Apply sealer to the flange of the stationary gear.

5. Install the stationary gear on the housing so that the slot on its flange aligns with the pin on the rear housing.

CAUTION: *Use care not to damage the O-ring during installation.*

6. Tighten the stationary gear bolts evenly, and in several stages, to 15 ft.lb.

Rotor Housings

1. Examine the inner margin of both housings for signs of gas or water leakage.
2. Wipe the inner surface of each housing with a clean cloth to remove the carbon deposits.

NOTE: *If the carbon deposits are stubborn, soak the cloth in a solution made for carbon removal. Do not scrape or sand the chrome plated surfaces of the rotor chamber.*

3. Clean all of the rust deposits out of the cooling passages of each rotor housing.
4. Remove the old sealer with a cloth soaked in ketone.
5. Examine the chromium plate inner surfaces for scoring, flaking, or other signs of damage. If any are present, the housing must be replaced.
6. Check the rotor housing for distortion by placing a straightedge on the areas illustrated.

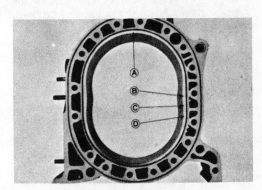

Check the rotor housing width at points A, B, C and D

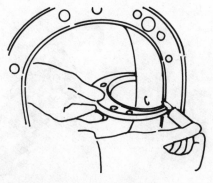

Checking the rotor housing width

If the distortion exceeds 0.0016 in. (0.04mm) have the housing refaced or replace it.

7. Measure the clearance between the straightedge and the housing with a feeler gauge. If the gap exceeds 0.002 in., replace the rotor housing.

8. Check the widths of both rotor housings, at a minimum of eight points near the trochoid surfaces of each housing, with a vernier caliper.

If the difference between the maximum and minimum valves obtained is greater than 0.0024 in., replace the housing. A housing in this condition will be prone to gas and coolant leakage.

NOTE: *Standard rotor housing width is 2.7559 in.*

Rotors

1. Check the rotor for signs of blow-by around the side and corner seal areas.

2. The color of the carbon deposits on the rotor should be brown, just as in a piston engine.

NOTE: *Usually the carbon on the leading side of the rotor is brown, while the carbon on the trailing side tends toward black, as viewed from the direction of rotation.*

3. Remove the carbon on the rotor with a scraper or extra fine emery paper. Use the scraper carefully when doing the seal grooves, so that no damage is done to them.

4. Wash the rotor in solvent and blow it dry with compressed air after removing the carbon.

5. Examine the internal gear for cracks or damaged teeth.

NOTE: *If the internal gear is damaged, the rotor and gear must be replaced as a single assembly.*

6. With the oil seal removed, check the land protrusions by placing a straightedge over the lands. Measure the gap between the rotor surface and the straightedge with a feeler gauge. The standard specification is 0.004–0.008 in.;

Checking the rotor width

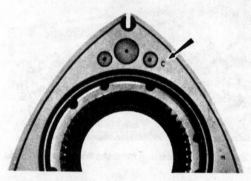
Rotor weight mark

if it is less than this, the rotor must be replaced.

7. Check the gaps between the housing and the rotor on both sides:

a. Measure the rotor width with a vernier caliper. The standard rotor width is 2.7500 in.

b. Compare the rotor width with the width of the rotor housing measured above. The standard rotor housing width is 2.7559 in.

c. Replace the rotor if the difference between the two measurements is not within 0.0051–0.0067 in.

8. Check the rotor bearing for flaking, wearing, or scoring and proceed as indicated in the next section, if any of these are present.

The rotors are classified into five lettered grades, according to their weight. A letter between A and E is stamped on the internal gear side of the rotor. If it becomes necessary to replace a rotor, use one marked with a C because this is the standard replacement rotor.

Rotor Bearing Replacement

Special service tools are required to replace a rotor bearing. Replacement is also a tricky procedure which, if done improperly, could result in serious damage to the rotor and could even make replacement of the entire rotor necessary. Therefore, this service procedure is best

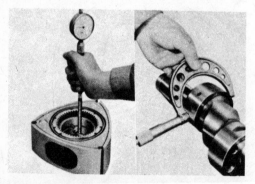
Checking the rotor bearing oil clearance

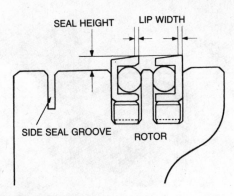

Checking the oil seal

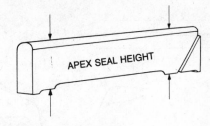

Checking the apex seal height

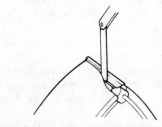

Apex seal spring free height

left to an authorized service facility or a qualified machine shop.

Oil Seal Inspection

NOTE: *Inspect the oil seal while it is mounted in the rotor.*

1. Examine the oil seal for signs of wear or damage.

2. Measure the width of the oil seal lip. If it is greater than 0.031 in., replace the oil seal.

3. Measure the protrusion of the oil seal, it should be greater than 0.020 in. Replace the seal, as detailed below, if it is not.

Oil Seal Replacement

NOTE: *Replace the rubber O-ring in the oil seal as a normal part of engine overhaul.*

1. Pry the seal out gently by inserting a screwdriver in the slots on the rotor. Do not remove the seal by prying it at only one point as seal deformation will result.

CAUTION: *Be careful not to deform the lip of the oil seal if it is to be reinstalled.*

2. Fit both of the oil seal springs into their respective grooves, so that their ends are facing upward and their gaps are opposite each other on the rotor.

3. Insert a new rubber O-ring into each of the oil seals.

NOTE: *Before installing the O-rings into the oil seals, fit each of the seals into its proper groove on the rotor. Check to see that all of the seals move smoothly and freely.*

4. Coat the oil seal groove and the oil seal with engine oil.

5. Gently press the oil seal into the groove with your fingers. Be careful not to distort the seal.

NOTE: *Be sure that the white mark is on the bottom side of each seal when it is installed.*

6. Repeat the installation procedure for the oil seals on both sides of each rotor.

Apex Seals

CAUTION: *Although the apex seals are extremely durable when in service, they are*

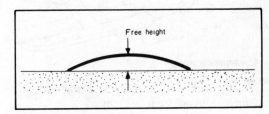

Checking the gap between the apex seal and the groove

Measure the apex seal length

Checking the apex seal

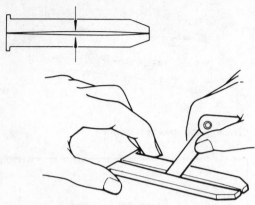

Apex seal warpage

Checking the side seal gap

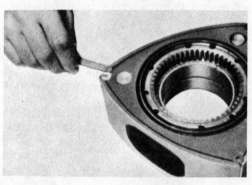

Checking the side seal-to-corner seal gap

easily broken when they are being handles. Be careful not to drop them.

1. Remove the carbon deposits from the apex seals and their springs. Do not use emery cloth on the seals as it will damage their finish.

2. Wash the seals and the springs in cleaning solution.

3. Check the apex seals for cracks and other signs of wear or damage.

4. Test the seal springs for weakness.

5. Use a micrometer to check the seal height. Replace any seal if its height is less than 0.275 in.

6. With a feeler gauge, check the side clearance between the apex seal and the groove in the rotor. Insert the gauge until its tip contacts the bottom of the groove. If the gap is greater than 0.006 in., replace the seal.

7. Check the gap between the apex seals and the side housing, in the following manner:

    a. Use a vernier caliper to measure the length of each apex seal.

    b. Compare this measurement to the minimum figure obtained when rotor housing width was being measured.

    c. If the difference is more than 0.0118 in., replace the seal. The standard gap is 0.0051–0.0067 in.

    d. If, on the other hand, the seal is too long, sand the ends of the seal with emery cloth until the proper length is reached.

CAUTION: *Do not use the emery cloth on the faces of the seal.*

Side Seals

1. Remove the carbon deposits from the side seals and their springs with a carbon scraper.

2. Check the protrusion of the side seals. It should be 0.02 in. or more.

3. Check the side seals for cracks or wear. Replace any of the seals found to be defective.

4. Check the clearance between the side seals and their grooves with a feeler gauge. Replace any side seals if they have a clearance of more than 0.0039 in. The standard clearance is 0.002–0.003 in.

5. Check the clearance between the side seals and the corner seals with both of them installed in the rotor.

    a. Insert the gauge against the direction of the rotor's rotation.

    b. Replace the side seal if the clearance is greater than 0.016 in.

6. If the side seal is replaced, adjust the clearance between it and the corner seal as follows:

    a. File the side seal on its reverse side, in the same rotational direction of the rotor, along the outline made by the corner seal.

    b. The clearance obtained should be 0.002–0.006 in. If it exceeds this, the performance of the seals will deteriorate.

CAUTION: *There are four different types of side seals, depending upon their location. Do not mix the seals up and be sure to use the proper type of seal for replacement.*

Corner Seals

1. Clean the carbon deposits from the corner seals.

2. Examine each of the seals for wear or damage.

3. Check the corner seal protrusion from the rotor surface. It should be free to move under

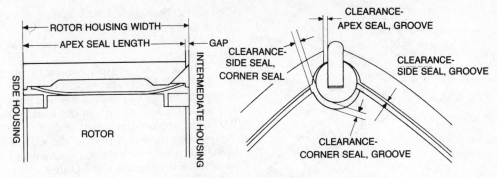

Side clearance measurements

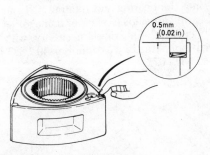

Checking the corner seal groove

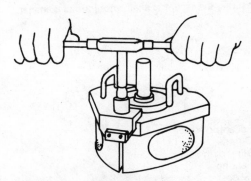

Reaming the corner seal groove

the finger pressure and protrude 0.02 in. or more.

4. Measure the clearance between the corner seal and its groove. The clearance should be 0.0018–0019 in. The wear limit of the gap is 0.0031 in.

5. If the wear is between the corner seal and the groove is uneven, check the clearance with the special bar limit gauge (Mazda part number 49 0839 165). The gauge has a go end and a no go end. Use the gauge in the following manner:

    a. If neither end of the gauge goes into the groove, the clearance is within specifications.

    b. If the go end of the gauge fits into the groove, but the no go end does not, replace the corner seal with one that is 0.0012 in. oversize.

    c. If both ends of the gauge fit into the groove, then the groove must be reamed out as detailed below. Replace the corner seal with one which is 0.0072 in. oversize, after completing reaming.

NOTE: *Take the measurement of the groove in the direction of maximum wear, i.e., that of rotation.*

Corner Seal Groove Reaming

NOTE: *This procedure requires the use of special tools; if attempted without them, damage to the rotor could result.*

1. Carefully remove all of the deposits which remain in the groove.

2. Fit the jig (Mazda part number 49 2113 030) over the rotor. Tighten its adjusting bar, being careful not to damage the rotor bearing or the apex seal grooves.

3. Use the corner seal groove reamer (Mazda part number 49 0839 170) to ream the groove.

4. Rotate the reamer at least 20 times while applying engine oil as a coolant.

NOTE: *If engine oil is not used, it will be impossible to obtain the proper groove surfacing.*

5. Remove the reamer and the jig.

6. Repeat Steps 1–5 for each of the corner seal grooves.

7. Clean the rotor completely and check it for any signs of damage.

8. Fit a 0.0079 in. oversize corner seal into the groove and check its clearance. Clearance should be 0.008–0.0019 in.

Seal Springs

Check the seal springs for damage or weakness. Be exceptionally careful when checking the spring areas which contact either the rotor or the seal.

Eccentric Shaft

1. Wash the eccentric shaft in solvent and blow its oil passages dry with compressed air.

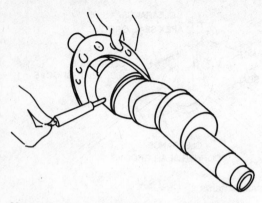

Measuring the eccentric shaft rotor journal diameter

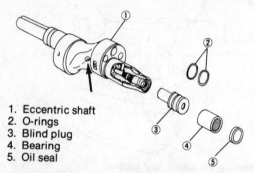

1. Eccentric shaft
2. O-rings
3. Blind plug
4. Bearing
5. Oil seal

Eccentric shaft—arrow points to oil jet plug: remove to check spring and steel ball

Checking the eccentric shaft runout

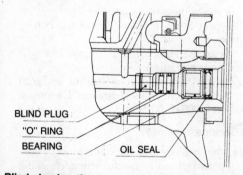

BLIND PLUG
"O" RING
BEARING
OIL SEAL

Blind plug location

2. Check the shaft for wear, cracks, or other signs of damage. Make sure that none of the oil passages are clogged.

3. Measure the shaft journals with a vernier caliper. The standard specifications are:

- Main journals—1.6929 in.
- Rotor journals—2.9134 in.

Replace the shaft if any of its journals show excessive wear.

4. Check eccentric shaft run-out by placing the shaft on V-blocks and using a dial indicator as shown. Rotate the shaft slowly and note the dial indicator reading. If run-out is more than 0.0024 in., replace the eccentric shaft.

5. Check the blind plug at the end of the shaft. If it is loose or leaking, remove it with an allen wrench and replace the O-ring.

6. Check the operation of the needle roller bearing for smoothness by inserting a mainshaft into the bearing and rotating it. Examine the bearing for signs of wear or damage.

7. Replace the bearing if necessary, with the special tool, Mazda part number 49 0823 073 and 49 0823 072.

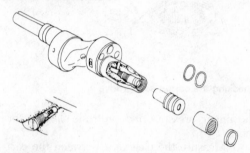

Roller bearing and oil jet

ENGINE ASSEMBLY

1. Place the rotor in a rubber pad or cloth.
2. Install the oil seal rings in their respective grooves in the rotors with the edge of the spring in the stopper hole. The oil springs are painted cream or blue in color. The cream colored springs must be installed on the front faces of both rotors. The blue colored springs must be installed on the rear faces of both rotors. When installing each oil seal spring, the painted side (square side) of the spring must face upward (toward the oil seal).
3. Install a new O-ring in each groove. Place each oil seal in the groove so that the square

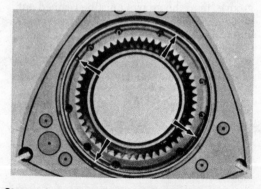

Stopper holes (arrows) of the oil seal spring

Torque Specifications
Rotary Engine
(All specifications in ft. lb.)

| Tension Bolts | Eccentric Shaft Pulley | Flywheel | Manifolds | | Oil Pump Sprocket |
			Intake	Exhaust	
23–27	72–87	289–362	12–17	32–43	22–25

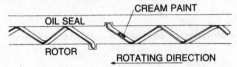

ON THE FRONT FACE OF ROTOR

CREAM PAINT
OIL SEAL
ROTOR
ROTATING DIRECTION

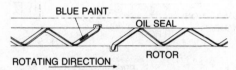

ON THE REAR FACE OF ROTOR

BLUE PAINT
OIL SEAL
ROTOR
ROTATING DIRECTION

Installation of the oil seal spring

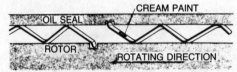

ON THE FRONT FACE OF ROTOR

CREAM PAINT
OIL SEAL
ROTOR
ROTATING DIRECTION

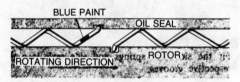

ON THE REAR FACE OF ROTOR

BLUE PAINT
OIL SEAL
ROTOR
ROTATING DIRECTION

Installing the oil seal

edge of the spring fits in the stopper hole of the oil seal. Push the head of the oil seal slowly with the fingers, being careful that the seal is not deformed. Be sure that the oil seal moves smoothly in the grooves before installing the O-ring.

4. Lubricate each oil seal and groove with engine oil and check the movement of the seal. It should move freely when the head of the seal is pressed.

5. Check the oil seal protrusion and install the seals on the other side of each rotor.

6. Install the apex seals without springs and side pieces into their respective grooves so that each side piece positions on the side of each rotor.

7. Install the corner seal springs and corner seals into their respective grooves.

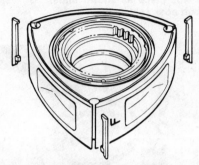

Install apex seals without springs or side pieces—"F" indicates front rotor

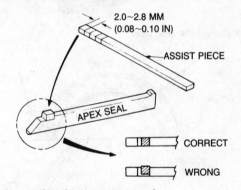

2.0~2.8 MM (0.08~0.10 IN)
ASSIST PIECE
APEX SEAL
CORRECT
WRONG

Fitting assist piece on apex seal

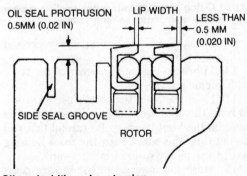

OIL SEAL PROTRUSION 0.5MM (0.02 IN)
LIP WIDTH
LESS THAN 0.5 MM (0.020 IN)
SIDE SEAL GROOVE
ROTOR

Oil seal width and protrusion

8. Install the side seal springs and side seals into their respective grooves.

9. Apply engine oil to each spring and check each spring for smooth movement.

10. Check each seal protrusion.

11. Invert the rotor being careful that the seals do not fall out, and install the oil seals on the other side in the same manner.

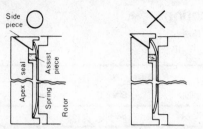

Install side piece as shown under "O"—spring must butt apex seal lip

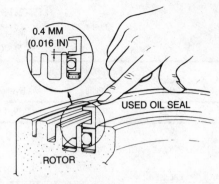

Install inner oil seal with a used inner oil seal

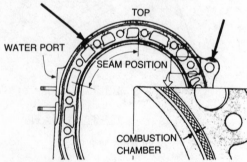

Installing the side seal

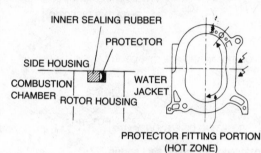

Install protector behind inner sealing rubber

Install O-ring (right arrow), outer sealing rubber (left arrow) and inner sealing rubber

Positioning the front rotor

12. Mount the front housing on a workstand so that the top of the housing is up.

13. Lubricate the internal gear of the rotor with engine oil.

14. Hold the apex seals with used O-rings to keep the apex seals installed and place the rotor on the front housing. Be careful that you do not drop the seals. Turn the front housing so that the sliding surfaces face upward.

15. Mesh the internal and stationary gears so that one of the rotor apexes is at any one of the four places shown and remove the old O-ring which is holding the apex seals in position.

16. Lubricate the front rotor journal of the eccentric shaft with engine oil and lubricate the eccentric shaft main journal.

17. Insert the eccentric shaft. Be careful that you do not damage the rotor bearing and main bearing.

18. Apply sealing agent to the front side of the front rotor housing.

19. Apply a light coat of petroleum jelly onto new O-rings and rubber seals (to prevent them from coming off) and install the O-rings and rubber seals on the front side of the rotor housing.

NOTE: *The inner rubber seal is of the square type. The wider white line of the rubber seal should face the combustion chamber and the seam of the rubber seal should be positioned as shown. Do not stretch the rubber seal.*

20. If the engine is being overhauled, install the seal protector to only the inner rubber seal to improve durability.

21. Invert the front rotor housing, being careful not to let the rubber seals and O-rings

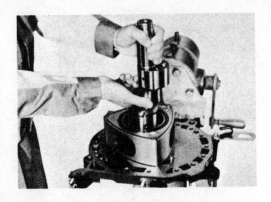

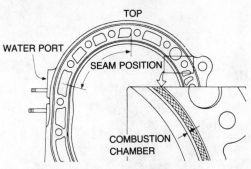

Proper positioning of the inner rubber seal

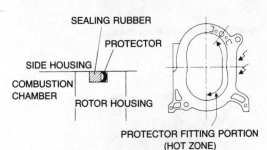

Installation of the rubber seal protector

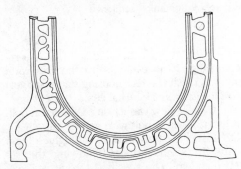

Apply sealer to the shaded areas

Installing the side piece and spring

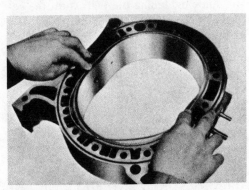

Installing the rubber seal

fall from their grooves, and mount it on the front housing.

22. Lubricate the dowels with engine oil and insert them through the front rotor housing holes and into the front housing.

23. Apply sealer to the front side of the rotor housing.

24. Install new O-rings and rubber seals on the front rotor housing in the same manner as for the other side.

25. Insert each apex spring seal, making sure that the seal is installed in the proper direction.

26. Install each side piece in its original position and be sure that the springs seat on the side piece.

27. Lubricate the side pieces with engine oil. Make sure that the front rotor housing is free of foreign matter and lubricate the sliding surface of the front housing with engine oil.

28. Turn the front housing assembly with the rotor, so that the top of the housing is up. Pull the eccentric shaft about 1 in.

29. Position the eccentric portion of the eccentric shaft diagonally, to the upper right.

30. Install the intermediate housing over the eccentric shaft onto the front rotor housing. Turn the engine so that the rear of the engine is up.

31. Install the rear rotor and rear rotor housing following the same steps as for the front rotor and the front housing.

32. Turn the engine so that the rear of the engine is up.

33. Lubricate the stationary gear and main bearing.

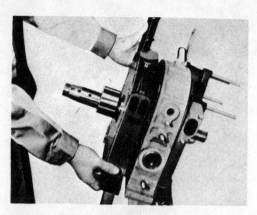

Installing the intermediate housing

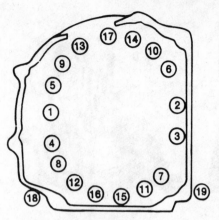

Tension bolt tightening sequence

Installing the rear rotor

Installing the rear rotor housing

34. Install the rear housing onto the rear rotor housing. If necessary, turn the rear rotor slightly to mesh the rear housing stationary gear with the rear rotor internal gear.

35. Install a new washer on each tension bolt, and lubricate each bolt with engine oil.

36. Install the tension bolts and tighten them evenly, in several stages following the sequence shown. The specified torque is 23–27 ft.lb.

37. After tightening the bolts, turn the eccentric shaft to be sure that the shaft and rotors turn smoothly and easily.

38. Lubricate the oil seal in the rear housing.

39. On trucks with manual transmission, install the flywheel on the rear of the eccentric shaft so that the keyway of the flywheel fits the key on the shaft.

40. Apply sealer to both sides of the flywheel lockwasher and install the lockwasher.

41. Install the flywheel locknut. Hold the flywheel SECURELY and tighten the nut to THREE HUNDRED AND FIFTY ft.lb. (350 ft.lb.) of torque.

NOTE: *350 ft.lb. is a great deal of torque.*

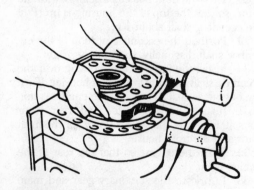

Installing the rear engine housing

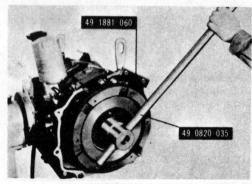

Tightening the flywheel nut

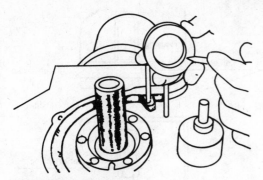

Installing the thrust plate

In actual practice, it is practically impossible to accurately measure that much torque on the nut. At least a 3 ft. bar will be required to generate sufficient torque. Tighten it as tightly as possible, with no longer than 3 ft. of leverage. Be sure the engine is held SE-CURELY.

42. On trucks with automatic transmission, install the key, counterweight, lockwasher and nut. Tighten the nut to 350 ft.lb. SEE STEP 41 AND THE NOTE FOLLOWING STEP 41.

43. Turn the engine so that the front faces up.

44. Install the thrust plate with the tapered face down, and install the needle bearing on the eccentric shaft. Lubricate with engine oil.

45. Install the bearing housing on the front housing. Tighten the bolts and bend up the lockwasher tabs. The spacer should be installed so that the center of the needle bearing comes to the center of the eccentric shaft and the spacer should be seated on the thrust plate.

46. Install the needle bearing on the shaft and lubricate it with engine oil.

47. Install the balancer and thrust washer on the eccentric shaft.

48. Install the oil pump drive chain over both of the sprockets. Install the sprocket and chain assembly over the eccentric shaft and oil pump shafts simultaneously. Install the key on the eccentric shaft.

Checking the eccentric shaft endplay

NOTE: *Be sure that both of the sprockets are engaged with the chain before installing them over the shafts.*

49. Install the distributor drive gear onto the eccentric shaft with the F mark on the gear facing the front of the engine. Slide the spacer and oil slinger onto the eccentric shaft.

50. Align the keyway and install the eccentric shaft pulley. Tighten the pulley bolt to 60 ft.lb.

51. Turn the engine so that the top of the engine faces up.

52. Check eccentric shaft end-play in the following manner:

   a. Attach a dial indicator to the flywheel. Move the flywheel forward and backward.

   b. Note the reading on the dial indicator; it should be 0.0016–0.0028 in.

   c. If the endplay is not within specifications, adjust it by replacing the front spacer. Spacers come in four sizes, ranging from

Eccentric Shaft Spacer Thickness Chart

I.D. Mark	mm	in.
V	8.02 [±] 0.01	0.3158 [±] 0.0004
X	8.08 [±] 0.01	0.3181 [±] 0.0004
Y	8.04 [±] 0.01	0.3165 [±] 0.0004
Z	8.00 [±] 0.01	0.3150 [±] 0.0004

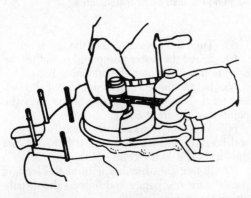

Install the oil pump chain and sprockets

Installing a new O-ring in the front cover oil passage

0.3150–0.3181 in. If necessary, a spacer can be ground on a surface plate with emery paper.

d. Check the endplay again and, if it is now within specifications, proceed with the next step.

53. Remove the pulley from the front of the eccentric shaft. Tighten the oil pump drive sprocket nut and bend the locktabs on the lockwasher.

54. Fit a new O-ring over the front cover oil passages.

55. Install the chain tensioner and tighten its securing bolts.

56. Position the front cover gasket and the front cover on the front housing, then secure the front cover with its attachment bolts.

57. Install the eccentric shaft pulley again. Tighten its bolt to 60 ft.lb.

58. Turn the engine so that the bottom faces up.

59. Cut off the excess gasket on the front cover along the mounting surface of the oil pan.

60. Install the oil strainer gasket and strainer on the front housing and tighten the attaching bolts.

61. Apply sealer to the joint surfaces of each housing.

62. Install the gasket and oil pan. Tighten the bolts evenly in two stages to 3.5 ft.lb.

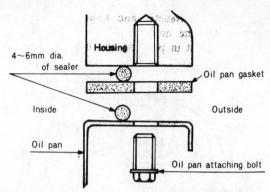

Apply sealant to both the top and bottom of the oil pan gasket

Installing the water pump

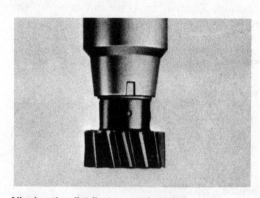

Aligning the distributor matchmarks

Installing the oil strainer

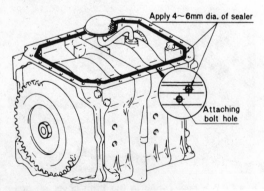

Apply sealant before installing oil pan

63. Turn the engine so that the top is up.

64. Install the water pump and gasket on the front housing. Tighten the attaching bolts.

65. Rotate the eccentric shaft until the yellow mark (leading side mark) aligns with the pointer on the front cover.

66. Align the marks on the distributor gear and housing and install the distributor so that the lockbolt is in the center of the slot.

67. Rotate the distributor until the leading points start to separate and tighten the distributor locknut.

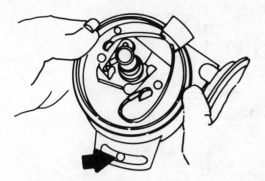

Install the distributor so that the lockbolt (arrow) is centered in the slot

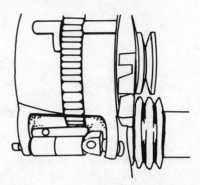

Adjusting the alternator bracket clearance (arrow)

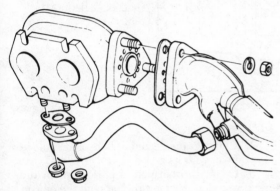

Thermal reactor

68. Install the gaskets and thermal reactor and tighten the attaching nuts.

69. Install the hot air duct.

70. Install the carburetor and intake manifold assembly with a new gasket. Tighten the attaching nuts.

71. Connect the oil tubes vacuum tube and metering oil pump connecting rod to the carburetor.

72. Install the decel valve and connect the vacuum lines, air hoses and wires.

73. Install the alternator bracket, alternator and bolt and check the clearance. If the clearance is more than 0.006 in., adjust the clear-

ance using a shim. Shims are available in three sizes: 0.0059 in., 0.0118 in., and 0.0197 in.

74. Install the alternator drive belt. Attach the alternator to the adjusting brace and adjust the belt tension to specification.

75. Install the air pump with the adjusting brace and install the air pump drive belt. Adjust the air pump drive belt to specifications.

76. Install the engine hanger bracket to the front cover.

77. Remove the engine from the stand.

78. Install the engine in the truck.

79. Fill the engine with fresh engine oil and install a new filter. Fill the engine with coolant. Start the engine, check the oil pressure, and warm it to normal operating temperature. Adjust the idle speed, timing and dwell. Recheck all capacities and refill if necessary. Check for leaks.

Intake Manifold
REMOVAL AND INSTALLATION

To remove the intake manifold and carburetor assembly, with the engine remaining in the automobile, proceed in the following manner:

1. Perform Steps 2, 3, 4, 5, 7, and 13 of Engine Removal and Installation, above. Do not remove the engine. Do not drain the engine oil; merely remove the metering oil pump hose from the carburetor.

2. Perform Steps 2, 3, and 4 of Engine Disassembly, above.

Install the intake manifold and carburetor assembly in the reverse order of removal. Tighten the manifold securing nuts working from the inside out, and in two or three stages, to the specifications in the Torque Chart. Refill the cooling system.

Thermal Reactor
REMOVAL AND INSTALLATION

CAUTION: *The thermal reactor operates at extremely high temperatures. Allow the en-*

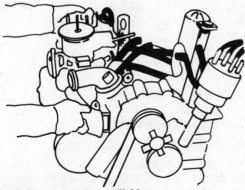

Installing the intake manifold

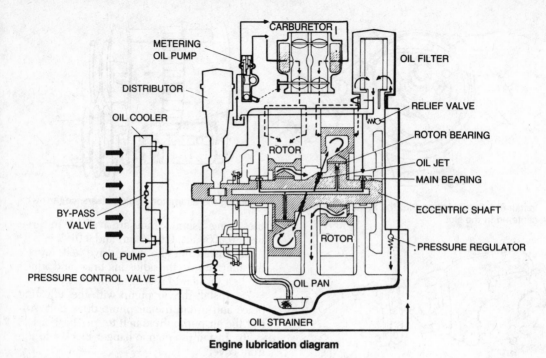

Engine lubrication diagram

gine to cool completely before attempting its removal.

To remove the thermal reactor, which replaces the exhaust manifold, proceed in the following manner:

1. Remove the air cleaner assembly from the carburetor.

2. Unbolt and remove the air injection pump, as outlined in Emission Controls Chapter 4.

3. Remove the intake manifold assembly, complete with carburetor.

4. Remove the heat stove from the thermal reactor.

5. Unfasten the thermal reactor securing nuts.

NOTE: *The bottom nut is difficult to reach. Mazda makes a special wrench, part number 49 2133 001, to remove it. If the wrench is unavailable, a flexible drive metric socket wrench can be substituted.*

6. Lift the thermal reactor away from the engine.

7. Installation is the reverse of removal.

Oil Pan
REMOVAL AND INSTALLATION

1. Raise the front of the car and support it with jackstands.

2. Remove the drain plug and drain the engine oil.

3. Remove the nuts and bolts which secure the gravel shield and withdraw it from underneath the car.

4. Unfasten the retaining bolts and remove the oil pan with its gasket.

5. Oil pan installation is performed in the reverse order of removal. Coat both the oil pan flange and its mounting flange with sealer, prior to assembly.

Oil Pump
REMOVAL AND INSTALLATION

A conventional oil pump, which is chain driven, circulates oil through the rotary engine. A full-flow filter is mounted on the top of the rear housing and an oil cooler is used to reduce the temperature of the engine oil.

An unusual feature of the rotary engine lubrication system is a metering oil pump which injects oil into the float chamber of the carburetor. Once there, it is mixed with the fuel which is to be burned, thus providing extra lubrication for the seals. The metering oil pump is designed to work only when the engine is operating under a load.

Oil pump removal and installation is contained in the Engine Overhaul section above. Perform only those steps needed in order to remove the oil pump.

Metering Oil Pump
OPERATION

A metering oil pump, mounted on the top of the engine, is used to provide additional lubrication to the engine when it is operating under

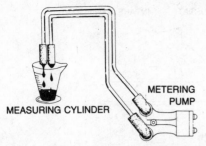

Checking the discharge rate of the oil metering pump

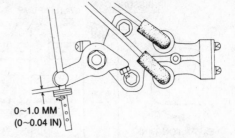

Metering oil pump connecting rod setting

a load. The pump provides oil to the carburetor, where it is mixed in the float chamber with the fuel which is to be burned.

The metering pump is a plunger type and is controlled by the throttle opening. A cam arrangement, connected to the carburetor throttle lever, operates a plunger. The plunger in turn, acts on a differential plunger, the stroke of which determines the amount of oil flow.

When the throttle opening is small, the amount of the plunger stroke is small; as the throttle opening increases, so does the amount of the plunger stroke.

TESTING

1. Disconnect the oil lines which run from the metering oil pump to the carburetor, at the carburetor end.

2. Use a container which has a scale calibrated in cubic centimeters (cc) to catch the pump discharge from the oil lines.

NOTE: *Such a container is available from a scientific equipment supply house.*

3. Run the engine at 2,000 rpm for six minutes.

4. At the end of this time, 2.2cc of oil should be collected in the container. If not, adjust the pump as explained below.

ADJUSTMENTS

Rotate the adjusting screw on the metering oil pump to obtain the proper oil flow. Clockwise

rotation of the screw increases the flow; counterclockwise rotation decreases the flow.

If necessary, the oil discharge rate may further be adjusted by changing the position of the cam in the pump connecting rod. The shorter the rod throw the more oil will be pumped. Adjust the throw by means of three holes provided.

NOTE: *After adjusting the metering oil pump, check the discharge rate again.*

Oil Cooler

REMOVAL AND INSTALLATION

1. Raise the car and support it with jackstands.

2. Drain the engine oil.

3. Unfasten the screws which retain the gravel shield and remove the shield.

4. Remove the oil lines from the oil cooler.

5. Unfasten the nuts which secure the oil cooler to the radiator.

6. Remove the oil cooler.

7. Examine the oil cooler for signs of leakage. Solder any leaks found. Blow the fins of the cooler clean with compressed air.

8. Installation is the reverse of removal.

Radiator

REMOVAL AND INSTALLATION

CAUTION: *Perform this operation when the engine has cooled completely.*

1. Drain the engine coolant into a large, clean container so that it may be reused.

CAUTION: *When draining the coolant, keep in mind that cats and dogs are attracted by the etheylne glycol antifreeze, and are quite likely to drink any that is left in an uncovered container or in puddles on the ground. This will prove fatal in sufficient quantity. Always drain the coolant into a sealable container. Coolant should be reused unless it is contaminated or several years old.*

2. Remove the nuts and bolts which attach the shroud to the radiator.

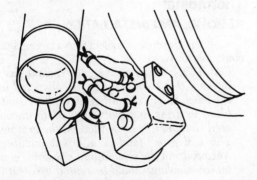

Metering oil pump adjusting screw

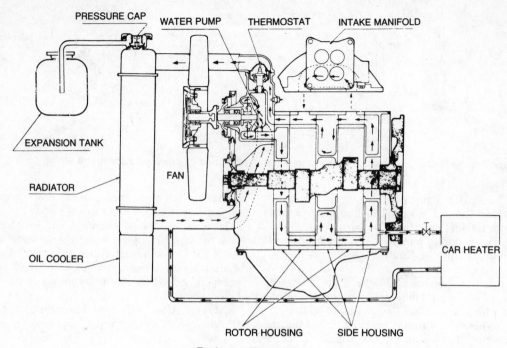

PRESSURE CAP   WATER PUMP   THERMOSTAT   INTAKE MANIFOLD

EXPANSION TANK

RADIATOR

FAN

OIL COOLER

CAR HEATER

ROTOR HOUSING   SIDE HOUSING

Engine cooling system

3. Remove the upper, lower and expansion tank hoses from the radiator.

4. Unfasten the bolts which attach the radiator to its mounting bracket. Remove the oil cooler nuts and bolts.

5. Withdraw the radiator from the car.

6. Install the radiator in the reverse order of removal.

Water Pump

REMOVAL AND INSTALLATION

1. Drain the cooling system.

CAUTION: *When draining the coolant, keep in mind that cats and dogs are attracted by the ethelyne glycol antifreeze, and are quite likely to drink any that is left in an uncovered container or in puddles on the ground. This will prove fatal in sufficient quantity. Always drain the coolant into a sealable container. Coolant should be reused unless it is contaminated or several years old.*

2. Remove the air cleaner.

3. Remove the bolts attaching the rear of the fan drive and remove the fan drive.

4. If necessary to disassemble the water pump, loosen the bolts attaching the water pump pulley to the water pump boss.

5. Remove the air pump and drive belt.

6. Remove the alternator and disconnect the drive belt.

7. If necessary, remove the water pump pulley and bolts.

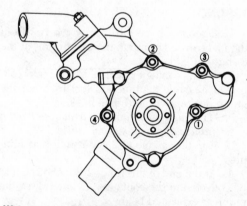

Water pump attaching bolts

8. Unbolt and remove the water pump.

9. Installation is the reverse of removal.

Thermostat

REMOVAL AND INSTALLATION

1. Drain the engine coolant into a large, clean container for reuse.

CAUTION: *When draining the coolant, keep in mind that cats and dogs are attracted by the ethelyne glycol antifreeze, and are quite likely to drink any that is left in an uncovered container or in puddles on the ground. This will prove fatal in sufficient quantity. Always drain the coolant into a sealable container. Coolant should be reused unless it is contaminated or several years old.*

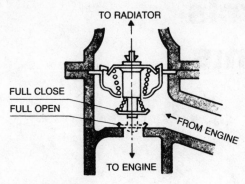

TO RADIATOR

FULL CLOSE

FULL OPEN

FROM ENGINE

TO ENGINE

Engine thermostat

2. Remove the nuts which secure the thermostat housing to the water pump.

3. Lift the thermostat out.

4. Thermostat installation is performed in the reverse order of removal.

CAUTION: *The thermostat is equipped with a plunger which covers and uncovers a bypass hole at its bottom. Because of its unusual construction, only the specified Mazda thermostat or an aftermarket thermostat equipped with this feature should be used for replacement. Use of a standard thermostat will cause the engine to overheat.*

Emission Controls and Fuel Systems

EMISSION CONTROLS-PISTON ENGINES

Gasoline Engines

The B1600 uses three emission control systems: a throttle positioner system, a positive crankcase ventilation system and evaporative emission control system, and a Thermactor air injection system.

The B1800 and B2000 employ six basic systems. A thermactor air injection system is used to control harmful composites in the exhaust gases by introducing fresh air to aid in more complete combustion. A positive crankcase ventilation (PCV) system is used on all trucks to route blow-by gases from the crankcase into the combustion chamber. All Mazdas use an evaporative emission control system to absorb fuel vapors emitted from the fuel tank by evaporation. All Mazdas also use a deceleration control system to augment the Thermactor air pump. Exhaust gas recirculation (EGR) is used on 1976 California Mazdas with manual transmission, and all 1977 and later models. Its purpose is to recycle a small portion of the exhaust gas by returning it to the combustion chamber, thus reducing combustion temperatures and the formation of No. The catalytic converter, used on some 1976–78 California trucks and most 1979 and later models, chemically alters the composition of exhaust gases which pass through it. In addition, a spark delay system is used on 1977 and later 1.8 and 2.0 engines, which retards the ignition spark curve during acceleration to promote more thorough combustion.

Diesel Engines

The diesel has only 2 basic emission control systems: a crankcase ventilation system, and a system which maintains a slight vacuum in the intake manifold, known as the Intake Shutter Valve System. The only maintenance required of the crankcase ventilation system is to occasionally check the cleanliness of the inside of the hose.

Intake Shutter Valve System

The intake shutter valve system may require checking of the vacuum it generates and adjustment of the diaphragm that operates the air shutter. To check, remove the plug in the intake manifold. Install an adapter with metric threads in place of the plug, and connect a vacuum gauge. Disconnect the electrical connector at the 3-way valve. Then, start the engine and run it at idle. Now, read the vacuum gauge. It should read approx. 16.92 in. Hg.

If the reading is not correct, adjust the adjusting screw on the shutter valve (located just to the right of the vacuum gauge on the air intake). Then, stop the engine, reconnect the electrical connector, and replace the plug in the intake manifold.

Throttle Positioner

The throttle positioner system consists of a servo diaphragm connected to the throttle lever and a vacuum control valve which controls intake manifold vacuum through the servo diaphragm.

TESTING THE SYSTEM

Servo Diaphragm

1. Start the engine and set the idle speed to 800 rpm. Stop the engine.
2. Disconnect the vacuum sensing tube between the servo diaphragm and the vacuum control valve at the servo diaphragm.
3. Remove the intake manifold suction hole plug.
4. Connect the intake manifold and the servo diaphragm with a tube so that the intake man-

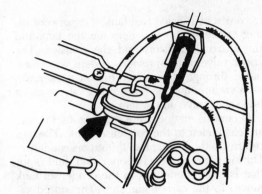
Servo diapnragm

ifold vacuum goes directly to the servo diaphragm.

5. Connect a tachometer and remove the vacuum sensing tube between the carburetor and distributor.

6. Start the engine and read the speed. If the engine is running between 1,300–1,500 rpm, the servo diaphragm is operating normally. If the engine speed is 800–1,500 rpm, adjust the speed with the throttle opening screw. If the engine speed remains normal, about 800 rpm, the servo diaphragm is defective and should be replaced.

SERVICE

Servo Diaphragm Replacement

1. Remove the air cleaner.
2. Disconnect the vacuum sensing tube from the servo diaphragm.
3. Remove the cotter pin and link.
4. Loosen the locknut and remove the servo diaphragm.
5. Installation is the reverse of removal. Adjust the servo diaphragm.

Vacuum Control Valve Replacement

1. Remove the air cleaner.
2. Disconnect the vacuum sensing tubes from the vacuum control valve.

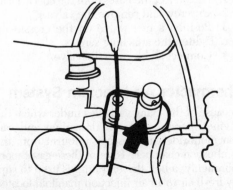
Vacuum control valve

3. Unbolt and remove the vacuum control valve.
4. Installation is the reverse of removal.

ADJUSTMENTS

Throttle Opener

1. Install a tachometer on the engine.
2. Start the engine and set the idle speed.
3. Stop the engine.
4. Disconnect the vacuum sensing tube between the servo diaphragm and the vacuum control valve from the servo diaphragm.
5. Remove the plug from the intake manifold suction hole.
6. Attach a test tube between the intake manifold between the intake manifold and the servo diaphragm to route intake manifold vacuum directly to the servo diaphragm.
7. Start the engine and note the speed.
8. Set the engine speed to 1,400 rpm using the throttle opener screw. Turning the adjusting screw clockwise increases engine speed.
9. Stop the engine and disconnect the tachometer. Reconnect all lines.

Adjusting the throttle positioner

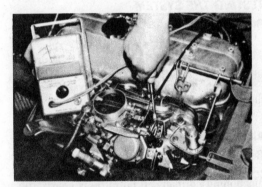
Intake manifold suction hole plug

Positive Crankcase Ventilation (PCV) System

The function of the PCV valve is to divert blow-by gases from the crankcase to the intake man-

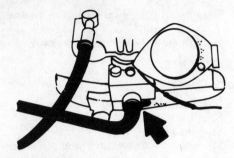

Typical 1972–84 PCV valve

ifold to be burned in the cylinders. The system consists of a PCV valve, an oil separator and the hoses necessary to connect the components.

Ventilating air is routed into the rocker cover from the air cleaner. The air is then moved to the oil separator and from the separator to the PCV valve. The PCV valve is operated by differences in air pressure between the intake manifold and the rocker cover.

TESTING THE SYSTEM

Standard Test

1. Remove the hose from the PCV valve.
2. Start the engine and run it at approximately 700–1,000 rpm.
3. Cover the end of the PCV valve with a finger. A distinct vacuum should be felt. If no vacuum is felt, replace the valve.

Alternate Test

Remove the valve from its fitting. Shake the valve. If a rattle is heard, the valve is probably functioning normally. If no rattle is heard, the valve is probably stuck (open or shut) and should be replaced.

REPLACEMENT

1. Remove the air cleaner.
2. Disconnect the hose from the PCV valve.
3. Remove the valve from the intake manifold fitting.
4. Install the valve in the fitting.
5. Connect the hose to the valve.
6. Install the air cleaner.

Evaporative Emission Control System

The evaporative emission control system is designed to control the emission of gasoline vapors into the atmosphere. The system consists of a fuel tank, a condenser tank and a check valve. In 1977, the system was changed slightly

to consist of a sealed fuel tank, a vapor controlling orifice in the line between the tank and the charcoal canister, and the canister. The check valve of the previous system was eliminated through the substitution of a filler cap with vacuum and pressure relief valves, and a fuel vapor valve on the tank.

When the engine is not running, fuel vapors are channeled to the condenser tank. The fuel returns to the fuel tank as the vapors condense. During periods of engine operation, fuel vapor that has not condensed in the condenser tank moves to the carbon canister. The stored vapors are removed from the charcoal by fresh air moving through the inlet hole in the bottom of the canister.

The check valve (1972–76), located between the condenser tank and the canister, allows fuel vapor and ventilation to flow during normal operation. If the system becomes clogged or frozen, the valve opens (by negative pressure in the fuel tank) to allow fuel to be drawn from the tank. The valve also opens to vent internal tank pressure under hot conditions. The fuel tank cap and fuel vapor valve replace the check valve in 1977 and later, and perform essentially the same functions.

The only service necessary for this system is replacement of the charcoal canister at regular intervals and inspection of the rubber hoses at the same time for cracks or breaks. Any deterioration hoses should be replaced.

CONDENSER TANK REMOVAL AND INSTALLATION

1. Raise and support the rear of the truck.
2. Disconnect the hoses from the condenser tank.
3. Unbolt and remove the condenser tank.
4. Install the tank and tighten the bolts.
5. Connect the hoses to the tank.
6. Lower the truck.

CHECK VALVE REMOVAL AND INSTALLATION

1. Disconnect the hoses from the check valve.
2. Unscrew and remove the valve.
3. Position a new valve on the crossmember. Tighten the attaching screws.
4. Connect all hoses to the valve.

Thermactor Air Injection System

Because of the many variables under which the engine operates, some hydrocarbon and carbon monoxide gases escape unburnt from the combustion chamber. To burn these gases more thoroughly, a belt-driven pump is used to supply fresh air to an air injection manifold located on the exhaust manifold. The injection of fresh

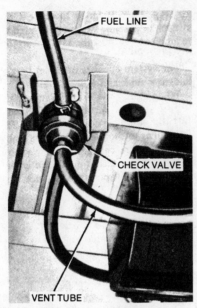

Three-way check valve—1972-76

FUEL LINE

CHECK VALVE

VENT TUBE

air supports combustion of the hot unburned HC and CO gases within the exhaust manifold.

The Thermactor system, used on California trucks only in 1972 and 1973, and all trucks thereafter, consists of an air pump with relief valve, a check valve, four air injection nozzles (one for each cylinder) connected to an air injection manifold, an air by-pass valve, and hoses from 1972-74. The air pump pushes air through the one way check valve into the injection manifold and through the nozzles. The check valve prevents any backfire of gases into the system. An air by-pass valve is used to prevent air injection during cold choke operation. Pulling the choke cable closes both the choke and the air by-pass valve, venting all pumped air into the air cleaner. This prevents overheating of the rich mixture exhaust. The air pump relief valve vents excess pressure to the atmosphere.

1975-76 trucks use a slightly modified version of the system. The principle and main components remain the same, but an air control valve, incorporating two relief valves, replaces the air by-pass valve. The no.1 relief valve is activated by a control unit (an engine rpm switch) located on the kick panel beneath the parking brake lever; the No. 2 relief valve is activated by engine vacuum. Below 4,000 rpm (4,300 with automatic transmission), no.1 directs air to the injection manifold. Above that engine speed, no.1 opens and vents air to the air cleaner. Number 2 opens when intake manifold vacuum exceeds 6.3 in. of mercury, reducing air flow to the injection manifold during low engine loads.

1977-78 1,796cc engines are the same, except that only trucks sold in California have the air control valve, with one relief valve activated by intake manifold vacuum. In addition, trucks sold in California have a vacuum delay valve.

The systems used in 1979 and later are slightly different. 1,970cc engines sold for 49 States use do not have an air pump. Instead, air injection is controlled by exhaust system back pressure. The air injection pipe runs from the air cleaner case to the exhaust manifold. A one-way check valve is installed in the pipe. During periods of negative exhaust pulsation, air is drawn from the air cleaner, through the check valve, and

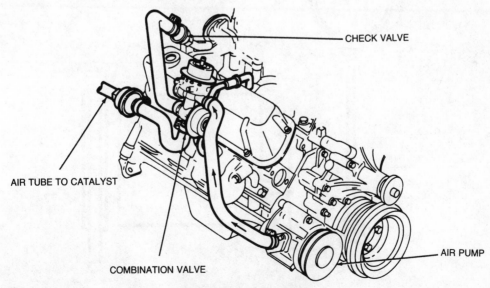

CHECK VALVE

AIR TUBE TO CATALYST

COMBINATION VALVE

AIR PUMP

Typical Thermactor system

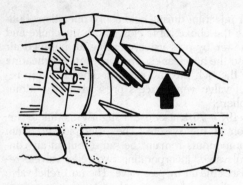

Control unit location

into the exhaust manifold. During periods of positive exhaust back pressure (positive pulsation), the check valve closes and no air is drawn into the exhaust system.

Models sold in California have an air pump, a check valve, and an air control valve. The air control valve has a no.1 relief valve, activated by intake manifold vacuum, and a No. 2 relief valve, which modulates the amount of secondary air. The No. 2 relief valve is not used with automatic transmissions.

TESTING THE SYSTEM

Air Pump Drive Belt

Be sure that the air pump drive belt is adjusted to the proper tension. See Chapter 1.

Air Pump

1. Disconnect the air pump outlet hose from the air by-pass valve.
2. Connect a T-fitting and pressure gauge into the outlet line. The other end of the fitting should have a plug with an $^{11}/_{32}$ in. hole drilled through it.
3. Start the engine and run it briefly at 1,500 rpm. Be sure the choke is fully open (pushed in).
4. If the pressure reading is below 1 psi, replace the pump

Air Pump Relief Valve

1. Operate the engine at idle.
2. Check the relief valve for airflow. No flow should be evident. If airflow out is noted, replace the relief valve and air pump.
3. Increase the engine speed to 3,000 rpm (4,500 rpm, 1978 and later). If air flows out of the relief valve, the valve is in good condition. If air does not flow from the relief valve, or if the valve is excessively noisy, the relief valve and air pump assembly should be replaced.

Air Manifold Check Valve

Remove the check valve from the air injection manifold. Blow through the valve from the intake side of the outlet side. Air should pass through the valve from the intake side only. If air passes through the valve from the outlet side, replace the valve.

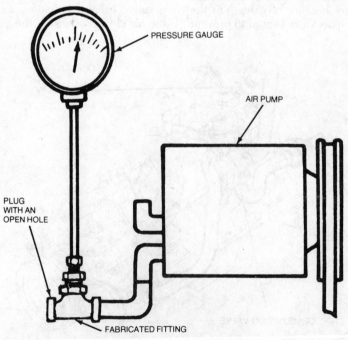

Checking air pump pressure

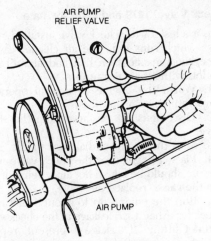

Checking the air pump relief valve

Air By-pass Valve 1972–74

1. Disconnect the air line at the check valve.
2. Push the choke knob all the way in.
3. Run the engine at 1,500 rpm.
4. Hold your hand over the end of the air pump air line. Air should flow from the hose.
5. Pull the choke knob all the way out. No air should flow from the air line.
6. If the valve is not operating properly, replace the valve.

Air Control Valve, 1975–76

1. Disconnect the outlet hose from the bottom of the air control valve at the air cleaner. Start the engine and let it idle. Air should not be discharged from the outlet.
2. Unplug the air control valve solenoid electrical connector. With the engine still idling, check for air discharge from the valve outlet.

3. Reconnect the electrical connectors. Increase the engine speed above 4,000 rpm (4,300 with automatic transmission), and check that air is discharged from the valve outlet. When the engine speed falls, the air discharge should stop.
4. If the valve is not operating properly, check the hoses for leaks, breaks, kinks, or improper connections. Replace the valve as necessary.

Control Unit, 1975–76

1. Attach a test light to the unit connector as shown.
2. Start the engine. The light should be on with the engine idling.
3. Increase the speed above 4,000 rpm (4,300 with automatic transmission). The light should go off.
4. If the light does not go off when specified, or does not remain on with the engine idling, replace the unit.

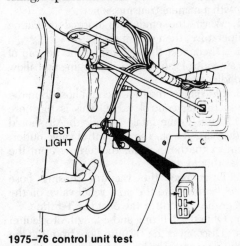

1975–76 control unit test

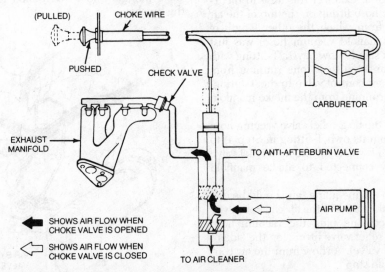

Operation of the air by-pass valve, 1972–74

Air Control Valve, 1977–78

This procedure is for all 1,796cc engines. Only California trucks have this valve.

1. Disconnect the outlet hose at the bottom of the valve. Start the engine and let it idle.

2. Check that air is not discharged from the outlet.

3. Disconnect the small diameter hose from the top of the valve. Air should now be felt at the valve outlet.

4. If the valve is not operating properly, check the hoses for leaks, kinks, breaks, or improper connections, and inspect the check valve for proper operation. Replace the air control valve if necessary. Reconnect the hoses after the test.

Air Control Valve, 1980 and Later With Manual Transmission

This test is for all 1980 models sold in California with a manual transmission.

1. Warm the engine to normal operating temperature, then shut it off.

2. Disconnect the air hose at the bottom of the air control valve. Start the engine and allow it to idle.

3. Disconnect the thin vacuum hose from the top of the air control valve. This is the hose which runs to the intake manifold. Air should be discharged from the air control valve outlet. Connect the hose again; the airflow from the outlet should stop.

4. Disconnect the vacuum sensing hose (which connects to the no.2 relief valve on the side of the air control valve) at the T-fitting.

5. Obtain a T fitting and a length of vacuum hose. Disconnect the vacuum hose from the top of the air control valve (same hose as disconnected in Step 3). Connect this hose to the T-fitting and the hose fitting on the top of the air control valve from which the other length of hose (intake manifold vacuum hose) was just removed. You should now have a T-fitting with two hoses connected to it: one running from the top of the air control valve to the T-fitting, and the other running from the intake manifold to the T-fitting.

6. Connect the no.2 relief valve vacuum hose (disconnect from its own T-fitting in Step 4) to the T-fitting. This will allow the no.2 relief valve to be directly connected to intake manifold vacuum.

7. With the engine idling, air should be discharged from the outlet of the air control valve.

8. Disconnect and plug the vacuum hose from the no.2 relief valve fitting (on the side of the air control valve). Airflow from the air control valve should stop.

9. If the air control valve does not operate correctly, replace it.

Check Valve, 1979 and Later 49 States

This is a test for the check valve installed in the hose which runs from the air cleaner case to the exhaust manifold, on 1979 and later 49 State models without an air pump.

1. Warm the engine to normal operating temperature, then shut it off.

2. Disconnect the air hose from the check valve.

3. Start the engine and allow it to idle.

4. Place a finger over the check valve inlet; vacuum should be felt. If not air is being drawn into the valve, replace the valve.

5. Run the engine up to about 1,500 rpm. Check for exhaust gas leakage at the check valve air inlet fitting. If leakage is present, replace the valve.

ADJUSTMENTS

Air Pump Drive Belt

Adjustment of the air pump drive belt is covered in Chapter 1.

Air By-Pass Valve, 1972–74

1. Push the choke handle all the way in. Be sure that the choke plate is fully open.

2. Loosen the cable retaining screw in the valve plunger and the screw in the cable retaining bracket.

3. Be sure that the plunger is fully bottomed.

4. Insert the cable in the plunger and tighten the retaining screw.

5. Push down on the cable as much as possible without bending the control wire, then tighten the bracket screw.

6. Pull the choke knob all the way out. The valve plunger should be pulled to the top of the bracket.

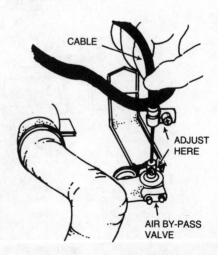

Adjusting the air by-pass valve, 1972–74

SERVICE

Air Pump Removal and Installation

1. Remove the battery, alternator and alternator drive belt.
2. Disconnect the inlet and outlet hoses from the air pump.
3. Remove the adjusting bar bolt and disengage the air pump drive belt.
4. Remove the air pump mounting bolt and remove the air pump.
5. Position the pump on the mounting bracket and loosely install the attaching and adjusting bolts.
6. Install the air pump drive belt.
7. Adjust the air pump belt tension and tighten the mounting and adjusting bolts.
8. Connect the inlet and outlet lines to the air pump.
9. Install the battery, alternator and alternator drive belt. Adjust the drive belt tension.

Air Pump Check Valve Removal and Installation

1. Disconnect the air hose from the check valve.
2. Unscrew the check valve from the air manifold.
3. Screw the check valve from the air manifold. Tighten the check valve to 20 ft.lb.
4. Connect the air hose to the check valve.

Air Manifold Removal and Installation, 1,796cc and 1,970cc

1. Remove the check valve.
2. Loosen the nuts securing the manifold to the cylinder head. Remove the nozzles from the manifold by removing the attaching nuts from the nozzles.
3. Unbolt and remove the manifold.
4. Install the nozzles in the manifold. Torque the nuts to 20 ft.lb.
5. Install the manifold and torque the nuts to 15 ft.lb.
6. Install the check valve.

Air Injection Nozzle Removal and Installation, 1,796cc and 1,970cc

1. Disconnect the air line from the check valve.
2. Remove the nozzles from the manifold by unscrewing the nuts.
3. Remove the heat stove from the exhaust manifold.
4. Remove the nozzles.
5. Install the nozzles. Torque the nuts to 20 ft.lb.
6. Install the heat stove on the exhaust manifold.
7. Connect the air line to the manifold check valve.

Air By-Pass Valve Removal and Installation, 1972–74

1. Loosen the cable attaching screws at the valve plunger and cable retaining bracket.
2. Pull the cable out of the valve.
3. Unscrew and remove the valve from the mounting bracket.
4. Install the valve on the mounting bracket.
5. Push the choke knob all the way in.
6. Insert the end of the cable in the valve plunger and tighten the retaining screw.
7. Pull the cable to remove all slack between the plunger and cable bracket. Tighten the cable retaining screw at the bracket.

Deceleration Control System

The deceleration control system is designed to maintain a balanced air/fuel mixture during periods of engine deceleration. Although the components used vary in some years, the basic theory remains the same: To more thoroughly burn or dilute the initial rich mixture formed when throttle is suddenly closed, and to smooth out the transition to a lean mixture by enriching the mixture slightly after the throttle has closed. Although the process may seem contradictory, they act in sequence to provide an overall ideal mixture.

The 1972 49 States and Canada Mazdas use a vacuum control valve, an accelerator switch, a servo diaphragm, and a set of spark retard points in the distributor. The vacuum control valve controls spark retard, through the ignition points, and throttle opening through the servo diaphragm, and a set of spark retard points in the distributor. The vacuum control valve controls spark retard, through the ignition points, and throttle opening through the servo diaphragm. During deceleration, the vacuum control valve applies vacuum to the servo diaphragm, slightly opening the primary throttle plate to admit additional fuel to the lean mixture. At the same time, it activates the retard points through a vacuum switch. At idle, the accelerator switch activates the retard points; above idle speed, the accelerator switch is off and the standard point set is used.

1972 Mazdas sold in California, and all 1973–74 Mazdas use an anti-afterburn valve, and a coasting richer valve on the carburetor which is controlled by three switches: speedometer, accelerator, and clutch. 1975–76 Mazdas use the same system, but the clutch switch is not used. The anti-afterburn valve has a diaphragm controlled engine vacuum. During deceleration, the diaphragm lifts allow the air pump to inject air into the intake manifold. This dilutes the incoming rich mixture, preventing detonation in the exhaust system, which would oc-

Deceleration Control System—1972 California only and 1973–74 models. 1975–76 models are the same, except that the air by-pass valve becomes an air control valve, used in the Thermactor system.

cur if the injected air from the air pump were to burn this rich mixture in the exhaust manifold. The coasting richer valve acts to add additional fuel to the lean intake mixture as soon as the anti-afterburn valve has shut off. The speed, accelerator and clutch switches must be closed to allow the coasting richer valve to operate. The accelerator switch closes when the accelerator pedal is released. The speedometer switch closes when the truck speed is above 17–23 mph. The clutch switch, used from 1972–74, is closed when the clutch pedal is released.

1977–78 1,796cc 49 States and Canada Mazdas use an air by-pass valve, a carburetor dashpot, and a throttle opener system comprised of a servo diaphragm connected to the throttle and a vacuum control valve. This is essentially the same as the 1972 49 States model. The air by-pass valve prevents afterburn in the exhaust by shutting off air to the exhaust manifold from the air pump during deceleration. The dashpot holds the throttle open slightly for an instant during sudden deceleration. The throttle opener system is the same as that used in the 1972 49 States models.

1977–78 California Mazdas use an anti-afterburn valve and a throttle opener system. The anti-afterburn valve is the same as that used from 1973–76, and the throttle opener is the same as that used in 1977–78 49 States models.

1979 and later 1,970cc 49 States models use an anti-afterburn valve and a throttle positioner. California models have an air by-pass

valve and a throttle positioner. Canadian models have an air by-pass valve, a dashpot, and a throttle positioner.

In addition to the above components, 1974–75 Rotary Pick-Ups have an altitude compensator which provides air to lean out the overly rich mixture which occurs at high altitudes.

On 1974 models with automatic transmission, a kick-down control system is used. Regardless of the gear selected, the transmission will not go above Second gear when the choke knob is pulled out.

TESTING

Combination Anti-Afterburn and Coasting Valve

1974

1. Disconnect the hose which runs from the air cleaner to the combination valve at the air cleaner end.

2. Start the engine and run it at curb idle.

3. There should be no vacuum present at the end of the hose which you disconnect in Step 1.

4. Turn the engine off.

5. Disconnect the hose which runs from coasting valve portion of the combination valve to the intake manifold from the coasting valve end and plug up the port.

6. Operate the engine at idle.

7. Disconnect the anti-afterburn valve solenoid connector.

Testing the anti-afterburn valve

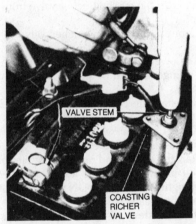

Testing the coasting richer valve with the battery

8. Check for vacuum at the end of the hose which you disconnect in Step 1; there should be vacuum present. If not, the anti-afterburn valve is defective.

9. Turn the engine off. Reconnect the anti-afterburn valve electrical leads and the hose to the coasting valve.

10. Disconnect the intake manifold-to-anti-afterburn valve vacuum line at the valve end, and plug the vacuum fitting on the valve.

11. Start the engine and allow it to idle.

12. Disconnect the coasting valve solenoid at the multiconnector.

13. Hold your hand over the end of the vacuum line which you disconnected in Step 10. Vacuum should be felt; if not, replace the defective coasting valve.

14. Turn the engine off and reconnect the leads and hoses which were disconnected above.

Altitude Compensator

1975

1. Detach the air intake hose from the altitude compensator.

2. Start the engine and run it at idle.

3. Hold your finger over the altitude compensator air intake; the engine speed should decrease. If it doesn't, replace the compensator.

4. Reconnect the air intake hose, if the compensator is in good working order.

Idle Switch

1. Unfasten the idle switch leads.

2. Connect the test meter to the switch terminals.

3. With the engine at idle, the meter should indicate a complete circuit.

4. Depress the plunger on the idle switch; the circuit should be broken (on meter reading). If the idle switch is not functioning properly, replace it with a new one.

Coolant Temperature Switch

1974–75

Start this test with the coolant temperature below 68°F.

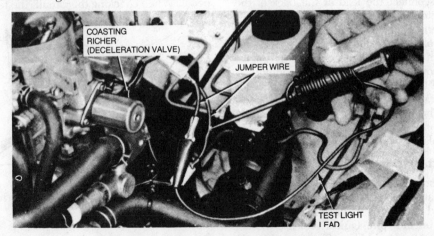

Testing the coaster richer valve with a test light

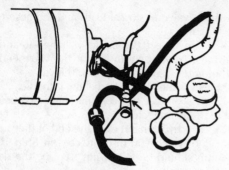

Altitude compensator (arrow)

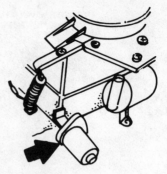

Anti-afterburn valve (arrow)

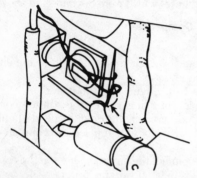

Idle switch (arrow)

1. Disconnect the electrical lead from the temperature switch.

2. Connect a test light between one terminal of the switch and a 12v battery. Ground the other terminal.

3. The test light should light.

4. Start the engine and allow it to warm up. Once the engine reaches normal operating temperature, the test light should go out.

5. Replace the switch if it doesn't work as outlined

Choke Switch (Semi-Automatic Choke)

1. Working underneath the instrument panel, disconnect the lead at the back of the choke switch.

2. Connect an ohmmeter to the terminals on the choke switch side of the connector.

3. With the choke knob on (off), the meter should show continuity (resistance reading).

4. Pull the choke knob out, about ½ in. for manual transmission trucks or 1 in. for automatics. The meter should show no continuity (read zero).

5. Replace the switch if defective.

Anti-Afterburn Valve

1. Remove the outlet hose from the anti-afterburn valve.

2. Hold a hand over the outlet fitting and raise the engine rpm. Quickly release the accelerator. Air should flow for approximately three seconds. If the valve passes air for more than three seconds, or does not pass air at all, it should be replaced.

Coasting Richer Valve (Deceleration Valve)

1. Remove the coasting richer valve from the carburetor.

2. Connect the coasting richer valve to the battery.

3. As power is applied to the valve, the solenoid plunger should be pulled into the valve body.

4. Reinstall the coasting richer valve. Connect a test light.

5. Raise the rear wheels and support the truck on stands. Block the front wheels.

6. Start the engine and raise the engine speed above 30 mph. Release the accelerator pedal. The test light should come ON and remain ON until the speed falls below 17–23 mph.

7. If the system is operating properly, no further tests are required. If not, proceed with the other tests.

8. Remove the stands and lower the truck. Disconnect the test light.

Clutch Switch

The clutch switch is activated by the clutch pedal. When checking the circuit, the test light

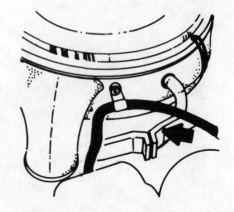

Coasting richer valve (arrow)

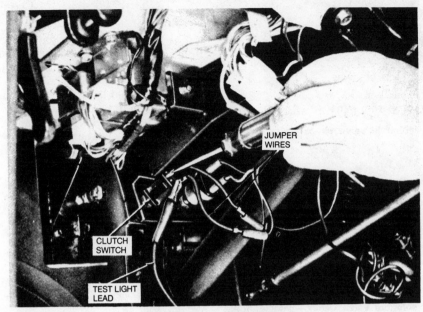

Checking the clutch switch

should be ON when the clutch pedal is fully released, and should be OFF when the clutch pedal is fully depressed.

Accelerator Switch

The accelerator switch is actuated by a throttle lever link on the carburetor through 1978; the switch is located on the accelerator pedal on 1979 and later models. When checking the switch with a circuit tester, the test light should be ON when the accelerator pedal is fully released and should be OFF when the pedal is depressed.

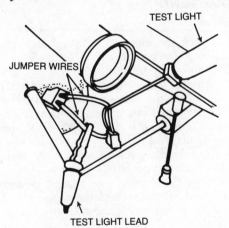

Checking the accelerator switch

Speed Switch

1. Remove the instrument cluster and attach a test light to the speedometer switch.

2. Reconnect the speedometer cable and ground wire.

3. Raise both wheels off the ground and support the truck on stands. Block the front wheels.

4. Start the engine.

5. Depress the accelerator pedal to accelerate the engine and confirm that the speed switch is ON at speeds of 17–23 mph and OFF at speeds below 17–23 mph.

6. If not, replace the switch.

7. Lower the truck and remove the test light. Reinstall the instrument cluster.

Speed Switch Relay

Check the speed switch relay with a test light to be sure that it is operating at 17–23 mph.

Three Way Solenoid Valve

1,970cc ENGINES

1. Start the engine and allow it to reach normal operating temperature. Check the idle speed and adjust as necessary.

2. Disconnect the wire at the three way solenoid valve. This wire is coded either black with a white stripe or brown with a red stripe on some models.

3. When the wire is disconnected, the engine speed should increase to 1,000 rpm for 49 States trucks, or 1,100 rpm for California models.

4. If the engine speed does not increase, the three way solenoid valve or the servo diaphragm is not operating correctly. Check the servo diaphragm using the following procedure; if the servo diaphragm is operating cor-

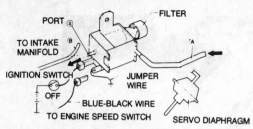

Three way solenoid valve check—with ignition switch off

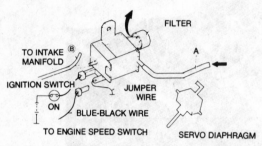

Three way solenoid valve check—with ignition switch on

rectly, the three way valve is faulty and should be replaced.

Servo Diaphragm

1. Start the engine and set the idle speed to specification.

2. Stop the engine and disconnect the vacuum line between the vacuum control valve and the diaphragm at the diaphragm.

3. Disconnect the vacuum line between the intake manifold and the vacuum control valve at the manifold on models through 1978. On 1979 and later models, disconnect the vacuum hose at the vacuum amplifier and the vacuum hose at the three way solenoid valve. Connect the vacuum hose from the servo diaphragm to the vacuum amplifier so that the intake manifold vacuum is applied directly to the servo diaphragm.

4. Disconnect and plug the vacuum line between the carburetor and distributor.

5. Connect a vacuum line from the intake manifold to the servo diaphragm on models through 1978.

6. Connect a tachometer and start the engine. The engine should idle at 1,300–1,500 rpm for models through 1978, or 900–1,100 rpm, 1979 (1,000–1,200 rpm for 1979 and later California models). If the engine speed is not correct, adjust by means of the servo diaphragm adjusting screw. If the correct speed is not obtainable, replace the diaphragm.

Vacuum Control Valve

1. Disconnect the vacuum hose between the vacuum control valve and the intake manifold at the manifold.

2. Attach a vacuum gauge in the line using a T-fitting.

3. Connect a tachometer to the engine. Start the engine and raise the speed to 3000 rpm, then suddenly release the throttle. The vacuum reading should rise above 21.3 in., drop to that figure and hesitate there for one or two seconds, then drop to the normal idle vacuum of 16–18 in. Note that these readings are for sea level, and should be corrected accordingly.

4. If the vacuum reading is not within specification, adjust the vacuum control valve by turning the adjusting screw in the top of the valve. If the correct reading is unobtainable, replace the valve.

Vacuum Switch

1. Disconnect the vacuum hose between the vacuum switch and the vacuum control valve.

2. Using a T-fitting, connect a vacuum gauge between the vacuum switch and an external vacuum source.

3. Raise the vacuum reading above 8 in., then allow the vacuum to drop. The switch should click at approximately 6 in. If it does not, or if it clicks at a higher reading, replace the switch.

Air By-Pass Valve

1. Disconnect the air hose from the side of the air by-pass valve.

2. Connect a tachometer to the engine. Start the engine and raise the speed above 2,000 rpm.

3. Release the throttle and check for air flow from the port on the side of the air by-pass valve. If there is no airflow, replace the valve.

ADJUSTMENTS

Dashpot

1. Check the engine idle speed and mixture, and adjust as necessary.

2. Remove the air cleaner.

3. With the tachometer still connected to the engine, loosen the dashpot locknut. Move the throttle lever and hold to maintain the engine speed at 2,400–2,600 rpm (2,100–2,300 rpm for California trucks).

4. Turn the dashpot until its rod contacts the throttle lever and tighten the locknut.

5. Move the throttle lever until it contacts the dashpot rod and recheck the engine speed. Repeat the adjustment if necessary.

Accelerator Switch Adjustment

1972–78

1. Be sure that the throttle valve is fully closed.

2. Loosen the switch adjusting screw and turn the switch off.

3. Gradually tighten the adjusting screw un-

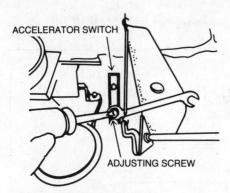

Adjusting the accelerator switch

til the switch produces a clicking sound and is turned on.

4. Tighten the adjusting screw another 1½ turns.

1979 AND LATER

The accelerator switch is mounted on the arm of the accelerator pedal.

1. Check the accelerator pedal to make sure that it moves freely.

2. Loosen the accelerator switch locknut.

3. Gradually turn the adjusting screw until the accelerator switch clicks.

4. Tighten the locknut.

Idle Switch

1. Warm up the engine until the water temperature is at least 156°F.

2. Make sure that the mixture and idle speed are properly adjusted.

3. Adjust the idle speed to 1,075–1,100 rpm on models with manual transmission; 1,200–1,300 rpm on models with automatic transmission, by rotating the throttle adjusting screw.

4. Rotate the idle switch adjusting screw until the switch changes from OFF to ON position.

5. Slowly turn the idle switch adjusting screw back to the point where the switch just changes from ON to OFF.

6. Turn the throttle screw back so that the engine returns to idle.

NOTE: *Be sure that the idle switch goes on when the idle speed is still above 1,000 rpm.*

REMOVAL AND INSTALLATION

Speed Switch

The speed switch is integral with the speedometer head located in the instrument panel. To replace the speed switch, refer to Instrument Cluster Removal and Installation in Chapter 5.

Anti-Afterburn Valve

1. Remove the air cleaner assembly.

2. Disconnect the air hoses and vacuum lines from the valve.

3. Unfasten the solenoid wiring.

4. Remove the securing nuts and withdraw the valve.

5. Installation is performed in the reverse order of removal.

Coasting Valve

The coasting valve is removed and installed in the same manner as the anti-afterburn valve.

Idle Switch

1. Remove the coasting valve. See the section above.

2. Remove the carburetor as detailed elsewhere in this chapter.

3. Disconnect the wiring from the switch.

4. Unfasten the securing screws and remove the switch.

5. Installation is performed in the reverse order of removal. After installing the switch, adjust it as outlined under Adjustments, below.

Air Supply Valve

1. Remove the air cleaner and the hot air duct.

2. Disconnect the air hose, the vacuum lines, and the solenoid wiring from the valve.

3. Unfasten the screws which secure the valve and remove it.

4. Air supply valve installation is performed in the reverse order of removal.

Altitude Compensator

1. Disconnect both hoses from the altitude compensator. Be sure to note their positions for correct hook-up.

2. Unfasten the altitude compensator securing bolts.

3. Remove the compensator from its bracket.

4. Installation is the reverse of removal.

Coolant Temperature Switch

1. Drain the coolant from the radiator enough to bring the coolant level below the temperature switch.

CAUTION: *When draining the coolant, keep in mind that cats and dogs are attracted by the ethylene glycol antifreeze, and are quite likely to drink any that is left in an uncovered container or in puddles on the ground. This will prove fatal in sufficient quantity. Always drain the coolant into a sealable container. Coolant should be reused unless it is contaminated or several years old.*

2. Remove the alternator and drive belt if they are in the way.

3. Disconnect the switch multiconnector.

4. Use an open-end wrench to remove the switch.

5. Installation is the reverse of removal.

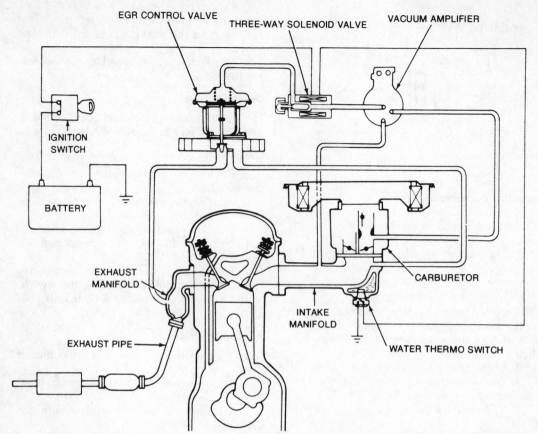

EGR CONTROL VALVE
THREE-WAY SOLENOID VALVE
VACUUM AMPLIFIER
IGNITION SWITCH
BATTERY
EXHAUST MANIFOLD
EXHAUST PIPE
INTAKE MANIFOLD
CARBURETOR
WATER THERMO SWITCH

Typical EGR system layout on trucks without electronic engine control

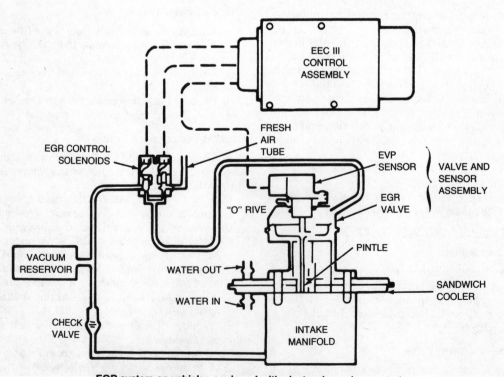

EEC III CONTROL ASSEMBLY
FRESH AIR TUBE
EGR CONTROL SOLENOIDS
EVP SENSOR
VALVE AND SENSOR ASSEMBLY
EGR VALVE
"O" RIVE
VACUUM RESERVOIR
WATER OUT
WATER IN
PINTLE
SANDWICH COOLER
CHECK VALVE
INTAKE MANIFOLD

EGR system on vehicles equipped with electronic engine control

Exhaust Gas Recirculation System

Oxides of nitrogen are formed under conditions of high temperatures and high pressure. By eliminating one of these conditions, the production of NOx is restricted. The exhaust gas recirculation system (EGR) reintroduces a small portion of the exhaust gases into the combustion chamber with the intake charge, thus reducing spark combustion temperature. The EGR system is used on 1976 Mazdas, and all 1977 and later trucks.

Components used through 1978 include an EGR control valve, a three-way solenoid valve, a vacuum amplifier, and a water thermo switch. The control valve, operated by engine vacuum, opens to allow exhaust gases into the intake manifold, and closes to shut them off. The solenoid valve regulates vacuum to the EGR valve. It is governed by the thermo switch. At coolant temperatures below 122°F (131°F for 1976 only), the thermo switch is closed. This closes the vacuum passage in the solenoid valve, cutting vacuum to the control valve which prevents exhaust recirculation when the engine is cold. At temperatures above 131°F, the thermo switch opens, allowing intake manifold vacuum to raise the control valve diaphragm, allowing recirculation of exhaust gases. The vacuum amplifier supplies varying amounts of vacuum to the control valve through the solenoid valve, opening or closing it during acceleration or at varying engine speeds.

A slightly different EGR system is used on 1979 and later models. Components include the EGR valve, a water thermo valve, and a vacuum amplifier. The three-way solenoid valve is used on 2.0 liter engines only. The EGR valve is the same vacuum operated unit used in earlier years, and operates in the same manner. The water thermo valve controls the EGR valve, except on California models; on California models, the thermo valve actuates the No. 2 relief valve in the air control valve, and the air control valve regulates the EGR vacuum signal. The thermo valve is closed when coolant temperatures are below 115°F. Above that temperature, the valve opens, allowing vacuum to be transmitted to the EGR valve. The vacuum amplifier performs the same function as in earlier years.

NOTE: *1,970cc Mazdas sold in California (1979–80) have two water thermo valves. One is for the EGR system and the other is for the Spark Timing Control System. The thermo valve used in the EGR system has two vacuum hoses; one runs to the vacuum amplifier, and the other runs to the EGR valve.*

EGR CONTROL VALVE TEST

1. Start the engine and allow it to idle.
2. On 1976 trucks, disconnect the vacuum hose from the EGR valve. Disconnect the intake manifold vacuum hose from the vacuum amplifier, and connect it to the EGR valve.
3. On 1977–78 trucks, disconnect the vac-

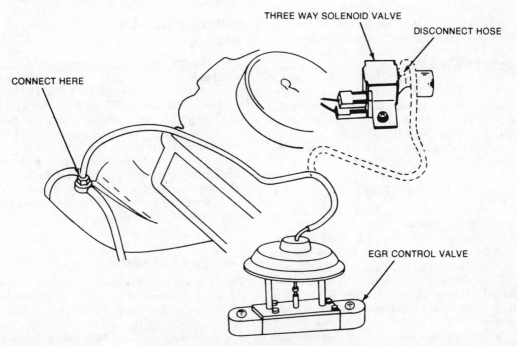

1977–78 EGR valve test; 1979 and later similar

uum hose which runs form the EGR valve to the three-way solenoid valve at the solenoid valve. Disconnect the intake manifold vacuum hose at the manifold, and connect the EGR valve vacuum hose to the intake manifold fitting.

4. On 1979 and later models, disconnect the vacuum hose from the water thermo valve. The valve is installed in the intake manifold. Disconnect the intake manifold vacuum hose and connect the EGR valve vacuum hose to the intake manifold vacuum fitting.

5. The engine should stall or idle roughly. If it does not, shut off the engine and remove the EGR valve and pipe from the engine. Clean the passages of the valve and pipe with a brush and a wire. Reinstall the parts and repeat the test.

6. If the test is not successful, replace the EGR valve. When engine stall or idle roughness occurs with the manifold vacuum hose connected to the EGR valve, return the hoses to their original positions.

THREE-WAY SOLENOID VALVE TEST

1. Disconnect the electrical connectors from the thermo switch. Connect a jumper wire between the connectors to simulate a complete circuit.

2. Turn the ignition switch ON.

3. Disconnect the vacuum hose from the EGR valve and blow into the hose. Air should be discharged from the three-way solenoid valve relief port. If it is not, replace the three-way valve.

4. Turn the ignition switch off, and remove the jumper wire from the thermo switch connectors. Disconnect the vacuum amplifier vacuum line from the three-way solenoid. Turn the ignition switch back to ON.

5. Blow into the vacuum line disconnected from the EGR valve, and check for air discharge from the vacuum amplifier port on the three-way solenoid valve. If there is no discharge, replace the solenoid valve.

6. After completion of all tests, reconnect the hoses to their original locations.

VACUUM AMPLIFIER TEST

1. Start the engine and warm it to normal operating temperature.

2. Disconnect the vacuum amplifier vacuum hose from the solenoid valve or thermo valve. Connect a vacuum gauge to this hose.

3. Disconnect the vacuum amplifier vacuum hose from the carburetor. The vacuum hose to the intake manifold should remain connected.

4. Depress and release the accelerator several times, then allow the engine to idle. The

vacuum gauge reading should be 2.0 ± .04 in. Hg.

5. Reconnect the vacuum amplifier vacuum hose to the carburetor.

6. Increase engine speed to 3,500 rpm. The vacuum gauge reading should be 3.54 in. Hg. If the vacuum amplifier does not test properly, replace it.

7. After all tests are completed, return the hoses to their original positions.

WATER THERMO VALVE TEST

1. Drain the cooling system until the coolant level is below the intake manifold. Remove the water thermo valve from the manifold.

CAUTION: *When draining the coolant, keep in mind that cats and dogs are attracted by the ethelyne glycol antifreeze, and are quite likely to drink any that is left in an uncovered container or in puddles on the ground. This will prove fatal in sufficient quantity. Always drain the coolant into a sealable container. Coolant should be reused unless it is contaminated or several years old.*

2. Place a valve in a container of water. Attach a length of vacuum hose to each of the two fittings.

3. Gradually heat the water while observing the temperature.

4. By blowing through one of the vacuum hoses, you will be able to tell when the valve opens. The valve should block the passage of air until the water temperature reaches approximately 115°F. If this is not the case, the valve is faulty and must be replaced.

EGR WARNING LIGHT

1976 Only

1976 Mazdas with EGR are equipped with a maintenance warning light on the instrument panel, which lights every 12,500 miles. The light indicates that the EGR system should be checked for proper operation, using the procedures outlined. The EGR valve should be removed and cleaned every 25,000 miles.

The switch controlling the light is installed behind the speedometer. To reset the switch after the maintenance has been performed, remove the cover from the switch, and move the switch knob to the opposite position.

Catalytic Converter

The 1976 and later trucks sold in California and almost all 1979 and later trucks have a catalytic converter installed in the exhaust system to aid in the reduction of HC and CO emissions. The only exceptions are some 1979–80 models sold in Canada.

The catalytic converter is a muffler-shaped device located between the exhaust manifold and the muffler. It is filled with beads containing platinum and palladium which, through catalytic action, enables the HC and CO gases to be converted into water vapor (H_2O) and carbon dioxide (CO_2). The converter has a warning system (1976 only), consisting of a thermo sensor inserted into the side of the converter, which monitors temperatures, and a warning light on the instrument panel which lights when the sensor detects converter temperatures exceeding 1,742°F. The converter should be inspected periodically for cracks, corrosion, and any signs of external burning, and replaced as required.

WARNING SYSTEM TEST

(1976 Only)

1. Turn the ignition switch ON. The warning light on the instrument panel should light. Start the engine. The warning light should go off.
2. If the light does not light, check the bulb. If burned out, replace and retest the system.
3. If the light does not go out after the engine has started, shut off the engine and tilt the seatback forward.
4. Disconnect the thermo sensor wire electrical connectors.
5. Using an ohmmeter, check the thermo sensor circuit for continuity, on the sensor side of the wiring. If there is no continuity, replace the sensor. Reconnect the wires and repeat the test.

REMOVAL AND INSTALLATION

1. Raise the truck and support it on safety stands.
   CAUTION: *Be very careful when working on or near the converter. External temperatures can reach 1,500°F. and more, causing severe burns. Removal or installation should only be performed on a cold exhaust system.*
2. Loosen the nut and remove the thermo sensor from the side of the converter (1976 models).
3. Remove the front and rear flange attaching nuts.
4. Remove the nut and rubber support which secures the converter bracket, and remove the converter.
5. Installation is the reverse of removal.

Spark Timing Control System

A spark delay system is used on 1977–78 1,796cc engines, and 1979 and later 1,970cc engines. Its purpose is to reduce the formation of CO

and NO_2 emissions by delaying the vacuum advance to the distributor during normal acceleration. The system consists of a spark delay valve installed in the vacuum hose between the carburetor and the distributor vacuum advance diaphragm, on all 1977–78 models, and all 1979 and later 49 States models. The spark delay valve is installed in the vacuum line between the water thermo valve and the distributor diaphragm on 1979 and later models sold in California. The water thermo valve is installed in the intake manifold. The spark delay valve has an internal restrictor to slow the air flow in one direction and a check valve which allows air to flow freely in the opposite direction.

SYSTEM TEST

1. Remove the air cleaner. Disconnect the vacuum hose from the distributor.
2. On 1977–78 models, disconnect the vacuum control valve hose at the intake manifold fitting, and install the distributor hose on that fitting. On 1979 and later 49 States models, disconnect the anti-afterburn valve line at the intake manifold fitting and install the distributor vacuum line to the intake manifold fitting. On 1979 and later California models, disconnect the air bypass valve hose from the intake manifold fitting and install the distributor vacuum line to the intake manifold fitting.
3. Remove the vacuum hose from the carburetor side of the spark delay valve. Plug this hose, and attach a vacuum gauge to the delay valve.
4. Start the engine and allow it to idle.
5. Disconnect the vacuum hose from the intake manifold fitting (the hose from the spark delay valve to the distributor which has been connected to the intake manifold in Step 2) and note the time for the vacuum gauge reading to drop to 11.8 in. Hg. It should drop to this figure within 2–7 seconds (1–10 seconds on California models), 1977–78, or 4–6 seconds, 1979 and later. If the reading is not correct, replace the spark delay valve.
6. After all tests have been completed, return the hoses to their original positions.

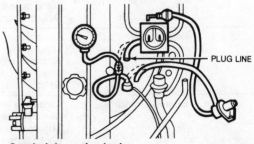

Spark delay valve test

DISTRIBUTOR SOLENOID VALVE TEST

1. Start the engine and allow it to idle.
2. Separate the connector at the distributor solenoid valve and apply battery power to the terminals to energize the valve.
3. Disconnect the vacuum hose from the vacuum advance unit. There should be no vacuum at the hose.
4. Remove the battery power to the solenoid valve. The valve is operating properly if air is drawn (by vacuum) into the vacuum hose as soon as power is removed.

WATER THERMO SWITCH TEST

1. Remove the switch.
2. Connect an ohmmeter across the switch terminals and place the sensor in water. Heat the water gradually. Using a thermometer check the water temperature as it is heated.
3. Note the temperature at which continuity exists between both poles. The specified temperature is 131°F. If the temperature is not within specifications, replace the switch.

TIMER TEST

1. Remove the timer.
2. Connect suitable test wires to terminals A, B, and C, respectively.
3. Connect a test wire with a 30KΩ resistor to terminal D.
4. Connect a test wire with a 3.4w lamp to terminal E.
5. Connect the positive test lead of a voltmeter to terminal D and the negative lead to the battery negative terminal.
6. Connect test wires A, D, and E to the positive terminal. Do not connect Terminal B in this step.

7. Connect the wire from terminal C to the battery negative terminal.
8. Check the voltmeter reading. It should read about 6v or above.
9. Connect the test wire from terminal B to the positive battery terminal. At the moment the connection is complete, the voltmeter should read less than 1 volt, and the lamp will light. Maintain this connection for 2 minutes. The voltmeter should read about 8v.

EMISSION CONTROLS-ROTARY ENGINE

Positive Crankcase Ventilation (PCV) System

The positive crankcase ventilation (PCV) valve is located on the intake manifold below the carburetor. In this case, the word "crankcase" is not quite correct, as the Mazda rotary engine has no crankcase in the normal sense of the term. Rather, the valve, which is operated by intake manifold vacuum, is used to meter the flow of fuel and air vapors through the rotor housings.

TESTING AND REPLACEMENT

The procedures for PCV valve testing and replacement may be found under Routine Maintenance, in Chapter 1.

Air Injection System

The air injection system used on the Mazda rotary engine differs from the type used on a conventional piston engine in two respects:
1. Air is not only supplied to burn the gases

Air Injection System Diagnosis Chart

Problem	Cause	Cure
Noisy drive belt	Loose belt	Tighten belt
	Seized pump	Replace pump
Noisy pump	Leaking hose	Find and fix leak
	Loose hose	Tighten clamp
	Hose rubbing	Reposition
	Air control valve failure	Replace
	Check valve failure	Replace
	Pump mounting loose	Tighten mounting bolts
	Defective pump	Replace
No air supply	Loose belt	Tighten belt
	Leaking hose	Find and fix leak
	Air control valve failure	Replace
	Check valve failure	Replace
	Defective pump	Replace
Exhaust backfire	Vacuum or air leaks	Find and fix
	Air control valve failure	Replace
	Sticking choke	Repair
	Choke setting too rich	Adjust

in the exhaust ports, but it is also used to cool the thermal reactor.

2. A three-way air control valve is used in place of the conventional anti-backfire and diverter valves. It contains an air cut-out valve, a relief valve, and a safety valve.

Air is supplied to the system by a normal vane type air pump. The air flows from the pump to the air control valve, where it is routed to the air injection nozzles to cool the thermal reactor or, in the case of a system malfunction, to the air cleaner. A check valve, located beneath the air control valve seat, prevents the back-flow of hot exhaust gases into the air injection system in case of air pressure loss.

Air injection nozzles are used to feed air into the exhaust ports, just as in a conventional piston engine.

COMPONENT TESTING

Air Pump

1. Check the air pump drive belt tension by applying 22 lbs. of pressure halfway between the water pump and air pump pulleys. The belt should deflect 0.23–0.35 in. Adjust the belt if necessary, or replace it if it is cracked or worn.

2. Turn the pump by hand. If it has seized, the drive belt will slip, producing noise.

NOTE: *Disregard any chirping, squealing, or rolling sounds coming from inside the pump; these are normal when it is being turned by hand.*

3. Check the hoses and connections for leaks. Hissing or a blast of air is indicative of a leak. Soapy water, applied around the area in question, is a good method of detecting leaks.

4. Connect a pressure gauge between the air pump and the air control valve with a T-fitting.

5. Plug the other hose connections (outlets) on the air control valve, as illustrated.

CAUTION: *Be careful not to touch the thermal reactor; severe burns will result.*

6. With the engine at normal idle speed, the pressure gauge should read 0.48–0.68 psi. Replace the air pump if it is less than this.

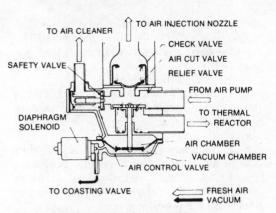

Cross-section of the air control valve

7. If the air pump is not defective, leave the pressure gauge connected but unplug the connections at the air control valve and proceed with the next test.

Air Control Valve

CAUTION: *When testing the air control valve, avoid touching the thermal reactor as severe burns will result.*

1. Test the air control valve solenoid as follows:

a. Turn the ignition switch off and on. A click should be heard coming from the solenoid. If no sound is audible, check the solenoid wiring.

b. If no defect is found in the solenoid wiring, connect the solenoid directly to the truck's battery. If the solenoid still does not click, it is defective and must be replaced. If the solenoid works, then check the components of the air flow control system. See below.

2. Start the engine and run it at idle speed. The pressure gauge should still read 0.37–0.75 psi. No air should leak from the two outlets which were unplugged.

3. Increase the engine speed to 3,500 rpm (3,000 rpm—automatic transmission). The pressure gauge should now read 1.2–2.8 psi and the two outlets still should not be leaking air.

4. Return the engine to idle.

5. Disconnect the solenoid wiring. Air should

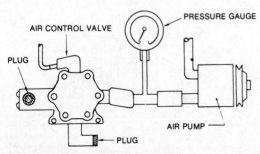

Test connections for the air pump

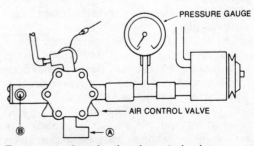

Test connections for the air control valve

now flow from the outlet marked A in the illustration, but not from the outlet marked B. The pressure gauge reading should remain the same as in Step 2.

6. Reconnect the solenoid.

7. If the relief valve is faulty, air sent from the air pump will flow into the cooling passages of the thermal reactor when the engine is at idle speed.

8. If the safety valve is faulty, air will flow into the air cleaner when the engine is idling.

9. Replace the air control valve if it fails to pass any one of the above tests. Remember to disconnect the pressure gauge.

Check Valve

1. Remove the check valve, as detailed below.

2. Depress the valve plate to see if it will seat properly.

3. Measure the free length of the valve spring; it should be 1.22 in.

NOTE: *The spring free length should be 0.75 in. on automatic transmission equipped models.*

4. Measure the installed length of the spring; it should be 0.68 in. Replace the check valve if it is not up to specifications.

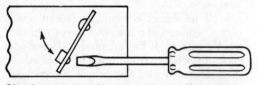

Check one-way valve operation, as illustrated

REMOVAL AND INSTALLATION
Air Pump

1. Remove the air cleaner assembly from the carburetor.

2. Loosen, but do not remove, the adjusting link bolt.

3. Push the pump toward the engine to slacken belt tension and remove drive belt.

4. Disconnect the air supply hoses from the pump.

5. Unfasten the pump securing bolts and remove the pump.

CAUTION: *Do not pry on the air pump housing during removal and do not clamp the housing in a vise once the pump has been removed. Any type of heavy pressure applied to the housing will distort it.*

6. Installation is performed in the reverse order of removal. Adjust the belt tension by moving the air pump to the specification given in the Testing section, above.

Air Control Valve

CAUTION: *Remove the air control valve only after the thermal reactor has cooled sufficiently to prevent the danger of a serious burn.*

1. Remove the air cleaner assembly.

2. Unfasten the leads from the air control valve solenoid.

3. Disconnect the air hoses from the valve.

4. Loosen the screws which secure the air control valve and remove the valve.

5. Valve installation is performed in the reverse order of removal.

Check Valve

1. Perform the air control valve removal procedure, detailed above. Be sure to pay attention to the CAUTION.

2. Remove the check valve seat.

3. Withdraw the valve plate and spring.

4. Install the check valve in the reverse order of removal.

Air Injection Nozzle

1. Remove the gravel shield from underneath the truck.

2. Perform the oil pan removal procedure as detailed in "Engine Lubrication," above.

3. Unbolt the air injection nozzles from both of the rotor housings.

4. Nozzle installation is performed in the reverse order of removal.

Thermal Reactor

A thermal reactor is used in place of a conventional exhaust manifold. It is used to oxidize unburned hydrocarbons and carbon monoxide before they can be released into the atmosphere.

If the engine speed exceeds 4,000 rpm, or if the truck is decelerating, the air control valve diverts air into passages in the thermal reactor housing in order to cool the reactor.

A one-way valve prevents hot exhaust gases from flowing back into the air injection system. The valve is located at the reactor air intake.

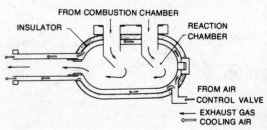

Thermal reactor cooling circuit

INSPECTION

CAUTION: *Perform thermal reactor inspection only after the reactor has cooled sufficiently to prevent the danger of being severely burned.*

1. Examine the reactor housing for cracks or other signs of damage.

2. Remove the air supply hose from the one-way valve. Insert a screwdriver into the valve and test the butterfly for smooth operation. Replace the valve if necessary.

3. If the valve is functioning properly, connect the hose to it.

NOTE: *Remember to check the components of the air injection system which are related to the thermal reactor.*

REMOVAL AND INSTALLATION

Thermal reactor removal and installation are given in the Engine Mechanical section of Chapter 3.

Airflow Control System

The airflow control system consists of a thermosensor, thermodetector, vacuum switch and a control box.

The system determines when the trailing distributor should be used, depending upon engine temperature and speed (rpm). The airflow control system also operates the solenoid on the airflow control valve.

When the engine is cold, the thermosensor sends a signal to the control box which, in turn, activates the distributor. The thermodetector is used to keep the thermosensor from being influenced by ambient temperatures. This ensures easier cold starting and better drivability. The thermosensor and control box are located, in order, beneath the dash, next to the fuse box, and behind the grille.

COMPONENT TESTING

No.1 Thermosensor

ALL MODELS

NOTE: *Begin this test procedure with the engine cold.*

1. Remove the air cleaner.

2. Examine the no.1 thermosensor, which is located next to the thermostat housing, for leakage around the boot and for signs of wax leakage.

3. Disconnect the multiconnector from the thermosensor and place the prods of an ohmmeter on the thermosensor terminals. The ohmmeter should read over 7kΩ with the engine cold and less than 2.3kΩ after the engine has been warmed up.

4. Replace the thermosensor with a new one,

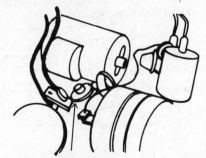

No. 1 thermosensor location

if the reading on the ohmmeter is not within specifications.

5. If the no.1 thermosensor is functioning properly, proceed with the appropriate test for the thermodetector below.

Thermodetector

Use the following chart to determine the correct ohmmeter reading for the ambient temperature at the time of the test:

Thermodetector Resistence Specifications

Ambient Temperature Degrees F	Resistence K[om] [+ −] 5%
[N−]4	10.0
+32	3.0
+68	1.2
+105	0.5

Thermodector location

No.1 Control Box

ALL MODELS

NOTE: *If all of the other components of the airflow control system are functioning properly and the system wiring and vacuum lines are in good condition, then the fault proba-*

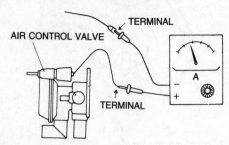

Testing the no. 1 control box

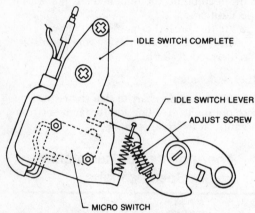

1972 idle switch—the 1973 switch uses a multi-connector

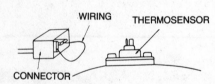

Using a jumper wire, short together the pins of the no. 1 thermosensor

bly lies in the no.1 control box. Perform the following tests to verify this.

1. Disconnect the no.1 thermosensor. Disconnect the idle switch multiconnector.

2. Start the engine and run it to the speeds specified below. The timing light should come on in these speed ranges:

Manual Transmission: 3,600–4,400 rpm
Automatic Transmission: 4,300–5,300 rpm
NOTE: *These speeds should be held for an instant only.*

3. Connect an ammeter to the air control valve solenoid leads and to ground.

 a. Current should flow when the engine speed is between 900–4,000 ± 200 rpm, manual or 5,500–5,200, automatic.

 b. Current flow should cease above 3,600–4,400 rpm, manual transmission or 4,300–5,300 rpm, automatic transmission.

4. Short together the pins of the no.1 thermosensor multiconnector with a jumper wire. Connect the timing light to the trailing side of the distributor, if it is not already in place.

 a. The timing light should go on when the engine is below 3,600–4,400 rpm, automatic, or below 4,300–5,200 rpm, manual.

 b. On automatic transmission equipped models, connect an ammeter to the air control valve solenoid. Current should flow to the solenoid when the engine speed is below 3,400 ± 200 rpm and should cease flowing above this speed.

5. Remove the jumper wire from the multiconnector and reconnect the No. 1 thermosensor. Reconnect the vacuum switch if it was disconnected.

6. Connect the prods of the ammeter to the coasting valve solenoid terminals.

NOTE: *For a further description of coasting valve operation, see Deceleration Control Systems, below.*

7. No current should flow to the solenoid with the engine at idle. Increase the engine speed; current should begin flowing between 1,250 and 1,500 rpm. Decrease engine speed; current should cease flowing between 1,300 and 1,100 rpm (1,400 rpm—automatic transmission). If the no.1 control box proves to be defective, replace it. Remember to disconnect all of the test equipment and reconnect the system components when the tests are completed.

REMOVAL AND INSTALLATION

No.1 Thermosensor

1. Remove the air cleaner assembly.

2. If necessary, remove the starter motor as detailed under Engine Electrical.

3. Unplug the thermosensor multiconnector.

4. Withdraw the boot from the thermosensor.

5. Unfasten its securing nuts and remove the switch.

6. Installation is the reverse of removal.

Control Box

1974–75

CAUTION: *Be sure that the ignition switch is turned off to prevent damage to the control box.*

1. Working from underneath the instrument panel, locate and disconnect the control box multiconnector.

2. Remove the screws which secure the control box.

3. Remove the control box.

4. Installation is performed in the reverse order of removal.

Other Components

Any of the other components used in the air-flow control system are removed by unfastening their multiconnectors and removing the screws which secure them.

GASOLINE FUEL SYSTEM

Electric Fuel Pump

All models, through 1984, use an external electric fuel pump, mounted on the left frame rail adjacent to the fuel tank. Current is supplied to the pump through the ignition circuit and the pump will operate with the key in the RUN position.

TESTING THE FUEL PUMP

To determine that the fuel pump is in good operating condition, test for both volume and pressure should be performed. The tests are performed with the fuel pump installed, and the engine at normal operating temperature and idle speed.

Be sure that the fuel filter has been changed within the specified interval. If in doubt, install a new filter.

Electric fuel pump location

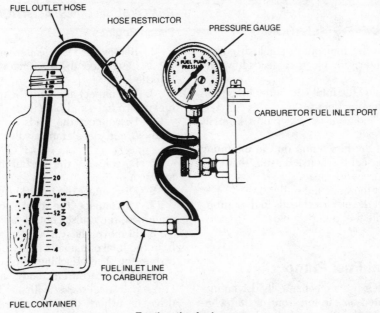

Testing the fuel pump

Pressure Test

1. Remove the air cleaner.
2. Disconnect the fuel inlet line at the carburetor.
3. Connect a pressure gauge, a restrictor and a flexible hose between the fuel filter and the carburetor. Position the flexible hose and restrictor so that the fuel can be discharged into a suitable graduated container.
4. Before taking a pressure reading, operate the engine at idle speed and vent the system into the container by momentarily opening the hose restrictor.
5. Close the hose restrictor and allow the pressure to stabilize and note the reading. It should be 2.8–3.6 psi or 3.6–5.0 psi on the Rotary Pick-Up.
6. If the pump pressure is not within specifications, and the fuel filter and fuel lines are not blocked, the pump is malfunctioning and should be replaced.
7. If the pressure is within specifications, perform the volume test.

Volume Test

1. Open the hose restrictor and expel the fuel into the container, while observing the time required to discharge 1 pint. Close the restrictor. Fuel pump volume should be approximately 2 pints/minute or 1.2 quarts/minutes on the Rotary Pick-Up.
2. If the pump volume is below specifications, repeat the test using an auxiliary fuel supply and a new filter. If the pump volume meets specifications while using an auxiliary fuel supply, check for a restriction in the fuel lines.

REMOVAL AND INSTALLATION

1. Remove the fuel pump shield from the frame. Disconnect the electrical leads from the pump.
2. Disconnect the inlet and outlet lines from the pump. Plug the lines.
3. Unbolt and remove the pump from its mounting bracket.
4. Position the fuel pump on the mounting bracket and install the bolts. Be sure that both mounting surfaces are clean.
5. Connect the inlet and outlet hoses.
6. Connect the electrical leads to the pump.
7. Install the fuel pump shield.

Mechanical Fuel Pump

All 1986 models use a mechanically driven fuel pump, mounted on the left front of the cylinder head, driven by the camshaft.

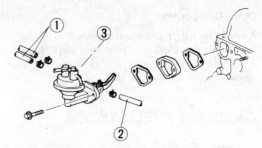

Mechanical fuel pump mounting

PRESSURE TEST

1. Disconnect the pump-to-carburetor hose at the carburetor. Connect a pressure gauge.
2. Disconnect the fuel return hose from the pump and plug the pump return and the return port on the carburetor.
3. Run the engine at idle and check the pressure. Pressure should be 3.9–4.4 psi. If not, replace the pump.

REMOVAL AND INSTALLATION

1. Disconnect the outlet, inlet and return hoses at the pump.
2. Unbolt and remove the pump and insulator. Discard the gaskets.
3. Installation is the reverse of removal. Use new gaskets coated with sealer.

Carburetor

The Mazda Rotary Pick-Up uses a 4-barrel downdraft carburetor, while the piston engines use 2-barrel downdraft units.

REMOVAL AND INSTALLATION

Piston Engines

1. Remove the air cleaner and duct.
2. Disconnect the accelerator shaft from the throttle lever.
3. Disconnect and plug the fuel supply and fuel return lines and plug these.
4. Disconnect the leads from the throttle solenoid and deceleration valve at the quick-disconnects.
5. Disconnect the carburetor-to-distributor vacuum line.
6. Disconnect the throttle return spring.
7. Disconnect the choke cable, and, if equipped, the cruise control cable.
8. Remove the carburetor attaching nuts from the intake manifold studs and remove the carburetor. The attaching nuts are tucked underneath the carburetor body and are difficult to reach; a small socket with an "L" shaped hex drive, or a short, thin wrench sold for work on ignition systems will make removal easier.

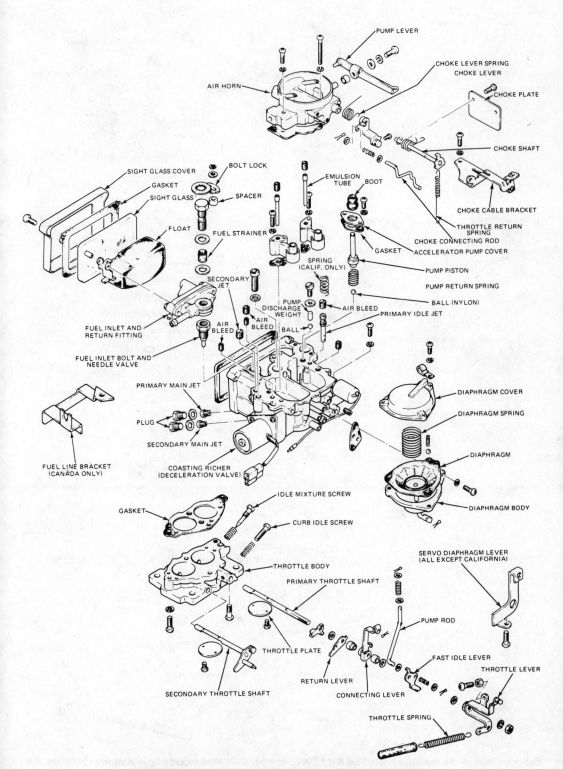

Exploded view of the carburetor used on the 1,586cc engine

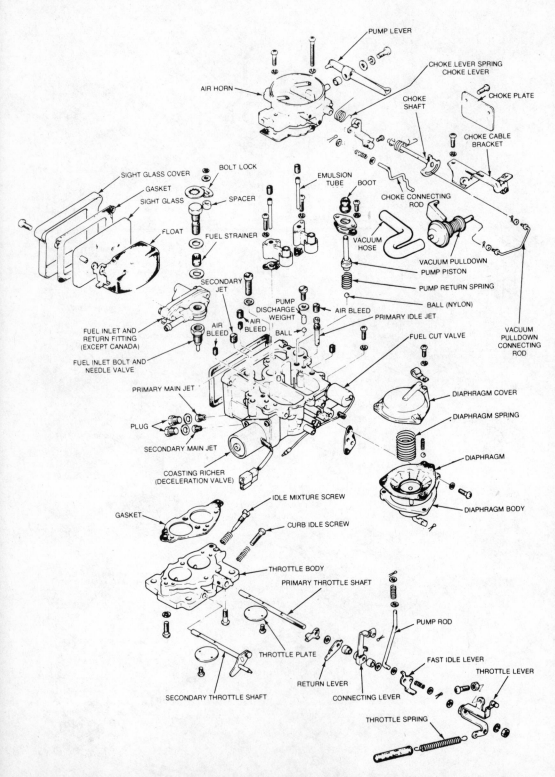

Exploded view of the carburetor used on the 1,796cc engine. California models have a spring above the primary idle jet air bleed

9. Install a new carburetor gasket on the manifold.

10. Install the carburetor and tighten the carburetor attaching nuts.

11. Connect the throttle return spring.

12. Connect the accelerator shaft to the throttle shaft.

13. Connect the electrical leads to the throttle solenoid and deceleration valve.

14. Connect the distributor vacuum line.

15. Connect the fuel supply and fuel return lines.

16. Connect and adjust the choke cable and, if equipped, the cruise control cable.

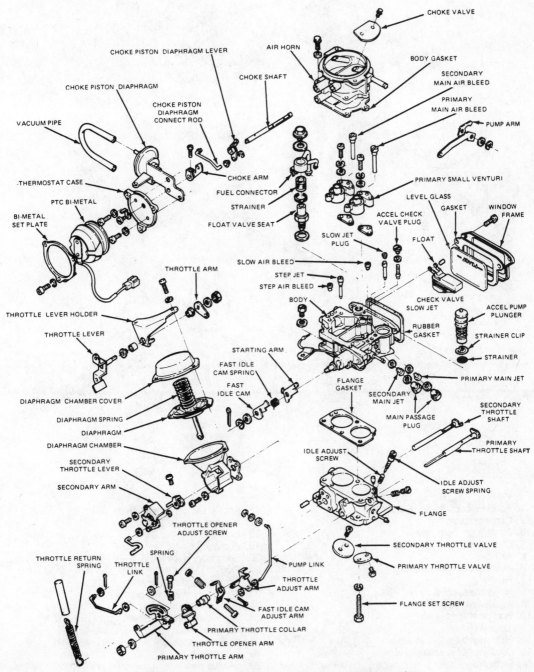

Exploded view of the carburetor used on the 1,970cc engine

17. Install the air cleaner and duct.

18. Start the engine and check for fuel leaks.

Rotary Engine

1. Remove the air cleaner assembly, complete with its hoses and mounting bracket.

2. Detach the choke and accelerator cables from the carburetor.

3. Disconnect the fuel and vacuum lines from the carburetor.

4. Remove the oil line which runs to the metering oil pump, at the carburetor.

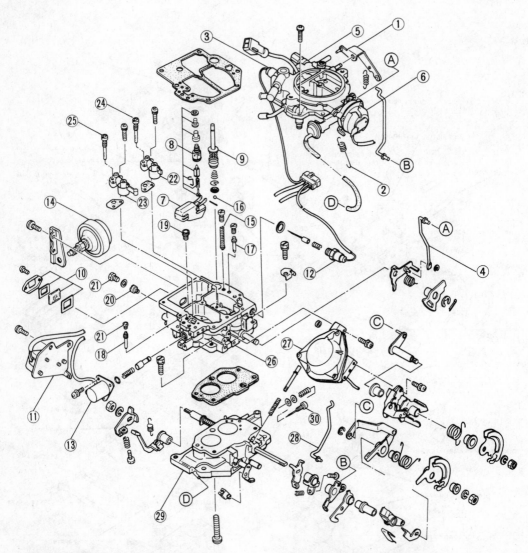

1. Accelerator pump connecting rod
2. Connect spring
3. Air vent solenoid valve
4. Choke rod
5. Air horn
6. Automatic choke assembly
7. Float
8. Needle valve assembly
9. Accelerator pump
10. Fuel bowl sight glass
11. Idle switch
12. Slow fuel cut solenoid valve
13. Coasting richer solenoid valve
14. Dash pot
15. Accelerator pump outlet check ball
16. Accelerator pump inlet check ball
17. Slow jet
18. Step jet
19. Primary main jet
20. Secondary main jet
21. Plug
22. Primary ventury & nozzle
23. Secondary ventury & nozzle
24. Primary main air bleed
25. Secondary main air bleed
26. Main body
27. Vacuum diaphragm
28. Throttle link
29. Throttle body
30. Mixture adjusting screw

Exploded view of the carburetor used on the 1,998cc engine

5. Unfasten the idle sensor switch wiring, if so equipped.

6. Remove the carburetor attaching nuts and/or bolts, gasket or heat insulator, and remove the carburetor.

7. Installation is performed in the reverse order of removal. Use a new gasket. Fill the float bowl with gasoline to aid in engine starting.

OVERHAUL

The following instructions are general overhaul procedures. Most good carburetor rebuilding kits come replete with exploded views and specific instructions.

Efficient carburetion depends greatly on careful cleaning and inspection during overhaul, since dirt, gum, water, or varnish in or on the carburetor parts are often responsible for poor performance.

Overhaul your carburetor in a clean, dust-free area. Carefully disassemble the carburetor, referring often to the exploded views. Keep all similar and look alike parts segregated during disassembly and cleaning to avoid accidental interchange during assembly. Make a note of all jet sizes.

When the carburetor is disassembled, wash all parts (except diaphragms, electric choke units, pump plunger, and any other plastic, leather, fiber or rubber parts) in clean carburetor solvent. Do not leave parts in the solvent any longer than is necessary to sufficiently loosen the deposits. Excessive cleaning may remove the special finish from the float bowl and choke valve bodies, leaving these parts unfit for service. Rinse all parts in clean solvent and blow them dry with compressed air or allow them to air dry. Wipe clean all cork, plastic, leather, and fiber parts with a clean, lint-free cloth.

Blow out all passages and jets with compressed air and be sure that there are no restrictions or blockages. Never use wire or similar tools to clean jets, fuel passages, or air bleeds. Clean all jets and valves separately to avoid accidental interchange.

Check all parts for wear or damage. If wear or damage is found, replace the defective parts. Especially check the following:

1. Check the float needle and seat for wear. If wear is found, replace the complete assembly.

2. Check the float hinge pin for wear and the float(s) for dents or distortion. Replace the float if fuel has leaked into it.

3. Check the throttle and choke shaft bores for wear or an out-of-round condition. Damage or wear to the throttle arm, shaft, or shaft bore will often require replacement of the throttle body. These parts require a close tolerance of fit; wear may allow air leakage, which could affect starting and idling.

NOTE: *Throttle shafts and bushings are not included in overhaul kits. They can be purchased separately.*

4. Inspect the idle moisture adjusting needles for burrs or grooves. Any such condition requires replacement of the needle, since you will not be able to obtain a satisfactory idle.

5. Test the accelerator pump check valves. They should pass air one way but not the other. Test for proper seating by blowing and sucking on the valve. Replace the valve if necessary. If the valve is satisfactory, wash the valve again to remove breath moisture.

6. Check the bowl cover for warped surfaces with a straightedge.

7. Closely inspect the valves and seats for wear or damage, replacing as necessary.

8. After the carburetor is assembled, check the choke valve for freedom of operation.

Carburetor overhaul kits are recommended for each overhaul. These kits contain all gaskets and new parts to replace those that deteriorate most rapidly. Failure to replace all parts supplied with the kit (especially gaskets) can result in poor performance later.

Some carburetor manufacturers supply overhaul kits of three basic types: minor repair, major repair, and gasket kits. Basically, they contain the following:

Minor Repair Kits:
- All gaskets
- Float needle valve
- Volume control screw
- All diaphragms
- Spring for the pump diaphragm

Major Repair Kits:
- All jets and gaskets
- All diaphragms
- Float needle valve
- Volume control screw
- Pump ball valve
- Main jet carrier
- Float
- Complete intermediate rod
- Intermediate pump lever
- Complete injector tube
- Some cover hold-down screws and washers

Gasket Kits:
- All gaskets

After cleaning and checking all components, reassemble the carburetor, using new parts and referring to the exploded view. When reassembling, make sure that all screws and jets are tight in their seats, but do not overtighten as the tips will be distorted. Tighten all screws gradually, in rotation. Do not tighten needle valves into their seats; uneven jetting will re-

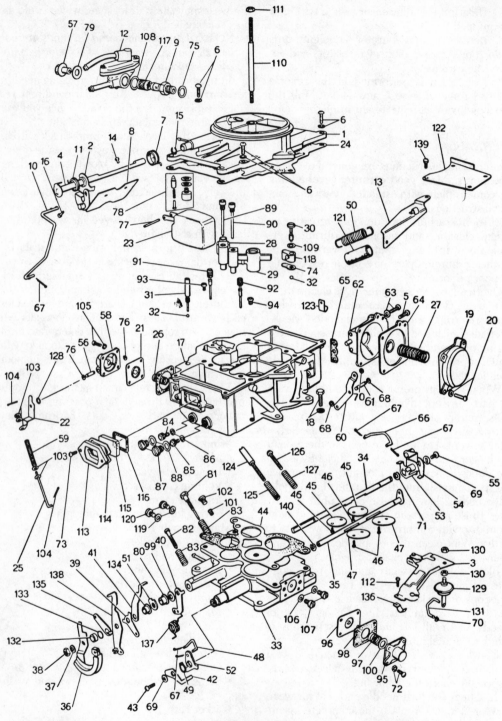

1. Air horn	11. Spring	21. Diaphragm
2. Choke valve lever	12. Fuel return valve	22. Accelerator pump arm
3. Clip	13. Hanger	23. Float
4. Choke lever shaft	14. Screw	24. Gasket
5. Screw	15. Ring	25. Connecting rod
6. Setscrew	16. Bolt	26. Spring
7. Spring	17. Carburetor body	27. Spring
8. Choke valve	18. Bolt	28. Small venturi
9. Connector	19. Diaphragm cover	29. Small venturi
10. Connecting rod	20. Screw	30. Bolt

sult. Always use new gaskets. Be sure to adjust the float lever when reassembling.

FLOAT AND FUEL LEVEL ADJUSTMENT

1,586cc, 1,796cc and 1,970cc Engines

1. With the engine running, check the fuel level in the sight glass (in the fuel bowl).

2. If the fuel level is not at the specified mark on the sight glass, remove the carburetor from the truck.

3. Remove the fuel bowl cover.

4. Invert the carburetor and lower the float until the tang on the float just contacts the needle valve.

5. Measure the clearance between the float and the edge of the bowl. Clearance should be:

1,586cc—0.0256 in.
1,796cc—0.0236 in.
1,970cc—0.0335 in.

6. If the clearance is not as specified, bend the float seal lip until the proper clearance is obtained.

7. Turn the carburetor right side up and

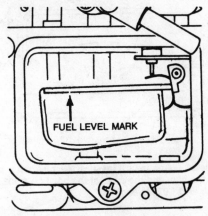

Fuel level mark on the sight glass of 1,586cc, 1,796cc and 1,970cc engines

measure the clearance between the bottom of the float and the bowl. Clearance should be:

1,586cc and 1,796cc — 0.047 in.
1,970cc — 0.039 in.

8. If not, bend the float stopper until the correct clearance is obtained.

31. Check ball plug	68. Ring	105. Screw
32. Steel ball	69. Washer	106. Gasket
33. Flange	70. Diaphragm stop ring	107. Plug
34. Throttle shaft	71. Diaphragm stop ring	108. Gasket
35. Throttle shaft	72. Screw	109. Gasket
36. Throttle lever	73. Level gauge screw	110. Bolt
37. Spring washer	74. Gasket	111. Nut
38. Nut	75. Gasket	112. Screw
39. Lock	76. Stop ring	113. Cover
40. Adjusting arm	77. Float pin	114. Gasket
41. Starting lever	78. Needle valve seat	115. Sight glass
42. Arm	79. Gasket	116. Gasket
43. Screw	80. Collar	117. Filter
44. Gasket	81. Throttle adjusting screw	118. Accelerator nozzle
45. Valve	82. Idle adjusting screw	119. Gasket
46. Screw	83. Spring	120. Plug
47. Throttle valve	84. Main jet	121. Cover
48. Throttle lever link	85. Main jet	122. Coasting valve bracket
49. Ring	86. Gasket	123. Clip
50. Throttle return spring	87. Plug	124. Screw
51. Arm	88. Gasket	125. Spring
52. Retainer	89. Air bleed	126. Screw
53. Metering pump lever	90. Air bleed	127. Spring
54. Metering pump arm	91. Slow jet	128. Shim
55. Screw	92. Step jet	129. Throttle positioner
56. Pin	93. Air bleed screw	130. Nut
57. Union bolt	94. Air bleed step	131. Rod
58. Cover	95. Cover	132. Collar
59. Diaphragm spring	96. Diaphragm	133. Shim
60. Diaphragm lever	97. Spring	134. Collar
61. Diaphragm pin	98. Gasket	135. Arm
62. Diaphragm chamber	99. Washer	136. Plate
63. Screw	100. Shim	137. Retaining spring
64. Diaphragm	101. Jet	138. Lever
65. Gasket	102. Bleed plug	139. Setscrew
66. Connecting rod	103. Retainer	140. Ring
67. Pin	104. Pin	

Exploded view of the carburetor used on the rotary engine

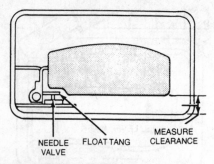

Float level adjustment. Measure the clearance between the float and the edge of the bowl on 1,586cc, 1,796cc and 1,970cc engines

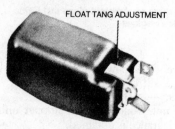

Bend the tang to adjust the float level

9. Install the fuel bowl cover.
10. Reinstall the carburetor on the truck.
11. Recheck the fuel level at the sight glass.

1,998cc

1. Remove the air horn from the carburetor.
2. Turn the air horn upside down on a level surface. Allow the float to hang under its own weight.
3. Measure the clearance between the float and the air horn gasket surface. The gap should be 11.5–12.5mm. If not, bend the float seat lip to obtain the correct gap.
4. Turn the air horn right side up and allow the float to hang under its own weight.
5. Measure the gap between the BOTTOM of the float and the air horn gasket surface. The

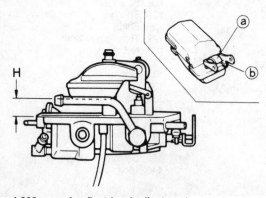

1,998cc engine float level adjustment

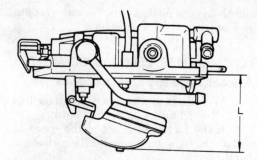

1,998cc engine float drop adjustment

gap should be 46.0–47.0mm. If not, bend the float stopper until it is.

FLOAT LEVEL ADJUSTMENT

Rotary Engine

1. With the engine running, check the fuel level in the sight glass, using a mirror.
2. If the fuel levels are not within the specified marks on the sight glass, remove the air horn with the floats.
3. Invert the air horn and let the float hang so that it just contacts the needle valve.
4. Measure the clearance between the float and the air horn gasket, which should be 0.043 in. Bend the float seat lip to adjust the clearance if necessary.
5. Install the air horn and recheck the fuel levels in the sight glass.

Checking the fuel level in the sight glass on the rotary engine

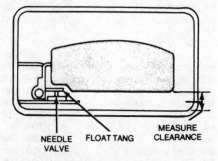

Checking the float level with the air horn removed, on the rotary engine

FLOAT DROP

Rotary Engine

1. Remove the air horn with the floats and allow the floats to hang free.

2. Measure the clearance between the bottom of the float and the air horn gasket. The clearance should be 2.03–2.07 in.

3. If not, adjust the distance by bending the float stopper.

4. Install the air horn and recheck the fuel level in the sight glass.

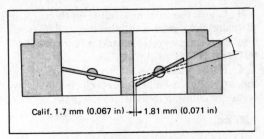

Calif. 1.7 mm (0.067 in) → 1.81 mm (0.071 in)

Fast idle adjustment points for 1,796cc engine carburetors. Bend the link at the point indicated by the arrow

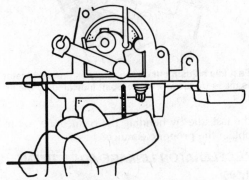

Checking the float drop on the rotary engine

1,796cc

1. Remove the air cleaner.

2. With the choke plate fully closed, measure the clearance between the primary throttle plate and the wall of the throttle bore. The clearance should measure 0.063–0.067 in. through 1976, and 0.071 in 1977–78, or 0.967 in for 1977–78 California models.

3. If the clearance is not as specified, bend the fast idle lever where it contacts the throttle lever tang until the proper clearance is obtained.

4. Install the air cleaner.

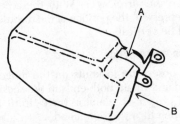

On the rotary engine, adjust the float drop at the float stopper, B, and the float level seat lip, A

1,970cc

1. Close the choke fully.

2. Place the fast idle adjusting screw on the first step of the fast idle cam.

FAST IDLE

1,586cc

The fast idle can be adjusted by turning the fast idle adjusting screw. Check the choke plate for free operation.

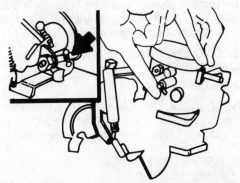

1,586cc engine fast idle adjusting screw location, (arrow)

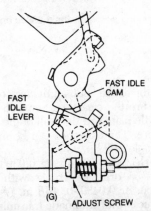

Fast idle adjustment for the 1,970cc carburetor

3. Check the clearance between the throttle plate and the inside of the throttle wall (G) with a wire feeler gauge. It should measure 0.051–0.059 in.

4. If the clearance is incorrect, adjust by means of the fast idle screw, clockwise to increase or counterclockwise to decrease.

1,998cc

1. Set the fast idle cam so that the fast idle lever rests on the second step of the cam.

2. Adjust the clearance between the air horn wall and the lower edge of the throttle plates, (G) by turning the fast idle adjusting screw. Clearance should be 0.75–1.13mm.

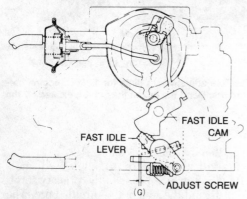

Fast idle adjustment for the 1,998cc carburetor

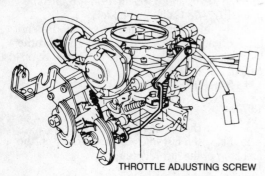

THROTTLE ADJUSTING SCREW

Throttle adjusting screw on the 1,998cc engine carburetor

Rotary Engine

1. Pull the choke knob all the way out.

2. Measure the clearance between the primary throttle plate and the wall of the primary throttle bore. The clearance can be measured with a suitable drill bit.

3. The clearance should be 0.0398–0.0524 in. (#61–#55 drill) for trucks with manual transmission, or 0.0480–0.0618 in. (#55–#53 drill) for trucks with automatic transmission.

4. If the clearance is not as specified, adjust

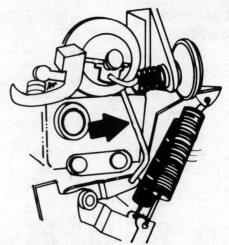

Fast idle adjustment on the rotary engine carburetor is made by the link at the point indicated by the arrow

the fast idle by bending the connecting rod to obtain the proper clearance.

ACCELERATOR LINKAGE ADJUSTMENT

1,586cc

Inspect the throttle linkage for free operation. Remove the air cleaner. With the accelerator fully depressed, the position of the throttle plates should be vertical.

1,796cc and 1,970cc

1. Loosen the locknuts on the longer linkage rod and rotate both ends in the sockets until the proper accelerator travel from idle to wide-open throttle is obtained.

2. Tighten the locknuts to set the adjustment.

1,998cc

1. Check the cable deflection at the carburetor. Deflection should be 1.0–3.0mm. If not, adjust it by turning the adjusting nut at the bracket near the carburetor.

2. Depress the accelerator pedal to the floor. The throttle plates should be vertical. If not, adjust their position by turning the adjusting nut on the accelerator pedal bracket.

SECONDARY THROTTLE VALVE ADJUSTMENT

All Models

The clearance between the primary throttle valve and the air horn wall, when the secondary throttle valve just starts to open should be:

- 1,586cc: 0.199–0.222 in.
- 1,796cc: 0.186–0.209 in.
- 1,970cc: 0.256 ± 0.015 in.
- 1,998cc: 0.289–0.325 in.

If not, bend the fast idle link (1972–84) or the tab B (1986, illustrated).

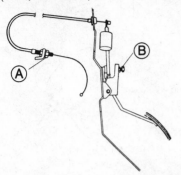

Throttle cable adjustment points for the 1,998cc engine

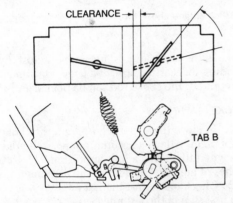

Bend the tab, B, to adjust the secondary throttle valve on 1986 models

VACUUM PULLDOWN ADJUSTMENT

1976–78 Only

1. On California Mazdas, unplug the electrical connectors from the water thermo switch

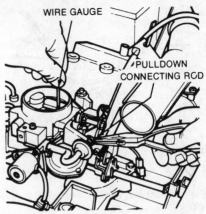

Vacuum pulldown adjustment

and connect a jumper wire between the connectors. Turn the ignition switch on.

2. Pull the choke knob out to fully close the choke.

3. Disconnect the vacuum source to the pulldown diaphragm.

4. Connect an external vacuum source to the pulldown diaphragm. Gradually apply vacuum. The pulldown should start to operate (open the choke) at 5.9–7.5 in. Hg.

5. Increase the vacuum to 9.8–12.0 in. Hg. Check the clearance between the carburetor air horn wall and the choke plate using a wire gauge. The clearance should measure 0.06–0.08 in. 1976, 0.066–0.075 in. all 1977–78

6. Adjust the clearance if necessary by bending the pulldown connecting rod.

CHOKE ADJUSTMENT

1,586cc and 1,796cc Engines

1. Push the choke knob all the way in.
2. Loosen the choke cable attaching screws

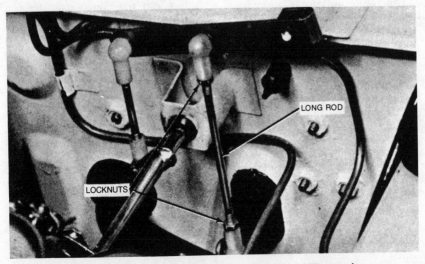

Throttle linkage adjustment on the 1,796cc and 1,970cc engine

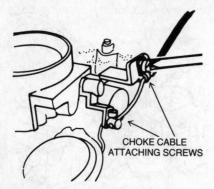

Choke adjustment for 1,586cc and 1,796cc engine carburetors

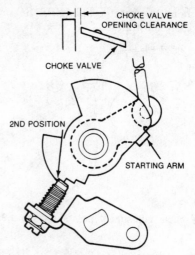

1,970cc engine choke throttle valve opening adjustment

at the choke lever and the choke cable bracket.

3. Be sure that the choke plate is fully open.

4. Insert the choke cable into the choke lever. Tighten the attaching screw.

5. Pull the cable outward to remove all slack between the choke lever and choke cable bracket and tighten the attaching screw at the choke cable bracket.

6. Operate the choke to be sure that there is no binding and that is is operating properly.

1,970cc Engine

There are four adjustments to be made to the choke in these years; choke/throttle valve opening adjustment; choke diaphragm adjustment; choke unloader adjustment; and choke thermostat (bi-metal) adjustment.

CHOKE/THROTTLE VALVE OPENING ANGLE

1. Adjust the fast idle cam as previously outlined before making this adjustment.

2. Place the fast idle screw on the second step of the fast idle cam.

3. Measure the clearance between the edge of the choke plate and the throttle bore with a wire gauge. Clearance should be 0.016–0.028 in.

4. If the clearance is incorrect, adjust by bending the starting arm. If a large adjustment is required, the choke rod can be bent slightly.

CHOKE DIAPHRAGM

1. Remove the vacuum hose from the choke diaphragm. Attach a vacuum pump to the diaphragm fitting and apply approximately 15.6 inches of mercury vacuum to the diaphragm.

2. Check to see that the fast idle screw is on the first step of the fast idle cam.

3. Press on the choke plate slightly to settle it. Measure the clearance between the edge of the choke plate an the throttle bore. Clearance should be 0.047–0.067 in.

4. If the clearance is incorrect, adjust by bending the choke lever.

CHOKE UNLOADER

1. Close the choke plate fully. Open the throttle plate fully.

2. Measure the clearance between the edge

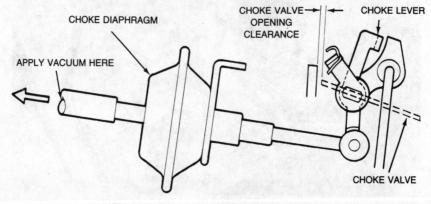

1,970cc engine choke diaphragm adjustment

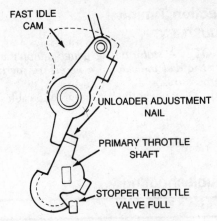

FAST IDLE CAM

UNLOADER ADJUSTMENT NAIL

PRIMARY THROTTLE SHAFT

STOPPER THROTTLE VALVE FULL

1,970cc engine choke unloader adjustment

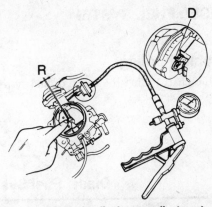

1,998cc engine choke diaphragm adjustment

of the choke plate and the throttle bore with a wire gauge. Clearance should be 0.079–0.099 in.

3. If the clearance is incorrect, bend the choke unloader adjusting nail (tang).

THERMOSTAT

1. The index mark on the thermostat cover should be aligned with the center mark on the choke housing.

2. Adjust by loosening the thermostat cover retaining screws slightly and shifting the position of the cover. Tighten the screws after adjustment.

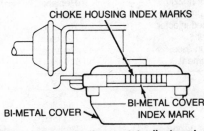

CHOKE HOUSING INDEX MARKS

BI-METAL COVER INDEX MARK

BI-METAL COVER

1,970cc engine choke thermostat adjustment

1,998cc Engine

Three choke related adjustments are performed on these units.

CHOKE DIAPHRAGM

1. Disconnect the vacuum line from the choke diaphragm unit.

2. Using a vacuum pump, apply 15.7 inHg to the diaphragm.

3. Using light finger pressure, close the choke valve. Check the clearance at the upper edge of the choke valve. Clearance should be 0.066–0.084 in.

4. If not, bend the tab on the choke lever to adjust it.

CHOKE VALVE CLEARANCE

1. Position the fast idle lever on the second step of the fast idle cam.

2. The leading edge of the choke valve should be 0.60–1.0mm from fully closed. If not, bend either the tab on the cam or the choke rod to adjust. The tab will give smaller adjustment increments.

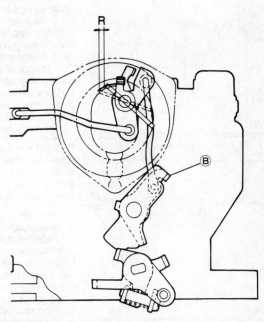

1,998cc engine choke valve clearance adjustment

CHOKE UNLOADER

1. Open the primary throttle valve all the way and hold it in this position.

2. The leading edge of the choke valve should be 2.74–3.60mm from fully closed. If not, bend the tab on the throttle lever.

DIESEL FUEL SYSTEM

Troubleshooting

Use the chart to find the cause of fuel system related problems:

Injection Timing
ADJUSTMENT

NOTE: *A static timing gauge adapter and metric dial indicator are necessary for this procedure.*

1. Disconnect the battery ground cables.

Diesel Fuel System Troubleshooting

Problem	Possible Causes	Remedy
Hard Starting	Clogged fuel filter	Replace
	Water or air in the fuel filter	Replace
	Faulty fuel cut-off solenoid	Replace
	Incorrect injection timing	Adjust
	Air in the injection pump	Repair
	Incorrect stop lever position	Adjust
	Mechanical problems in the injection pump	Replace
	Seized injector needle valve	Replace
	Fuel leakage at the injector nozzle	Replace
	Incorrect injector opening pressure	Repair
	Bad glow plug	Replace
Rough Idle	Clogged fuel filter	Replace
	Water or air in the fuel filter	Replace
	Faulty fuel cut-off solenoid	Replace
	Incorrect injection timing	Adjust
	Air in the injection pump	Repair
	Incorrect stop lever position	Adjust
	Mechanical problems in the injection pump	Replace
	Seized injector needle valve	Replace
	Fuel leakage at the injector nozzle	Replace
	Incorrect injector opening pressure	Repair
	Loose or incorrectly installed injector	Replace
	Bad injector copper washer	Replace
	Cracked or leaking injection lines	Replace
	Incorrect idle speed adjustment	Adjust
Engine Knock	Incorrect injection timing	Adjust
	Poor quality fuel	Replace
	Incorrect injector opening pressure	Repair
	Seized injector needle valve	Replace
	Fuel leakage at the injector nozzle	Replace
High Fuel Consumption	Incorrect idle speed adjustment	Adjust
	Incorrect injection timing	Adjust
	Fuel leakage at the injector nozzle	Replace
	Incorrect injector opening pressure	Repair
	Loose or incorrectly installed injector	Replace
	Bad injector copper washer	Replace
	Cracked or leaking injection lines	Replace
	Clogged fuel filter	Replace
	Clogged air cleaner	Replace
Poor Acceleration	Clogged air cleaner	Replace
	Seized injector needle valve	Replace
	Fuel leakage at the injector nozzle	Replace
	Faulty fuel cut-off solenoid	Replace
	Incorrect injection timing	Adjust
	Air in the injection pump	Repair
	Incorrect stop lever position	Adjust
	Mechanical problems in the injection pump	Replace
	Cracked or leaking injection lines	Replace
	Water or air in the fuel filter	Replace

55 WAYS TO IMPROVE FUEL ECONOMY

CHILTON'S
FUEL ECONOMY
& TUNE-UP TIPS

Tune-up • Spark Plug Diagnosis • Emission Controls

Fuel System • Cooling System • Tires and Wheels

General Maintenance

CHILTON'S FUEL ECONOMY & TUNE-UP TIPS

Fuel economy is important to everyone, no matter what kind of vehicle you drive. The maintenance-minded motorist can save both money and fuel using these tips and the periodic maintenance and tune-up procedures in this Repair and Tune-Up Guide.

There are more than 130,000,000 cars and trucks registered for private use in the United States. Each travels an average of 10-12,000 miles per year, and, and in total they consume close to 70 billion gallons of fuel each year. This represents nearly ⅔ of the oil imported by the United States each year. The Federal government's goal is to reduce consumption 10% by 1985. A variety of methods are either already in use or under serious consideration, and they all affect you driving and the cars you will drive. In addition to "down-sizing", the auto industry is using or investigating the use of electronic fuel delivery, electronic engine controls and alternative engines for use in smaller and lighter vehicles, among other alternatives to meet the federally mandated Corporate Average Fuel Economy (CAFE) of 27.5 mpg by 1985. The government, for its part, is considering rationing, mandatory driving curtailments and tax increases on motor vehicle fuel in an effort to reduce consumption. The government's goal of a 10% reduction could be realized — and further government regulation avoided — if every private vehicle could use just 1 less gallon of fuel per week.

How Much Can You Save?

Tests have proven that almost anyone can make at least a 10% reduction in fuel consumption through regular maintenance and tune-ups. When a major manufacturer of spark plugs sur-

TUNE-UP

1. Check the cylinder compression to be sure the engine will really benefit from a tune-up and that it is capable of producing good fuel economy. A tune-up will be wasted on an engine in poor mechanical condition.

2. Replace spark plugs regularly. New spark plugs alone can increase fuel economy 3%.

3. Be sure the spark plugs are the correct type (heat range) for your vehicle. See the Tune-Up Specifications.

Heat range refers to the spark plug's ability to conduct heat away from the firing end. It must conduct the heat away in an even pattern to avoid becoming a source of pre-ignition, yet it must also operate hot enough to burn off conductive deposits that could cause misfiring.

The heat range is usually indicated by a number on the spark plug, part of the manufacturer's designation for each individual spark plug. The numbers in bold-face indicate the heat range in each manufacturer's identification system.

Periodically, check the spark plugs to be sure they are firing efficiently. They are excellent indicators of the internal condition of your engine.

Manufacturer	Typical Designation
AC	R **45** TS
Bosch (old)	WA **145** T30
Bosch (new)	HR **8** Y
Champion	RBL **15** Y
Fram/Autolite	4**15**
Mopar	P-**62** PR
Motorcraft	BRF-**42**
NGK	BP **5** ES-15
Nippondenso	W **16** EP
Prestolite	14GR **5** 2A

On AC, Bosch (new), Champion, Fram/Autolite, Mopar, Motorcraft and Prestolite, a higher number indicates a hotter plug. On Bosch (old), NGK and Nippondenso, a higher number indicates a colder plug.

4. Make sure the spark plugs are properly gapped. See the Tune-Up Specifications in this book.

5. Be sure the spark plugs are firing efficiently. The illustrations on the next 2 pages show you how to "read" the firing end of the spark plug.

6. Check the ignition timing and set it to specifications. Tests show that almost all cars have incorrect ignition timing by more than 2°.

veyed over 6,000 cars nationwide, they found that a tune-up, on cars that needed one, increased fuel economy over 11%. Replacing worn plugs alone, accounted for a 3% increase. The same test also revealed that 8 out of every 10 vehicles will have some maintenance deficiency that will directly affect fuel economy, emissions or performance. Most of this mileage-robbing neglect could be prevented with regular maintenance.

Modern engines require that all of the functioning systems operate properly for maximum efficiency. A malfunction anywhere wastes fuel. You can keep your vehicle running as efficiently and economically as possible, by being aware of your vehicle's operating and performance characteristics. If your vehicle suddenly develops performance or fuel economy problems it could be due to one or more of the following:

PROBLEM	POSSIBLE CAUSE
Engine Idles Rough	Ignition timing, idle mixture, vacuum leak or something amiss in the emission control system.
Hesitates on Acceleration	Dirty carburetor or fuel filter, improper accelerator pump setting, ignition timing or fouled spark plugs.
Starts Hard or Fails to Start	Worn spark plugs, improperly set automatic choke, ice (or water) in fuel system.
Stalls Frequently	Automatic choke improperly adjusted and possible dirty air filter or fuel filter.
Performs Sluggishly	Worn spark plugs, dirty fuel or air filter, ignition timing or automatic choke out of adjustment.

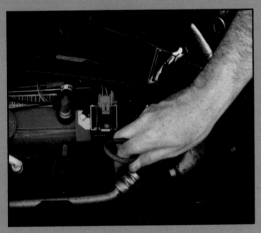

Check spark plug wires on conventional point type ignition for cracks by bending them in a loop around your finger.

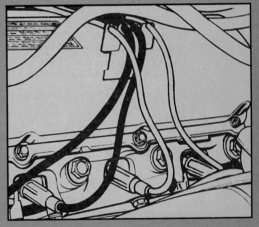

Be sure that spark plug wires leading to adjacent cylinders do not run too close together. (Photo courtesy Champion Spark Plug Co.)

7. If your vehicle does not have electronic ignition, check the points, rotor and cap as specified.

8. Check the spark plug wires (used with conventional point-type ignitions) for cracks and burned or broken insulation by bending them in a loop around your finger. Cracked wires decrease fuel efficiency by failing to deliver full voltage to the spark plugs. One misfiring spark plug can cost you as much as 2 mpg.

9. Check the routing of the plug wires. Misfiring can be the result of spark plug leads to adjacent cylinders running parallel to each other and too close together. One wire tends to pick up voltage from the other causing it to fire "out of time".

10. Check all electrical and ignition circuits for voltage drop and resistance.

11. Check the distributor mechanical and/or vacuum advance mechanisms for proper functioning. The vacuum advance can be checked by twisting the distributor plate in the opposite direction of rotation. It should spring back when released.

12. Check and adjust the valve clearance on engines with mechanical lifters. The clearance should be slightly loose rather than too tight.

SPARK PLUG DIAGNOSIS

Normal

APPEARANCE: This plug is typical of one operating normally. The insulator nose varies from a light tan to grayish color with slight electrode wear. The presence of slight deposits is normal on used plugs and will have no adverse effect on engine performance. The spark plug heat range is correct for the engine and the engine is running normally.

CAUSE: Properly running engine.

RECOMMENDATION: Before reinstalling this plug, the electrodes should be cleaned and filed square. Set the gap to specifications. If the plug has been in service for more than 10-12,000 miles, the entire set should probably be replaced with a fresh set of the same heat range.

Oil Deposits

APPEARANCE: The firing end of the plug is covered with a wet, oily coating.

CAUSE: The problem is poor oil control. On high mileage engines, oil is leaking past the rings or valve guides into the combustion chamber. A common cause is also a plugged PCV valve, and a ruptured fuel pump diaphragm can also cause this condition. Oil fouled plugs such as these are often found in new or recently overhauled engines, before normal oil control is achieved, and can be cleaned and reinstalled.

RECOMMENDATION: A hotter spark plug may temporarily relieve the problem, but the engine is probably in need of work.

Incorrect Heat Range

APPEARANCE: The effects of high temperature on a spark plug are indicated by clean white, often blistered insulator. This can also be accompanied by excessive wear of the electrode, and the absence of deposits.

CAUSE: Check for the correct spark plug heat range. A plug which is too hot for the engine can result in overheating. A car operated mostly at high speeds can require a colder plug. Also check ignition timing, cooling system level, fuel mixture and leaking intake manifold.

RECOMMENDATION: If all ignition and engine adjustments are known to be correct, and no other malfunction exists, install spark plugs one heat range colder.

Carbon Deposits

APPEARANCE: Carbon fouling is easily identified by the presence of dry, soft, black, sooty deposits.

CAUSE: Changing the heat range can often lead to carbon fouling, as can prolonged slow, stop-and-start driving. If the heat range is correct, carbon fouling can be attributed to a rich fuel mixture, sticking choke, clogged air cleaner, worn breaker points, retarded timing or low compression. If only one or two plugs are carbon fouled, check for corroded or cracked wires on the affected plugs. Also look for cracks in the distributor cap between the towers of affected cylinders.

RECOMMENDATION: After the problem is corrected, these plugs can be cleaned and reinstalled if not worn severely.

Photos Courtesy Fram Corporation

MMT Fouled

APPEARANCE: Spark plugs fouled by MMT (Methycyclopentadienyl Maganese Tricarbonyl) have reddish, rusty appearance on the insulator and side electrode.

CAUSE: MMT is an anti-knock additive in gasoline used to replace lead. During the combustion process, the MMT leaves a reddish deposit on the insulator and side electrode.

RECOMMENDATION: No engine malfunction is indicated and the deposits will not affect plug performance any more than lead deposits (see Ash Deposits). MMT fouled plugs can be cleaned, regapped and reinstalled.

High Speed Glazing

APPEARANCE: Glazing appears as shiny coating on the plug, either yellow or tan in color.

CAUSE: During hard, fast acceleration, plug temperatures rise suddenly. Deposits from normal combustion have no chance to fluff-off; instead, they melt on the insulator forming an electrically conductive coating which causes misfiring.

RECOMMENDATION: Glazed plugs are not easily cleaned. They should be replaced with a fresh set of plugs of the correct heat range. If the condition recurs, using plugs with a heat range one step colder may cure the problem.

Ash (Lead) Deposits

APPEARANCE: Ash deposits are characterized by light brown or white colored deposits crusted on the side or center electrodes. In some cases it may give the plug a rusty appearance.

CAUSE: Ash deposits are normally derived from oil or fuel additives burned during normal combustion. Normally they are harmless, though excessive amounts can cause misfiring. If deposits are excessive in short mileage, the valve guides may be worn.

RECOMMENDATION: Ash-fouled plugs can be cleaned, gapped and reinstalled.

Detonation

APPEARANCE: Detonation is usually characterized by a broken plug insulator.

CAUSE: A portion of the fuel charge will begin to burn spontaneously, from the increased heat following ignition. The explosion that results applies extreme pressure to engine components, frequently damaging spark plugs and pistons.

Detonation can result by over-advanced ignition timing, inferior gasoline (low octane) lean air/fuel mixture, poor carburetion, engine lugging or an increase in compression ratio due to combustion chamber deposits or engine modification.

RECOMMENDATION: Replace the plugs after correcting the problem.

Photos Courtesy Champion Spark Plug Co.

EMISSION CONTROLS

13. Be aware of the general condition of the emission control system. It contributes to reduced pollution and should be serviced regularly to maintain efficient engine operation.

14. Check all vacuum lines for dried, cracked or brittle conditions. Something as simple as a leaking vacuum hose can cause poor performance and loss of economy.

15. Avoid tampering with the emission control system. Attempting to improve fuel econ-

FUEL SYSTEM

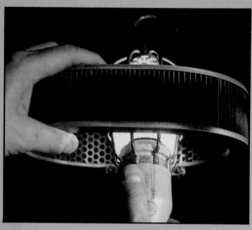

Check the air filter with a light behind it. If you can see light through the filter it can be reused.

Extremely clogged filters should be discarded and replaced with a new one.

18. Replace the air filter regularly. A dirty air filter richens the air/fuel mixture and can increase fuel consumption as much as 10%. Tests show that ⅓ of all vehicles have air filters in need of replacement.

19. Replace the fuel filter at least as often as recommended.

20. Set the idle speed and carburetor mixture to specifications.

21. Check the automatic choke. A sticking or malfunctioning choke wastes gas.

22. During the summer months, adjust the automatic choke for a leaner mixture which will produce faster engine warm-ups.

COOLING SYSTEM

29. Be sure all accessory drive belts are in good condition. Check for cracks or wear.

30. Adjust all accessory drive belts to proper tension.

31. Check all hoses for swollen areas, worn spots, or loose clamps.

32. Check coolant level in the radiator or expansion tank.

33. Be sure the thermostat is operating properly. A stuck thermostat delays engine warm-up and a cold engine uses nearly twice as much fuel as a warm engine.

34. Drain and replace the engine coolant at least as often as recommended. Rust and scale

TIRES & WHEELS

38. Check the tire pressure often with a pencil type gauge. Tests by a major tire manufacturer show that 90% of all vehicles have at least 1 tire improperly inflated. Better mileage can be achieved by over-inflating tires, but never exceed the maximum inflation pressure on the side of the tire.

39. If possible, install radial tires. Radial tires deliver as much as ½ mpg more than bias belted tires.

40. Avoid installing super-wide tires. They only create extra rolling resistance and decrease fuel mileage. Stick to the manufacturer's recommendations.

41. Have the wheels properly balanced.

omy by tampering with emission controls is more likely to worsen fuel economy than improve it. Emission control changes on modern engines are not readily reversible.

16. Clean (or replace) the EGR valve and lines as recommended.

17. Be sure that all vacuum lines and hoses are reconnected properly after working under the hood. An unconnected or misrouted vacuum line can wreak havoc with engine performance.

23. Check for fuel leaks at the carburetor, fuel pump, fuel lines and fuel tank. Be sure all lines and connections are tight.

24. Periodically check the tightness of the carburetor and intake manifold attaching nuts and bolts. These are a common place for vacuum leaks to occur.

25. Clean the carburetor periodically and lubricate the linkage.

26. The condition of the tailpipe can be an excellent indicator of proper engine combustion. After a long drive at highway speeds, the inside of the tailpipe should be a light grey in color. Black or soot on the insides indicates an overly rich mixture.

27. Check the fuel pump pressure. The fuel pump may be supplying more fuel than the engine needs.

28. Use the proper grade of gasoline for your engine. Don't try to compensate for knocking or "pinging" by advancing the ignition timing. This practice will only increase plug temperature and the chances of detonation or pre-ignition with relatively little performance gain.

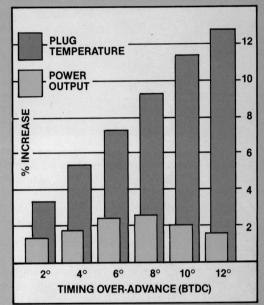

Increasing ignition timing past the specified setting results in a drastic increase in spark plug temperature with increased chance of detonation or preignition. Performance increase is considerably less. (Photo courtesy Champion Spark Plug Co.)

that form in the engine should be flushed out to allow the engine to operate at peak efficiency.

35. Clean the radiator of debris that can decrease cooling efficiency.

36. Install a flex-type or electric cooling fan, if you don't have a clutch type fan. Flex fans use curved plastic blades to push more air at low speeds when more cooling is needed; at high speeds the blades flatten out for less resistance. Electric fans only run when the engine temperature reaches a predetermined level.

37. Check the radiator cap for a worn or cracked gasket. If the cap does not seal properly, the cooling system will not function properly.

42. Be sure the front end is correctly aligned. A misaligned front end actually has wheels going in differed directions. The increased drag can reduce fuel economy by .3 mpg.

43. Correctly adjust the wheel bearings. Wheel bearings that are adjusted too tight increase rolling resistance.

Check tire pressures regularly with a reliable pocket type gauge. Be sure to check the pressure on a cold tire.

GENERAL MAINTENANCE

Check the fluid levels (particularly engine oil) on a regular basis. Be sure to check the oil for grit, water or other contamination.

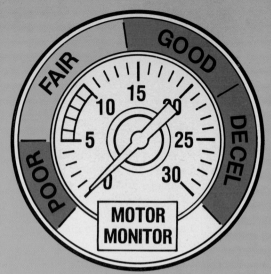

A vacuum gauge is another excellent indicator of internal engine condition and can also be installed in the dash as a mileage indicator.

44. Periodically check the fluid levels in the engine, power steering pump, master cylinder, automatic transmission and drive axle.

45. Change the oil at the recommended interval and change the filter at every oil change. Dirty oil is thick and causes extra friction between moving parts, cutting efficiency and increasing wear. A worn engine requires more frequent tune-ups and gets progressively worse fuel economy. In general, use the lightest viscosity oil for the driving conditions you will encounter.

46. Use the recommended viscosity fluids in the transmission and axle.

47. Be sure the battery is fully charged for fast starts. A slow starting engine wastes fuel.

48. Be sure battery terminals are clean and tight.

49. Check the battery electrolyte level and add distilled water if necessary.

50. Check the exhaust system for crushed pipes, blockages and leaks.

51. Adjust the brakes. Dragging brakes or brakes that are not releasing create increased drag on the engine.

52. Install a vacuum gauge or miles-per-gallon gauge. These gauges visually indicate engine vacuum in the intake manifold. High vacuum = good mileage and low vacuum = poorer mileage. The gauge can also be an excellent indicator of internal engine conditions.

53. Be sure the clutch is properly adjusted. A slipping clutch wastes fuel.

54. Check and periodically lubricate the heat control valve in the exhaust manifold. A sticking or inoperative valve prevents engine warm-up and wastes gas.

55. Keep accurate records to check fuel economy over a period of time. A sudden drop in fuel economy may signal a need for tune-up or other maintenance.

© 1980 Chilton Book Company, Radnor, PA 19089

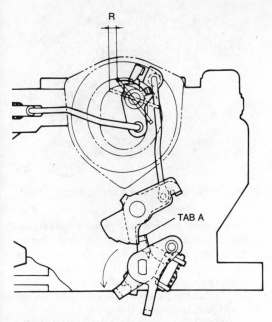

1,998cc engine choke unloader adjustment

2. Remove the distributor head plug bolt from the injection pump.

3. Install the timing gauge adapter and metric dial indicator so that the indicator pointer is in contact with the injection pump plunger and the gauge reads 2.0mm.

4. Align the 2°ATDC mark on the crankshaft pulley with the indicator on the timing gear case cover.

5. Slowly turn the engine counterclock-

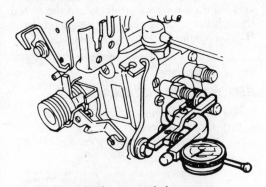

Installing the injection pump timing gauge

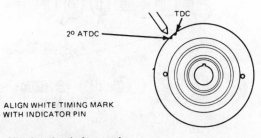

ALIGN WHITE TIMING MARK
WITH INDICATOR PIN

Aligning the timing mark

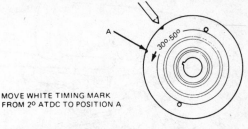

MOVE WHITE TIMING MARK
FROM 2° ATDC TO POSITION A

Moving the crankshaft pulley timing mark

wise until the dial indicator pointer stops moving (approximately 30°–50° pulley travel).

6. Adjust the dial indicator to 0. Confirm that the dial indicator does not move from 0, by rotating the crankshaft slightly from right to left.

7. Turn the crankshaft clockwise until the timing mark is once again aligned with the cover pointer. The dial indicator should read 1mm ± 0.02mm. If not, proceed to step 8.

8. Loosen the injection pump mounting nuts and bolts.

9. Rotate the pump counterclockwise past the correct timing position, then clockwise until timing is correct.

10. Repeat the timing check to make sure the adjustment is correct.

Fuel Filter and Priming Pump
REMOVAL AND INSTALLATION

1. Disconnect both battery ground cables.
2. Disconnect and cap the filter lines.
3. The filter is removed with a band wrench.
4. Remove the two bolts attaching the priming pump to its bracket and lift off the pump.
5. Unbolt and remove the bracket from the engine.
6. Installation is the reverse of removal. Apply clean fuel to the filter O-ring prior to installation. Loosen the vent screw and prime the pump to expel air. Close the vent screw.

Injection Pump
REMOVAL AND INSTALLATION

1. Disconnect both battery ground cables.
2. Remove the radiator fan and shroud.
3. Remove the air conditioning compressor/power steering drive belt and idler pulley.
4. Remove the injection pump cover and gasket.
5. Turn the crankshaft until the injection pump drive gear keyway is at TDC.
6. Remove the large nut and washer attaching the drive gear to the injection pump.

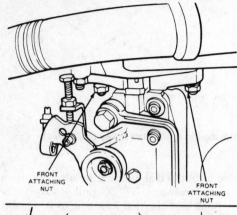

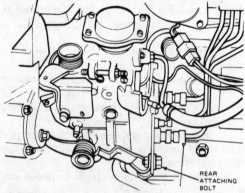

Injection pump attaching locations

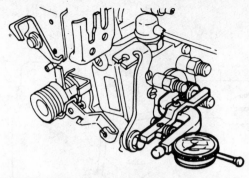

Installing the injection pump timing gauge

NOTE: *Be careful! It's easy to accidently drop the washer into the timing case.*

7. Remove the intake hose from the air cleaner and manifold.

8. Disconnect the throttle cable and, if equipped, the cruise control cable, from the pump.

9. Disconnect the fuel inlet line from the pump. Cap the line and pump fitting immediately.

10. Disconnect the fuel shut-off solenoid lead at the pump.

11. Disconnect the injection lines from the nozzle and pump. Cap the lines, nozzles and pump openings immediately.

12. Disconnect the lower fuel return line at the pump and fuel hoses. Cap all openings.

13. Loosen the lower no.3 intake port nut and remove the fuel return line.

14. Remove the two nuts attaching the injection pump to the front timing gear cover, and the one bolt attaching the pump to the rear support bracket.

15. Install a gear and hub remover in the drive gear cover and attach it to the injection pump drive gear. Rotate the screw clockwise until the gear separates from the pump. Remove the pump.

NOTE: *When removing the pump, be care-*

ful to avoid dropping the pump shaft key into the timing case. Disconnect the cold start cable before lifting the pump clear of the engine, and reconnect it when lowering the pump into place for installation.

16. Install the pump in the case, aligning the key with the keyway in the gear.

17. Install the nuts and washers attaching the pump and draw the pump into position. Do not tighten the fasteners completely, at this time.

18. Install the bolt attaching the pump to the rear support. Install the washer and nut attaching the pump to the drive gear. Torque the nut to 50 ft.lb.

19. Install the pump drive gear cover and new gasket.

20. Adjust the injection timing as described above.

21. Connect all other components in the reverse of their removal order. Bleed the system through the priming pump, as described above. Run the engine and check for leaks.

Fuel Injectors
REMOVAL AND INSTALLATION

NOTE: *A 27mm deep well socket is necessary for this procedure.*

1. Disconnect both battery ground cables.

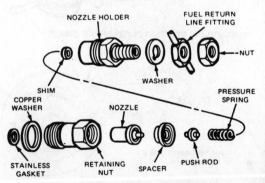

Fuel injection nozzle assembly components

2. Disconnect the injection lines at the nozzle and pump. Cap all openings immediately.

3. Remove the fuel return line and gaskets.

4. Unbolt the fuel line heater from the head and position it out of the way.

5. Unscrew the nozzles.

6. Remove the copper washer and steel gasket from the nozzle. Discard them.

7. Clean the nozzles and seats with a cleaning kit made for diesel nozzles.

8. Using new gaskets and washers, install the nozzles in the head. Torque them to 50 ft.lb.

NOTE: *The gaskets are installed with the blue side up.*

9. Install all other parts in reverse of their removal order.

Water Separator

DRAINING

1. Loosen the drain plug and allow the water to drain out.

2. If the water won't drain freely, or at all, loosen the vent plug on the priming pump.

3. When the water has drained, prime the system with the priming pump. Bleed the system at the priming pump.

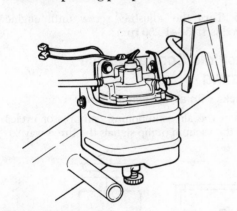

Diesel water separator

REMOVAL AND INSTALLATION

1. Disconnect the wiring.

2. Disconnect and cap the fuel lines.

3. Remove the protective cover.

4. Unbolt and remove the separator.

5. Installation is the reverse of removal. Bleed the system.

Fuel Cut-Off Solenoid

REMOVAL AND INSTALLATION

1. Disconnect the battery ground cables.

2. Disconnect the wiring.

3. Unscrew the cut-off solenoid and discard the O-ring.

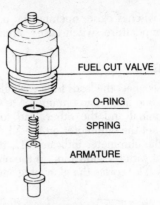

Diesel fuel cut-off solenoid

4. Installation is the reverse of removal. Use a new O-ring coated with clean diesel fuel.

Glow Plugs

OPERATION

This engine uses a quick start glow plug system, enabling the operator to start the engine relatively quickly after the key-on sequence. One glow plug per cylinder is used, controlled by a control module, two relays, a resistor, a coolant temperature switch, and clutch and neutral switches.

Relay, power, and feedback circuits are protected by fusible links in the harness. The control module is protected by a 10A fuse in the fuse panel.

When the ignition switch is turned ON, a Wait-to-Start signal appears near the cold start knob on the instrument panel. At this time, relay no.1 closes and full system voltage is applied to the glow plugs. If coolant temperature is below 86°F (30°C), relay no.2 also closes. After three seconds, the module turns off the Wait-to-Start light. If the operator does not start the engine and the key is left ON, the no.1 relay opens and cuts off voltage to the glow plugs within three seconds.

However, if coolant temperature is below 86°F when the no.1 relay opens, the no.2 relay will remain closed, continuing reduced voltage to the glow plugs until the ignition switch is turned OFF.

When the engine is cranked, the control module cycles relay no.1 intermittently, providing the glow plugs with between 4 and 12v, depending on which replay is closed.

Once the engine has started, the alternator output signals the control module to open the no.1 relay and the afterglow function takes over, supplying between 4 and 5v to the glow plugs through the no.2 relay as long as the coolant temperature remains below 86°F.

Once the truck is in motion, the clutch and

neutral switches close, opening the no.2 relay if the temperature switch hasn't already done so.

TESTING

1. Disconnect the leads from each glow plug. Connect one lead of an ohmmeter to the glow plug terminal and the other lead to a good ground. Set the ohmmeter on the X1 scale.

2. If the ohmmeter indicates 1Ω, the problem is not with the glow plug. If the ohmmeter indicates 1Ω, replace the glow plug and retest.

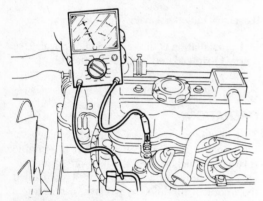

Testing the glow plugs

REMOVAL AND INSTALLATION

1. Disconnect the battery ground cables.
2. Disconnect the glow plug harness.
3. Using a 12mm deep well socket, unscrew the glow plugs.
4. Installation is the reverse of removal. Torque the glow plugs to 11–15 ft.lb.

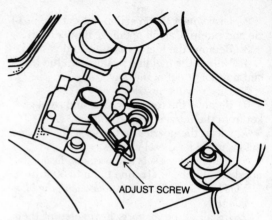

Cold start device adjusting screw location

Cold Start Device

ADJUSTMENT

1. Disconnect the cable from the advance lever on the pump.
2. Pull the control knob under the dash to the full out position.
3. Connect a tachometer to the engine.
4. Start the engine and push the advance lever all the way to the stopper. Connect the cable.
5. Turn the adjusting screw until engine speed is 1,150–1,250 rpm.

Fast Idle Control Device

TESTING

Trucks with air conditioning only

When the air conditioning compressor cycles on, the vacuum pump signals the three-way so-

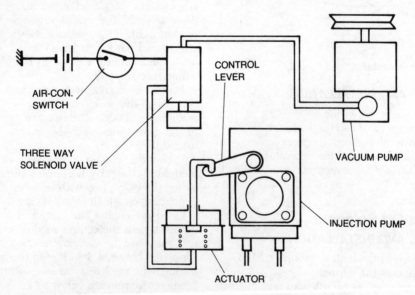

Fast idle control device schematic

lenoid valve, which in turn applies vacuum to a vacuum diaphragm unit connected to a control lever on the injection pump. Engine speed should be held at 700 rpm or increase to no more than 750 rpm. If engine speed drops below 700 rpm with the air conditioning compressor on, there is a leak in the vacuum circuit.

FUEL TANK

REMOVAL AND INSTALLATION

1. Raise and support the rear of the truck.
2. Remove the fuel tank drain plug and drain the gasoline into a metal container.
3. Install the drain plug.
4. Disconnect and plug the fuel pump line at the tank.
5. Disconnect the line from the condenser tank or vapor valve at the fuel tank.
6. If so equipped, disconnect the fuel return line.
7. Disconnect the fuel sending unit lead and the electrical connector.
8. Remove the fuel tank attaching bolts at the mounting bracket and lower the tank.
9. Installation is the reverse of removal.

Chassis Electrical

5

UNDERSTANDING AND TROUBLESHOOTING ELECTRICAL SYSTEMS

For any electrical system to operate, it must make a complete circuit. This simply means that the power flow from the battery must make a complete circle. When an electrical component is operating, power flows from the battery to the component, passes through the component causing it to perform its function (lighting a light bulb), and then returns to the battery through the ground of the circuit. This ground is usually (but not always) the metal part of the truck on which the electrical component is mounted.

Perhaps the easiest way to visualize this is to think of connecting a light bulb, with two wires attached to it, to the battery. If one of the two wires attached to the light bulb were attached to the negative post of the battery and the other were attached to the positive post of the battery, you would have a complete circuit. Current from the battery would flow to the light bulb, causing it to light, and return to the negative post of the battery.

The normal automotive circuit differs from this simple example in two ways. First, instead of having a return wire from the bulb to the battery, the light bulb returns the current to the battery through the chassis of the vehicle. Since the negative battery cable is attached to the chassis and the chassis is made of electrically conductive metal, the chassis of the vehicle can serve as ground wire to complete the circuit. Second, most automotive circuits contain switches to turn components on and off as required.

Every complete circuit from a power source must include a component which is using the power from the power source. If you were to disconnect the light bulb from the wires and touch the two wires together (don't do this) the power supply wire to the component would be grounded before the normal ground connection for the circuit.

Because grounding a wire from a power source makes a complete circuit, less the required component to use the power, this phenomenon is called a short circuit. Common causes are: broken insulation (exposing the metal wire to a metal part of the truck), or a shorted switch.

Some electrical components which require a large amount of current to operate also have a relay in their circuit. Since these circuits carry a large amount of current, the thickness of the wire in the circuit (gauge size) is also greater. If this large wire were connected from the component to the control switch on the instrument panel, and then back to the component, a voltage drop would occur in the circuit. To prevent this potential drop in voltage, an electromagnetic switch (relay) is used. The large wires in the circuit are connected from the battery to one side of the relay, and from the opposite side of the relay to the component. The relay is normally open, preventing current from passing through the circuit. An additional, smaller, wire is connected from the relay to the control switch for the circuit. When the control switch is turned on, it grounds the smaller wire from the relay and completes the circuit. This closes the relay and allows current to flow from the battery to the component. The horn, headlight, and starter circuits are three which use relays.

It is possible for larger surges of current to pass through the electrical system of your truck. If this surge of current were to reach an electrical component, it could burn it out. To prevent this, fuses, circuit breakers or fusible links are connected into the current supply wires of most of the major electrical systems. When an electrical current of excessive power passes throughout the component's fuse, the fuse blows out and breaks the circuit, saving the component from destruction.

A circuit breaker is basically a self-repairing fuse. The circuit breaker opens the circuit the same way a fuse does. However, when either the short is removed from the circuit or the surge subsides, the circuit breaker resets itself and does not have to be replaced as a fuse does.

A fuse link is a wire that acts as a fuse. It is normally connected between the starter relay and the main wiring harness. This connection is usually under the hood. The fuse link (if installed) protects all the chassis electrical components, and is the probable cause of trouble when none of the electrical components function, unless the battery is disconnected or dead.

Electrical problems generally fall into one of three areas:

1. The component that is not functioning is not receiving current.
2. The component itself is not functioning.
3. The component is not properly grounded.

The electrical system can be checked with a test light and a jumper wire. A test light is a device that looks like a pointed screwdriver with a wire attached to it and has a light bulb in its handle. A jumper wire is a piece of insulated wire with an alligator clip attached to each end.

If a component is not working, you must follow a systematic plan to determine which of the three causes is at fault.

1. Turn on the switch that controls the inoperable component.
2. Disconnect the power supply wire from the component.
3. Attach the ground wire on the test light to a good metal ground.
4. Touch the probe end of the test light to the end of the power supply wire that was disconnected from the component. If the component is receiving current, the test light will go on.

NOTE: *Some components work only when the ignition switch is turned on.*

If the test light does not go on, then the problem is in the circuit between the battery and the component. This includes all the switches, fuses and relays in the system. Follow the wire that runs back to the battery. The problem is an open circuit between the battery and the component. If the fuse is blown and, when replaced, immediately blows again, there is a short circuit in the system which must be located and repaired. If there is a switch in the system, bypass it with a jumper wire. This is done by connecting one end of the jumper wire to the power supply wire into the switch and the other end of the jumper wire to the wire coming out of the switch. If the test light lights

with the jumper wire installed, the switch or whatever was bypassed is defective.

NOTE: *Never substitute the jumper wire for the component, since it is required to use the power from the power source.*

5. If the bulb in the test light goes on, then the current is getting to the component that is not working. This eliminates the first of the three possible causes. Connect the power supply wire and connect a jumper wire from the component to a good metal ground. Do this with the switch which controls the component turned on, and also the ignition switch turned on if it is required for the component to work. If the component works with the jumper wire installed, then it has a bad ground. This is usually caused by the metal area on which the component mounts to the chassis being coated with some type of foreign matter.

6. If neither test located the source of the trouble, then the component itself is defective. Remember that for any electrical system to work, all connections must be clean and tight.

HEATER

Heater Assembly
REMOVAL AND INSTALLATION

1. Disconnect the battery ground cable.
2. Drain the cooling system.

CAUTION: *When draining the coolant, keep in mind that cats and dogs are attracted by the ethylene glycol antifreeze, and are quite likely to drink any that is left in an uncovered container or in puddles on the ground. This will prove fatal in sufficient quantity. Always drain the coolant into a sealable container. Coolant should be reused unless it is contaminated or several years old.*

3. Remove the water valve shield at the left side of the heater.
4. Disconnect the two hoses from the left side of the heater.
5. At the heat-defroster door, the water valve and the outside recirculation door, disengage the control cable housing from the mounting clip on the heater. Disconnect each of the three cable wires from the crank arms.
6. Disconnect the fan motor electrical lead.
7. Remove the glove compartment for clearance.
8. Working inside the engine compartment, remove the two retaining nuts and the single bolt and washer which hold the heater to the firewall. Later models also have a retaining bolt inside the passenger compartment which must be removed.

9. Disconnect the two defroster ducts from the heater and remove the heater.

10. Install the heater on the dash so that the heater duct indexes with the air intake duct and the two mounting studs enter their respective holes.

11. From the engine side of the firewall, install the nuts on the mounting studs. While an assistant holds the heater in position, install the mounting bolt.

12. Connect the defroster ducts.

13. Connect the heat-defrost door control cable to the door crank arm. Set the control lever (upper) in the HEAT position and turn the crank arm toward the mounting clip as far as it will go. Engage the cable housing in the clip and install the screw in the clip.

14. Connect the water valve control cable wire to the crank arm on the water valve lever. Locate the cable housing in the mounting clip. Set the control lever in the HOT position and pull the valve plunger and lever to the full outward position. This will move the lever crank arm toward the cable mounting clip as far as it will go. Tighten the clip and screw.

15. Insert the outside recirculation door control cable into the hole in the door crank arm. Bend the wire over and tighten the screw. Set the center control lever in the REC position and turn the door crank arm toward the mounting clip as far as it will go. Engage the cable housing in the clip and install the screw in the clip.

16. Connect the fan motor electrical lead.

17. Connect the two hoses to the heater core tubes, at the left side of the heater, and tighten the clamp.

18. Install the water valve shield and tighten the three screws (left side of the heater).

19. Refill the cooling system and connect the battery ground cable.

20. Run the engine and check for leaks. Check the operation of the heater.

21. Replace the glove compartment.

Heater Motor and Blower Fan
REMOVAL AND INSTALLATION

1. Remove the heater assembly.

2. Remove the five screws and separate the halves of the heater assembly.

3. Loosen the fan retaining nut. Lightly tap on the nut to loosen the fan. Remove the fan and nut from the motor shaft.

4. Remove the three motor-to-case retaining screws and disconnect the bullet connector to the resistor and ground screw.

5. Rotate the motor and remove it from the case.

6. Install the motor in the case, rotating it slightly.

7. Install the retaining screws and connect the bullet connector and ground wire.

8. Install the fan on the shaft and install the nut.

9. Assemble the halves together and install the five retaining screws.

10. Install the heater in the trucks. Check the operation of the heater.

Heater Core
REMOVAL AND INSTALLATION

1. Remove the heater from the truck.

2. Remove the five screws and separate the halves of the case.

3. Loosen the hose clamps and slide the heater core from the case.

4. Slide the replacement core into the case. At the same time, connect the core tube to the water valve tube with the short hose and clamps.

5. Assemble the halves of the heater and install the five screws.

6. Install the heater in the truck. Check the operation of the heater.

RADIO

For best FM reception, adjust the antenna to a height of 31 inches. For best AM reception, extend the antenna to its full height.

CAUTION: *Never operate the radio with the speaker lead or antenna disconnected. Operation of the radio without a load will damage the amplifier's output transistors. If a replacement speaker is installed, be sure it is of the same impedance (resistance in ohms) as the original.*

REMOVAL AND INSTALLATION
1972–78

1. Remove the ash tray, ash tray retainer and rear retainer support. Remove the heater control knobs, heater control bezel and right-hand defroster hose.

2. Remove the heater control and position it to the left.

3. Remove the radio chassis rear support bracket.

4. Bend the bracket down 90°.

5. Remove the radio knobs, attaching nuts and bezel.

6. Pull the chassis forward until the control shafts clear the holes in the instrument panel. Disconnect the speaker wires, power lead and antenna lead. Rotate the chassis so that the

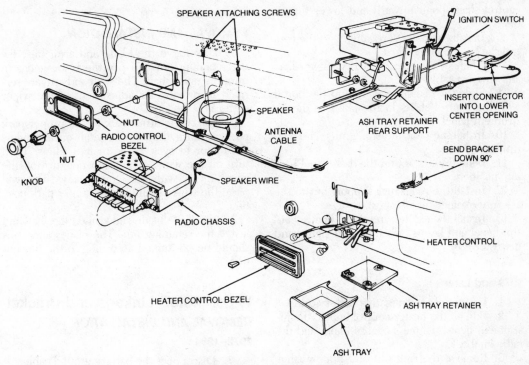

SPEAKER ATTACHING SCREWS

IGNITION SWITCH

SPEAKER

NUT

ANTENNA CABLE

RADIO CONTROL BEZEL

NUT

INSERT CONNECTOR INTO LOWER CENTER OPENING

ASH TRAY RETAINER REAR SUPPORT

KNOB

BEND BRACKET DOWN 90°

SPEAKER WIRE

RADIO CHASSIS

HEATER CONTROL

HEATER CONTROL BEZEL

ASH TRAY RETAINER

ASH TRAY

1972–78 radio installation details

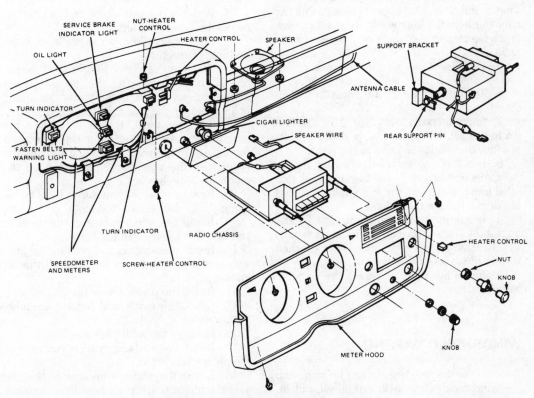

SERVICE BRAKE INDICATOR LIGHT

NUT-HEATER CONTROL

HEATER CONTROL

SPEAKER

SUPPORT BRACKET

OIL LIGHT

ANTENNA CABLE

TURN INDICATOR

CIGAR LIGHTER

FASTEN BELTS WARNING LIGHT

SPEAKER WIRE

REAR SUPPORT PIN

TURN INDICATOR

RADIO CHASSIS

HEATER CONTROL

NUT

KNOB

SPEEDOMETER AND METERS

SCREW-HEATER CONTROL

METER HOOD

KNOB

1979 and later radio installation details

control shafts point upward and lower the radio.

7. Install the radio vertically, with the control shafts pointed upward.

8. Connect the speaker wires, power lead and antenna cable.

9. Slide the chassis upward and position it with the control shafts in the holes in the instrument panel.

10. Install the radio attaching nuts, and control knobs.

11. Bend the bracket on the dash panel back into position.

12. Install the radio rear support nut to the ash tray retainer rear support.

13. Install the ash tray retainer, heater control bezel and knobs, ash tray, and right-hand defroster hose.

1979 and Later

1. Disconnect the negative battery cable.

2. Pull off the heater control knobs, the instrument light brightness control knob, and the radio knobs.

3. Remove the ring nut and fiber washer for the brightness control. Remove the radio attaching nuts (shaft nuts). Remove the four screws from the meter hood (instrument trim panel) and remove the hood.

4. Slide the radio to the left until the rear support pin clears the support bracket. Pull the radio out from the instrument panel far enough to gain access to the wires at the rear of the radio chassis.

5. Disconnect the power lead, speaker leads and the antenna cable. Remove the radio.

6. To install, connect the wires to the radio.

7. Slide the radio into place. Move the radio to the left, engage the support pin with its bracket, then slide the radio to the right.

8. Install the meter hood, inserting the radio shafts and heater knobs through it as it is fitted into place. Install the four retaining screws but do not tighten them yet.

9. Install the washer and ring nut for the brightness control. Install the radio shaft nuts loosely. Tighten the meter hood screws, then tighten the radio shaft nuts.

10. Install the knobs. Connect the negative battery cable.

WINDSHIELD WIPERS

Because the steering wheel must be removed, the windshield wiper switch removal and installation procedure is in Chapter 8.

Blade and Arm
REMOVAL AND INSTALLATION

1. To remove the blade and arm, unscrew the retaining nut and pry the blade and arm from the pivot shaft. The shaft and arm are serrated to provide for adjustment of the wiper pattern on the glass.

2. To set the arms back in the proper park position, turn the wiper switch on and allow the motor to cycle three or four times. Then turn off the wiper switch (do not turn off the wiper motor with the ignition key). This will place the wiper shafts in the proper park position.

3. Install the blade and arm on the shaft and install the retaining nut. The blades and arms should be positioned according to the illustration.

Wiper Motor, Linkage and Bracket
REMOVAL AND INSTALLATION
1972–1984

1. Disconnect the battery ground cable.

2. Remove the wiper arms and blades by removing the retaining nuts.

3. Remove the rubber cap, nut, tapered spacer and rubber grommet from each pivot shaft.

4. Remove the two motor and bracket retaining bolts and washers.

5. Disconnect the wiper motor leads at the multiple connector.

6. Remove the motor and bracket assembly. Note the position of the ground washer and the rubber washer at the bracket mounting holes. Remove the plastic water shield.

7. To disconnect the motor from the bracket, remove the retaining clip that holds the linkage to the motor output arm. Note the position of the washers before removing the motor from the bracket.

8. Remove the four motor-to-bracket retaining bolts and remove the motor.

9. Install the wiper motor on the bracket and install the four retaining bolts.

10. Install the washers and position the linkage on the motor output arm. Install the retaining clip.

11. Install the plastic water shield.

12. Install the motor and bracket assembly in the truck.

13. Connect the multiple connector.

14. Install the washers, spacers and nuts on the pivot shafts.

15. Install the wiper arms and blades. Be sure the motor is in the Park position. This can be determined by cycling the motor several

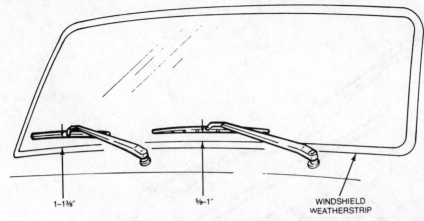

Wiper blade and arm positioning for 1972–84 models

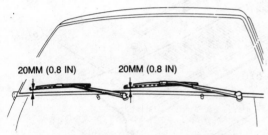

Wiper blade and arm positioning for 1986 models

times. Adjust the position of the wipers. The clearance between the tips of the blades and the windshield moulding should be 20mm at park.

16. Connect the battery cable and check the operation of the wipers.

1986

1. Remove the wiper arm/blade assembly. Note that the arms are different. Don't confuse them.

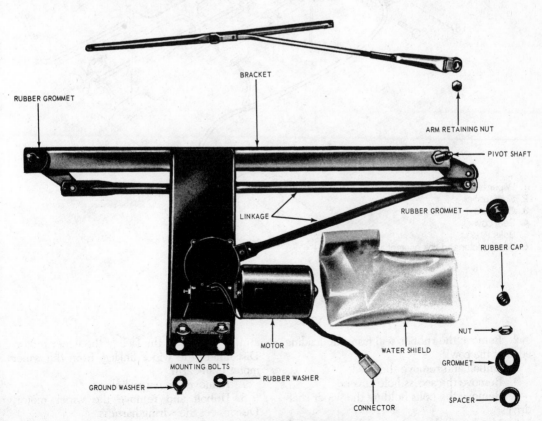

1972–84 wiper motor and linkage

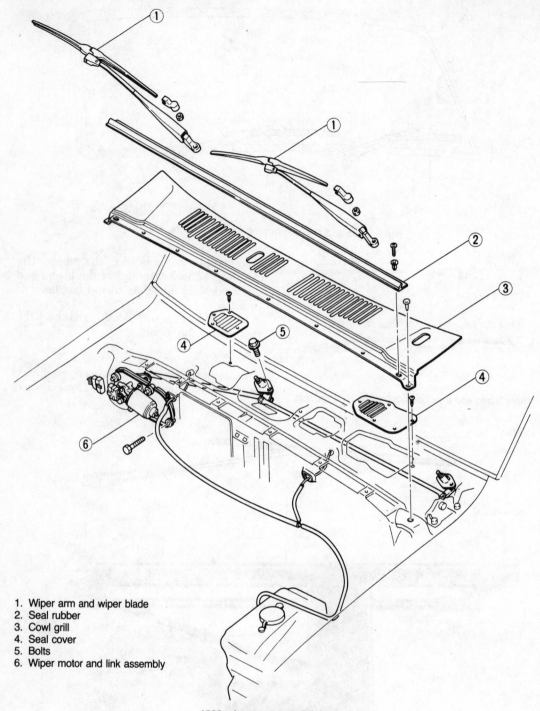

1. Wiper arm and wiper blade
2. Seal rubber
3. Cowl grill
4. Seal cover
5. Bolts
6. Wiper motor and link assembly

1986 wiper motor and linkage

2. Remove the rubber seal from the leading edge of the cowl.

3. Unbolt and remove the cowl.

4. Remove the access hole covers.

5. Remove the bolts holding the wiper shaft drives.

6. Matchmark the position of the wiper crank arm in relation to the face of the wiper motor. Disconnect the wiper linkage from the wiper motor crank arm.

7. Remove the wiper linkage.

8. Unbolt and remove the wiper motor. Disconnect the wiring harness.

9. Installation is the reverse of removal. Make

sure that the parked height of the wiper arms, measured from the blade tips to the windshield moulding is 20mm. Torque the arm retaining nuts to 8–10 ft.lb.

INSTRUMENT PANEL

Instrument Cluster

REMOVAL AND INSTALLATION

1972–84

1. Disconnect the battery ground cable.
2. On 1979 and later models only, the meter hood (instrument cluster trim panel) must be removed for access to the cluster. See Steps 1–3 of the 1979 and later radio removal and installation procedure for details on meter hood removal.
3. Remove the screws holding the cluster to the instrument panel.
4. Pull the cluster rearward enough to gain access to the cluster assembly.
5. Reach behind the cluster and disconnect the speedometer cable.
6. Pull the multiple connector from the printed circuit.
7. Note the position of the two ammeter leads and disconnect them.
8. Remove the screw attaching the ground wire to the rear of the cluster. On trucks equipped with a coasting richer valve, remove the two connectors at the speedometer sensor switch.
9. Remove the instrument cluster.

10. Position the cluster assembly near the opening and connect the ground lead.
11. Connect the two ammeter leads to the ammeter.
12. Install the multiple connector at the rear of the cluster. On trucks equipped with a coasting richer valve, connect the two wires to the speedometer speed sensor.
13. Connect the speedometer cable to the speedometer head.
14. Install the four attaching screws.
15. On 1979 and later models, replace the meter hood.
16. connect the battery cable.
17. Run the engine and check the operation of all gauges.

1986

1. Disconnect the battery ground cable.
2. Reach behind the cluster and disconnect the speedometer cable.
3. Remove the screws attaching the cluster hood and carefully lift the hood off.
4. Remove the screw attaching the cluster pod to the dash panel and pull the pod out toward you, gradually. Reach behind the pod and disconnect the wiring connectors.
5. Remove the trip meter knob, and, on cluster w/tachometer, the clock adjust knob.
6. Remove the screws retaining the lens cover and lift off the cover.
7. Remove the screws retaining the cluster bezel and lift off the bezel.
8. Lift out the warning light plate.
9. On clusters wo/tachometer, remove, in order:

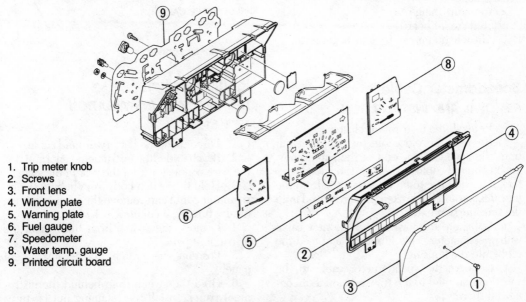

1. Trip meter knob
2. Screws
3. Front lens
4. Window plate
5. Warning plate
6. Fuel gauge
7. Speedometer
8. Water temp. gauge
9. Printed circuit board

1986 standard instrument cluster

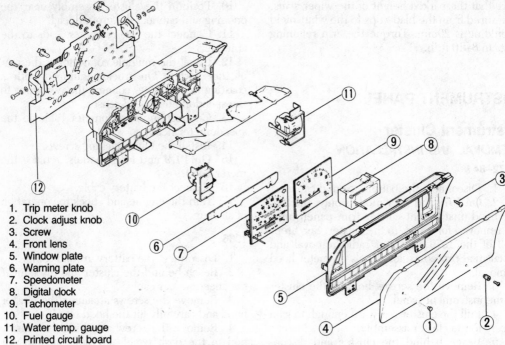

1. Trip meter knob
2. Clock adjust knob
3. Screw
4. Front lens
5. Window plate
6. Warning plate
7. Speedometer
8. Digital clock
9. Tachometer
10. Fuel gauge
11. Water temp. gauge
12. Printed circuit board

1986 electronic instrument cluster

fuel gauge
speedometer
temperature gauge
printed circuit board
10. On cluster w/tachometer, remove, in order:
speedometer
digital clock
tachometer
fuel gauge
temperature gauge
printed circuit board
11. Installation is the reverse of removal.

Speedometer Cable

REMOVAL AND INSTALLATION

1. Remove the instrument cluster.
2. Remove the old cable by pulling it out from the speedometer end of the cable housing. If the old cable is broken, the speedometer cable will have to be disconnected from the transmission and the broken piece removed from the transmission end.
3. Lubricate the lower ¾ of the new cable with speedometer cable lubricant, and feed the cable into the housing.
4. Connect the speedometer cable to the speedometer, and to the transmission if disconnected there.
5. Replace the instrument cluster.

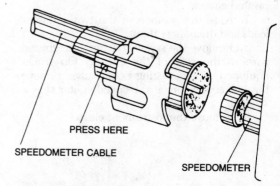

PRESS HERE

SPEEDOMETER CABLE

SPEEDOMETER

Speedometer connector

Ignition Switch

REMOVAL AND INSTALLATION

1972–81

1. Disconnect the battery ground cable.
2. Reach under the instrument panel and pull the wire connector from the rear of the switch.
3. Hold the switch body from behind the instrument panel and remove the black retaining nut by turning it counterclockwise.
4. Remove the switch from the rear of the instrument panel.
5. Position the switch in the instrument panel.
6. Hold the switch from behind the instrument panel. Install the retaining nut by turning it clockwise.

7. Plug the multiple connector into the back of the switch.

8. Connect the battery ground cable and check the operation of the switch.

1982–84

1. Disconnect the negative battery terminal.

2. Remove the steering wheel.

3. Remove the steering column shroud.

4. Disconnect the multiple connectors at the base of the combination switch.

5. Remove the switch retaining snap ring. Pull the turn signal indicator cancelling cam off the shaft.

6. Remove the switch retaining bolt and remove the complete switch from the column.

7. Installation is the reverse of removal.

1986

1. Disconnect the battery ground cable.

2. Remove the steering column covers.

3. Disconnect the wiring harness connector at the switch.

4. Remove the attaching screw and lift out the switch.

5. Installation is the reverse of removal.

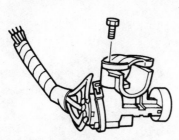

Ignition switch used in 1986 models

Ignition Lock

REMOVAL AND INSTALLATION

1. Disconnect the negative battery terminal.

2. Remove the steering wheel.

3. Remove the steering column shroud.

4. Disconnect the multiple connectors at the base of the combination switch.

5. Remove the switch retaining snap ring. Pull the turn signal indicator cancelling cam off the shaft.

6. Remove the switch retaining bolt and remove the complete switch from the column.

NOTE: *Make a groove on the head of the bolts attaching the steering lock body to the column shaft using a saw. A screwdriver can be used to loosen the screws.*

7. Remove the steering lock attaching bolts. Remove the steering lock.

8. Installation is the reverse of removal. During installation position a new steering lock on the column shaft. Tighten the bolts until the neads break off.

HEADLIGHTS

REMOVAL AND INSTALLATION

1. Remove the radiator grille attaching screws and remove the grille.

2. Remove the headlight bulb trim ring, by removing the three screws and rotating the ring clockwise. Support the headlight bulb and remove the trim ring.

NOTE: *Do not disturb the headlight aiming screws, which are installed in the housing next to the retaining screws.*

3. Pull the plug connector from the rear of the bulb and remove the bulb.

4. Connect the plug connector to the rear of a new headlight.

5. Install the headlight in the housing, and locate the bulb tabs in the slots and the housing.

6. Position the trim ring over the bulb and loosely install the retaining screws. Rotate the ring counterclockwise to lock it in position. Tighten the three attaching screws. Check the headlight operation.

7. Install the grille.

8. Have the headlight aim checked.

CIRCUIT PROTECTION

The fuse box, on trucks through 1984, is located on the left side of the engine compartment near the windshield. On 1986 trucks, the fuse box is located under the instrument panel, on the left of the driver.

When a fuse blows out, inspect the electrical system for shorts or other faults. Fuses of specified capacity should be installed in their respective positions. Oversize fuses will allow excessive current to flow and should not be used.

Spare fuses should be kept in a vinyl bag in the glove compartment.

1972–76 trucks have a 40 amp master fuse located underneath a plastic cover on the right hand fender apron in the engine compartment, just behind the battery tray support. It protects the entire electrical system; all systems will be dead if it has blown. To replace it, first disconnect the battery ground cable. Then remove the plastic cover and the fuse.

1977–84 trucks have a fusible link instead of

the master fuse. The fusible link is a length of wire specially designed to melt under excessive electrical loads. It protects the entire electrical system. Replacements are made by splicing a new section into place. To replace the fusible link, first disconnect the battery negative cable. Then remove the old link and replace it with a link of similar capacity, available at your dealer.

1986 trucks have replaced the fusible link with an 80 amp fuse located under a protective cover on the right fender apron. This fuse is a push-in type block fuse.

Flashers and Relays

The hazard warning flasher is located to the left of the steering column, beneath the instrument panel, and is secured by a clamp and one screw. To remove it, simply unplug the electrical connector, loosen the screw, and slide the flasher out of the clamp. The turn signal flasher is located to the right of the steering column, beneath the instrument panel, and is secured in the same way as the hazard flasher.

The turn the signal relay is located to the immediate right of the hazard flasher, and is secured by two screws. To remove it, unplug the electrical connector and remove the screws.

WIRING DIAGRAMS

Wiring diagrams have been omitted from this book. As trucks have become more complex, and available with longer and longer option lists, wiring diagrams have grown in size and complexity also. It has become virtually impossible to provide a readable reproduction in a reasonable number of pages. Information on ordering wiring diagrams from Mazda can be found in the owner's manual.

Drive Train
6

CLUTCH

The clutch is a dry single disc type, consisting of a clutch disc, clutch cover and pressure plate and a clutch release mechanism. It is hydraulically operated by a firewall mounted master cylinder and a clutch release slave cylinder mounted on the clutch housing.

CAUTION: *The clutch driven disc contains asbestos, which has been determined to be a cancer causing agent. Never clean clutch surfaces with compressed air! Avoid inhaling any dust from any clutch surface! When cleaning clutch surfaces, use a commercially available brake cleaning fluid.*

Adjustments

CLUTCH PEDAL FREE-PLAY

1972–75

The free-play of the clutch pedal before the pushrod contacts the piston in the master cylinder should be 0.02–0.12 in. To adjust the free-play, loosen the locknut and turn the pushrod until the proper adjustment is obtained. Tighten the locknut after the adjustment is complete.

1976–86

The clutch pedal free-play is measured from the top of the pedal pad at rest to the point at which it stops when the pushrod hits the master cylinder piston. Free-play is adjusted by loosening the locknut on the pushrod and adjusting the pushrod length by rotating the rod. The clutch should have a free travel, measured at the pedal pad, of 0.025–0.121 in. for 1976–84 trucks, and 0.20–0.50 in. for 1986 trucks. Tighten the locknut when the adjustment is complete.

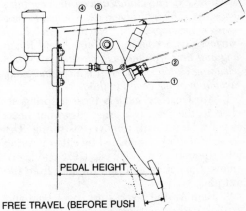

FREE TRAVEL (BEFORE PUSH ROD CONTACTS WITH PISTON)

1. Locknut   3. Locknut
2. Stopper   4. Pushrod

Clutch pedal adjustment points:

PEDAL HEIGHT

Pedal height is measured from the top of the pedal at rest, to the floor board, horizontally behind the pedal. Adjustment is made by loosening the locknut on the pedal stopper and turning the adjusting bolt. Pedal height should be:

- 1972–81: 215mm
- 1982–84 Gasoline engine: 205mm
- Diesel engine: 215mm
- 1986: 215mm

CLUTCH RELEASE LEVER ADJUSTMENT

1972–75

NOTE: *This adjustment must be maintained to prevent release bearing and clutch damage.*

1. Raise and support the truck.
2. Disconnect the release lever return spring at the lever.
3. Loosen the locknut and rotate the adjusting nut until a clearance of 0.14–0.18 in. is ob-

tained between the bullet nosed end of the adjusting nut and the release lever.

4. Tighten the locknut and hook the return spring.

5. Lower the truck.

1976 and later

No adjustment is possible on 1976 and later trucks. Instead, the stroke can be checked by raising the truck and moving the release rod. If the stroke measures less than 5mm (0.196 in.) the clutch pedal should be replaced.

Release Lever and Bearing
REMOVAL AND INSTALLATION

CAUTION: *The clutch driven disc contains asbestos, which has been determined to be a cancer causing agent. Never clean clutch surfaces with compressed air! Avoid inhaling any dust from any clutch surface! When cleaning clutch surfaces, use a commercially available brake cleaning fluid.*

1. Most earlier models have a spring attached to the release bearing (throwout bearing) collar. If present, remove this spring. The release lever (fork) is retained by either a spring (earlier models) or a spring clip (1976 and later). Remove the spring and pull the fork from the pivot pin.

2. Remove the lever, dust cover boot and the release (throwout) bearing.

3. Inspect the parts carefully. Wipe off all the oil and dirt from the bearing, but do not soak it in solvent; it is prelubricated. Any burrs should be smoothed with crocus cloth. If burrs are present, inspect the transmission input shaft bearing retainer, and smooth any scoring with crocus cloth.

4. Coat the bearing retainer with a thin film of lithium base grease. Apply a thin film of this grease to both sides of the fork at contact points. Also lightly coat the release bearing surface where it contacts the pressure plate fingers.

5. Fill the grease groove inside the bearing hub with the lithium grease. Do not use polyethylene grease. Clean any excess grease from the bore of the hub, because excess grease will eventually work its way into the clutch disc.

6. Before installing the bearing, hold the inner race and rotate the outer race, applying pressure. If the rotation is noisy or rough, replace the bearing. Bearing failure is generally caused by improper free play settings at the release cylinder or pedal. Riding the pedal can reduce clearance, causing the bearing to constantly spin, increasing wear. The bearing can also fail due to release lever misalignment (bent out of plane or not centered on the housing

bracket) or misalignment between the engine and transmission.

7. Apply a thin film of lithium grease to the input shaft bearing retainer portion of the clutch housing.

8. Dab the end of the pivot pin with grease, and drive the release lever onto it. Apply a thin film of grease to the contact points of the release lever, and install the release bearing. Hook the release collar spring back into place (if applicable).

9. Check the operation of the release bearing hub. It should slide freely on the input shaft bearing retainer.

10. Install the dust boot.

Clutch Unit

CAUTION: *The clutch driven disc contains asbestos, which has been determined to be a cancer causing agent. Never clean clutch surfaces with compressed air! Avoid inhaling any dust from any clutch surface! When cleaning clutch surfaces, use a commercially available brake cleaning fluid.*

REMOVAL AND INSTALLATION
All Models

1. Remove the transmission.

2. Remove the four attaching and two pilot bolts holding the clutch cover to the flywheel. Loosen the bolts evenly and a turn or two at a time. If the clutch cover is to be reinstalled, mark the flywheel and clutch cover to show the location of the two pilot holes.

3. Remove the clutch disc.

4. Install the clutch disc on the flywheel. Do not touch the facing or allow the facing to come in contact with grease or oil. The clutch disc can be aligned using a tool made for that purpose, or with an old mainshaft.

5. Install the clutch cover on the flywheel and install the four standard bolts and the two pilot bolts.

6. To avoid distorting the pressure plate, tighten the bolts evenly a few turns at a time until they are all tight.

7. Torque the bolts to 13–20 ft.lbs. using a crossing pattern.

8. Remove the aligning tool.

9. Apply a light film of lubricant to the release bearing, release lever contact area on the release bearing hub and to the input shaft bearing retainer.

10. Install the transmission.

11. Check the operation of the clutch and if necessary, adjust the pedal free-play and the release lever.

1. Clutch disc
2. Clutch cover
3. Bolt
4. Service hole cover
5. Reamer bolt
6. Pivot pin
7. Release bearing
8. Spring
9. Clutch housing
10. Release fork
11. Oil seal
12. Dust boot

Rotary engine clutch assembly

Clutch Master Cylinder

REMOVAL AND INSTALLATION

All Models

1. Disconnect and plug the fluid outlet line at the outlet fitting on the master cylinder one-way valve.

2. Remove the nuts and bolts attaching the master cylinder to the firewall.

3. Remove the cylinder straight out away from the firewall.

4. Start the pedal pushrod into the master cylinder and position the master cylinder on the firewall.

5. Install the attaching nuts and bolts. Torque the nuts to 12–17 ft.lb.

6. Connect the fluid outlet line to the master cylinder fitting.

7. Bleed the hydraulic system.

8. Check the clutch pedal free-travel and adjust as necessary.

OVERHAUL

1972–84

1. Remove the master cylinder.

2. Clean the outside of the cylinder thoroughly and drain the fluid.

3. On models through 1975, remove the dust cover.

4. Pry out the piston stop ring and remove the stop washer.

5. Remove the piston, piston cup and spring from the cylinder.

6. On all models except the 1976–78 B1800, carefully remove and disassemble the one-way valve.

7. Clean all parts thoroughly using clean brake fluid.

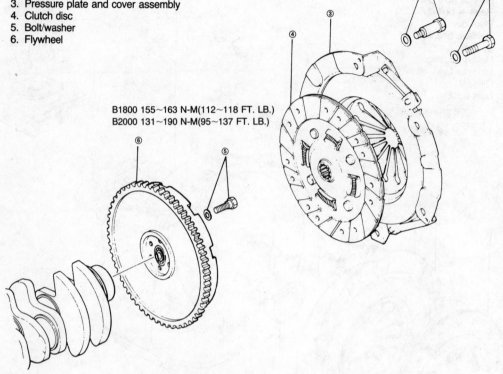

B1800 18~27 N-M(13~20 FT. LB.)
B2000 19~27 N-M(13.7~20 FT. LB.)

1. Bolt/washer
2. Reamer bolt/washer
3. Pressure plate and cover assembly
4. Clutch disc
5. Bolt/washer
6. Flywheel

B1800 155~163 N-M(112~118 FT. LB.)
B2000 131~190 N-M(95~137 FT. LB.)

1976–84 piston engine clutch assembly

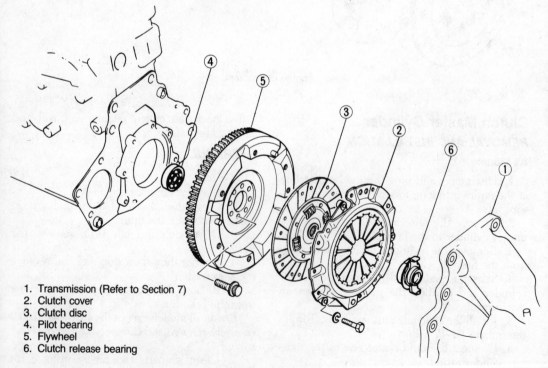

1. Transmission (Refer to Section 7)
2. Clutch cover
3. Clutch disc
4. Pilot bearing
5. Flywheel
6. Clutch release bearing

1986 clutch assembly

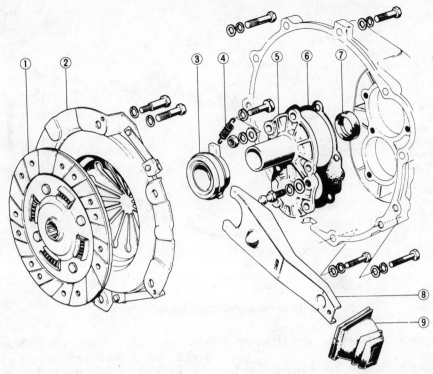

1. Clutch disc
2. Clutch cover and pressure plate assembly
3. Release bearing

4. Spring
5. Front cover
6. Gasket

7. Oil seal
8. Release fork
9. Dust cover

1972–75 piston engine clutch assembly

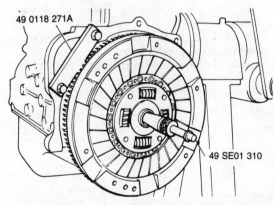

Clutch aligning tool and flywheel holding tool in place

8. Discard any worn, damaged or misshapen parts.

9. Check the piston-to-bore clearance. Clearance should be 0.006 in. If clearance exceeds this figure, replace the unit.

10. If the cylinder bore is lightly scored or brinnelled, it may be honed to restore the finish.

11. Assembly is the reverse of disassembly. Coat all parts with clean brake fluid prior to assembly. On 1976–78 B1800 models, be sure

that the compensating port is open. Fill and bleed the system.

1986

1. Remove the master cylinder.

2. Using snapring pliers, press down on the piston and remove the snapring from the cylinder bore.

3. Remove the piston and secondary cup, primary cup protector, primary cup, return spring, reservoir and bushing.

4. The secondary piston and cup must be blown out with compressed air applied to the fluid pipe hole. Be careful to cover the bore opening with a heavy rag to catch the piston.

5. Inspect all parts for wear or damage. Clean all parts in clean brake fluid.

6. Assembly is the reverse of disassembly. Coat all parts with clean brake fluid prior to assembly.

ONE-WAY VALVE REMOVAL AND INSTALLATION

A one-way valve is used on all master cylinders except 1976–78 1.8 liter models, which have a compensating port instead.

1. Pin
2. Spring
3. Piston
4. Gasket
5. Nut
6. Filler cap
7. Baffle
8. Baffle plate
9. Cylinder and reservoir
10. Return spring
11. Primary cup
12. Piston
13. Secondary cup
14. Washer
15. Stop ring
16. Dust boot

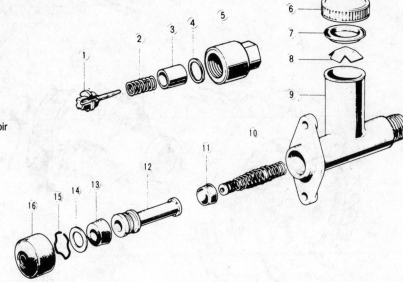

1972–75 piston engine clutch master cylinder

1. Remove the cap from the side of the master cylinder.

2. Remove the washer, one-way valve, and the spring.

3. Installation is the reverse.

Clutch Slave Cylinder

REMOVAL AND INSTALLATION

1972–84

1. Disconnect and plug the line at the cylinder.

2. On models through 1975, unhook the re-lease lever return spring. On 1976 and later models, unhook the lever from the pushrod.

3. Remove the nuts and washers attaching the slave cylinder to the clutch housing.

4. Installation is the reverse of removal. Torque the mounting nuts to 12–17 ft.lb. Fill and bleed the system.

1986

1. Raise and support the front end on jackstands.

2. Back off the flare nut on the fluid pipe to free the slave cylinder hose.

3. Pull off the hose-to-bracket retaining clip

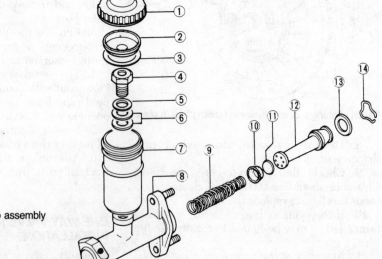

1. Cap
2. Fluid baffle
3. Packing
4. Bolt
5. Washer
6. Corn spring
7. Reservoir
8. Cylinder
9. Spring
10. Primary piston cup
11. Spacer
12. Piston and secondary cup assembly
13. Piston stop washer
14. Piston stop ring

1976–78 piston engine clutch master cylinder

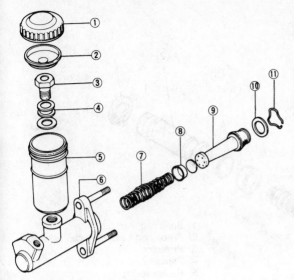

1. Cap
2. Fluid baffle
3. Bolt
4. Washer
5. Reservoir
6. Cylinder
7. Spring
8. Primary piston cup
9. Piston and secondary cup assembly
10. Piston stop washer
11. Piston stop wire

Rotary engine clutch master cylinder

and pull the hose from the bracket. Cap the pipe to prevent fluid loss.

4. Unbolt and remove the slave cylinder.

5. Installation is the reverse of removal. Torque the bolt to 12–17 ft.lb.

OVERHAUL

1972–84

1. Remove the cylinder.
2. Clean the outside thoroughly.
3. Remove the dust cover and release rod.
4. Remove the piston from the cylinder.
5. Disassemble the bleeder valve.
6. Discard any worn, damaged or distorted parts.
7. Clean all parts in clean brake fluid.
8. The cylinder bore may be honed to remove slight surface damage.
9. Assembly is the reverse of disassembly. Coat all parts in clean brake fluid prior to assembly.

1986

1. Remove the cylinder.
2. Clean the outside thoroughly.
3. Remove the dust cover and release rod.
4. Remove the piston from the cylinder.
5. Remove the return spring.
6. Remove the bleeder screw and the small steel check ball underneath it.

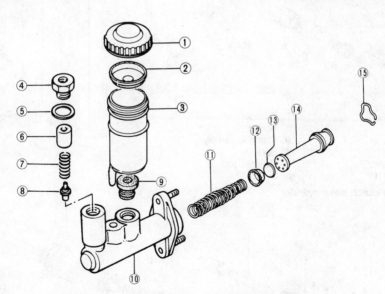

1. Cap
2. Fluid baffle
3. Reservoir
4. Joint bolt
5. Packing
6. Piston-oneway valve
7. Return spring
8. Pin
9. Elbow joint bush
10. Cylinder
11. Spring
12. Primary piston cup
13. Spacer
14. Piston and secondary cup assembly
15. Piston stop ring

1979–84 clutch master cylinder

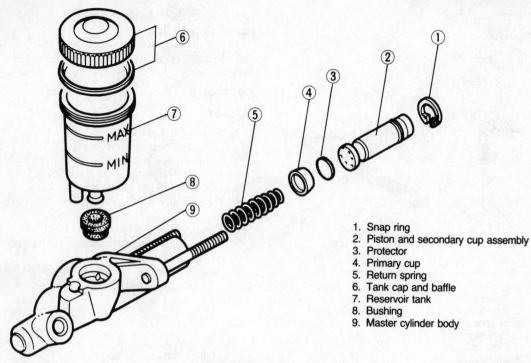

1. Snap ring
2. Piston and secondary cup assembly
3. Protector
4. Primary cup
5. Return spring
6. Tank cap and baffle
7. Reservoir tank
8. Bushing
9. Master cylinder body

1986 clutch master cylinder

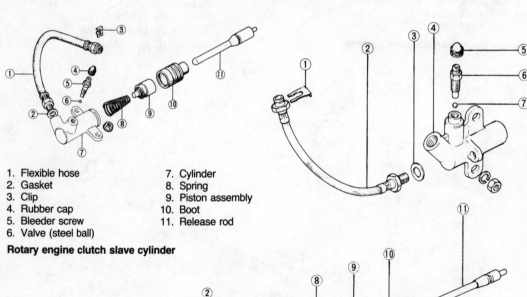

1. Flexible hose   7. Cylinder
2. Gasket   8. Spring
3. Clip   9. Piston assembly
4. Rubber cap   10. Boot
5. Bleeder screw   11. Release rod
6. Valve (steel ball)

Rotary engine clutch slave cylinder

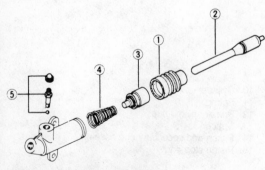

1979–84 clutch slave cylinder

1. Clip   7. Valve (steel ball)
2. Flexible hose   8. Spring
3. Gasket   9. Piston assembly
4. Cylinder   10. Boot
5. Rubber cap   11. Release rod
6. Bleeder screw

1972–78 piston engine clutch slave cylinder

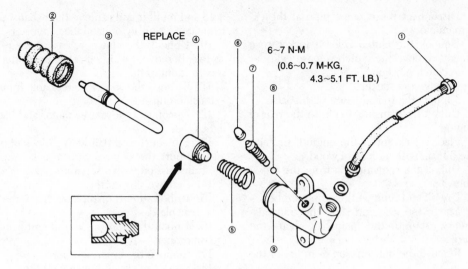

6~7 N-M
(0.6~0.7 M-KG,
4.3~5.1 FT. LB.)

1986 clutch slave cylinder

7. Discard any worn, damaged or distorted parts.

8. Clean all parts in clean brake fluid.

9. The cylinder bore may be honed to remove slight surface damage.

10. Assembly is the reverse of disassembly. Coat all parts in clean brake fluid prior to assembly.

BLEEDING THE HYDRAULIC SYSTEM

The clutch hydraulic system must be bled whenever the line has been disconnected or air has entered the system.

To bleed the system, remove the rubber cap from the bleeder valve and attach a rubber hose to the valve. Submerge the other end of the hose in a large jar of clean brake fluid. Open the bleeder valve. Depress the clutch pedal and allow it to return slowly. Continue this pumping action and watch the jar of brake fluid. When air bubbles stop appearing, close the bleeder valve and remove the tube.

During the bleeding process, the master cylinder must be kept at least ¾ full. After the bleeding operation is finished, install the cap on the bleeder valve and fill the master cylinder to the proper level. Always use fresh brake fluid, and above all, do not use the fluid that was in the jar for bleeding, since it contains air. Install the master cylinder reservoir cap.

MANUAL TRANSMISSION

The 4-speed manual transmission, used from 1972 though 1984, is synchronized in all forward gears. The transmission case is of light metal construction, manufactured as two mated halves. There is no external shift linkage; all

the shifting mechanisms are contained within the case. There are no linkage or shifter adjustments.

An optional 5-speed manual, first available in 1976 and used through 1984, has the same ratio in the first four gears as the 4-speed, but has an overdrive 5th gear with a 0.875:1 ratio. It is synchronized in all forward gears. The transmission case is cast aluminum, with a bottom cover and removable clutch and extension housings. The gearshift lever is connected directly to the shift forks; thus, there is no external linkage, and no adjustments are necessary.

In 1986 a completely different unit was introduced. This transmission is a 4-speed unit which, in its optional form, is converted to a 5-speed overdrive gearbox with the addition of an intermediate housing containing the overdrive gearing.

REMOVAL AND INSTALLATION

B1600

1. Raise and support the truck. Drain the lubricant from the transmission.

2. Disconnect the ground wire from the battery.

3. Remove the gearshift lever boot.

4. Unbolt the cover plate from the gearshift lever retainer.

5. Pull the gearshift lever, shim and bushing straight up and away from the gearshift lever retainer.

6. Disconnect the wires from the starter motor and back-up light switch.

7. Disconnect the speedometer cable from the extension housing.

8. Remove the driveshaft.

9. Unbolt the exhaust pipe from the bracket on the transmission case.

10. Disconnect the exhaust pipe at the exhaust manifold.

11. Unhook the clutch release fork return spring and remove the clutch release cylinder from the clutch housing.

12. Remove the starter.

13. Support the transmission with a jack.

14. Unbolt the transmission from the rear of the engine.

15. Place a jack under the engine, protecting the oil pan with a block of wood.

16. Unbolt the transmission from the crossmember.

17. Unbolt and remove the crossmember.

18. Lower the jack and slide the transmission rearward until the mainshaft clears the clutch disc.

19. Remove the transmission from under the trunk.

20. Installation is the reverse of removal.

B1800, B2200, 1979–84 B2000

1. Put the gearshift in Neutral.

2. Lift up the boot covering the shift lever and detach the gearshift tower from the extension housing. Remove the shift lever, tower and gasket as an assembly.

3. Cover the opening in the case with a heavy rag to keep dirt out.

4. Remove the negative battery cable. Raise and support the truck.

5. Disconnect the driveshaft at the rear axle.

6. Remove the driveshaft center bearing support and pull the driveshaft rearward to disconnect the driveshaft from the transmission. Install a plug in the extension housing to prevent lubricant from leaking out.

7. Remove the exhaust pipe brackets from the transmission case.

8. Disconnect the exhaust pipe hanger from the clutch housing.

9. Disconnect the exhaust pipe at the manifold and muffler and remove the exhaust pipe-resonator assembly or catalytic converter.

10. Unhook the clutch release lever return spring. Remove the clutch release cylinder and secure it out of the way.

11. Remove the speedometer cable from the extension housing.

12. Disconnect the starter motor and backup light wires.

13. Protect the oil pan with a block of wood and support the engine with a jack. Support the transmission with a separate jack.

14. Remove the starter.

15. Unbolt the transmission from the engine rear plate.

16. Unbolt the transmission mount from the crossmember.

17. Remove the crossmember.

18. Work the clutch housing off the locating dowels. Slide the transmission rearward until the input shaft spline clears the clutch disc.

19. Remove the transmission from the truck.

20. Be sure that all mating surfaces are free of dirt, burrs and paint.

21. Lift the transmission into place and start the input shaft into the clutch disc. Be sure that the splines align and move the transmission forward until the clutch housing seats on the locating dowels of the engine rear plate.

22. Bolt the clutch housing to the rear plate.

23. Install the starter motor.

24. Raise the engine and install the rear crossmember.

25. Install the rear transmission mount on the crossmember. Bolt the transmission to the rear mount.

26. Remove the jacks.

27. Install the driveshaft in the transmission extension housing. Install the center bearing.

28. Connect the driveshaft to the rear axle flange.

29. Install the exhaust pipe and resonator.

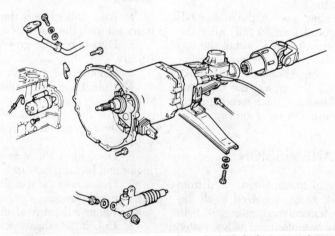

Typical 1972–84 piston engine manual transmission mounting

30. Connect the exhaust pipe to the fly-wheel housing and transmission brackets.

31. Connect the starter and back-up light wires.

32. Install the clutch release cylinder.

33. Adjust the clutch release lever free travel. Connect the return spring.

34. Connect the speedometer cable.

35. Fill the transmission with lubricant.

36. Lower the truck.

37. Install the shift tower and gasket. Install the boot.

38. Road test the truck and check for leaks.

1986 B2000

1. Disconnect the battery ground cable.

2. Raise and support the truck on jack-stands.

3. Drain the transmission oil.

4. Remove the gearshift knob, remove the shift console attaching screws, and lift off the console.

5. Remove the shift lever-to-extension housing attaching bolts and remove the shift lever.

6. Remove the driveshaft.

7. Disconnect the speedometer cable from the transmission.

8. Disconnect the wiring at the starter and remove the starter.

9. Disconnect and tag all wiring at the transmission.

10. Disconnect the parking brake return spring, and disconnect the parking brake cables.

11. Remove the clutch slave cylinder.

12. Remove the transmission front support bracket.

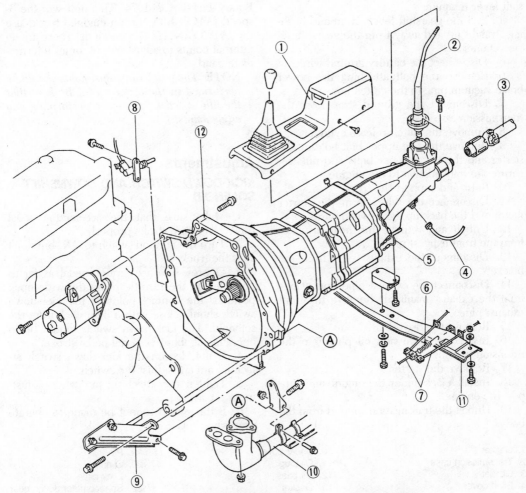

1. Console	5. Wiring harnesses	9. Gusset plate
2. Gearshift lever	6. Return spring	10. Exhaust pipe
3. Propeller shaft	7. Parking brake cables	11. Transmission cross member
4. Speedometer cable	8. Release cylinder	12. Transmission

Typical 1986 manual transmission mounting

13. Disconnect the exhaust pipe at the transmission and manifold.

14. Support the weight of the transmission with a floor jack or transmission jack.

15. Remove the transmission crossmember.

16. Lower the transmission to get access to the top bolts and remove the transmission-to-engine bolts.

17. Pull the transmission straight back and away from the engine. When clear, lower it and remove it from under the truck.

18. Installation is the reverse of removal. Torque the transmission-to-engine bolts to 60–65 ft.lb.; the gearshift lever bolts to 6–8 ft.lb.

Rotary Pick-Up

1. Remove the knob from the gearshift lever.

2. Remove the gearshift lever.

3. Unbolt the retainer cover from the gearshift lever retainer.

4. Pull the gearshift lever, shim and bushing straight up and away from the gearshift lever retainer.

5. Disconnect the battery ground wire.

6. Remove the bolt attaching the power brake vacuum pipe to the clutch housing.

7. Disconnect the ground strap from the transmission case.

8. Remove the clutch release cylinder.

9. Remove the one upper bolt holding the starter and the three upper bolts and nuts securing the transmission to the engine.

10. Raise and support the truck.

11. Disconnect the wires from the starter motor and the back-up light switch wires.

12. Unbolt and remove the heat insulator from the front exhaust pipe.

13. Disconnect the exhaust pipe from the brackets.

14. Disconnect the exhaust pipe front flange from the exhaust manifold. Remove the front exhaust pipe.

15. Remove the driveshaft.

16. Insert a transmission oil plug into the extension housing.

17. Remove the starter.

18. Install a jack under the engine and support the engine.

19. Unbolt the transmission support from the body.

20. Remove the two lower bolts holding the transmission to the engine.

21. Slide the transmission rearward until the mainshaft clears the clutch disc and remove the transmission from under the truck.

22. Installation is the reverse of removal.

Back-Up Light Switch
REMOVAL AND INSTALLATION

The switch is located on the upper left rear of the transmission case. To replace it, disconnect the wiring and unscrew the switch from the case. Don't lose the washer.

AUTOMATIC TRANSMISSION

An automatic transmission was first used on the Rotary Pick-Up in 1974. This unit was the 3-speed JATCO R3A. Piston engined trucks use the JATCO 3N71B, 3-speed unit. There are no internal points to adjust except for an intermediate band.

NOTE: *The following adjustments should be performed in the order given. Be sure that the idle speed is set before performing any adjustments.*

Adjustments
KICK-DOWN SWITCH AND DOWNSHIFT SOLENOID

1. Make sure that the accelerator pedal travels its entire stroke properly.

2. Turn the ignition switch to ON, but don't start the truck.

3. Depress the accelerator pedal as far as possible. As the throttle nears the wide open position, the contact point of the kick-down switch should close with a light click from the solenoid. The kick-down switch should begin operation at about 7⁄8 of full pedal stroke.

4. If not, loosen the kick-down switch attaching nut and adjust the switch.

5. Tighten the attaching nut when adjustment is correct.

6. If the switch cannot be made to operate properly, replace it.

1. Gasket	10. Under cover	19. Pin
2. Transmission case	11. Oil plug	20. O ring
3. Gasket	12. Oil pass	21. Lock plate
4. Blind cover	13. Gasket	22. Speedometer driven gear
5. Clip	14. Extension housing	23. Sleeve
6. Intermediate housing	15. Blind cover	24. Oil seal
7. Rear bearing housing	16. Gasket	25. Cable joint
8. Oil plug	17. Oil seal	
9. Gasket	18. Pin	

Rotary engine manual transmission

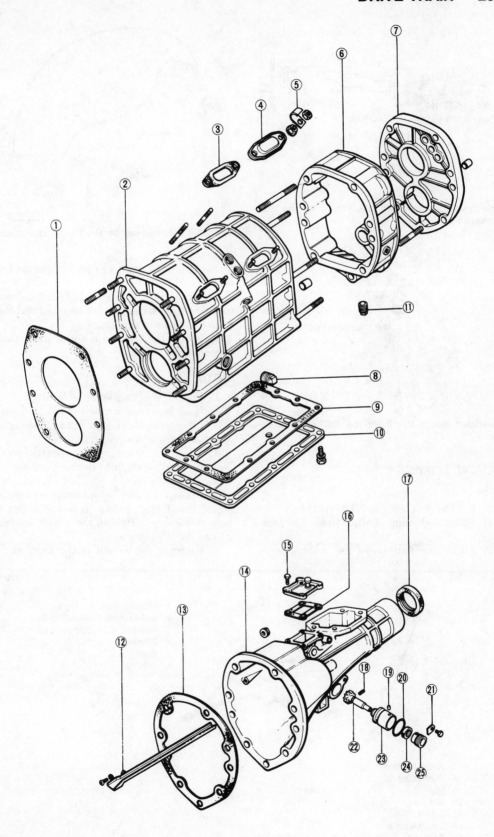

Rotary engine manual transmission

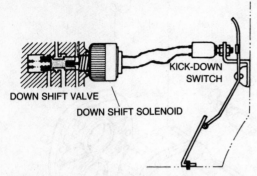

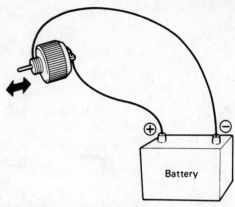

Kick-down and downshift adjustment for the R3A transmission

Downshift solenoid test for the 3N71B transmission

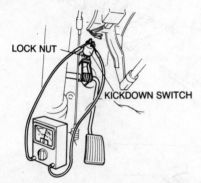

Kick-down switch check for the 3N71B transmission

MANUAL LINKAGE

R3A

1. Put the shift lever in NEUTRAL.
2. Raise and support the truck on jack-stands.
3. Adjust the position of the manual lever

by turning the T-joint so that the manual lever is in NEUTRAL.

4. Shift the gearshift lever to PARK and make sure that the parking pawl is engaged and there is no looseness in the linkage.
5. Lower the truck and check transmission operation.

3N71B

1. Put the gearshift lever in Neutral.
2. Raise and support the truck.
3. Disconnect the T-joint from the lower end of the selector lever operating arm.
4. Move the transmission manual lever to Neutral, the 3rd detent position from the rear of the transmission.
5. Loosen the two T-joint retaining nuts and adjust the T-joint so that it freely enters the hole of the lever. Tighten the retaining nuts to secure the adjustment.
6. Connect the T-joint to the lever and at-

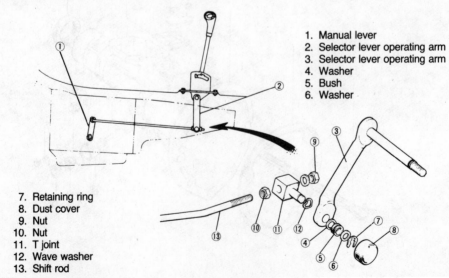

1. Manual lever
2. Selector lever operating arm
3. Selector lever operating arm
4. Washer
5. Bush
6. Washer
7. Retaining ring
8. Dust cover
9. Nut
10. Nut
11. T joint
12. Wave washer
13. Shift rod

R3A manual linkage

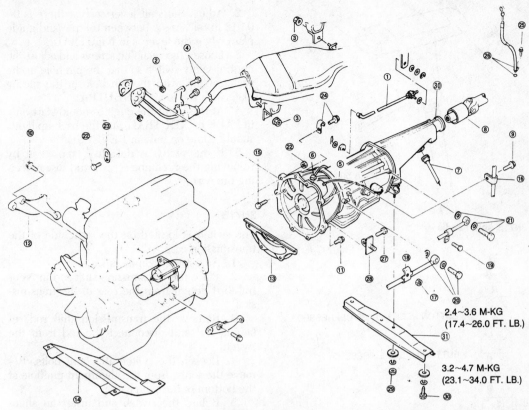

1. Shift rod
2. Nuts
3. Nuts
4. Bolts
5. Connector (for solenoid)
6. Connector (for inhibitor switch)
7. Speedometer cable
8. Propeller shaft

9. Starter-installation bolts
10. Bolts
11. Bolts
12. Gusset Plates
13. Lower cover
14. Under cover
15. Bolts
16. Vacuum-pipe clip

17. Nut
18. Pipe clip
19. Pipe-clip-installation bolt
20. Connector bolt and washers
21. Connector bolt and washers
22. Bolt and nut
23. Engine hanger

2.4~3.6 M-KG
(17.4~26.0 FT. LB.)

3.2~4.7 M-KG
(23.1~34.0 FT. LB.)

3N71B transmission, exploded view

tach it with the spring washer, flat washer and retaining clip.

7. Lower the truck and check the operation of the linkage. Be sure that all gears engage properly.

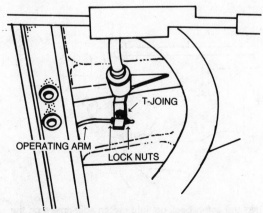

Manual linkage adjustment points for the 3N71B

SHIFT LEVER HANDLE INTERLOCK

3N71B

The interlock should be adjusted when it does not perform as shown in the accompanying illustration, or, whenever the handle has been removed.

1. Back off the locknut below the handle.
2. Position the shifter in either N or D.
3. Screw in the handle until no play is felt at the interlock button.
4. Turn the handle one additional turn, if necessary, to position the button on the driver's side.
5. Depress the button and shift to P. If the lever cannot be moved to the P position, screw in the handle an additional turn, repeating the shift move an additional turn, until P can be engaged smoothly. From this point, shift through the various positions, confirming that the shifter works as shown in the illustration. If the lever can be shifted to R from either P or

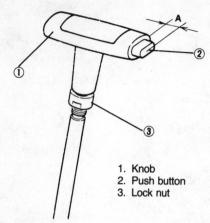

1. Knob
2. Push button
3. Lock nut

3N71B shift handle

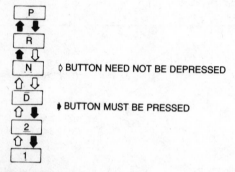

◊ BUTTON NEED NOT BE DEPRESSED

♦ BUTTON MUST BE PRESSED

3N71B shifter performance chart

N, or into 2 from D, without depressing the button, back out on the handle.

6. When the adjustment is completed, check that the button protrudes 6.0mm from the handle in the N or P position. Recheck the shift pattern.

7. Tighten the locknut to 15 ft.lb.

NEUTRAL SAFETY/BACK-UP LIGHT SWITCH

R3A

The switch is located at the base of the shift lever.

1. Remove the housing from the shift lever.

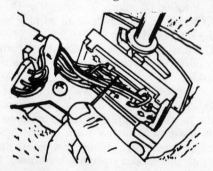

Neutral safety/back-up light switch adjustment on the R3A transmission

2. Adjust the shift lever so that there is 0–0.012 in. clearance between the pin and guide plate when the lever is in NEUTRAL.

3. Loosen the retaining screws and adjust the neutral safety switch so that the pin hole in the switch aligns with the pin hole in the sliding plate with the lever in NEUTRAL.

4. At this point the engine should start only in PARK or NEUTRAL, and the back-up lights should come on only in REVERSE.

5. If the switch is defective, replace it by removing the retaining screws and disconnecting the wiring.

3N71B

The switch is located on the right side of the transmission case.

1. Adjust the manual linkage.

2. Place the transmission shift rod in Neutral (3rd detent from the rear of the transmission).

3. Remove the transmission shift rod retaining nut and disconnect the rod from the switch.

4. Loosen the switch attaching bolts. Remove the screw from the alignment pin hole at the bottom of the switch.

5. Rotate the switch and insert an alignment pin, 1.5mm (0.059 in.) diameter into the alignment pin hole and internal rotor.

6. Tighten the two switch attaching bolts and remove the alignment pin.

7. Reinstall the alignment pin hole screw in the switch body.

8. Connect the shift rod.

9. Check the operation of the switch. The engine should start, only with the transmission selector lever in Neutral or Park. The back-up lights should come on, only with the lever in Reverse.

10. If the switch is defective, replace it by simply removing the attaching screws and disconnecting the wiring.

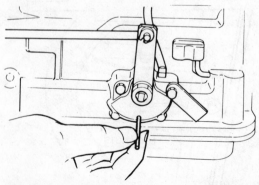

Neutral safety/back-up light switch adjustment on the 3N71B transmission

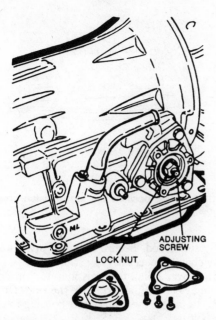

Intermediate band adjustment on the R3A transmission

INTERMEDIATE BAND ADJUSTMENT

1. Raise and support the truck.
2. Place a drain pan under the transmission and loosen the pan attaching bolts to drain the fluid. Finally remove all the bolts except the two at the front.
3. When the fluid has drained, remove and thoroughly clean the pan.
4. Discard the pan gasket.
5. Loosen the brake band adjusting screw locknut and tighten the adjusting screw to 9–11 ft.lb.
6. Back the adjusting screw off two turns.
7. Hold the adjusting screw locknut to 22–29 ft.lb.
8. Install a new pan gasket and install the pan on the transmission.
9. Lower the truck and fill the transmission with fluid.

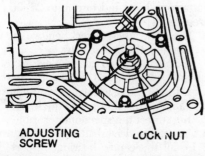

Intermediate band adjustment on the 3N71B transmission

Transmission Fluid Pan
REMOVAL AND INSTALLATION

1. Raise and support the truck on jackstands.
2. Place a drain pan under the transmission.
3. Remove all the pan bolts except the two at the front. Loosen these slightly and allow the fluid to drain. The pan may have to be carefully pried loose.
4. Remove the pan. Discard the gasket.
5. Clean the pan thoroughly in a safe solvent.
6. Installation is the reverse of removal. Torque the bolts to 5 ft.lb.

Transmission
REMOVAL AND INSTALLATION
R3A

1. Disconnect the battery ground.
2. Disconnect the power brake vacuum line from the converter housing.
3. Raise and support the truck on jackstands.
4. Remove the bell housing access cover and remove the four converter-to-drive plate bolts by turning the drive plate until the bolt appears and holding the drive pulley lockbolt with a wrench.
5. Remove the heat insulator from the exhaust pipe.
6. Disconnect the exhaust pipe at the manifold and the muffler and remove the pipe.
7. Remove the underbody heat shield.
8. Remove the driveshaft as explained in Chapter 7.
9. Disconnect the speedometer cable from the extension housing.
10. Disconnect the shift linkage at the transmission.
11. Remove the starter as explained in Chapter 3.
12. Remove the converter housing cover.
13. Support the transmission with a floor jack. Remove the transmission crossmember.
14. Lower the transmission slightly and remove the vacuum fitting bolt from the intake manifold.
15. Remove the vacuum line clips from the length of the transmission.
16. Disconnect and tag all wiring from the transmission.
17. Disconnect and plug the cooling lines from the transmission.
18. Remove the transmission-to-engine bolts.
19. Raise the transmission to its normal position and slide it rearward. It may be necessary to carefully pry the transmission from the

engine. Be careful! The torque converter will come off with the transmission, but can easily fall.

20. Lower the jack once the unit is clear.

21. Check the converter drive plate runout. Runout should be less than 0.012 in. If not, replace the drive plate.

22. If the converter was removed and installed, check the distance between the flat face of the converter and the mating surface of the housing. Distance should be 0.78 in. If not, remove and install the converter in a different position.

23. Installation is the reverse of removal. Torque the converter-to-drive plate bolts and the transmission-to-engine bolts to 40 ft.lb. Adjust the linkage.

3N71B

1. Disconnect the negative cable from the battery.

2. Raise and support the truck.

3. Drain the transmission fluid but do not remove the pan. After the fluid has drained, install a few bolts to hold the pan in place, temporarily.

4. Remove the exhaust pipe bracket bolt from the right side of the converter housing.

5. Remove the exhaust pipe flange bolts from the rear of the resonator or catalytic converter, and disconnect the pipe.

6. Disconnect the driveshaft from the rear axle flange.

7. Remove the driveshaft center bearing support nuts, washers, and lockwashers. Lower the driveshaft and remove it from the transmission.

8. Disconnect the speedometer cable.

9. Disconnect the shift rod from the manual lever.

10. Remove the vacuum hose from the diaphragm. Disconnect the electrical connectors from the downshift solenoid and inhibitor switch, and remove their wires from the clip.

11. Disconnect and plug the cooler lines from the radiator at the transmission. Use a flare nut wrench if one is available.

12. Remove the access cover from the lower front of the converter housing.

13. Matchmark the drive plate (flywheel) and torque converter for reassembly. Remove the four bolts holding the torque converter to the drive plate.

14. Remove the bolts connecting the crossmember to the transmission.

15. Support the transmission with a jack. Remove the crossmember-to-frame bolts, and remove the crossmember.

16. Make sure that the transmission is se-

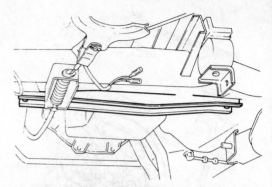

On 1984 trucks, position the transmission crossmember as shown

curely supported. Secure it to the jack with a safety chain, if necessary.

17. Lower the transmission to provide working clearance, and remove the starter.

18. Remove the converter housing-to-engine bolts.

19. Remove the fluid filler tube.

20. With a pry bar, exert light pressure between the converter and the drive plate to prevent the converter from disengaging from the transmission as it is removed.

21. Lower the transmission and converter as an assembly. Be careful not to let the converter fall out.

22. Place the transmission on the jack. Be sure that the converter is properly installed.

23. Raise the transmission into place. Install the converter housing-to-engine bolts, and torque in two stages to 23–34 ft.lb.

24. Lower the transmission on the jack and install the starter.

25. Install the fluid filler tube with a new O-ring.

26. Raise the transmission slightly, and install the crossmember to the frame. Tighten the bolts to 23–34 ft.lb.

27. Lower the transmission and install the transmission-to-crossmember bolts. Tighten to 23–34 ft.lb.

28. Align the matchmarks made earlier on the torque converter and drive plate. Install the four attaching bolts and torque to 25–36 ft.lb. in three stages.

29. Install the access cover. Remove the jack.

30. Connect the cooler lines.

31. Install the electrical connectors to the switch and solenoid, and replace the wires in the clip. Install the diaphragm vacuum hose.

32. Connect the shift rod to the lever.

33. Reconnect the speedometer cable.

34. Insert the driveshaft into the transmission. Install the center bearing support. Bolt the driveshaft to the rear of the axle flange.

35. Connect the exhaust pipe to the reson-

ator or catalytic converter, using a new gasket. Reinstall the exhaust pipe clamp onto the converter housing, and torque the bolt to 10–15 ft.lb.

36. Install a new pan gasket and the fluid pan, if this has not already been done.

37. Lower the truck. Connect the battery cable. Fill the transmission through the dipstick tube with the specified fluid, being careful not to overfill, and check for leaks.

DRIVESHAFT AND U-JOINTS

A 2-piece driveshaft is used on all models through 1976. Some 1977 and later models use a one piece driveshaft with U-joints at each end.

The 2-piece driveshaft assembly consists of the front shaft, the rear shaft, a center support bearing and U-joints and yokes. The rear end of the driveshaft is attached to a companion flange at the rear axle through a U-joint, and, at the front, to the mainshaft by means of a sliding yoke. This arrangement provides for fore-aft movement of the driveshaft as the truck moves up and down. The center of the drive-shaft is supported by the bearing attached to the underside of the truck.

Driveshaft

REMOVAL AND INSTALLATION

1. Matchmark the rear U-joint with the rear companion flange. Remove the bolts attaching the driveshaft to the rear companion flange.

2. On 2-piece units, remove the center support bearing bracket from the underbody.

3. Pull the driveshaft rearward and out of the transmission. Plug the rear seal opening.

4. Installation is the reverse of removal. Make sure that you align the matchmarks. Torque the rear companion flange bolts to 39–47 ft.lb.; the center bearing bracket nuts to 27–38 ft.lb.

U-Joint

OVERHAUL

1. Remove the driveshaft.

2. If the front yoke is to be disassembled, matchmark the driveshaft and sliding splined yoke (transmission yoke) so that driveline bal-

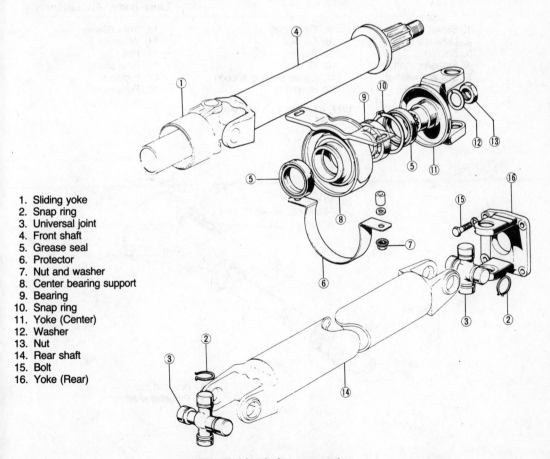

1. Sliding yoke
2. Snap ring
3. Universal joint
4. Front shaft
5. Grease seal
6. Protector
7. Nut and washer
8. Center bearing support
9. Bearing
10. Snap ring
11. Yoke (Center)
12. Washer
13. Nut
14. Rear shaft
15. Bolt
16. Yoke (Rear)

1972–76 driveshaft components

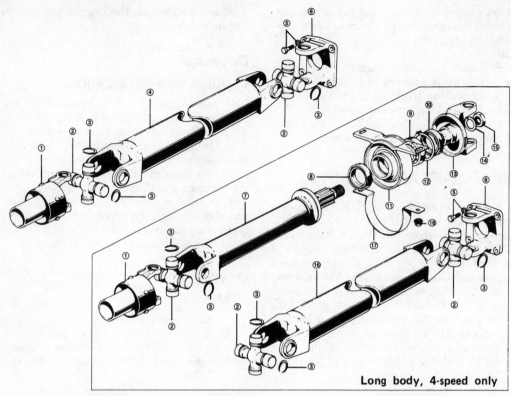

1. Sliding yoke
2. Universal joint
3. Snap ring
4. Propeller shaft
5. Bolt and washer
6. Yoke (Rear)
7. Front shaft
8. Oil seal
9. Bearing
10. Oil seal
11. Center bearing support
12. Snap ring
13. Yoke (Center)
14. Washer
15. Nut
16. Rear shaft
17. Protector
18. Flange nut

1977–83 driveshaft components

Long body, 4-speed only

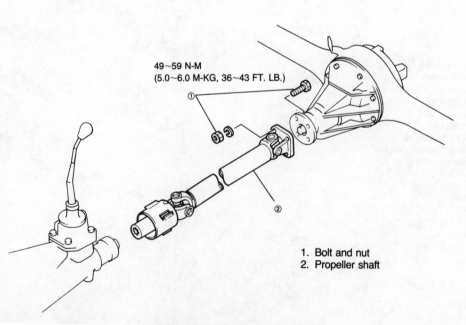

49~59 N-M
(5.0~6.0 M-KG, 36~43 FT. LB.)

1. Bolt and nut
2. Propeller shaft

1986 short bed driveshaft components

1. Yoke
2. Universal joint set
3. Propeller shaft
4. Universal joint yoke
5. Protector
6. Snap ring
7. Support
8. Ball bearing
9. Oil seal
10. Yoke

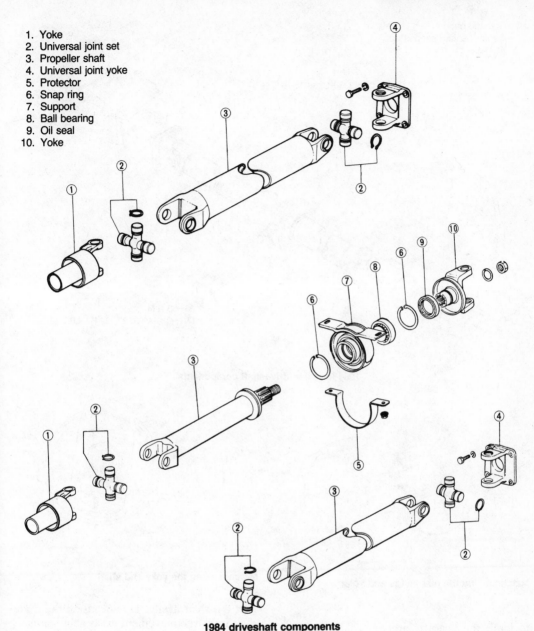

1984 driveshaft components

ance is preserved upon reassembly. Remove the snap rings which retain the bearing caps.

3. Select two sockets, one small enough to pass through the yoke holes for the bearing caps, the other large enough to receive the bearing cap.

4. Using a vise or a press, position the small and large sockets on either side of the U-joint. Press in on the smaller socket so that it presses the opposite bearing cap out of the yoke and into the larger socket. If the cap does not come all the way out, grasp it with a pair of pliers and work it out.

5. Reverse the position of the sockets so that the smaller socket presses on the cross. Press the other bearing cap out of the yoke.

6. Repeat the procedure on the other bearings.

7. To install, grease the bearing caps and needles throughly if they are not pregreased. Start a new bearing cap into one side of the yoke. Position the cross in the yoke.

8. Select two sockets small enough to pass through the yoke holes. Put the sockets against the cross and the cap, and press the bearing cap ¼ inch below the surface of the yoke. If there is a sudden increase in the force needed to press the cap into place, or if the cross starts

1. Bolt and nut
2. Center bearing support nut
3. Propeller shaft

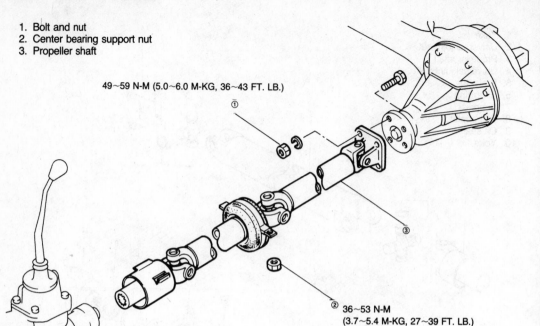

49~59 N-M (5.0~6.0 M-KG, 36~43 FT. LB.)

36~53 N-M
(3.7~5.4 M-KG, 27~39 FT. LB.)

1986 long bed driveshaft components

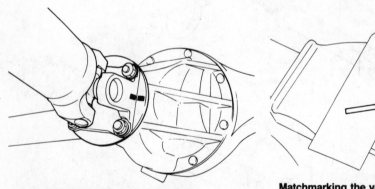

Matchmarking the rear flange and yoke

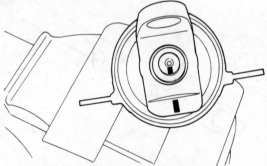

Matchmarking the yoke and shaft

to bind, the bearings are cocked. They must be removed and restarted in the yoke. Failure to do so will greatly reduce the life of the bearing.

9. Install a new snap ring.

10. Start a new bearing into the opposite side. Place a socket on it and press in until the opposite bearing contacts the snap ring.

11. Install a new snap ring. It may be necessary to grind the facing surface of the snap ring slightly to permit easier installation.

12. Install the other bearings in the same manner.

13. Check the joint for free movement. If binding exists, smack the yoke ears with a brass or plastic faced hammer to seat the bearing needles. Do not strike the bearings, and support the shaft firmly. Do not install the driveshaft until free movement exists at all joints.

14. The nut attaching the yoke and bearing to the front coupling is torqued to 115–130 ft.lb.

Center Bearing
REPLACEMENT

The center support bearing is a sealed unit which requires no periodic maintenance. The following procedure should be used if it becomes necessary to replace the bearing. You will need a pair of snap pliers for this job.

1. Remove the driveshaft assembly.

2. To maintain driveline balance, matchmark the rear driveshaft, the center yoke and the front driveshaft so that they may be installed in their original positions.

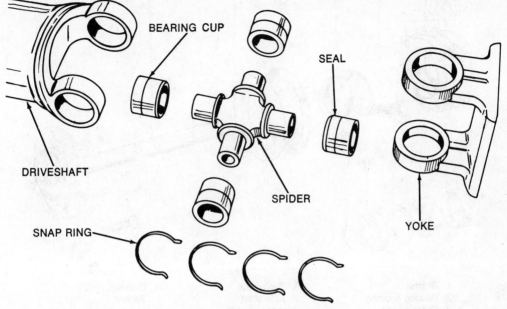

BEARING CUP

SEAL

DRIVESHAFT

SPIDER

YOKE

SNAP RING

Exploded view of a U-joint

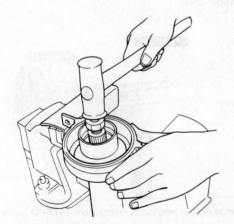

Place an old nut on the end of the driveshaft and tap the nut lightly to force off the center support and bearing assembly

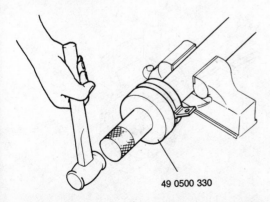

49 0500 330

Installing the center support and bearing assembly

3. Remove the center universal joint from the center yoke, leaving it attached to the rear driveshaft. See the following section for the correct procedure.

4. Remove the nut and washer securing the center yoke to the front driveshaft.

5. Slide the center yoke off the splines. The rear oil seal should slide off with it.

6. If the oil has remained on top of the snap ring, remove and discard the seal. Remove the snap ring from its groove. Remove the bearing.

7. Slide the center support and front oil seal from the front driveshaft. Discard the seal.

8. Install the new bearing into the center support. Secure it with the snap ring.

9. Apply a coat of grease to the lips of the new oil seals, and install them into the center support on either side of the bearing.

10. Coat the splines of the front driveshaft with grease. Install the center support assembly and the center yoke onto the front driveshaft, being sure to match up the marks made during disassembly.

11. Install the washer and nut. Torque the nut to 116–130 ft.lb.

12. Check that the center support assembly rotates smoothly around the driveshaft.

13. Align the mating marks on the center yoke and the rear driveshaft, and assemble the center universal joint.

14. Install the driveshaft. Be sure that the rear yoke and the axle flange are aligned properly.

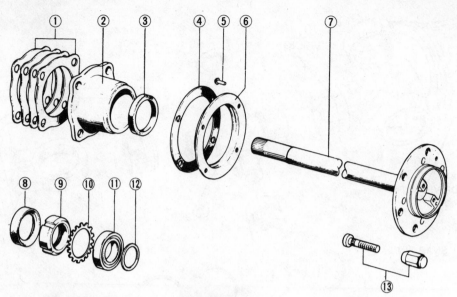

1. Shims
2. Bearing housing
3. Outer oil seal
4. Gasket
5. Rivet
6. Baffle seal
7. Axle shaft
8. Inner oil seal
9. Lock nut
10. Lock washer
11. Bearing
12. Spacer
13. Hub bolt and lug nut

1972–84 rear axle components

REAR AXLE

Mazda uses a removable carrier type rear axle.

Axle Shaft, Bearing and Seal
REMOVAL AND INSTALLATION
1972-84

1. Raise and support the rear end on jack-stands.

2. Remove the wheels and brake drums.

3. Remove the brake shoes.

4. Remove the parking brake cable retainer.

5. Disconnect and cap the brake lines at the wheel cylinders.

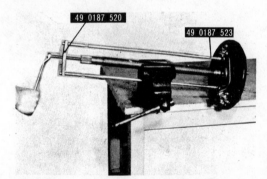

Removing the bearing housing from 1972–84 axles

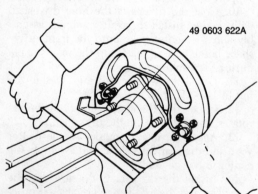

Removing the bearing housing locknut

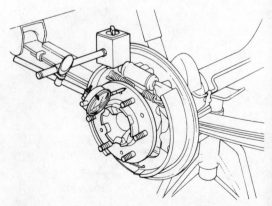

Measuring axleshaft endplay on 1972–84 axles

6. Remove the bolts securing the backing plate and bearing housing.

7. Slide the axle shaft from the axle housing.

8. Remove the oil seal from the axle housing and discard it. A puller may be necessary.

9. Straighten the tabs on the lockwasher and remove the nut and lockwasher from the axle shaft.

10. Remove the bearing and race from the shaft. A puller or press may be necessary. Discard the spacer.

11. Remove the outer seal from the bearing housing and discard it.

12. Discard the gasket from the baffle.

13. Using new seals and a new gasket, install all parts in reverse order of removal. Temporarily install the bearing/backing plate bolts, torquing them to 16 ft.lb. Don't install the brake shoes or drum yet.

14. Using a dial indicator mounted as shown, check axle shaft endplay. If only one shaft has been removed, endplay should be 0.002–0.006 in. If both shafts have been removed, check endplay immediately after the first shaft has been replaced. Endplay should be 0.026–0.033 in. Install the second shaft and check that endplay. Second shaft endplay should be 0.002–0.006 in. If endplay at any step is not within specifications, shims are available.

15. After endplay is adjusted, torque the bearing retainer/backing plate bolts to 40–50 ft.lb. and assemble all remaining parts.

1986

NOTE: *A bearing puller and a press are necessary for this procedure.*

1. Raise and support the rear end on jackstands.

2. Remove the wheel and brake drum.

3. Remove the brake shoes.

4. Remove the parking brake cable retainer.

5. Disconnect and cap the brake lines at the wheel cylinders.

6. Remove the bolts securing the backing plate and bearing housing.

7. Slide the axle shaft from the axle housing. Be careful to avoid damaging the oil seal with the shaft.

8. If the seal in the axle housing is damaged in any way, it must be replaced. The seal can be removed using a slide hammer and adapter.

9. Remove two of the backing plate bolts, diagonally from each other.

10. Using a grinding wheel, grind down the bearing retaining collar in one spot, until about 5mm remains before you get to the axle shaft. Place a chisel at this point and break the collar. Be careful to avoid damaging the shaft.

CAUTION: *Wear some kind of protective goggles when grinding the collar and breaking the collar from the shaft!*

11. Using a press or puller, remove the hub and bearing assembly from the shaft. Remove the spacer from the shaft.

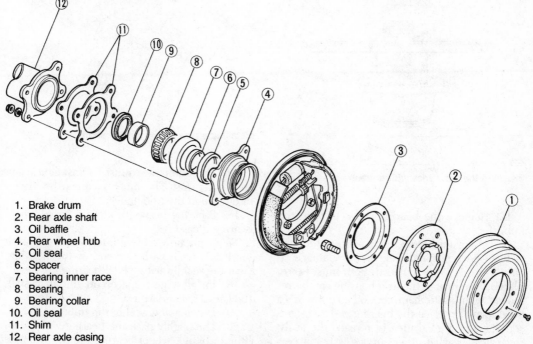

1. Brake drum
2. Rear axle shaft
3. Oil baffle
4. Rear wheel hub
5. Oil seal
6. Spacer
7. Bearing inner race
8. Bearing
9. Bearing collar
10. Oil seal
11. Shim
12. Rear axle casing

1986 rear axle outer end components

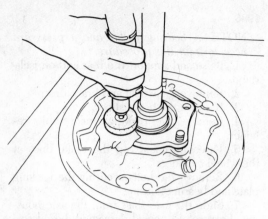

Grinding down the bearing collar on 1986 axles

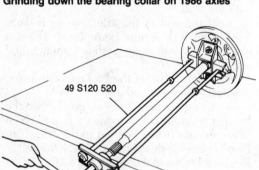

49 S120 520

Removing the bearing housing from 1986 axles

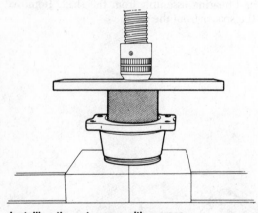

Installing the outer race with a press

Pack the hub at the places shaded, with lithium based wheel bearing grease

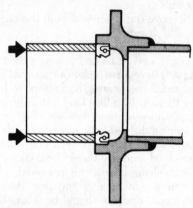

Installing a new oil seal

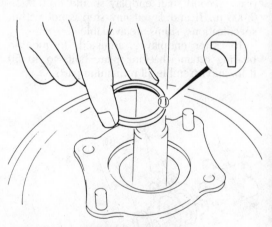

Installing a new spacer on the shaft

12. Remove the bearing and seal from the hub.

13. Using a drift, tap the race from the hub.

14. Check all parts for wear or damage. If either race is to be replaced, both must be replaced. The race in the axle housing can be removed with a slide hammer and adapter. It's a good idea to replace the bearing and races as a set. It's also a good idea to replace the seals, regardless of what other service is being performed.

15. The outer race must be installed using an arbor press. The inner race can be driven into place in the axle housing.

16. Pack the hub with lithium based wheel bearing grease.

17. Tap a new oil seal into the axle housing until it is flush with the end of the housing. Coat the seal lip with wheel bearing grease.

18. Install a new spacer on the shaft with the larger flat surface up.

19. Install a new seal in the hub.

20. Thoroughly pack the bearing with clean, lithium based, wheel bearing grease. If one is available, use a grease gun adapter meant for

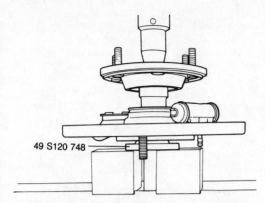

49 S120 748

Pressing a new bearing into position on the shaft

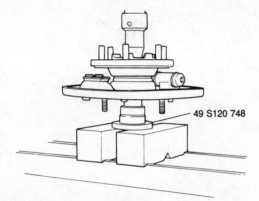

49 S120 748

Pressing a new retaining collar into position on the shaft

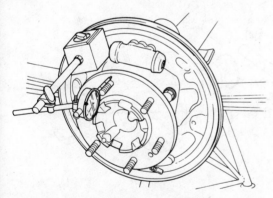

Checking axleshaft endplay on 1986 axles

packing bearings. These are available at all auto parts stores.

21. Place the bearing in the hub, and, using a press, press the hub and bearing assembly onto the shaft.

22. Press the new collar onto the shaft. The press pressure for the collar is critical. Press pressures should be 9,240–13,420 lb. (4,200–6,100 kg).

23. Install one shaft in the housing being very careful to avoid damaging the inner seal.

24. If only one shaft was being serviced, the

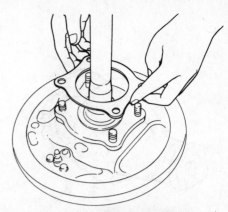

Using a shim to correct axleshaft endplay

other must now be removed to check bearing play on the serviced axle. If both shafts were removed, leave the other one out for now.

25. Tighten the backing plate bolts on the one installed axle to 80 ft.lb.

26. Mount a dial indicator on the backing plate, with the pointer resting on the axle shaft flange. Check the axial play. Standard bearing play should be 0.026–0.037 in. (0.65–0.95mm).

27. If play is not within specifications, shims are available for correcting it. See the table below:

Shim Selection Chart

Part Number	Thickness mm (in.)
S083 26 165	0.10 (0.004)
S083 26 166	0.15 (0.006)
S083 26 167	0.50 (0.020)
S083 23 168	0.75 (0.030)

28. Install the other shaft and torque the backing plate bolts. Check the play as on the first shaft. Play should be 0.002–0.010 in. If not, correct it with shims.

29. Install the brake drums and wheels. Bleed the brake system.

Differential

NOTE: *Differential service is best left to those extremely familiar with their vagaries and idiosyncrasies. A great many specialized tools are required as well as a good deal of experience.*

REMOVAL AND INSTALLATION

1. Raise the vehicle and support it safely with jackstands.

2. Remove the differential drain plug and drain the lubricant from the differential. Install the plug after all of the fluid has drained.

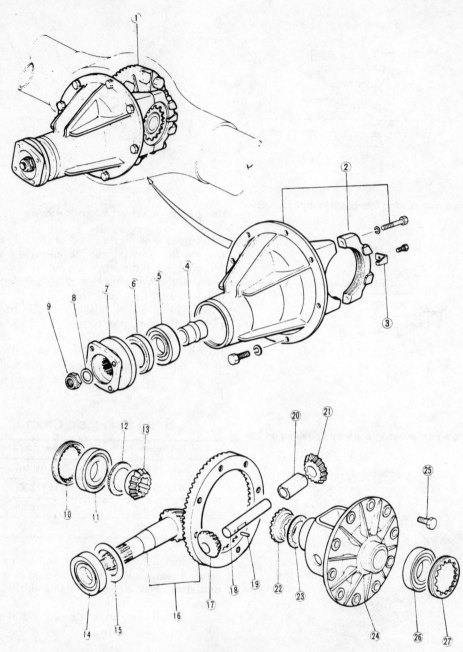

1. Driving & differential
2. Differential carrier
3. Lock plate
4. Distance piece
5. Front pinion bearing
6. Oil seal
7. Companion flange
8. Washer
9. Lock nut
10. Adjust screw
11. Bearing
12. Washer
13. Differential side gear
14. Rear pinion bearing
15. Spacer
16. Final gear set
17. Differential pinion
18. Differential pinion shaft
19. Pin
20. Thrust block
21. Differential pinion
22. Differential side gear
23. Washer
24. Case
25. Ring gear bolt
26. Bearing
27. Adjust screw

Differential carrier components

3. Remove the axle shafts as previously outlined.

4. Remove the driveshaft(s) as previously outlined.

5. Remove the carrier-to-differential housing retaining fasteners and remove the carrier assembly from the housing.

6. Clean the carrier and axle housing mating surfaces.

7. If the differential originally used a gasket between the carrier and the differential housing, replace the gasket. If the unit had no gasket, apply a thin film of oil-resistant silicone sealer to the mating surfaces of both the carrier and the housing and allow the sealer to set according to the manufacturer's instructions.

8. Place the carrier assembly onto the housing and install the carrier-to-housing fasteners. Torque the fasteners to 12–17 ft.lb.

9. Install the driveshaft(s) and axle shafts as previously outlined.

10. Install the brake drums and wheels.

11. Fill the differential with the proper amount of SAE 80W-90 fluid (see the Capacities Chart).

OPERATION

The differential is an arrangement of gears that permits the rear wheels to turn at different speeds when cornering and divides the torque between the axle shafts. The differential gears are mounted on a pinion shaft and the gears are free to rotate on this shaft. The pinion shaft is fitted in a bore in the differential case and is at right angles to the axle shafts.

Power flow through the differential is as follows. The drive pinion, which is turned by the driveshaft, turns the ring gear. The ring gear, which is bolted to the differential case, rotates the case. The differential pinion forces the pinion gears against the side gears. In cases where both wheels have equal traction, the pinion gears do not rotate on the pinion shaft, because the input force of the pinion gear is divided equally between the two side gears. Consequently the pinion gears revolve with the pinion shaft, although they do not revolve on the pinion shaft itself. The side gears, which are splined to the axle shafts, and meshed with the pinion gears, rotate the axle shafts.

When it becomes necessary to turn a corner, the differential becomes effective and allows the axle shafts to rotate at different speeds. As the inner wheel slows down, the side gear splined to the inner wheel axle shaft also slows down. The pinion gears act as balancing levers by maintaining equal tooth loads to both gears while allowing unequal speeds of rotation at the axle shafts. If the vehicle speed remains constant, the inner wheel slows down to 90 percent of vehicle speed, the outer wheel will speed up to 110 percent.

GEAR RATIO

Axle ratios for the Mazda are 4.11:1 for manual transmissions, and 4.65:1 for automatic transmissions through 1976. All 1977–79 Mazdas have a ratio of 3.64:1, 1980 and later models with the 2.0 liter engine have 3.31:1 ratios.

The axle ratio is obtained by dividing the number of teeth on the drive pinion gear into the number of teeth on the ring gear. It is always expressed as a proportion and is a simple expression of gear speed reduction and torque multiplication.

DIFFERENTIAL DIAGNOSIS

The most essential part of rear axle service is proper diagnosis of the problem. Bent or broken axle shafts or broken gears pose little problem, but isolating an axle noise and correctly interpreting the problem can be extremely difficult, even for an experienced mechanic.

Any gear driven unit will produce a certain amount of noise; therefore, a specific diagnosis for each individual unit is the best practice. Acceptable or normal noise can be classified as a slight noise heard only at certain speeds or under unusual conditions. This noise tends to reach a peak at 40–60 mph, depending on the road condition, load, gear ratio and tire size. Frequently, other noises are mistakenly diagnosed as coming from the rear axle. Vehicle noises from tires, transmission, driveshaft, U-joints and front and rear wheel bearings will often be mistaken as emanating from the rear axle. Raising the tire pressure to eliminate tire noise (although this will not silence mud or snow treads), listening for the noise at varying speeds and road conditions and listening for noise at drive and coast conditions will aid in diagnosing alleged rear axle noises. See the Troubleshooting section of this book for diagnosis procedures.

Suspension and Steering

FRONT SUSPENSION

On 1972–84 trucks, the front suspension consists of a wishbone-type, upper and lower control arm assembly with coil spring. Suspension travel is dampened by double acting shock absorbers.

1986 trucks use a torsion bar type front suspension, with upper and lower control arms. Conventional, double-acting shock absorbers are employed to dampen motion. A stabilizer bar is standard equipment.

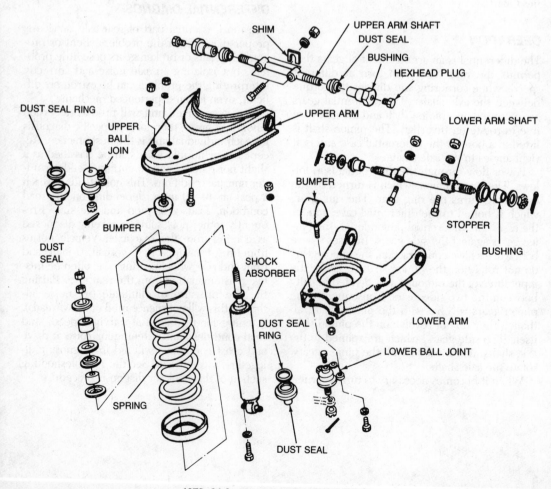

1972–84 front suspension components

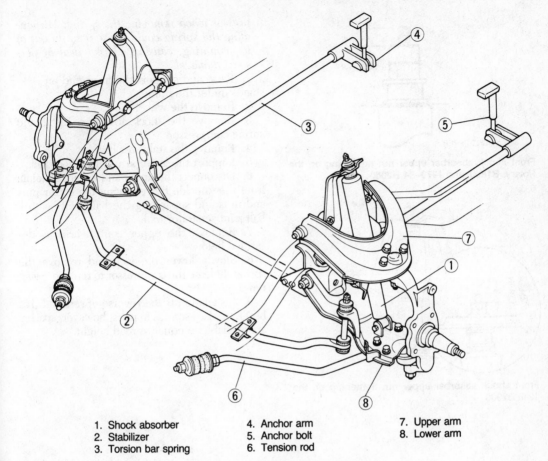

1. Shock absorber
2. Stabilizer
3. Torsion bar spring
4. Anchor arm
5. Anchor bolt
6. Tension rod
7. Upper arm
8. Lower arm

1986 front suspension components

Shock Absorber

TEST

The easiest way to check the performance of your shocks is to go to one corner of the truck and start it bouncing up and down. Get it going as much as you can and then release it. It should stop bouncing in less than two full bounces.

REMOVAL AND INSTALLATION

1. Raise and support the front end on jackstands.
2. Remove the upper end nut, bushings and washers from the shock stem.
3. Remove the lower end attaching bolts.
4. Remove the shock from beneath the lower control arm.
5. Installation is the reverse of removal. Tighten the lower bolts to 25 ft.lb. on 1972–84 trucks, and 55–59 ft.lb. on 1986 trucks. Tighten the upper nut until ¼ inch of thread is visible above the locknut on the Rotary Pick-Up, B1800, and 1979–84 B2000, or ⅛ inch on the B1600. On the 1986 B2000, tighten the upper

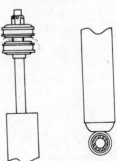

3.5MM(0.14IN)

Front shock absorber upper nut tightening on the B1600

nut to 17–25 ft.lb. At this point, 7mm of thread should be visible above the nut.

Coil Spring

REMOVAL AND INSTALLATION

1972–84

CAUTION: *The spring is under a great deal of tension! It's best to use a coil spring com-*

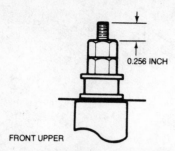

0.256 INCH

FRONT UPPER

Front shock absorber upper nut tightening on the Rotary, B1800, and 1979–84 B2000

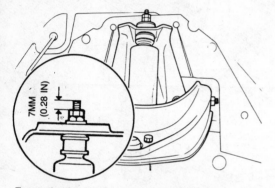

7MM (0.28 IN)

Front shock absorber upper nut tightening on the 1986 B2000

pressor when removing the spring. Mishandling the spring could cause it to fly out of its mounting, causing a great deal of personal damage!

1. Raise and support the front end on jackstands under the frame.

2. Remove the wheel.

3. Remove the shock absorber. Install the spring compressor.

4. Remove the stabilizer bar.

5. Support the lower arm with a floor jack.

6. Disconnect the upper and lower ball joints from the knuckle by removing the cotter pins and nuts and separating the ball joints with a ball joint separator tool.

7. Remove the upper control arm as described below.

8. Slowly lower the jack and remove the spring. Release the compressor to remove spring tension.

9. Installation is the reverse of removal. It's best to replace springs in pairs, however, spacers are available to equalize road height.

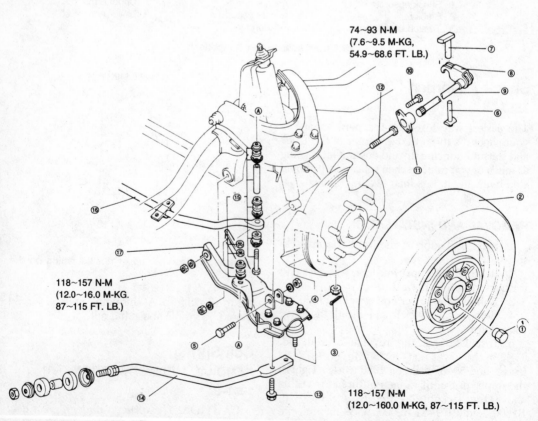

74~93 N-M
(7.6~9.5 M-KG,
54.9~68.6 FT. LB.)

118~157 N-M
(12.0~16.0 M-KG.
87~115 FT. LB.)

118~157 N-M
(12.0~160.0 M-KG, 87~115 FT. LB.)

Torsion bar removal from the 1986 front suspension

Torsion Bar and Lower Control Arm

REMOVAL AND INSTALLATION

1986 Only

NOTE: *Special tools are necessary for this procedure.*

1. Raise and support the front end on jackstands under the frame.

2. Remove the wheel.

3. Remove the cotter pin and nut from the lower ball joint.

4. Remove the lower shock absorber bolt.

5. Matchmark the anchor arm bolt and anchor swivel and remove the bolt and swivel.

6. Matchmark the torsion bar and anchor arm and the torsion bar and torque plate.

7. Remove the anchor arm and torsion bar from the torque plate. Separate the anchor arm from the torsion bar.

8. Unbolt and remove the torque plate.

9. Remove the lower arm-to-frame bolt. Separate the lower arm from the frame bracket with bushing puller/installer 49 0727 575.

10. Unbolt the tension rod from the lower arm and frame and remove it.

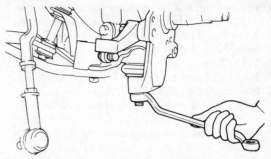

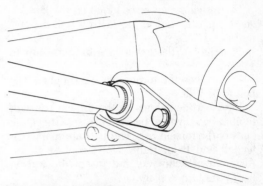

Installing the ball joint on the lower arm

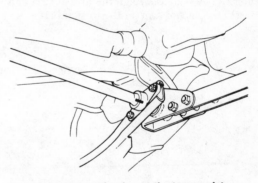

Torque plate installation

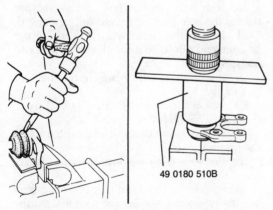

49 0180 510B

Removing and installing the ball joint dust boot

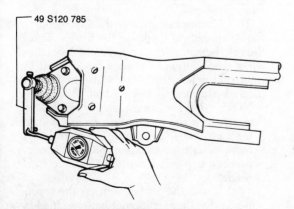

49 S120 785

Measuring ball joint preload

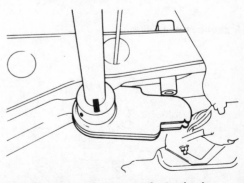

Connecting the torsion bar to the torque plate

Connecting the anchor arm to the torsion bar

NOTE: *Don't change the position of the double nut at the rear of the tension rod bushing, since it would affect caster.*

11. Remove the stabilizer bar bolt, bushing,

retainer and nut and remove the stabilizer bar.

12. Using a ball joint separator, separate the lower ball joint from the knuckle. Remove the lower control arm.

13. Inspect all parts for wear or damage. Replace any suspect parts. Using a spring scale and adapter 49 0180 510B, check the ball joint preload. Pull scale reading should be 39.6 lb. or less. Measure the preload after first shaking the ball joint stud 3 or 4 times to make sure it is free.

14. Install the lower arm on the frame bracket and hand tighten the nut.

15. Install the lower ball joint on the knuckle and torque the nut to 115 ft.lb. Install the cotter pin.

16. Tighten the lower arm-to-frame nut to 115 ft.lb.

17. Position the torque plate and tighten the bolt to 68 ft.lb.

18. Coat the splines on the torsion bar with lithium based wheel bearing grease. Check the ends of the torsion bar. The bars are marked L for left and R for right. Don't confuse them. Align the matchmarks and install the torsion bar in the torque plate.

19. Coat the splines on the torsion bar with lithium based grease. Align the matchmarks and install the anchor arm on the torsion bar.

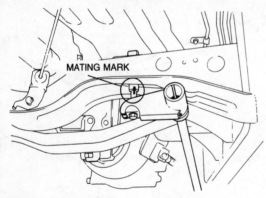

Anchor bolt installation

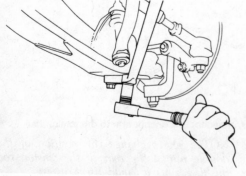

Connect the tension rod and stabilizer link

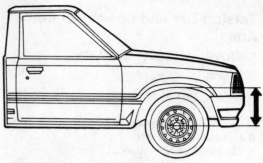

Ride height measuring points

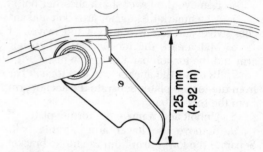

Anchor arm installation when reference marks aren't available

20. Install the anchor bolt and swivel and tighten the bolt until the matchmarks are mated.

21. Install the tension rod. Torque the bushing end nut to 90 ft.lb.; the lower arm end bolts to 85 ft.lb.

22. Install the stabilizer bar. Torque the bolt to 19 ft.lb.

23. Install the shock absorber bolt. Torque the bolt to 55–59 ft.lb.

24. Install the wheels and lower the truck to the ground.

25. Retorque the lower arm-to-frame bracket nut.

26. Check the front and rear tire pressures. Set the pressures to what are specified on the vehicle rating plate, except for P-metric radials. Set them at the maximum pressure shown on the side wall.

27. Measure the distance from the center of the wheel hub to the lip of the fender. This is the ride height. Proper ride height is obtained when the difference between the left and the right side is less than 10mm. Adjust the ride height by turning the anchor bolt.

NOTE: *If, for some reason, you didn't matchmark the torsion bar anchor bolt, or the matchmarks were lost, or you're installing a new, unmarked torsion bar, here's a procedure to help you attain the correct ride height:*

a. Install the anchor arm on the torsion bar so that there is 125mm between the lowest point on the arm and the crossmember directly above it.

b. Tighten the anchor bolt until the anchor arm contacts the swivel. Then, tighten the bolt an additional 45mm travel.

Stabilizer Bar

REMOVAL AND INSTALLATION

1. Raise and support the front end on jackstands.

2. Unbolt the stabilizer bar-to-frame clamps.

3. Unbolt the stabilizer bar from the lower control arms. Keep all the bushings, washers and spacers in order.

4. Check all parts for wear or damage and replace anything which looks suspicious.

5. Installation is the reverse of removal. Tighten all fasteners lightly, then torque them to specifications with the wheels on the ground. Stabilizer bar-to-control arm nut, 1972–84: 25 ft.lb.
1986: 34 ft.lb.
Stabilizer-to-frame clamp bolts: 16 ft.lb.

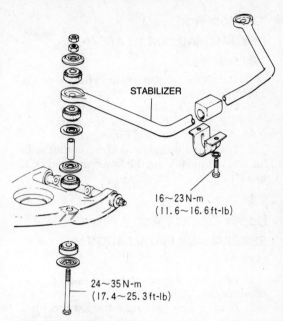

STABILIZER

16~23 N-m
(11.6~16.6 ft-lb)

24~35 N-m
(17.4~25.3 ft-lb)

1972–84 stabilizer bar

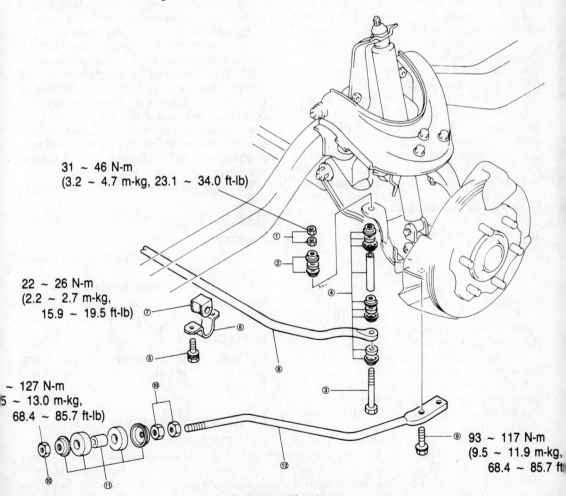

31 ~ 46 N-m
(3.2 ~ 4.7 m-kg, 23.1 ~ 34.0 ft-lb)

22 ~ 26 N-m
(2.2 ~ 2.7 m-kg,
15.9 ~ 19.5 ft-lb)

~ 127 N-m
5 ~ 13.0 m-kg,
68.4 ~ 85.7 ft-lb)

93 ~ 117 N-m
(9.5 ~ 11.9 m-kg,
68.4 ~ 85.7 ft

1986 stabilizer bar

Tension Rod

REMOVAL AND INSTALLATION

1986 Only

1. Unbolt the tension rod from the lower arm and frame and remove it.

NOTE: *Don't change the position of the double nut at the rear of the tension rod bushing, since it would affect caster.*

2. Install the tension rod. Torque the bushing end nut to 90 ft.lb.; the lower arm end bolts to 85 ft.lb.

Upper Control Arm

REMOVAL AND INSTALLATION

1972–84

1. Raise and support the front end on jackstands under the frame.

2. Using a floor jack, raise the lower control arm until the upper control arm is off the bumper stop.

3. Remove the wheel.

4. Place a chain through the coil spring as a safety measure, or install a spring compressor.

5. Remove the cotter pin and nut retaining the upper ball joint.

6. Using a ball joint separator, disconnect the ball joint from the spindle.

7. Working under the hood, remove the two upper arm retaining bolts and lift the arm from the truck. Note the number and position of any shims.

8. Installation is the reverse of removal. Place the shims in their original locations. Torque the two arm retaining bolts to 65–75 ft.lb.; the ball joint-to-arm bolts to 15–20 ft.lb.; the ball joint-to-spindle nut to 40–55 ft.lb.

1986

1. Raise and support the front end on jackstands placed under the frame.

2. Remove the wheels. Support the lower arm with a floor jack.

3. Remove the cotter pin and nut from the upper ball joint and separate the ball joint from the upper arm using a ball joint separator tool.

4. Remove the bushings and dust seals from the ends of the upper arm shaft.

5. Remove the nuts and bolts that retain the upper arm shaft to the support bracket. Note the number and location of the shims under the nuts. These must be installed in their exact locations for proper wheel alignment. Check all parts for wear or damage. Replace any suspect parts. Check the ball joint preload with a pull scale and adapter 49 0180 510B. Shake the ball joint stud a few times to make sure that it is

free, then take the reading. The pull scale reading should be 40 lb. or less.

6. Installation is the reverse of removal. Torque the upper arm shaft mounting bolts to 60–68 ft.lb.; the ball joint nut to 30–37 ft.lb.

Lower Control Arm

REMOVAL AND INSTALLATION

1972–84

1. Raise the front end and support it on jackstands under the frame.

2. Remove the wheels.

3. Remove the lower shock absorber bolts and push the shock up, out of the way.

4. Disconnect the front stabilizer bar from the control arms.

5. Place a floor jack under the lower arm and raise the arm to compress the spring. Install a safety chain or spring compressor.

6. Unbolt the ball joint from the lower arm.

7. Pull the spindle and ball joint away from the arm.

8. Carefully lower the jack. The spring is under pressure, so be very careful that it is secured with the chain or spring compressor.

9. Remove the three lower control arm retaining bolts and lift the arm from the frame.

10. When installing the arm, safety chain the spring to the arm prior to installing the arm, or use a spring compressor. When the arm is in position, loosely install the ball joint bolts and remove the chain or compressor, then, tighten the ball joint nut to 70 ft.lb.; the three ball joint retaining nuts to 70 ft.lb. Install all other parts in reverse order of removal.

11. Have the front end alignment checked.

Ball Joints

CHECKING

1. Inspect the dust seals. If cracked or brittle, replace them.

2. Check end play of both the upper and lower ball joints. If either exceeds 0.0039 in., it is defective.

REPLACEMENT

For replacement procedures, see the appropriate parts of either upper or lower control arm removal and installation.

Front Wheel Bearings

CAUTION: *Brake shoes contain asbestos, which has been determined to be a cancer causing agent. Never clean the brake surfaces with compressed air! Avoid inhaling any dust from any brake surface! When cleaning brake surfaces, use a commercially available brake cleaning fluid.*

ADJUSTMENT

1. Raise and support the front end on jackstands. Check both the bearing axial play and the ease and smoothness of rotation. Axial play should be 0; the wheel should rotate smoothly, with no perceptible bearing noise.

2. Remove the wheel. Remove the brake drum or disc brake caliper. Suspend the caliper out of the way. Don't disconnect the brake line.

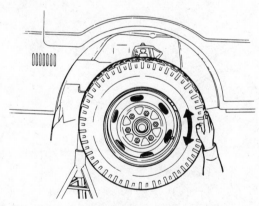

Checking bearing axial play

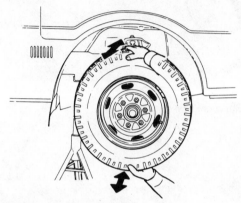

Checking bearing for smoothness of rotation

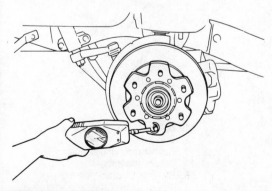

Checking rotational force

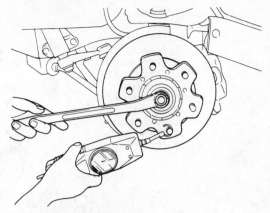

Adjusting rotational force

3. Attach a spring scale to a wheel lug.

4. Pull the scale horizontally and check the force needed to start the wheel turning. The force should be 1.3–2.4 lbs. If the reading is not correct, proceed.

5. Remove the grease cap and cotter pin.

6. Tighten or loosen the hub nut until the correct pull rating is obtained.

7. Align the cotter pin holes and insert a new cotter pin. Replace the grease cap and wheel.

REMOVAL, REPACKING, INSTALLATION

1. Raise and support the front end on jackstands.

2. Remove the wheel.

3. Remove the grease cap, cotter pin, hub nut and flat washer.

4. On trucks with disc brakes, remove the caliper and suspend it out of the way without disconnecting the brake line. Slowly pull the hub from the spindle, positioning your hand to catch the outer bearing.

5. Remove the spacer, inner seal and inner bearing. Discard the seal.

6. Thoroughly clean the bearings and inside of the hub with a nonflammable solvent. Allow them to air dry.

7. Inspect the bearings for wear, damage, heat discoloration or other signs of fatigue. If they are at all suspect, replace them. When replacing bearings, it is a good idea to replace the bearing races as a set, as bearings do wear the races in a definite pattern which may not be compatible with new bearings.

8. To replace the races, carefully drive them out of the hub with a drift.

9. Coat the outside of the new races with clean wheel bearing grease and drive them into place until they bottom in their bore. Make certain that they are completely bottomed! A drift can be used as a driver, if you hammer evenly around the rim of the race and are very careful not to slip and scratch the surface of the

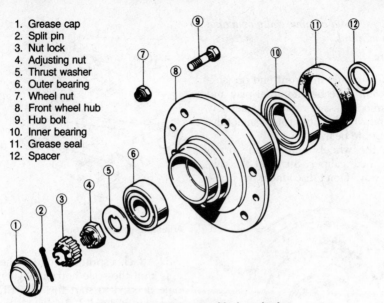

1. Grease cap
2. Split pin
3. Nut lock
4. Adjusting nut
5. Thrust washer
6. Outer bearing
7. Wheel nut
8. Front wheel hub
9. Hub bolt
10. Inner bearing
11. Grease seal
12. Spacer

Front hub components with drum brakes

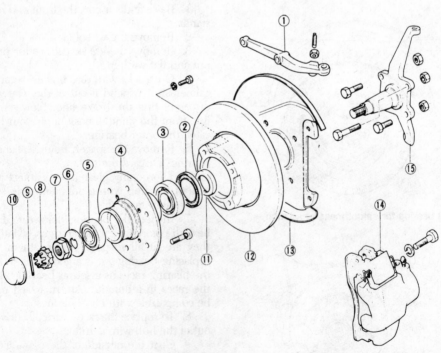

1. Knuckle arm
2. Grease seal
3. Inner bearing
4. Hub
5. Outer bearing

6. Washer
7. Adjusting nut
8. Nut lock
9. Split pin
10. Grease cap

11. Spacer
12. Brake disc
13. Caliper mounting adaptor
14. Caliper assembly
15. Steering knuckle

Front hub components with disc brakes, through 1984

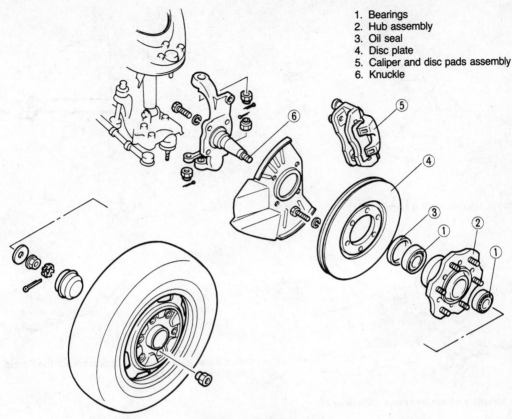

1. Bearings
2. Hub assembly
3. Oil seal
4. Disc plate
5. Caliper and disc pads assembly
6. Knuckle

1986 front hub components

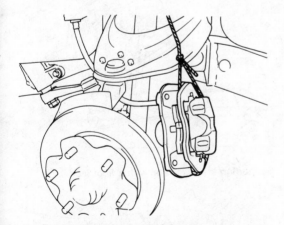

Suspending the caliper out of the way

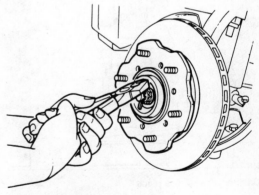

Removing the cotter pin

race. A driver made for the purpose is much easier to use.

10. Pack the inside of the hub with clean wheel bearing grease until it is flush packed.

11. Pack each bearing with clean grease, making sure that it is thoroughly packed. Special devices are sold for packing bearings. They are inexpensive and readily available. If you don't have one, just make certain that the bearing is as full of grease as possible by working it in with your fingers.

12. Install the inner bearing and seal. Drive the seal into place carefully until it is seated.

13. Install the spacer and the hub on the spindle.

14. Install the outer bearing, flat washer and hub nut.

15. Adjust the bearing as explained above.

16. Install the nut cap, cotter pin and grease cap. Install the wheel.

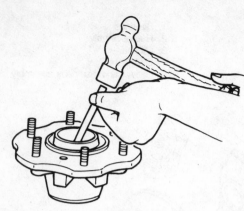

Driving out the bearing races

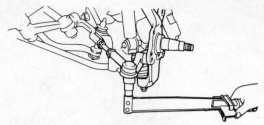

Removing the tie rod end nut

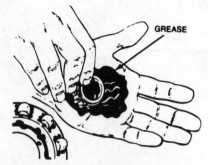

Packing the wheel bearings with grease

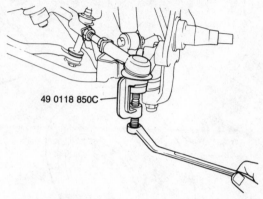

Using a ball joint separator to disconnect the tie rod end from the knuckle

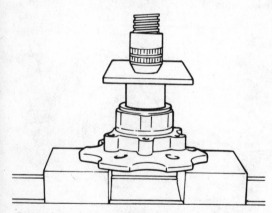

Driving the seal into place

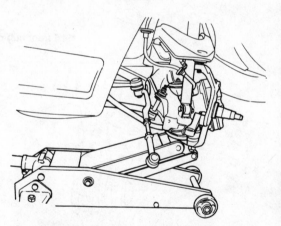

Supporting the lower arm with a floor jack

Knuckle and Spindle

REMOVAL AND INSTALLATION

CAUTION: *The coil spring on 1972–84 models is under great tension! Use a coil spring compressor for safety's sake.*

1. Raise and support the front end on jackstands.

2. Remove the wheels.

3. Remove the brake drums or calipers. Suspend the calipers out of the way with a wire. Don't disconnect the brake line.

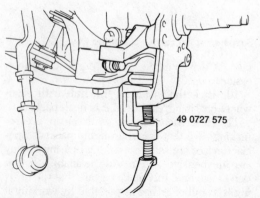

Disconnecting the lower ball joint

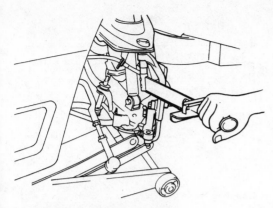

Removing the upper ball joint nut

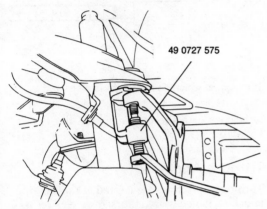

49 0727 575

Disconnecting the upper ball joint

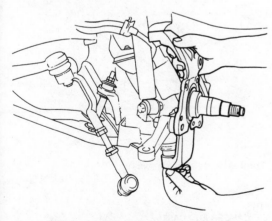

Removing the knuckle/spindle assembly

4. Remove the hub and bearings.
5. Remove the tie rod-to-knuckle nut, and, using a ball joint separator, remove the tie rod end from the knuckle.
6. On models through 1984, remove the shock absorber.
7. On models through 1984, install a spring compressor on the coil spring.
8. Support the lower arm with a floor jack.
9. Remove the cotter pin and nut from the

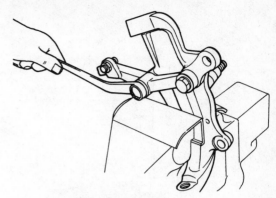

Removing the knuckle arm

lower ball joint, and, using a ball joint separator, disconnect the lower ball joint from the knuckle.
10. Remove the cotter pin and nut from the upper ball joint, and, using a ball joint separator, disconnect the upper ball joint from the knuckle.
11. Pull the knuckle and spindle assembly from the control arms.
12. The knuckle arm may now be removed.
13. Clean and inspect all parts for wear or damage. Replace parts as necessary.
14. Secure the knuckle in a vise and install the knuckle arm. Torque the bolts to 70–74 ft.lb.
15. Installation of the knuckle assembly is the reverse of removal. Observe the following torques:
• Upper ball joint-to-knuckle,
1972–84: 50–55 ft.lb.
1986: 35–38 ft.lb.
• Lower ball joint-to-knuckle,
1972–84: 70 ft.lb.
1986: 116 ft.lb.
• Tie rod end-to-knuckle: 22–29 ft.lb.

FRONT END ALIGNMENT

Caster

Caster is the forward or rearward tilt of the upper ball joint. Rearward tilt is positive caster; forward tilt is negative caster. Caster is adjusted by changing the shims between the upper arm shaft and the frame, or, by turning the shaft until the correct angle is obtained.

Camber

Camber is the outward or inward tilting of the wheels at the top. Camber is adjusted by adding or subtracting the shims between the upper arm shaft and the frame. Shims are available in thicknesses of 0.039, 0.063, 0.079, and 0.126 inch.

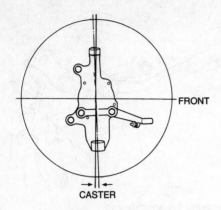

Caster angle computation

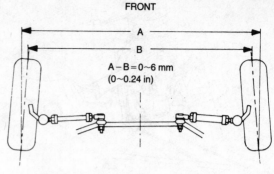

FRONT

A − B = 0~6 mm
(0~0.24 in)

Computing toe-in

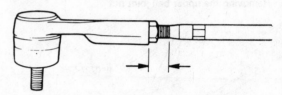

The point at which tie rod length is measured

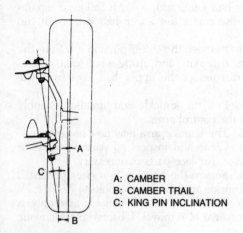

A: CAMBER
B: CAMBER TRAIL
C: KING PIN INCLINATION

Camber angle computation

Toe-In

Toe-in is the amount, measured in fractions of an inch, that the wheels are closer together in the front than the rear.

Toe-in can be changed by changing the length of the tie rods. Threaded sleeves on the rods are provided for this purpose. The clamps on the tie rods must be positioned to prevent in-

terference with the center link on the Rotary Pick-Up.

Turning Angle

Turning stop screws are located at the steering knuckle. If necessary, the screws can be adjusted.

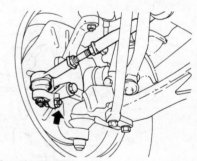

Turning angle stop screws

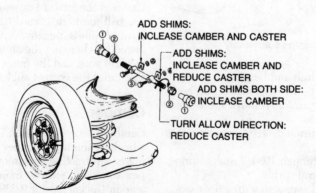

ADD SHIMS:
INCLEASE CAMBER AND CASTER

ADD SHIMS:
INCLEASE CAMBER AND
REDUCE CASTER

ADD SHIMS BOTH SIDE:
INCLEASE CAMBER

TURN ALLOW DIRECTION:
REDUCE CASTER

Adding shims to change caster and camber angle

REAR SUSPENSION

The suspension is made up of semi-eliptical leaf springs and double action shock absorbers.

Springs
REMOVAL AND INSTALLATION

1. Raise and support the rear of the truck on jackstands under the frame.

CAUTION: *The rear leaf springs are under considerable tension. Be very careful when removing and installing them; they can exert enough force to cause serious injuries.*

2. Place a floor jack under the rear axle to take up its weight.
3. Disconnect the lower end of the shock absorbers.
4. Remove the spring U-bolts and plate.
5. Remove the spring rear bolt.
6. Remove the front shackle nuts and the shackle.
7. Lift the spring from the truck.
8. Installation is the reverse of removal. Torque the spring rear shackle-to-frame nut to 58 ft.lb.; the rear shackle-to-spring nut to 72 ft.lb.; the U-bolt nuts to 58 ft.lb.; the front spring pin nut to 18 ft.lb.

Shock Absorbers
CHECKING

See the procedure for front shocks.

REMOVAL AND INSTALLATION
1972–84

1. Raise and support the truck on jackstands.
2. Unbolt the shock absorber at the top and bottom and remove it.
3. Installation is the reverse of removal. Tighten the nuts so that ¼ inch of thread is visible past the nut at each end of the shocks on all except the Rotary Pick-Up, or ⅛ inch on the Rotary Pick-Up.

1986

1. Raise and support the rear end on jackstands.
2. Remove the wheels.
3. Unbolt the shock absorber at each end and remove it.
4. Installation is the reverse of removal. Torque each bolt to 57 ft.lb.

STEERING

The steering system consists of a recirculating ball nut gear unit.

Steering Wheel
REMOVAL AND INSTALLATION

1. Disconnect the battery ground.
2. On the B1600, turn the horn button

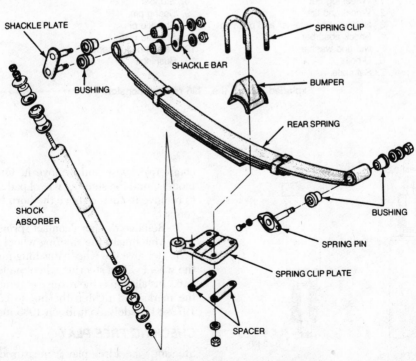

Exploded view of the 1972–84 rear suspension

SHACKLE PLATE

SHACKLE BAR

BUSHING

SPRING CLIP

BUMPER

REAR SPRING

BUSHING

SHOCK ABSORBER

SPRING PIN

SPRING CLIP PLATE

SPACER

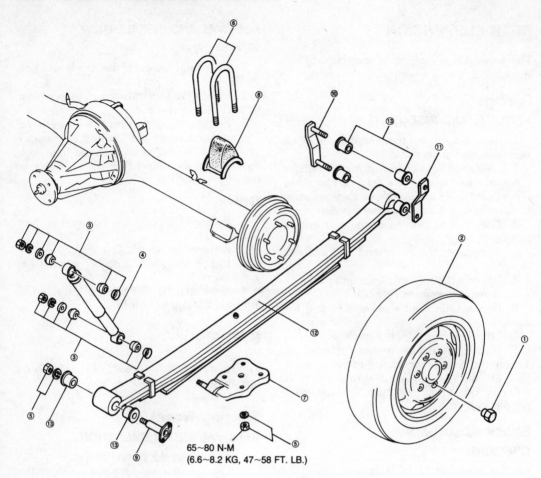

65~80 N-M
(6.6~8.2 KG, 47~58 FT. LB.)

1. Wheel lug nut
2. Wheel and tire
3. Nut, washer, retainer and bushing
4. Shock absorber
5. Nut and washer
6. U-bolts
7. Set plate
8. Stopper rubber
9. Spring pin
10. Shackle pin
11. Shackle plate
12. Leaf spring assembly
13. Bushings

Exploded view of the 1986 rear suspension

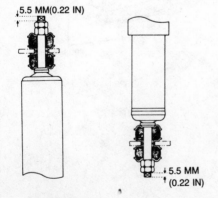

5.5 MM(0.22 IN)

5.5 MM
(0.22 IN)

Installing the upper nut on 1972–84 shock absorbers

counterclockwise and remove it. On all other models, pull the steering wheel pad straight up to remove it, then remove the horn button and contact.

3. Remove the horn contact spring.

4. Matchmark the steering wheel and shaft.

5. Remove the wheel attaching nut and pull the wheel with a steering wheel puller.

6. Installation is the reverse of removal. Align the marks and tighten the nut to 25 ft.lb. on 1972–84 models; 35 ft.lb. on 1986 models.

CHECKING FREE PLAY

Steering wheel free play is measured from any point on the outer circumference of the wheel.

Free play in either direction must not exceed ½ to 1 inch on 1972–84 models and ¼ to ¾ inch on 1986 models. If it does, check for:

a. worn ball joints
b. worn idler arm bushings
c. loose wheel bearings
d. worn or out-of-adjustment steering gear

Combination Switch

The combination turn signal, windshield wiper, and headlight switch is mounted on the steering column, and must be replaced as an assembly.

REMOVAL AND INSTALLATION

1. Disconnect the negative battery cable.
2. Remove the steering wheel.
3. Remove the "Lights-Hazard" Indicator and the steering column shroud.

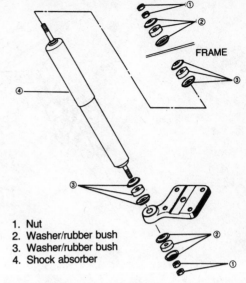

1. Nut
2. Washer/rubber bush
3. Washer/rubber bush
4. Shock absorber

1972–84 rear shock absorber

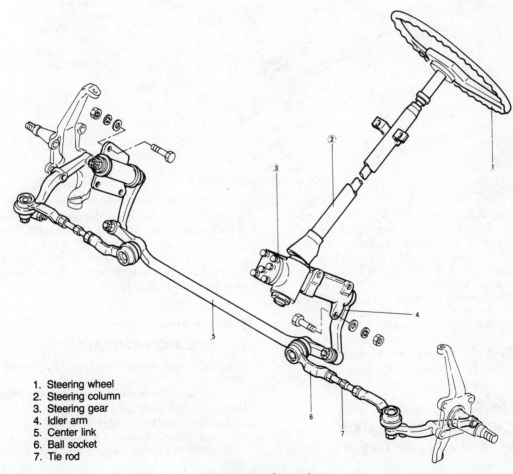

1. Steering wheel
2. Steering column
3. Steering gear
4. Idler arm
5. Center link
6. Ball socket
7. Tie rod

1972–84 steering system

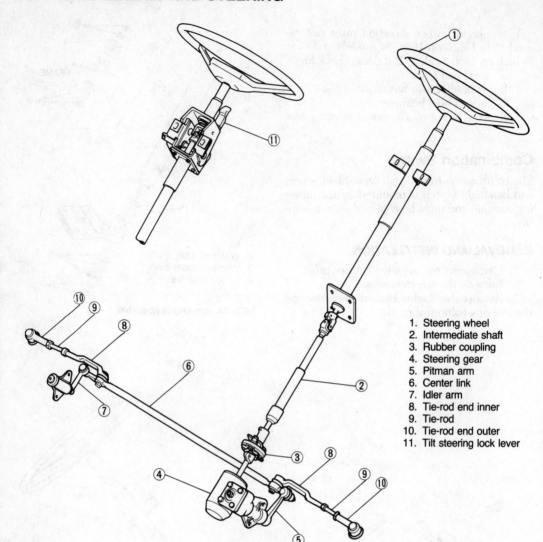

1. Steering wheel
2. Intermediate shaft
3. Rubber coupling
4. Steering gear
5. Pitman arm
6. Center link
7. Idler arm
8. Tie-rod end inner
9. Tie-rod
10. Tie-rod end outer
11. Tilt steering lock lever

1986 manual steering system

4. Unplug the electrical multiple connectors at the base of the steering column.

5. Pull the headlight knob from its shaft.

6. Remove the snap ring, which retains the switch, from the steering shaft. Pull the turn indicator canceling cam from the shaft.

7. Remove the single retaining bolt near the bottom of the switch. Remove the complete switch from the column.

8. Installation is the reverse of removal. Check the operation of the switch before installing the steering wheel.

Idler Arm

REMOVAL AND INSTALLATION

1. Raise and support the front end on jackstands.

2. Remove the idler arm-to-center link nut

and cotter pin. Disconnect the center link from the idler arm using a ball joint separator.

3. Unbolt and remove the idler arm.

4. Installation is the reverse of removal. Torque the center link nut to 40 ft.lb.; the frame mounting nut to 58 ft.lb.

Pitman Arm

REMOVAL AND INSTALLATION

1. Raise and support the front end on jackstands.

2. Remove the cotter pin and nut attaching the center link to the pitman arm.

3. Disconnect the center link from the pitman arm with a ball joint separator.

4. Matchmark the pitman arm and sector shaft.

5. Remove the pitman arm-to-sector shaft nut

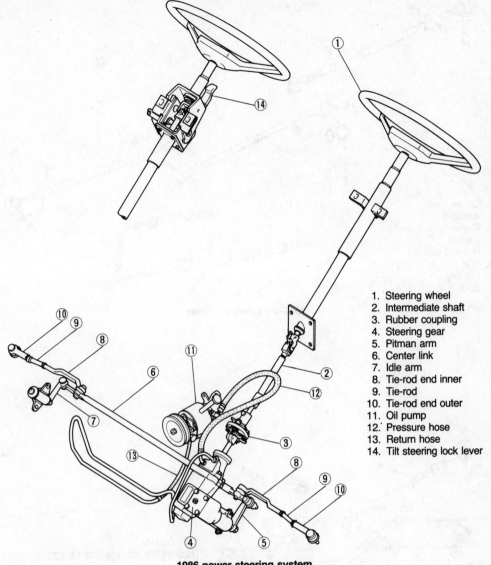

1. Steering wheel
2. Intermediate shaft
3. Rubber coupling
4. Steering gear
5. Pitman arm
6. Center link
7. Idle arm
8. Tie-rod end inner
9. Tie-rod
10. Tie-rod end outer
11. Oil pump
12. Pressure hose
13. Return hose
14. Tilt steering lock lever

1986 power steering system

and remove the pitman arm. It may be necessary to use a puller.

6. Installation is the reverse of removal. Make sure you align the matchmarks. Tighten the pitman arm-to-sector shaft nut to 130 ft.lb.; the pitman arm-to-center link nut to 32 ft.lb. If the cotter pin does not align, tighten the nut to make it line up; never loosen it!

Center Link

REMOVAL AND INSTALLATION

1. Raise and support the front end on jackstands.
2. Disconnect the center link at the tie rods, pitman arm and idler arm.

3. Installation is the reverse of removal. Tighten all of the nuts to 30 ft.lb.

Tie Rod Ends

REMOVAL AND INSTALLATION

1. Loosen the tie rod clamp nuts (jam nuts, 1977 and later).
2. Remove and discard the cotter pin from the ball socket end, and remove the nut.
3. Use a ball joint puller to loosen the ball socket stud from the center link. Remove the stud from the kingpin steering arm in the same way.
4. Unscrew the tie rod end from the threaded sleeve, counting the number of threads until

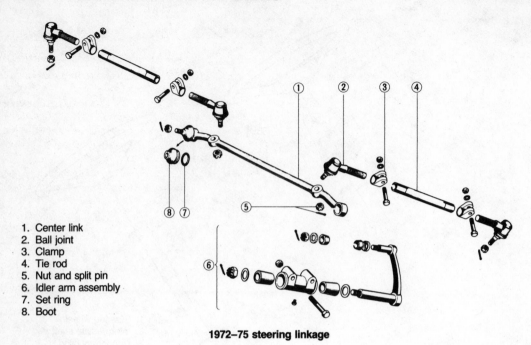

1. Center link
2. Ball joint
3. Clamp
4. Tie rod
5. Nut and split pin
6. Idler arm assembly
7. Set ring
8. Boot

1972–75 steering linkage

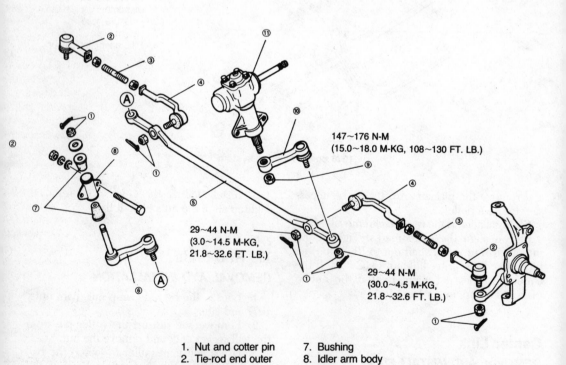

147~176 N-M
(15.0~18.0 M-KG, 108~130 FT. LB.)

29~44 N-M
(3.0~14.5 M-KG,
21.8~32.6 FT. LB.)

29~44 N-M
(30.0~4.5 M-KG,
21.8~32.6 FT. LB.)

1. Nut and cotter pin	7. Bushing
2. Tie-rod end outer	8. Idler arm body
3. Tie-rod	9. Nut
4. Tie-rod end inner	10. Pitman arm
5. Center link	11. Steering gear box
6. Idler arm	

1986 steering gear and linkage components

1. Dust seal
2. Dust seal ring
3. Ball joint
4. Tie rod clamp
5. Tie rod
6. Dust seal ring
7. Dust seal
8. Ball joint
9. Center link
10. Tapered bush
11. Idler bracket
12. Tapered bush
13. Idler arm
14. Insulator

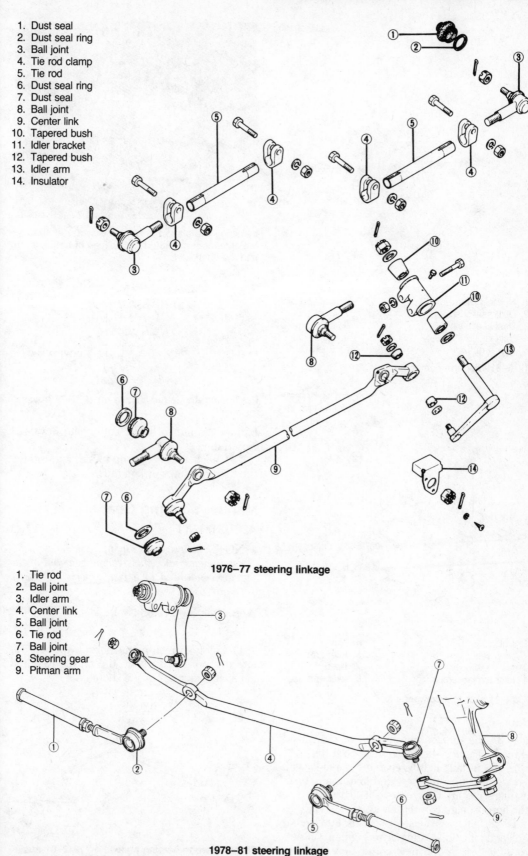

1976–77 steering linkage

1. Tie rod
2. Ball joint
3. Idler arm
4. Center link
5. Ball joint
6. Tie rod
7. Ball joint
8. Steering gear
9. Pitman arm

1978–81 steering linkage

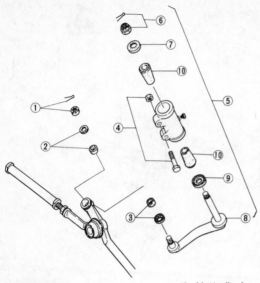

1. Nut/split pin
2. Dust seal/bush
3. Dust seal/bush
4. Bolt/nut
5. Idler arm ass'y
6. Nut/split pin
7. Dust seal
8. Idler arm
9. Dust seal
10. Bush

1978–81 idler arm components

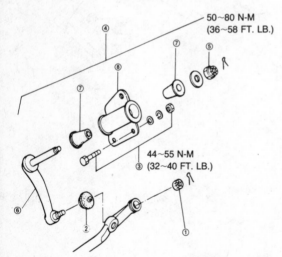

50~80 N-M
(36~58 FT. LB.)

44~55 N-M
(32~40 FT. LB.)

1. Nut
2. Dust seal
3. Nuts and bolts
4. Idler arm assembly
5. Nut
6. Idler arm
7. Bush
8. Idler arm body

1982–84 idler arm components

it's off. The threads may be left or right hand threads. Tighten the jam nuts to 58 ft.lb.

5. To install, lightly coat the threads with grease, and turn the new end in as many turns as were required to remove it. This will give the approximate correct toe-in.

6. Install the ball socket studs into center link and kingpin steering arm. Tighten the nuts to 30 ft.lb. Install a new cotter pin. You may

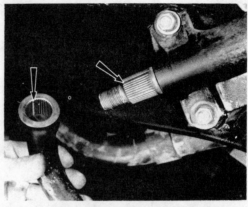

Installing the pitman arm on the sector shaft. Note the alignment marks on the splines of both the arm and the shaft

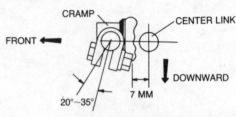

Positioning the tie rod clamps on 1972–76 trucks

tighten the nut to fit the cotter pin, but don't loosen it.

7. Check and adjust the toe-in, and tighten the tie rod clamps or jam nuts.

Manual Steering Gear

ADJUSTMENT

NOTE: *These adjustments are most accurately made with the steering gear out of the truck, mounted in a vise. Special tools are required.*

Worm Bearing Preload

1972–81

1. Using an inch pound torque wrench, rotate the wormshaft. Note the torque required for shaft rotation. Torque should be:

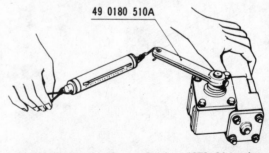

Checking worm bearing preload on 1972–81 trucks

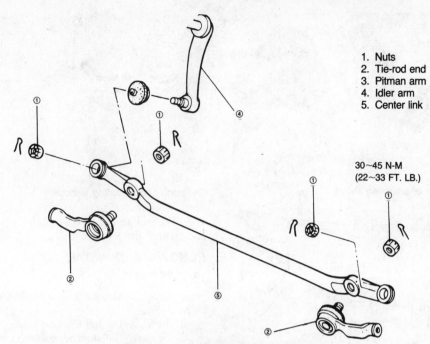

1. Nuts
2. Tie-rod end
3. Pitman arm
4. Idler arm
5. Center link

30~45 N-M
(22~33 FT. LB.)

1982–84 center link attachment points

- 1979–81: 5.2–7.8 in.lb.
- 1978: 7.9–10.4 in.lb.
- 1976–77: 0.9–3.5 in.lb.
- 1972–75: 7.9–10.4 in.lb.

2. If not, remove the end cover and correct it by adding or removing shims under the cover. Shims are available in sizes of 0.050mm, 0.060mm, 0.070mm, 0.075mm, 0.080mm, 0.100mm and 0.200mm.

1982–86

1. Install a spring scale and adapter 49 0180 510B to the wormshaft. Rotating torque should be ½–1.0 lb.

2. If not, loosen the wormshaft locknut and, using spanner 49 UB39 585, turn the adjuster until preload is within specifications.

3. Using wrench 49 1391 580, or equivalent, tighten the locknut to 140 ft.lb.

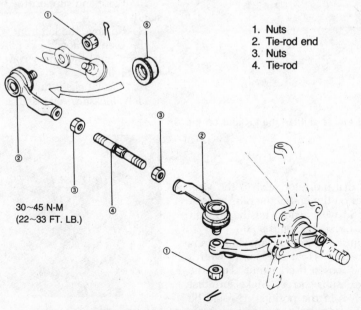

1. Nuts
2. Tie-rod end
3. Nuts
4. Tie-rod

30~45 N-M
(22~33 FT. LB.)

1982–84 tie rod attachment points

Installation of adjusting shims

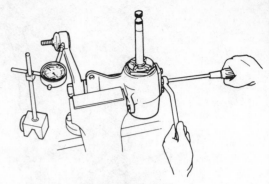

Checking and adjusting backlash

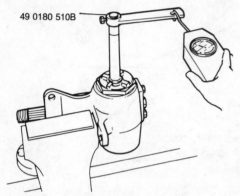

49 0180 510B

Checking worm bearing preload on 1982–86 trucks

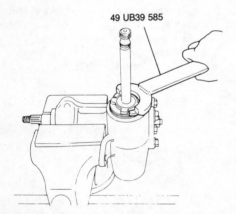

49 UB39 585

Using a special tool to tighten the locknut on the adjuster

Backlash

1. Mount a dial indicator next to the vise, with the pointer on the end of the pitman arm. With the gear in what would be the straight ahead position, backlash should be 0.

2. If not, adjust it using the adjusting screw on top of the gear. Hold the screw with a screwdriver and loosen the locknut. Turn the screw until backlash is correct. Make sure that the pitman arm is in the position it would be with the wheels straight ahead.

3. When backlash is correct, hold the screw and tighten the locknut.

REMOVAL AND INSTALLATION
1972–75 B1600

1. Remove the steering wheel as outlined above.

2. Remove the light switch knob.

3. Remove the steering column covers.

4. Remove the stop ring, cancelling cam and spring from the end of the column.

5. Disconnect the combination switch wiring.

6. Remove the combination switch from the column.

7. Remove the steering column support bracket.

8. Loosen the nut securing the bottom of the steering column jacket and pull the jacket off of the shaft.

9. Remove the dust cover from the firewall at the bottom of the shaft.

10. Raise and support the front end on jackstands.

11. Remove the left front wheel.

12. Using a floor jack, raise the lower control arm until the upper control arm is off the bumper stop.

13. Place a chain through the coil spring as a safety measure, or install a spring compressor.

Location of the steering column jacket securing nut

14. Remove the cotter pin and nut retaining the upper ball joint.

15. Using a ball joint separator, disconnect the ball joint from the spindle.

16. Working under the hood, remove the two upper arm retaining bolts and lift the arm from the truck. Note the number and position of any shims.

17. Disconnect the center link from the pitman arm.

18. Unbolt the steering gear from the frame. Lift the gear off of the frame, noting the position of the shim for installation.

19. Installation is the reverse of removal. Mount the steering gear, placing the shim in its original position. Place the upper control arm shaft shims in their original locations. Observe the following torques:
- Steering gear-to-frame: 40 ft.lb.
- Upper control arm shaft bolts: 65–75 ft.lb.
- Ball joint-to-knuckle: 40–55 ft.lb.
- Center link-to-pitman arm: 30 ft.lb.
- Pitman arm-to-sector shaft: 130 ft.lb.
- Steering wheel nut: 22–29 ft.lb.

1976–77 B1600

1. Raise and support the front end on jackstands. Remove the left front wheel.

2. Loosen the bolt securing the wormshaft to the steering shaft joint.

3. Remove the cotter pin and nut securing the pitman arm to the center link and separate the pitman arm from the link with a ball joint tool.

4. Remove the speedometer cable from the clips securing it to the steering gear housing and power brake booster.

5. Unbolt the steering gear from the frame.

6. If the pitman arm is to be removed from the sector shaft, first matchmark their positions, relative to each other.

7. Installation is the reverse of removal. Observe the following torques:
- Steering gear-to-frame: 40 ft.lb.
- Wormshaft-to-steering shaft yoke: 28 ft.lb.
- Pitman arm-to-sector shaft: 139 ft.lb.
- Pitman arm-to-center link: 30 ft.lb.

Rotary Pick-Up

1. Raise and support the front end on jackstands. Remove the left front wheel.

2. Loosen the bolt securing the wormshaft to the steering shaft joint.

3. Remove the cotter pin and nut securing the pitman arm to the center link and separate the pitman arm from the link with a ball joint tool.

4. Unbolt and remove the insulator from the pitman arm.

5. Unbolt the steering gear from the frame.

6. If the pitman arm is to be removed from the sector shaft, first matchmark their positions, relative to each other.

7. Installation is the reverse of removal. Observe the following torques:
- Steering gear-to-frame: 40 ft.lb.
- Wormshaft-to-steering shaft yoke: 28 ft.lb.
- Pitman arm-to-sector shaft: 139 ft.lb.
- Pitman arm-to-center link: 30 ft.lb.

B1800, 1979–81 B2000

1. Remove the steering wheel as outlined above.

2. Remove the light switch knob.

3. Remove the steering column covers.

4. Remove the stop ring, cancelling cam and spring from the end of the column.

5. Disconnect the combination switch wiring.

6. Remove the combination switch from the column.

7. Remove the steering column support bracket.

8. Loosen the nut securing the bottom of the steering column jacket and pull the jacket off of the shaft.

9. Remove the dust cover from the firewall at the bottom of the shaft.

10. Raise and support the front end on jackstands.

11. Remove the left front wheel. Remove the air cleaner.

12. Disconnect the fluid pipe at the clutch master cylinder, and cap the openings.

13. Disconnect the fluid pipes at the brake master cylinder, and cap the openings.

14. Remove the brake master cylinder.

15. Disconnect the pushrod at the pedal.

16. Unbolt and remove the power booster from the firewall.

17. Drain the cooling system.

CAUTION: *When draining the coolant, keep in mind that cats and dogs are attracted by the ethylene glycol antifreeze, and are quite likely to drink any that is left in an uncovered container or in puddles on the ground. This will prove fatal in sufficient quantity. Always drain the coolant into a sealable container. Coolant should be reused unless it is contaminated or several years old.*

18. Disconnect the EGR pipe.

19. Remove the accelerator linkage.

20. Disconnect the choke cable and fuel line. Plug the fuel line.

21. Disconnect the PCV valve hose.

22. Disconnect the heater return hose and by-pass hose.

23. Remove the intake manifold-to-cylinder head attaching nuts.

24. Remove the manifold and carburetor as an assembly.

25. Clean the gasket mating surfaces.

26. Using a floor jack, raise the lower control arm until the upper control arm is off the bumper stop.

27. Place a chain through the coil spring as a safety measure, or install a spring compressor.

28. Remove the cotter pin and nut retaining the upper ball joint.

29. Using a ball joint separator, disconnect the ball joint from the spindle.

30. Working under the hood, remove the two upper arm retaining bolts and lift the arm from the truck. Note the number and position of any shims.

31. Disconnect the center link from the pitman arm.

32. Unbolt the steering gear from the frame. Lift the gear off of the frame, noting the position of the shim for installation.

33. Installation of the steering gear and control arm is the reverse of removal. Mount the steering gear, placing the shim in its original position. Place the upper control arm shaft shims in their original locations. When installing the brake booster, check the clearance between the master cylinder piston and the power booster pushrod. Clearance should be 0.004–0.020 in. If not, adjust it at the pushrod. Observe the following torques:

- Steering gear-to-frame: 40 ft.lb.
- Wormshaft-to-steering shaft yoke: 20 ft.lb.
- Upper control arm shaft bolts: 65–75 ft.lb.
- Ball joint-to-knuckle: 40–55 ft.lb.
- Center link-to-pitman arm: 30 ft.lb.
- Pitman arm-to-sector shaft: 130 ft.lb.
- Steering wheel nut: 22–29 ft.lb.
- Power brake booster-to-firewall: 17 ft.lb.
- Master Cylinder-to-booster: 15 ft.lb.

34. Install a new gasket and the manifold on the studs. Torque the attaching nuts to specification, working from the center outward.

35. Connect the PCV valve hose to the manifold.

36. Connect the by-pass and heater return hoses.

37. Install the accelerator linkage.

38. Connect the fuel line and choke cable.

39. Replace the air cleaner.

40. Fill the cooling system. Bleed the brakes and clutch. Run the engine and check for leaks.

1982–84 B2000, B2200

1. Remove the steering wheel as outlined above.

2. Remove the steering column covers.

3. Remove the stop ring, cancelling cam and spring from the end of the column.

4. Disconnect the combination switch wiring.

5. Remove the combination switch from the column.

6. Remove the steering column support bracket.

7. Loosen the nut securing the bottom of the steering column jacket and pull the jacket off of the shaft.

8. Remove the dust cover from the firewall at the bottom of the shaft.

9. Remove the bolt securing the yoke joint to the wormshaft and remove the steering shaft.

10. Remove the air cleaner.

11. On trucks with column shift, unbolt the lower bracket from the gear select rod and the shift rod.

12. Remove the lower bracket from the steering gear.

13. Remove the brakes lines from the master cylinder and cap the lines.

14. Unbolt and remove the master cylinder from the firewall or power booster. These trucks have a remotely mounted reservoir, so the lines will have to be unclipped and plugged.

15. Remove the cotter pin and nut and disconnect the center link from the pitman arm using a ball joint tool.

16. Remove the cotter pin and nut, match-mark the pitman arm and sector shaft and disconnect the pitman arm from the sector shaft using a ball joint tool.

17. Unbolt the steering gear from the frame, noting the position of any shim that might be installed.

18. Installation is the reverse of removal. Mount the steering gear, placing the shim in its original position. Observe the following torques:

- Steering gear-to-frame: 40 ft.lb.
- Center link-to-pitman arm: 30 ft.lb.
- Pitman arm-to-sector shaft: 130 ft.lb.
- Steering wheel nut: 22–29 ft.lb.
- Master Cylinder-to-booster: 15 ft.lb.
- Wormshaft-to-steering shaft yoke: 20 ft.lb.

1986 B2000

1. Raise and support the front end on jackstands.

2. Remove the pinch bolt securing the wormshaft to the steering shaft coupling.

3. Remove the cotter pin and nut securing the pitman arm to the center link and separate the pitman arm from the link with a ball joint tool.

4. Unbolt the steering gear from the frame.

5. If the pitman arm is to be removed from the sector shaft, first matchmark their positions, relative to each other.

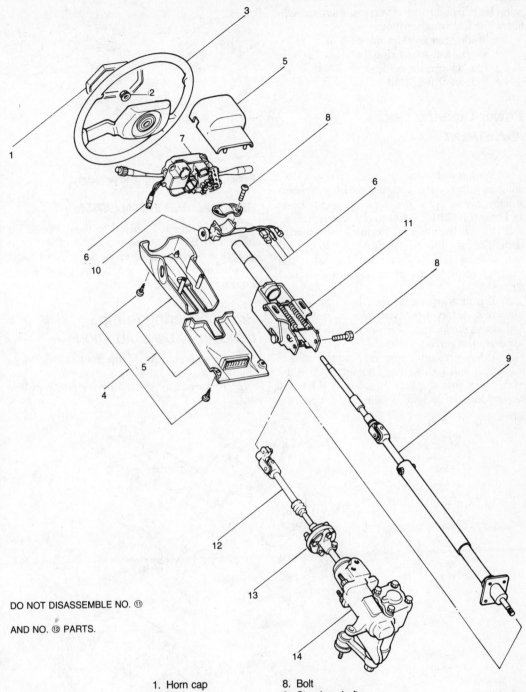

DO NOT DISASSEMBLE NO. ⑪

AND NO. ⑫ PARTS.

1. Horn cap
2. Lock nut
3. Steering wheel
4. Screw
5. Column cover
6. Harness couplers
7. Combination switch
8. Bolt
9. Steering shaft
10. Steering lock
11. Tilt bracket
12. Intermediate shaft
13. Rubber coupling
14. Steering gear box

1986 steering gear and column

6. Installation is the reverse of removal. Observe the following torques:
- Steering gear-to-frame: 40 ft.lb.
- Wormshaft-to-steering shaft yoke: 28 ft.lb.
- Pitman arm-to-sector shaft: 139 ft.lb.
- Pitman arm-to-center link: 30 ft.lb.

Power Steering Gear
ADJUSTMENT
Preload

1. With the steering gear mounted in a vise, and the pitman arm positioned in a "wheels straight ahead" position, attach a spring scale and adapter 49 0180 510B to the wormshaft.

2. Check the rotating torque of the wormshaft. Rotating torque should be 2.2 lb or less, but, at least ½ to 1 lb higher than what the rotating torque is at a point 360° from straight ahead.

3. If preload is not correct, hold the adjusting screw on top of the gear with a screwdriver and loosen the locknut. Turn the adjusting screw to obtain the correct preload.

4. When preload is correct, hold the adjusting screw and tighten the locknut to 35 ft.lb. Make sure that the adjusting screw does not move while the locknut is being tightened.

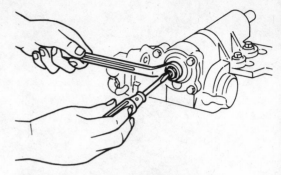

Power steering gear preload adjustment

REMOVAL AND INSTALLATION

This procedure is identical to the 1986 B2000 procedure for manual steering, with the exception that the power steering fluid hoses must be removed from the gear before the gear can be removed from the truck.

Power Steering Pump
REMOVAL AND INSTALLATION

1. Raise and support the front end on jackstands.

2. Remove the power steering pump pulley nut.

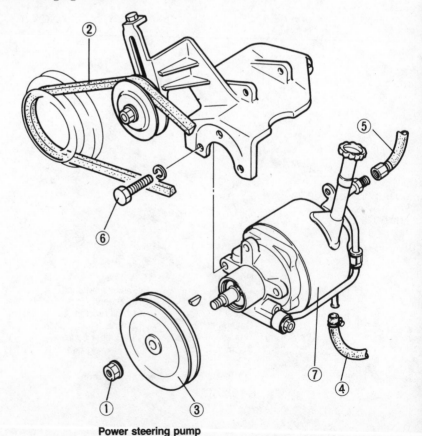

1. Nut
2. Oil pump belt
3. Oil pump pulley
4. Return hose
5. Pressure hose
6. Bolts
7. Oil pump

Power steering pump

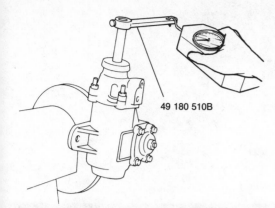

49 180 510B

Measuring power steering gear preload

3. Loosen the drive belt tensioner pulley and remove the belt.

4. Remove the pulley from the pump.

5. Position a drain pan under the pump and disconnect the hoses.

6. Remove the bracket-to-pump bolts and remove the pump from the truck.

7. Installation is the reverse of removal. Adjust the belt to give ½ inch deflection along its longest straight run. Bleed the system.

BLEEDING THE SYSTEM

1. Raise and support the front end on jackstands.

2. Check the fluid level and fill it, if necessary.

3. Start the engine and let it idle. Turn the steering wheel lock-to-lock, several times. Recheck the fluid level.

4. Lower the truck to the ground.

5. With the engine idling, turn the wheel lock-to-lock several times again. If noise is heard in the fluid lines, air is present.

6. Put the wheels in the straight ahead position and shut off the engine.

7. Check the fluid level. If it is higher than when you last checked it, air is in the system. Repeat step 5. Keep repeating step 5 until no air is present.

Wheel Alignment Specifications

Year & Model	Caster (deg.)		Camber (deg.)		Toe-in (in.)	Steering Axis Inclination (deg.)
	Range	Pref.	Range	Pref.		
1972–76 B1600	½P to 1½P	1P	1P to 2P	1½P	0–.25	8¼
Rotary Pick-Up	1½P to 2½P	2P	0 to ¾P	⅓P	0–.25	8¼
1977–78 B1800	⅔P to 1⅓P	1P	⅓P to 1¹⁄₁₂P	¾P	0–.25	8¼
1979–84 B2000 B2200	⅔P to 1⅓P	1P	⅓P to 1¼P	¾P	0–.25	8¼
1986 B2000	①	②	⅓P to 1¼P	¾P	0–.25	8¼

① Manual Steering: $1/12$P to $17/12$P
   Power Steering: $1\frac{1}{12}$P to $2\frac{7}{12}$P
② Manual Steering: $5/6$P
   Power Steering: $1\frac{5}{6}$P

Brakes

8

GENERAL BRAKE SYSTEM

CAUTION: *Brake shoes contain asbestos, which has been determined to be a cancer causing agent. Never clean the brake surfaces with compressed air! Avoid inhaling any dust from any brake surface! When cleaning brake surfaces, use a commercially available brake cleaning fluid.*

All Mazdas have a split hydraulic braking system. This system has separated hydraulic circuits for the front and rear brakes, using a master cylinder with two reservoirs. If a wheel cylinder or brake line should fail in either circuit, the other half of the braking system will still work.

The hydraulic lines run from the master cylinder to the pressure differential valve, located on the firewall, and from there to the brakes. The valve contains a warning switch connected to the valve piston. If unequal hydraulic pressure is applied, as in the case of a fluid leak, the piston moves off center, closing the switch and illuminating the warning light on the instrument panel.

Piston engine models, through 1976, have front drum brakes. Two single-piston wheel cylinders are used in each brake. The shoes and linings are interchangeable, as are the brake return springs. The Rotary Pick-Up uses disc brakes in the front and dual piston wheel cylinder drum brakes at the rear. 1977 and later Mazdas have single piston caliper front disc brakes. All Mazdas through 1978 have two dual piston wheel cylinders in each drum brake. The rear brakes are not self-adjusting on those models, and adjustments must be made to each of the two wheel cylinders in each brake. 1979 and later models have one dual piston wheel cylinder in each rear drum brake; the brakes are self-adjusting, requiring manual adjustment only when the linings are replaced. As in the front drum brakes, the shoes, linings, and

return springs are interchangeable in the rear brakes (but 1972–78 brake components are not interchangeable with 1979 and later brake parts). The brake system is a vacuum boosted in all 1977 and later models.

An independent hand-operated parking brake actuates the rear wheel brakes through a cable linkage. The parking brake operates off of the rear brake shoes.

ADJUSTMENTS

Front Drum Brakes

The brakes should be cool before adjustment.

1. Raise and support the front end on jackstands.
2. Remove the adjuster slot plugs from the backing plates.
3. Insert a brake adjusting tool in the slot and engage the starwheel. Rotate the starwheel until the drum is locked by the brake shoes, then back it off 5 notches. Repeat this for each starwheel.
4. When adjustment is complete, check that the wheels rotate freely, with no drag.

Rear Drum Brakes

1972–78

The brakes should be cool prior to adjustment.

1. Raise and support the rear end on jackstands.
2. Release the parking brake.
3. Disconnect the parking brake equalizer clevis pin.
4. Remove the adjusting slot plugs from the backing plates.
5. Insert a brake adjusting tool into the lower slot and engage the starwheel.
6. Turn the starwheel until the the brake shoes lock the wheel, then back it off 5 notches.
7. Repeat this procedure for the top starwheel, then continue on to the other wheel and adjust those brakes in the same sequence.

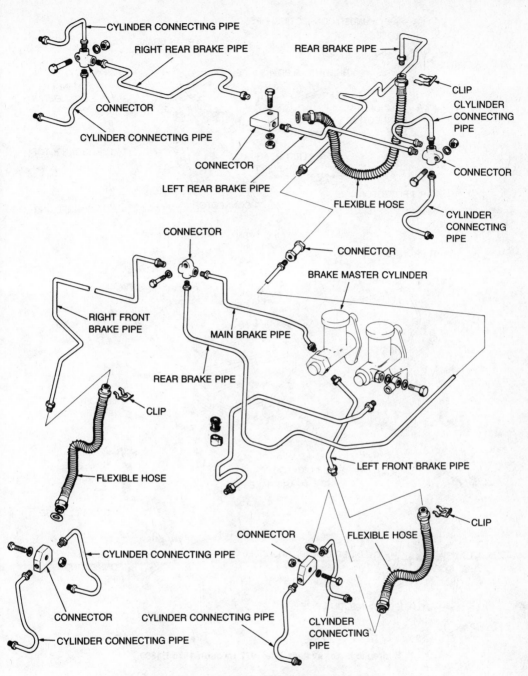

CYLINDER CONNECTING PIPE

RIGHT REAR BRAKE PIPE

REAR BRAKE PIPE

CLIP

CLYLINDER CONNECTING PIPE

CONNECTOR

CYLINDER CONNECTING PIPE

CONNECTOR

LEFT REAR BRAKE PIPE

CONNECTOR

FLEXIBLE HOSE

CONNECTOR

CYLINDER CONNECTING PIPE

CONNECTOR

CONNECTOR

BRAKE MASTER CYLINDER

RIGHT FRONT BRAKE PIPE

MAIN BRAKE PIPE

REAR BRAKE PIPE

CLIP

FLEXIBLE HOSE

LEFT FRONT BRAKE PIPE

CONNECTOR

FLEXIBLE HOSE

CLIP

CYLINDER CONNECTING PIPE

CONNECTOR

CYLINDER CONNECTING PIPE

CLYINDER CONNECTING PIPE

CONNECTOR

CYLINDER CONNECTING PIPE

Early 1972 B1600 hydraulic system components

8. When adjustment is complete, make sure that each wheel rotates freely, with no drag.

1979 AND LATER

The rear drum brakes are self-adjusting on 1979 and later models. Manual adjustment is required only when the brake shoes have been replaced, or when the length of the self-adjusting rod has been changed for some reason. The brakes should be cold (room temperature).

1. If the shoe retaining spring has been removed, first retract the pushrod fully (drum removed).

2. Raise and support the rear of the truck. The wheels must be free to turn.

3. Make sure the parking brake is fully released.

4. Remove the two adjusting hole plugs from the brake backing plate.

5. An arrow stamped on the backing plate

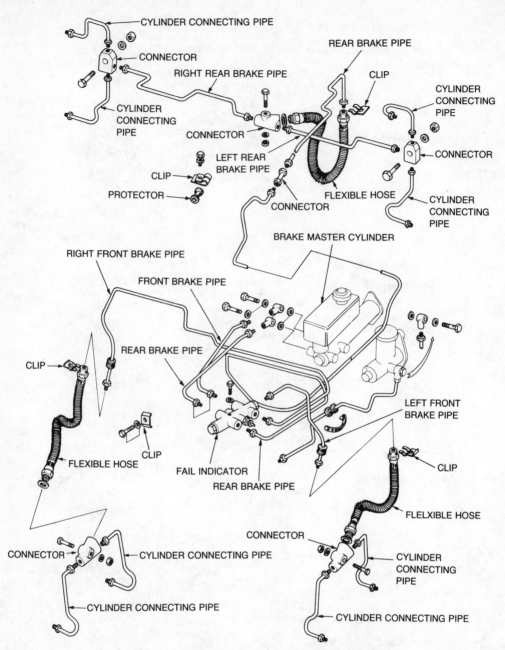

Hydraulic brake system, late 1972 through 1975 B1600

indicates the direction to turn the adjuster star-wheel to expand the shoes. Insert a brake spoon through the adjuster hole and turn the star-wheel until the brakes are locked.

6. Insert a drift through the other adjuster hole. Use the drift to hold the pole lever of the self-adjuster firmly. Back off the starwheel three or four notches; the wheel should rotate freely (no drag).

7. Repeat the adjustment on the other wheel. Make sure the adjustment is exactly the same.

Road test for equal brake action and readjust as necessary.

Disc Brakes

Disc brakes require no adjustments.

Brake Pedal Free-Play

Using the top of the pedal pad as a reference point, there should be 7.0–9.0mm on trucks through 1984 with power brakes, 4.0–7.0mm on 1986 trucks with power brakes, and, a little

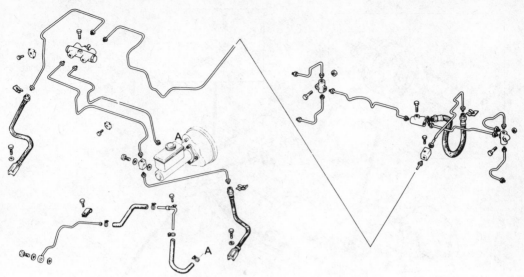

Hydraulic brake system, late 1978 through 1981

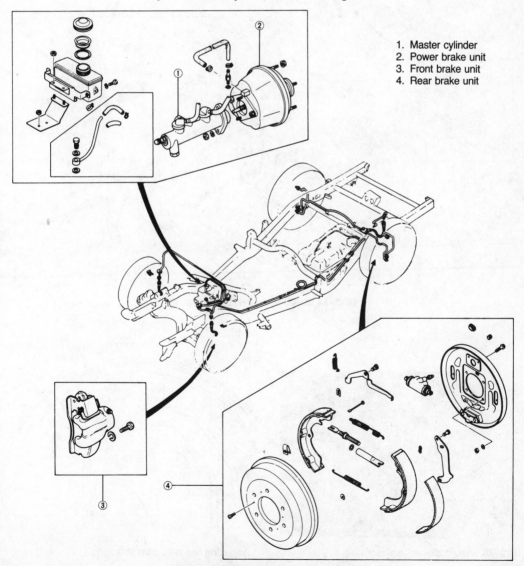

1. Master cylinder
2. Power brake unit
3. Front brake unit
4. Rear brake unit

1982–84 B2000 hydraulic brake system

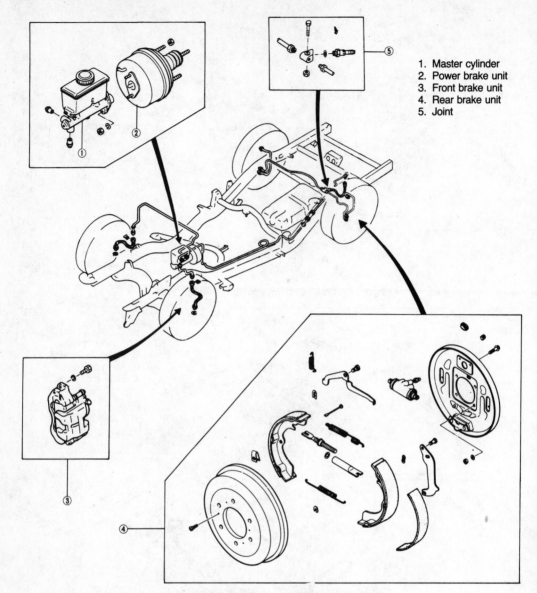

1. Master cylinder
2. Power brake unit
3. Front brake unit
4. Rear brake unit
5. Joint

1982–84 B2200 hydraulic brake system

1972–78 drum brake adjustment

Adjusting the hole plug locations

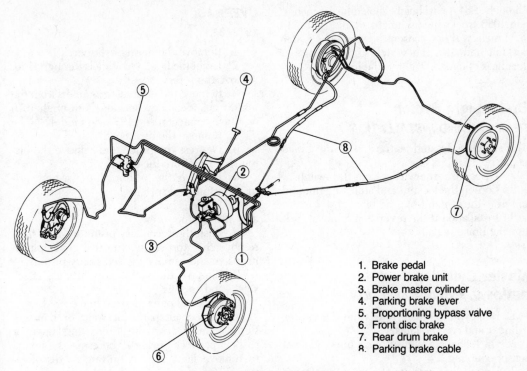

1. Brake pedal
2. Power brake unit
3. Brake master cylinder
4. Parking brake lever
5. Proportioning bypass valve
6. Front disc brake
7. Rear drum brake
8. Parking brake cable

1986 hydraulic brake system

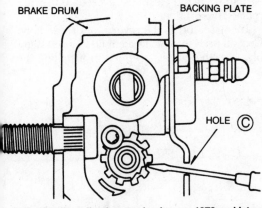

BRAKE DRUM   BACKING PLATE

HOLE Ⓒ

Activating the adjusting mechanism on 1979 and later rear brakes

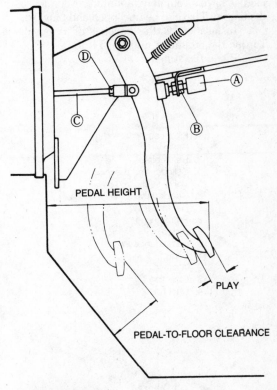

Ⓓ
Ⓒ
Ⓐ
Ⓑ

PEDAL HEIGHT

PLAY

PEDAL-TO-FLOOR CLEARANCE

less than ⅛ inch free-play before the pushrod contacts the master cylinder piston on models with non-power brakes.

1. Loosen the locknut on the master cylinder pushrod at the clevis.

2. Turn the pushrod to obtain the proper free-play, then tighten the nut.

Brake Pedal Height

Pedal height is measured from the center of the pedal pad surface, horizontally to the firewall. On the Rotary Pick-Up, pedal height should be 7.5 inches. On piston engine trucks

A. Brake light switch
B. Locknut
C. Pushrod
D. Locknut
Brake pedal adjustment points:

through 1984, pedal height should be 8.1 inches. On 1986 trucks, pedal height should be 8.23–8.43 inches. If not, loosen the stop light switch locknut and turn the switch until the proper height is obtained. Tighten the locknut.

Brake Light Switch

REMOVAL AND INSTALLATION

The switch is located at the top of the brake pedal.

1. Disconnect the wiring from the switch.
2. Loosen the locknut and adjusting nut and unscrew the switch from the bracket.
3. Installation is the reverse of removal. Adjust the brake pedal.

Master Cylinder

REMOVAL AND INSTALLATION

1. Remove the brakes lines from the master cylinder and cap the lines.
2. On 1986 models, disconnect the fluid level sensor coupling.
3. Unbolt and remove the master cylinder from the firewall or power booster. 1977–84 models have a remotely mounted reservoir, so the lines will have to be unclipped and plugged.
4. Installation is the reverse of removal. Torque the mounting nuts to 15 ft.lb.
5. Bleed the system.

OVERHAUL

1972–84

1. Remove the master cylinder.
2. Drain the fluid. On models through 1976, remove the reservoir.
3. Remove the reservoir grommets from the master cylinder body on models through 1976 or elbow connectors on 1977–84 models.
4. Remove the dust boot.
5. Depress the piston and remove the piston stop ring from the cylinder.
6. Remove the piston stop washer, primary piston, and spring.
7. Loosen, but do not remove, the secondary piston stop screw.
8. Push the secondary piston inward, then remove the stop screw. Insert a guide pin in its place, and remove the secondary piston.
9. Remove the outlet port fittings, check valves and springs.
10. Clean all parts in clean brake fluid.
11. Inspect all parts for wear or damage. Replace any worn, discolored, misshapen or suspect part. The cylinder bore may be honed to remove light scoring, pitting or discoloration. If honing cannot polish the interior, discard the cylinder. Check the piston-to-bore clearance. If the clearance exceeds 0.006 in., replace the cylinder.
12. Assembly is the reverse of disassembly. Coat all parts in clean brake fluid before assembly. Use the guide pin to aid in installing the

1. Filler cap
2. Baffle
3. Baffle plate
4. Cylinder and reservoir
5. Valve seat
6. Check valve
7. Return spring
8. Primary cup
9. Piston
10. Secondary cup
11. Clip
12. Washer
13. Stop ring
14. Dust boot

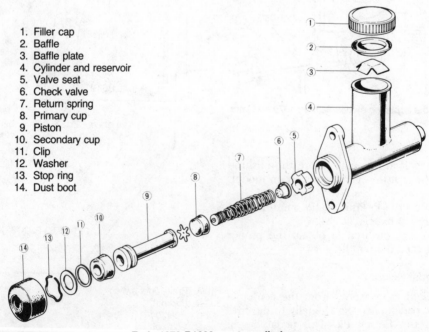

Early 1972 B1600 master cylinder

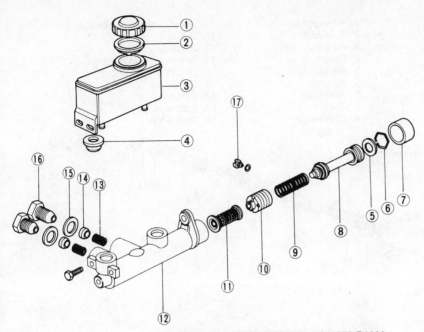

1. Filler cap
2. Baffle
3. Reservoir
4. Grommet
5. Washer
6. Stop ring
7. Dust boot
8. Primary piston
9. Spring
10. Secondary piston
11. Valve and spring
12. Cylinder
13. Spring
14. Check valve
15. Gasket
16. Outlet fitting
17. Stop bolt

Master cylinder, late 1972 through 1975 B1600

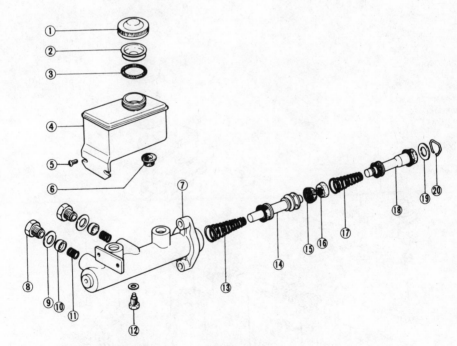

1. Reservoir cap
2. Fluid baffle
3. Packing
4. Reservoir
5. Bolt
6. Bushing
7. Cylinder
8. Joint bolt
9. Gasket
10. Check valve
11. Spring
12. Secondary piston stop bolt and O-ring
13. Spring
14. Secondary piston
15. Secondary piston cup
16. Secondary piston cup
17. Spring
18. Primary piston
19. Stop washer
20. Snap-ring

Rotary pick-up master cylinder

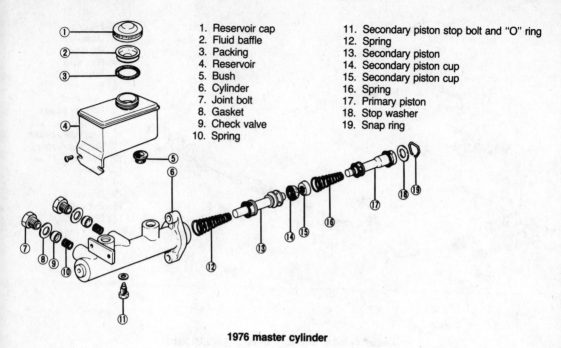

1. Reservoir cap
2. Fluid baffle
3. Packing
4. Reservoir
5. Bush
6. Cylinder
7. Joint bolt
8. Gasket
9. Check valve
10. Spring

11. Secondary piston stop bolt and "O" ring
12. Spring
13. Secondary piston
14. Secondary piston cup
15. Secondary piston cup
16. Spring
17. Primary piston
18. Stop washer
19. Snap ring

1976 master cylinder

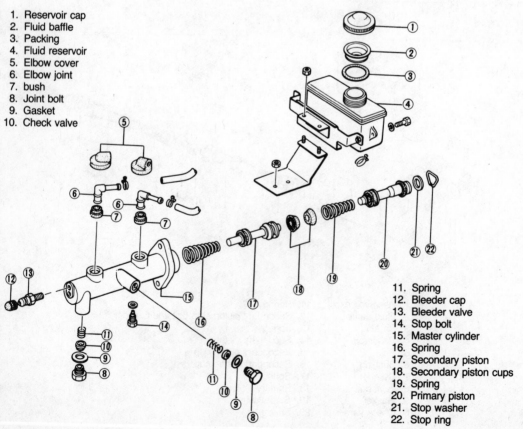

1. Reservoir cap
2. Fluid baffle
3. Packing
4. Fluid reservoir
5. Elbow cover
6. Elbow joint
7. bush
8. Joint bolt
9. Gasket
10. Check valve

11. Spring
12. Bleeder cap
13. Bleeder valve
14. Stop bolt
15. Master cylinder
16. Spring
17. Secondary piston
18. Secondary piston cups
19. Spring
20. Primary piston
21. Stop washer
22. Stop ring

1977–78 master cylinder

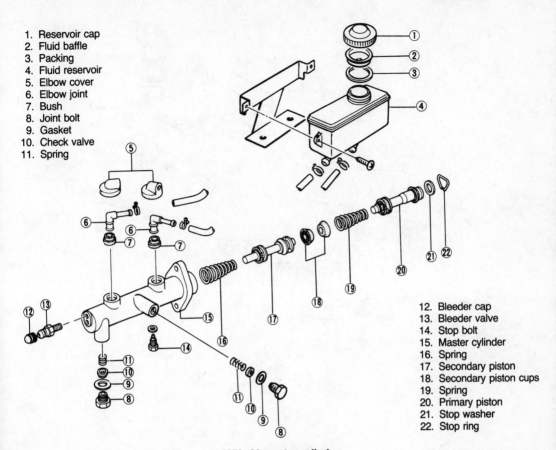

1. Reservoir cap
2. Fluid baffle
3. Packing
4. Fluid reservoir
5. Elbow cover
6. Elbow joint
7. Bush
8. Joint bolt
9. Gasket
10. Check valve
11. Spring

12. Bleeder cap
13. Bleeder valve
14. Stop bolt
15. Master cylinder
16. Spring
17. Secondary piston
18. Secondary piston cups
19. Spring
20. Primary piston
21. Stop washer
22. Stop ring

1979–80 master cylinder

secondary piston. Refill the master cylinder and pump the piston several times, until fluid flows from each outlet port.

1986

1. Rock the reservoir from side-to-side to remove it from the master cylinder.
2. Remove the reservoir grommets.
3. Remove the piston stopper screw from the bottom of the master cylinder.
4. Depress the piston and remove the snap ring.
5. Remove the primary piston assembly.
6. Remove the secondary piston assembly. Compressed air applied to the rearmost fluid port may be necessary to remove the secondary piston. If so, place a heavy rag over the cylinder bore to catch the piston.
7. Clean all parts in clean brake fluid.
8. Inspect all parts for wear or damage. Replace any worn, discolored, misshapen or suspect part. The cylinder bore may be honed to remove light scoring, pitting or discoloration. If honing cannot polish the interior, discard the cylinder. Check the piston-to-bore clearance. If the clearance exceeds 0.005 in., replace the cylinder.

Power Booster
REMOVAL AND INSTALLATION

1. Remove the master cylinder.
2. Disconnect the pushrod at the pedal.
3. Unbolt and remove the power booster from the firewall.
4. Installation is the reverse of removal. Check the clearance between the master cylinder piston and the power booster pushrod. Clearance should be 0.004–0.020 in. If not, adjust it at the pushrod. Torque the mounting nuts to 17 ft.lb.

Brake Hoses
INSPECTION AND REPLACEMENT

1. Clean the brake hose thoroughly before inspecting it.
2. Check all flexible hoses for any signs of swelling, cracking or brittleness. Replace any hose that shows any of these symptoms.
3. Check the hoses for any sign that they are rubbing against any other component. If shiny marks or scuffing is found. Determine what the

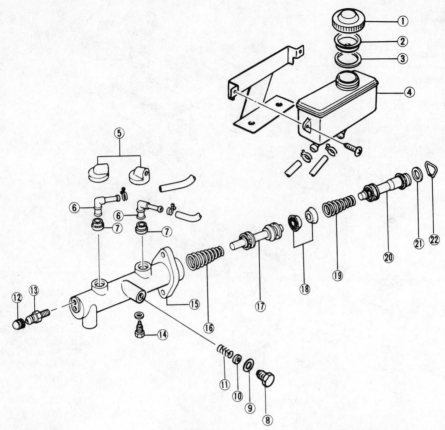

1. Reservoir cap	9. Gasket	17. Secondary piston
2. Fluid baffle	10. Check valve	18. Secondary piston cups
3. Packing	11. Spring	19. Spring
4. Fluid reservoir	12. Bleeder cap	20. Primary piston
5. Elbow cover	13. Bleeder valve	21. Stop washer
6. Elbow joint	14. Stop bolt	22. Stop ring
7. Bush	15. Master cylinder	
8. Joint bolt	16. Spring	

1981 master cylinder

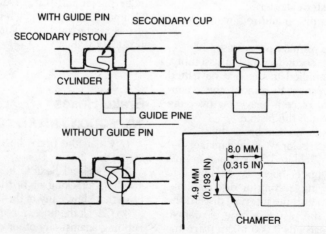

Guide pin usage

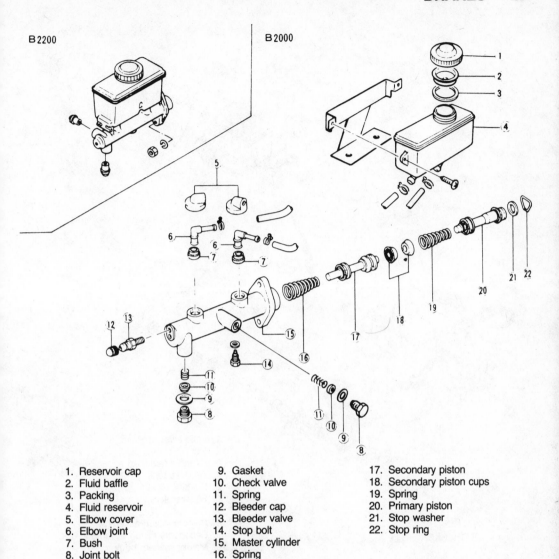

B 2200

B 2000

1. Reservoir cap
2. Fluid baffle
3. Packing
4. Fluid reservoir
5. Elbow cover
6. Elbow joint
7. Bush
8. Joint bolt
9. Gasket
10. Check valve
11. Spring
12. Bleeder cap
13. Bleeder valve
14. Stop bolt
15. Master cylinder
16. Spring
17. Secondary piston
18. Secondary piston cups
19. Spring
20. Primary piston
21. Stop washer
22. Stop ring

1982–84 master cylinder

hose is rubbing against and correct the problem. If scuffing has removed *any* material from the hose, replace it.

4. Check brake pipes for corrosion or dents. Replace any damaged pipe.

Checking piston-to-bore clearance

5. Check all connections for signs of leakage. Check threads for damage.

6. When disconnecting hoses and pipes, remove the retaining clip AFTER loosening the flare nut at the joint. When tightening fittings, install the clip, THEN, tighten the flare nut.

7. When installing a hose, make sure it is not twisted. Make absolutely certain, especially in the case of the hoses connected to the front calipers or wheel cylinders, that they will not come into contact with any other component with the front wheels in any position. Observe the following torques when installing lines:

Flexible hose-to-caliper or wheel cylinder: 16–19 ft.lb.

Flare nuts: 10–15 ft.lb.

8. When any brake line is opened, the system must be bled when the job is done.

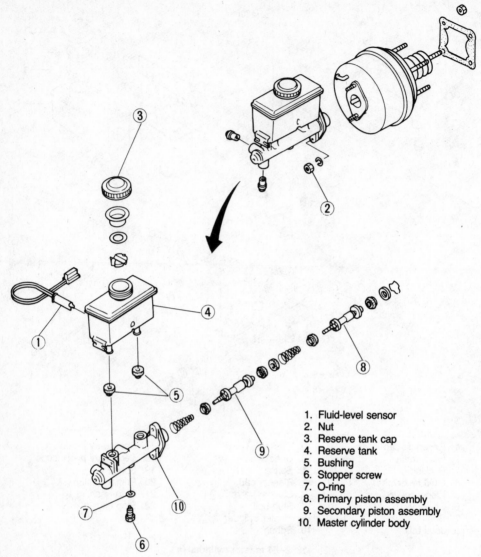

1. Fluid-level sensor
2. Nut
3. Reserve tank cap
4. Reserve tank
5. Bushing
6. Stopper screw
7. O-ring
8. Primary piston assembly
9. Secondary piston assembly
10. Master cylinder body

1986 master cylinder

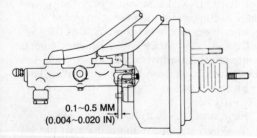

0.1~0.5 MM
(0.004~0.020 IN)

Checking clearance between the piston and rod

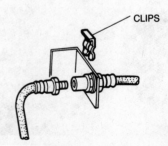

CLIPS

Brake hose clip installation

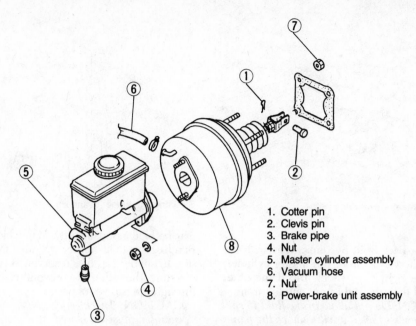

1. Cotter pin
2. Clevis pin
3. Brake pipe
4. Nut
5. Master cylinder assembly
6. Vacuum hose
7. Nut
8. Power-brake unit assembly

Power brake booster mounting

Pressure Differential Valve

REMOVAL AND INSTALLATION

1. Disconnect the brake warning light switch connector, at the switch.

2. Disconnect the brake lines at the valve, and plug the lines.

3. Unbolt and remove the valve.

4. Installation is the reverse of removal. Bleed the system.

CENTRALIZING THE PRESSURE DIFFERENTIAL VALVE

After the brake system has been opened for repairs, or bled, the brake light will remain on. The pressure differential valve must be centered to make the light go off.

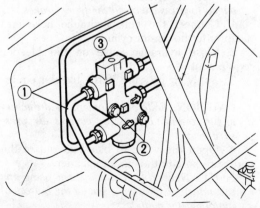

1. Brake line pipes   2. Bolts   3. Valve assembly

Typical pressure differential valve

1. Turn the ignition switch ON, but don't start the engine.

2. Make sure that the master cylinder reservoirs are filled.

3. Slowly depress the brake pedal. The valve should center itself and the light go off. If not, bleed the brakes again and repeat the above procedure.

Brake Bleeding

The hydraulic brake system must be free of air to operate properly. Air can enter the system when hydraulic parts are disconnected for servicing or replacement, or when the fluid level in the master cylinder reservoirs is very low. Air in the system will give the brake pedal a spongy feeling upon application.

The quickest and easiest of the two ways for system bleeding is the pressure method, but special equipment is needed to externally pressurize the hydraulic system. The other, more commonly used method of brake bleeding is done manually.

BLEEDING SEQUENCE

1. Master cylinder. If the cylinder is not equipped with bleeder screws, open the brake line(s) to the wheels slightly while pressure is applied to the brake pedal. Be sure to tighten the line before the brake pedal is released. The procedure for bench bleeding the master cylinder is covered below.

2. Pressure Differential Valve: If equipped with a bleeder screw.

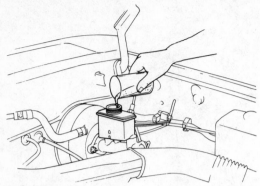

Filling the master cylinder

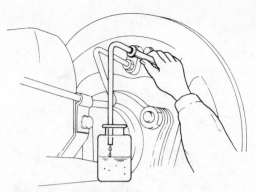

Bleeding the wheel cylinders

3. Front/Back Split Systems: Start with the wheel farthest away from the master cylinder, usually the right rear wheel. Bleed the other rear wheel then the right front and left front.

CAUTION: *Do not allow brake fluid to spill on the truck's finish, it will remove the paint. Flush the area with water.*

MANUAL BLEEDING

1. Clean the bleed screw at each wheel.

2. Start with the wheel farthest from master cylinder (right rear).

3. Attach a small rubber hose to the bleed screw and place the end in a container of clean brake fluid.

4. Fill the master cylinder with brake fluid. (Check often during bleeding). Have an assistant slowly pump up the brake pedal and hold pressure.

5. Open the bleed screw about one-quarter turn, press the brake pedal to the floor, close the bleed screw and slowly release the pedal. Continue until no more air bubbles are forced from the cylinder on application of the brake pedal.

6. Repeat procedure on remaining wheel cylinders and calipers, still working from cylinder/caliper farthest from the master cylinder. Master cylinders equipped with bleed screws

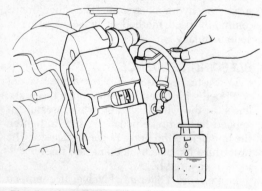

Bleeding the calipers

may be bled independently. When bleeding the Bendix-type dual master cylinder it is necessary to solidly cap one reservoir section while bleeding the other to prevent pressure loss through the cap vent hole.

CAUTION: *The bleeder valve at the wheel cylinder must be closed at the end of each stroke, and before the brake pedal is released, to insure that no air can enter the system. It is also important that the brake pedal be returned to the full up position so the piston in the master cylinder moves back enough to clear the bypass outlets.*

PRESSURE BLEEDING DISC BRAKES

CAUTION: *Special adapters are required when pressure bleeding cylinders with plastic reservoirs.*

Pressure bleeding equipment should be diaphragm type; placing a diaphragm between the pressurized air supply and the brake fluid. This prevents moisture and other contaminants from entering the hydraulic system.

NOTE: *Some front disc/rear drum equipped vehicles use a metering valve which closes off pressure to the front brakes under certain conditions. These systems contain manual release actuators, which must be engaged to pressure bleed the front brakes.*

1. Connect the tank hydraulic hose and adapter to the master cylinder.

2. Close hydraulic valve on the bleeder equipment.

3. Apply air pressure to the bleeder equipment.

CAUTION: *Follow equipment manufacturer's recommendations for correct air pressure.*

4. Open the valve to bleed air out of the pressure hose to the master cylinder.

NOTE: *Never bleed this system using the secondary piston stopscrew on the bottom of many master cylinders.*

5. Open the hydraulic valve and bleed each wheel cylinder and caliper. Bleed rear brake

system first when bleeding both front and rear systems.

FLUSHING HYDRAULIC BRAKE SYSTEMS

Hydraulic brake systems must be totally flushed if the fluid becomes contaminated with water, dirt or other corrosive chemicals. To flush, simply bleed the entire system until all fluid has been replaced with the correct type of new fluid.

BENCH BLEEDING MASTER CYLINDER

Bench bleeding the master cylinder before installing it on the truck reduces the possibility of getting air into the lines.

1. Connect two short pieces of brake line to the outlet fittings, bend them until the free end is below the fluid level in the master cylinder reservoirs.
2. Fill the reservoirs with fresh brake fluid. Pump the piston until no more air bubbles appear in the reservoir(s).
3. Disconnect the two short lines, refill the master cylinder and securely install the cylinder cap(s).
4. Install the master cylinder on the truck. Attach the lines but do not completely tighten them. Force any air that might have been trapped in the connection by slowly depressing the brake pedal. Tighten the lines before releasing the brake pedal.

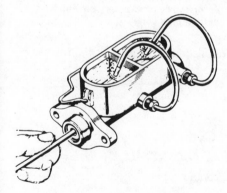

Pre-bleeding master cylinder

FRONT DRUM BRAKES

CAUTION: *Brake shoes contain asbestos, which has been determined to be a cancer causing agent. Never clean the brake surfaces with compressed air! Avoid inhaling any dust from any brake surface! When cleaning brake surfaces, use a commercially available brake cleaning fluid.*

Brake Drum
REMOVAL AND INSTALLATION

1. Raise and support the front end on jackstands.
2. Remove the wheels.
3. Remove the drum attaching screws and insert them in the threaded holes in the drum. Turn the screws inward, evenly, to force the drum off the hub.
4. Thoroughly inspect the drum. Discard a cracked drum. If the drum is suspected of being out of round, or shows signs of wear or has a ridged or rough surface, have it turned on a lathe at a machine shop. The maximum oversize is stamped into the drum.
5. Installation is the reverse of removal. Make sure that the holes are aligned for the attaching screws. Tighten the screws evenly to install the drum.

Removing the brake drum

Front drum brakes. The slots in the shoes should face the starwheels

Brake Shoes

REMOVAL AND INSTALLATION

The purchase of an inexpensive brake spring tool will make this job a lot easier.

1. Raise and support the front end on jack-stands.

2. Remove the drums.

3. Remove the retracting springs.

4. Remove the holddown springs and guide pins by turning the collars 90° with a pliers, or spring tool, releasing the springs.

5. Remove the shoes, noting in which place the shoe with the longer lining is installed.

6. Inspect the shoes for cracks, heat checking or contamination by oil or grease. Minimum lining thickness is 0.039 in. If heat checking or discoloration is noted, the wheel cylinder are probably at fault and will have to be rebuilt or replaced.

NOTE: *Never replace the shoes on one side of the truck, only! Always replace shoes on both sides!*

7. Clean the backing plate with an approved cleaning fluid.

8. Lubricate the threads of the starwheel with lithium based or silicone based grease. Apply a small dab of lithium or silicone based grease to the pads on which the brake shoes ride.

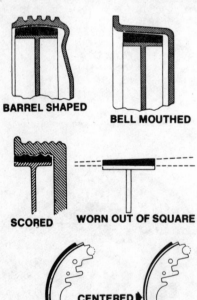

BARREL SHAPED

BELL MOUTHED

SCORED   **WORN OUT OF SQUARE**

CENTERED ▶

NOT CENTERED

Improperly worn linings are cause for concern, only if braking is unstable and/or noise is objectionable. Compare the lining and drum wear patterns. The drum pattern is more important since the drum shapes the wear of the shoe

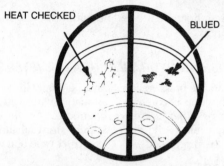

HEAT CHECKED

BLUED

A blued or severely heat checked drum, and charred or heavily glazed linings, are signs of overheating. The brakes should be replaced and the problem diagnosed and corrected

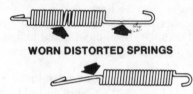

WORN DISTORTED SPRINGS

Replace weak or distorted springs

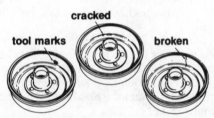

cracked

tool marks   **broken**

Check the drums for breaks. Replace broken drums. Tool marks or small cracks can be removed by turning the drum on a lathe

9. Installation of the shoes is the reverse of removal.

10. Check the action of the brakes at the pedal. If any sponginess is noted, bleed the brakes.

Wheel Cylinder

REMOVAL AND INSTALLATION

1. Raise and support the front end on jack-stands.

2. Remove the brake drum and shoes.

3. Disconnect the brake line at the wheel cylinder and plug it.

4. Remove the attaching nuts from behind the backing plate and remove the wheel cylinder.

5. Installation is the reverse of removal.

OVERHAUL

1. Remove the wheel cylinder.

2. Remove the piston and adjusting screw, then remove the boot and adjuster.

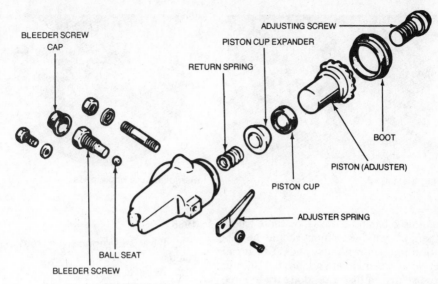

Exploded view of the front wheel cylinder

3. Using compressed air in the inlet port, blow out the piston cup, expander and spring.

4. Clean all parts in clean brake fluid.

5. Inspect all parts for wear or damage. Replace any worn, discolored, misshapen or suspect part. The cylinder bore may be honed to remove light scoring, pitting or discoloration. If honing cannot polish the interior, discard the cylinder. Check the piston-to-bore clearance. If the clearance exceeds 0.006 in., replace the cylinder.

6. Assembly is the reverse of disassembly. Coat all parts in clean brake fluid before assembly.

7. Install the wheel cylinder and all other parts. Bleed the system.

FRONT DISC BRAKES

CAUTION: *Brake shoes contain asbestos, which has been determined to be a cancer causing agent. Never clean the brake surfaces with compressed air! Avoid inhaling any dust from any brake surface! When cleaning brake surfaces, use a commercially available brake cleaning fluid.*

Brake Pads

REMOVAL AND INSTALLATION

NOTE: *Minimum thickness of the pad lining and backing plate combined should be 0.276 in.*

Through 1984

1. Raise and support the front end on jackstands.

Removing pin retainers from the caliper

Removing the holddown plates

2. Remove the wheels.

3. Remove the caliper retaining pins and holddown plates.

4. Lift off the caliper, remove the anti-rattle clips and remove the pads.

5. Remove about ½ of the fluid from the front brake reservoir of the master cylinder.

6. Position a large C-clamp on the caliper and force the piston back into its bore.

7. Installation is the reverse of removal.

Removing the caliper

Removing the brake pads

Shims are used behind the pads on these trucks from the factory. These shims should be discarded and replaced with new ones at each pad change. Some aftermarket pads are too thick to use these shims. In that case, don't try to force new shims in place. Do without them. Refill the master cylinder reservoir. Pump the brake pedal a few times to restore pressure.

1986

1. Raise and support the front end on jack-stands.
2. Remove the wheels.
3. Remove the caliper lockpin bolts.
4. Lift off the caliper and remove the brake pads.

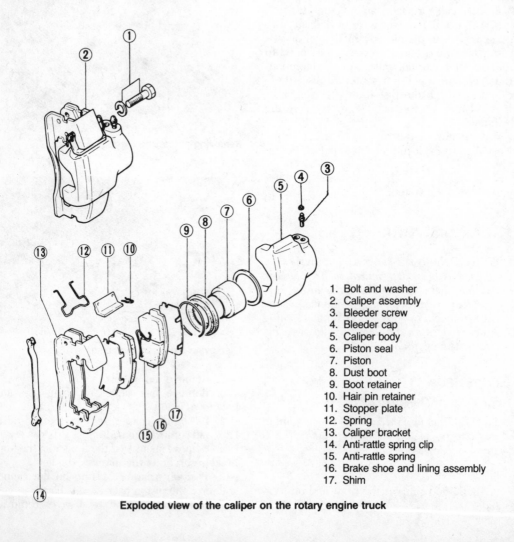

1. Bolt and washer
2. Caliper assembly
3. Bleeder screw
4. Bleeder cap
5. Caliper body
6. Piston seal
7. Piston
8. Dust boot
9. Boot retainer
10. Hair pin retainer
11. Stopper plate
12. Spring
13. Caliper bracket
14. Anti-rattle spring clip
15. Anti-rattle spring
16. Brake shoe and lining assembly
17. Shim

Exploded view of the caliper on the rotary engine truck

5. Remove about ½ of the fluid from the front brake reservoir of the master cylinder.

6. Position a large C-clamp on the caliper and force the piston back into its bore.

7. Install new pads in the caliper. Shims are used behind the pads on these trucks from the factory. These shims should be discarded and replaced with new ones at each pad change. Some aftermarket pads are too thick to use these shims. In that case, don't try to force new shims into place. Do without them.

8. Position the caliper on the mounting support, install the lockpins and tighten them to 30 ft.lb.

9. Install the wheels, lower the truck to the ground and refill the master cylinder. Pump the brake pedal a few times to restore pressure.

Caliper

REMOVAL AND INSTALLATION

1. Follow the procedure for removing the brake pads, above.

2. Disconnect the brake line at the caliper and plug the line.

3. Installation is the reverse of removal. Bleed the brakes.

OVERHAUL

1. Remove the caliper.

2. Place a thin piece of wood in the caliper, in front of the piston. Apply enough compressed air through the brake line inlet hole to force the piston out of the caliper. Don't try to catch the piston with your fingers. A set of mashed fingers will result. It's also a good idea

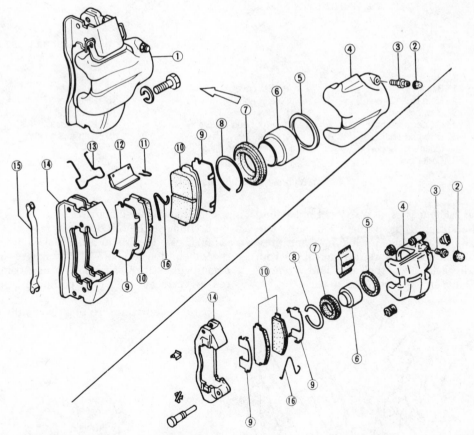

1. Caliper assembly	7. Dust boot	13. Spring
2. Bleeder cap	8. Boot retainer	14. Caliper bracket
3. Bleeder screw	9. Shim	15. Anti-rattle spring clip
4. Caliper body	10. Brake shoe and lining assembly	16. Anti-rattle spring
5. Piston seal	11. Locking clip	
6. Piston	12. Stopper plate	

Exploded views of the B1800 and 1979–84 B2000 caliper (top) and the B2200 caliper (bottom)

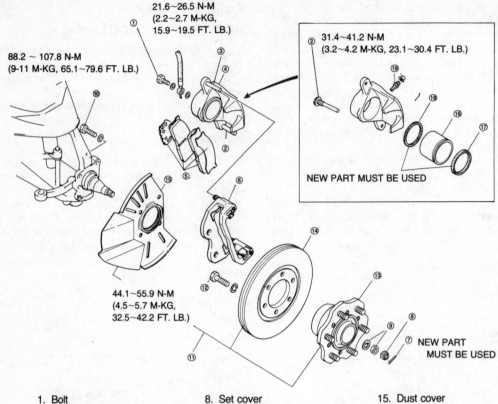

21.6~26.5 N-M
(2.2~2.7 M-KG,
15.9~19.5 FT. LB.)

88.2 ~ 107.8 N-M
(9-11 M-KG, 65.1~79.6 FT. LB.)

31.4~41.2 N-M
(3.2~4.2 M-KG, 23.1~30.4 FT. LB.)

NEW PART MUST BE USED

44.1~55.9 N-M
(4.5~5.7 M-KG,
32.5~42.2 FT. LB.)

NEW PART
MUST BE USED

1. Bolt	8. Set cover	15. Dust cover
2. Main lock pin bolt	9. Nut and washer	16. Piston
3. Sub lock pin bolt	10. Bolt	17. Dust seal
4. Caliper assembly	11. Front hub assembly	18. Piston seal
5. Disc pad and shim	12. Bolt	19. Cap and screw
6. Mounting support	13. Bearing housing	
7. Cotter pin	14. Disc plate	

1986 brake and hub assembly

to wear safety glasses, as a spray of brake fluid will often result. If the piston is seized, try tapping around the caliper while applying pressure. If that doesn't work, fill the caliper with a rust dissolving agent such as Liquid Wrench® or WD-40® and let it stand for a while.

3. Discard all rubber parts.
4. Remove the bleeder screw.
5. Clean all parts in clean brake fluid. Inspect the piston and bore for any signs of wear, damage or heat discoloration. Minor damage can be corrected with light polishing using a crocus cloth.
6. Rebuilding kits are equipped with two

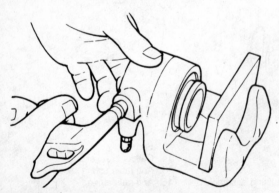

Forcing the piston from the caliper with compressed air. A thin block of wood is positioned to catch the piston

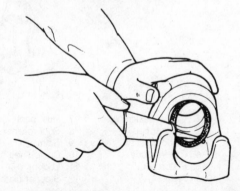

Removing the dust boot

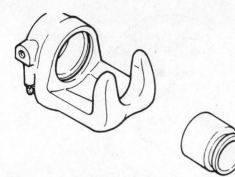

Piston removed from the caliper

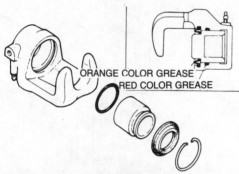

ORANGE COLOR GREASE
RED COLOR GREASE

Caliper components. The inset shows the application of the color coded grease

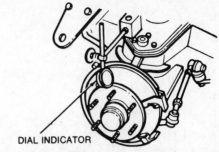

DIAL INDICATOR
Use a dial indicator to check disc runout.

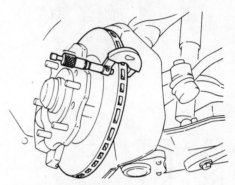

Checking caliper thickness

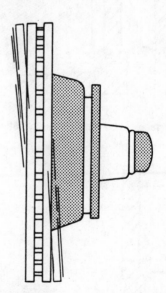

Excessive runout

kinds of grease, color coded orange and red. See the illustration for application details. Install a new seal, lubricated with clean brake fluid, on the piston. Be sure that the seal is not twisted!

7. Lubricate the piston and bore with clean brake fluid and insert the piston in the bore.

8. Install a new dust boot and retainer.

9. Install the bleeder screw.

10. Install the caliper in reverse of removal.

Brake Rotor

REMOVAL AND INSTALLATION

1. Raise and support the front end on jackstands.

2. Remove the wheel.

3. Remove the grease cap, cotter pin, hub nut and flat washer.

4. Remove the caliper and suspend it out of the way without disconnecting the brake line. At this point, check the disc runout using a dial indicator. Slowly pull the hub from the spindle, positioning your hand to catch the outer bearing.

5. Matchmark the hub and rotor. Unbolt the rotor from the hub.

6. Inspect the rotor for any signs of wear, damage, roughness, ridges, pitting or heat discoloration. If heat discoloration is noted, you probably have a problem with the caliper pis-

ton seizing. Rebuild the caliper. Check the rotor thickness. To correct most of the above problems, have the caliper turned at a machine shop. Minimum caliper thickness is 0.433 in.

7. When installing the rotor, make sure that the matchmarks are aligned. Tighten the rotor-to-hub bolts to 40 ft.lb.

8. Pack the inside of the hub with clean wheel bearing grease until it is flush packed.

9. Pack the bearing with clean grease,

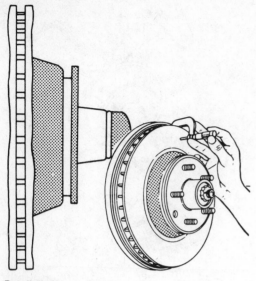

Parallelism

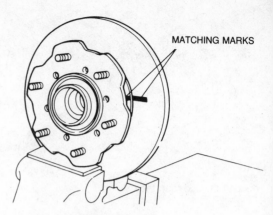

Aligning matchmarks

MATCHING MARKS

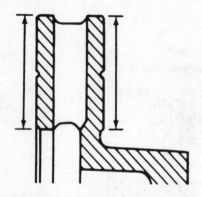

These surfaces to be flat and within .002 in.

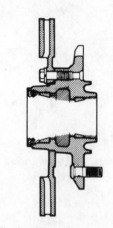

Fill the hub flush with grease

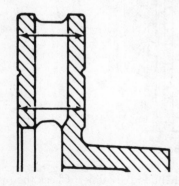

Taper variation not to exceed .003 in.

Pack the bearing with clean grease

making sure that it is thoroughly packed. Special devices are sold for packing bearings. They are inexpensive and readily available. If you don't have one, just make certain that the bearing is as full of grease as possible by working it in with your fingers.

10. If removed, install the inner bearing and seal. Drive the seal into place carefully until it is seated.

11. Install the spacer and the hub on the spindle.

12. Install the outer bearing, flat washer and hub nut. Torque the nut to 22 ft.lb. and turn the hub 2 or 3 times to seat the bearings. Back off the nut until it is loose. Rock the hub back and forth to make sure the pads are not causing

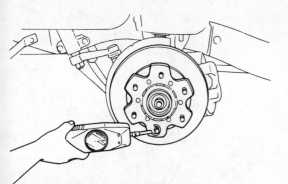

Checking bearing preload with a spring scale

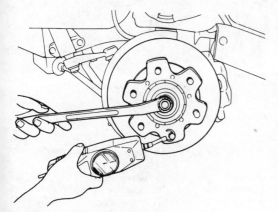

Setting bearing preload

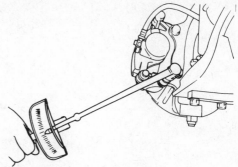

Tightening caliper mounting bolts

any drag on the rotor. It may be necessary to force the inner pad back using a C-clamp.

13. Attach a spring scale to a wheel lug.

14. Pull the scale horizontally and check the force needed to start the wheel turning. The force should be 1.3–2.4 lbs. If the reading is not correct, tighten or loosen the hub nut until the correct pull rating is obtained.

15. Install the nut cap, cotter pin and grease cap. Install the wheel.

REAR DRUM BRAKES

CAUTION: *Brake shoes contain asbestos, which has been determined to be a cancer causing agent. Never clean the brake sur-*

1. Drum attaching bolt
2. Drum
3. Brake shoe
4. Shoe return spring
5. Bolt and nut
6. Backing plate
7. Plug
8. Shoe hold-down spring pin
9. Wheel cylinder nut
10. Parking brake opening lever
11. Operating strut
12. Pushrod
13. Clip spring
14. Wave washer
15. Brake shoe retaining clip
16. Wheel cylinder
17. Brake lining
18. Brake pipe guard
19. Screw and washer
20. Wheel center cap
21. Set rubber
22. Wheel center cap adaptor
23. Balance weight
24. Rear wheel

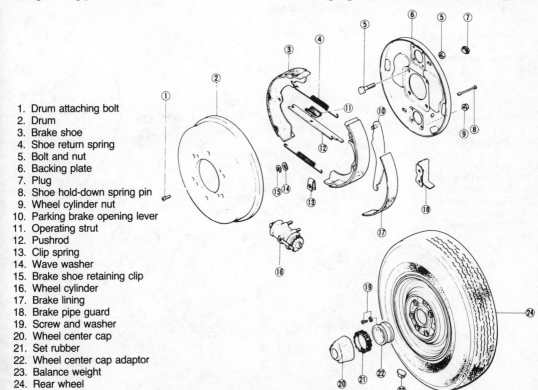

1972–76 rear brake components

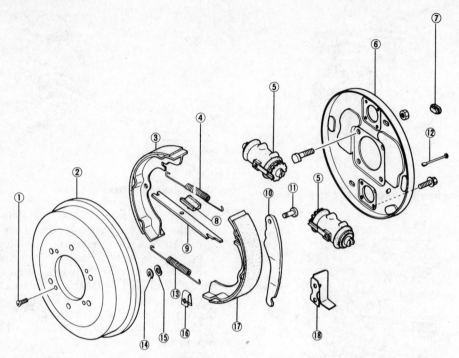

1. Screw
2. Drum
3. Brake shoe
4. Shoe return spring
5. Wheel cylinder
6. Backing plate

7. Plug
8. Strut holder
9. Parking brake strut rod
10. Parking brake operating lever
11. Pin
12. Guide pin

13. Shoe return spring
14. Clip
15. Wave washer
16. Retaining spring
17. Brake shoe
18. Brake pipe guard

1977–78 rear brake components

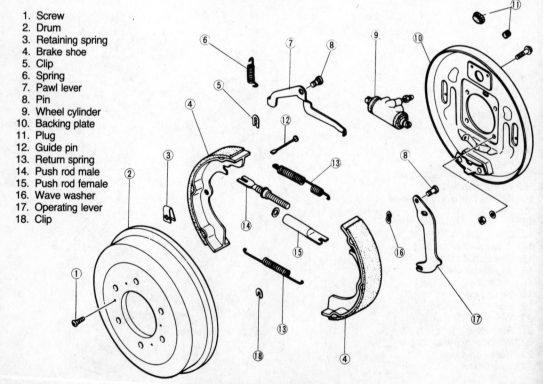

1. Screw
2. Drum
3. Retaining spring
4. Brake shoe
5. Clip
6. Spring
7. Pawl lever
8. Pin
9. Wheel cylinder
10. Backing plate
11. Plug
12. Guide pin
13. Return spring
14. Push rod male
15. Push rod female
16. Wave washer
17. Operating lever
18. Clip

1979–86 rear brake components

faces with compressed air! Avoid inhaling any dust from any brake surface! When cleaning brake surfaces, use a commercially available brake cleaning fluid.

Brake Drums
REMOVAL AND INSTALLATION

1. Raise and support the rear end on jack-stands.
2. Remove the wheels.
3. Remove the drum attaching screws and insert them in the threaded holes in the drum.

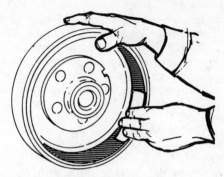

Sanding brake drums

Turn the screws inward, evenly, to force the drum off the hub.

4. Thoroughly inspect the drum. Discard a cracked drum. If the drum is suspected of being out of round, or shows signs of wear or has a ridged or rough surface, have it turned on a lathe at a machine shop. The maximum over-size is stamped into the drum.

5. Installation is the reverse of removal. Make sure that the holes are aligned for the attaching screws. Tighten the screws evenly to install the drum.

Brake Shoes
REMOVAL AND INSTALLATION

The purchase of an inexpensive brake spring tool will make this job a lot easier.

1. Raise and support the rear end on jack-stands.
2. Remove the drums.
3. Remove the retracting springs.
4. Remove the holddown springs and guide pins by turning the collars 90° with a pliers, or spring tool, releasing the springs.
5. Remove the parking brake link and dis-connect the parking brake cable from the lever.

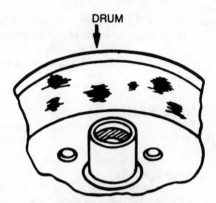

DRUM

Hard or Chill Spots

LOOK HERE FOR TURNED DRUM TOOL MARK RIDGE

0.60"

Oversize drum

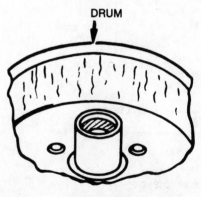

DRUM

Heat checks

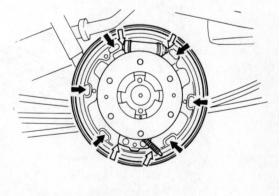

Lubrication points prior to installing the shoes

6. Remove the shoes, noting in which place the shoe with the longer lining is installed.

7. Inspect the shoes for cracks, heat checking or contamination by oil or grease. Minimum lining thickness is 0.039 in. If heat checking or discoloration is noted, the wheel cylinders are probably at fault and will have to be rebuilt or replaced.

NOTE: *Never replace the shoes on one side of the truck, only! Always replace shoes on both sides!*

8. Clean the backing plate with an approved cleaning fluid.

9. Lubricate the threads of the starwheel with lithium based or silicone based grease. Apply a small dab of lithium or silicone based grease to the pads on which the brake shoes ride.

10. Installation of the shoes is the reverse of removal.

11. Check the action of the brakes at the pedal. If any sponginess is noted, bleed the brakes.

Wheel Cylinder

REMOVAL AND INSTALLATION

1. Raise and support the rear end on jackstands.

2. Remove the brake drum and shoes.

3. Disconnect the brake line at the wheel cylinder and plug it.

4. Remove the attaching nuts from behind the backing plate and remove the wheel cylinder.

5. Installation is the reverse of removal.

OVERHAUL

1. Remove the wheel cylinder.

2. Remove the piston and adjusting screw, then remove the boot and adjuster.

3. Using compressed air in the inlet port, blow out the piston cup, expander and spring.

4. Clean all parts in clean brake fluid.

5. Inspect all parts for wear or damage. Replace any worn, discolored, misshapen or suspect part. The cylinder bore may be honed to remove light scoring, pitting or discoloration. If honing cannot polish the interior, discard the cylinder. Check the piston-to-bore clearance. If the clearance exceeds 0.006 in., replace the cylinder.

6. Assembly is the reverse of disassembly. Coat all parts in clean brake fluid before assembly.

7. Install the wheel cylinder and all other parts. Bleed the system.

PARKING BRAKE

ADJUSTMENT

1. Adjust the service brakes before attempting to adjust the parking brake.

2. Use the adjusting nut to adjust the length of the front cable so that the rear brakes are locked when the parking brake lever is pulled out 5–10 notches on trucks through 1984, and 11–13 notches on 1986 trucks.

3. After adjustment, apply the parking brake several times. Release the parking brake and make sure that the rear wheels rotate without dragging. If they drag, repeat the adjustment.

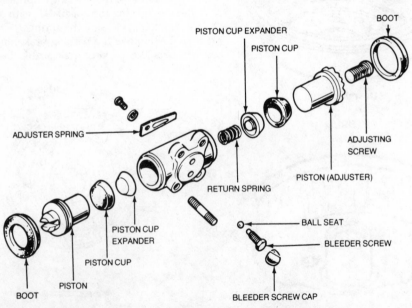

Exploded view of a rear wheel cylinder through 1978

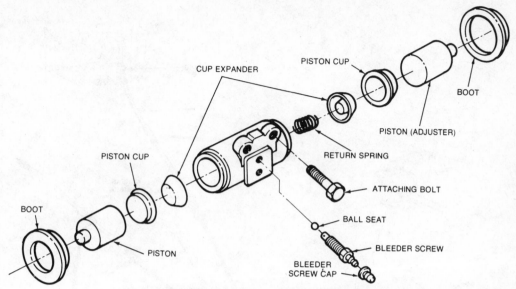

Exploded view of a rear wheel cylinder; 1979 and later

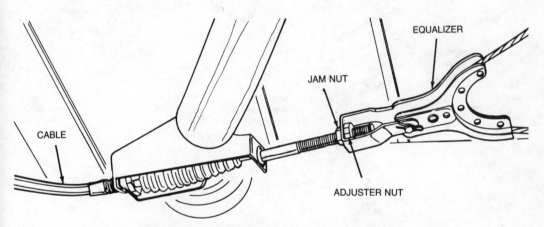

Parking brake adjusting point for trucks through 1984

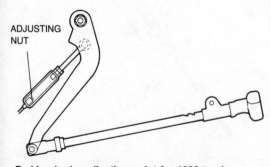

Parking brake adjusting point for 1986 trucks

NOTE: *If the parking brake cable is replaced, prestretch it by applying the parking brake hard three or four times before attempting adjustment.*

REMOVAL AND INSTALLATION

Front Cable

1. Raise and support the front end on jackstands.

2. Remove the adjusting nut.

3. Separate the front cable from the equalizer and remove the jam nut.

4. Remove the return spring and boot from the housing.

5. Pull the lower housing forward and out of the slotted frame bracket. Slip the cable shaft sideways through the slot until the cable and housing are free of the bracket.

6. Disengage the upper cable connector from the brake lever by removing the clevis pin and retainer.

7. Remove the upper cable housing retain-

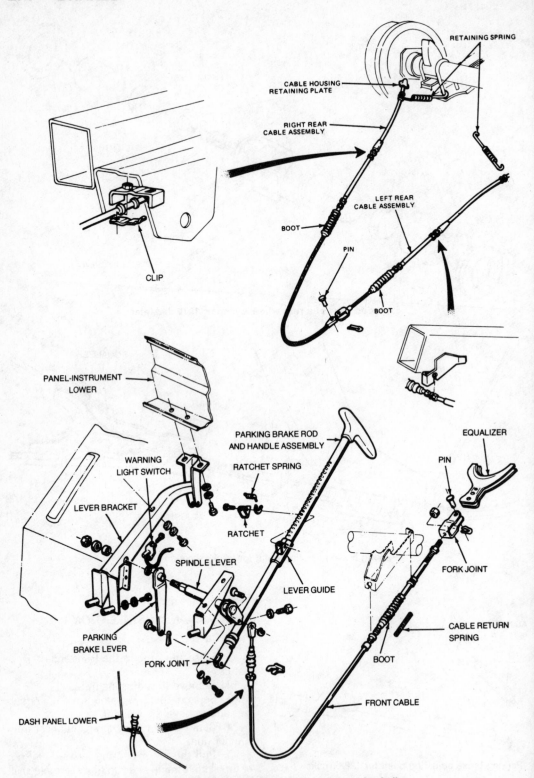

RETAINING SPRING

CABLE HOUSING
RETAINING PLATE

RIGHT REAR
CABLE ASSEMBLY

LEFT REAR
CABLE ASSEMBLY

BOOT

PIN

BOOT

CLIP

PANEL-INSTRUMENT
LOWER

PARKING BRAKE ROD
AND HANDLE ASSEMBLY

EQUALIZER

WARNING
LIGHT SWITCH

RATCHET SPRING

PIN

LEVER BRACKET

RATCHET

SPINDLE LEVER

FORK JOINT

PARKING
BRAKE LEVER

LEVER GUIDE

FORK JOINT

CABLE RETURN
SPRING

BOOT

DASH PANEL LOWER

FRONT CABLE

1972–74 parking brake linkage; 1975–84 linkage is similar

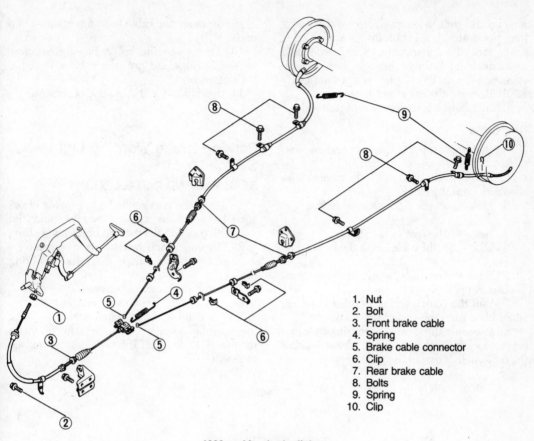

1. Nut
2. Bolt
3. Front brake cable
4. Spring
5. Brake cable connector
6. Clip
7. Rear brake cable
8. Bolts
9. Spring
10. Clip

1986 parking brake linkage

Brake Specifications

(All specifications in inches)

Year & Model	Master Cyl. Bore	Brake Disc			Brake Drum			Wheel Cyl. or Caliper Bore	
		Original Thickness	Minimum Thickness	Maximum Run-out	Orig. Inside Dia.	Max. Wear Limit	Maximum Machine O/S	Front	Rear
1972–76 B1600	0.750	—	—	—	10.24F 10.24R	10.28F 10.28R	10.30F 10.30R	1.000	0.813
Rotary Pick-Up	0.875	0.4724	0.4331	0.0039	10.24	10.28	10.30	2.125	0.750
1977–78 B1800	0.875	0.4724	0.4331	0.0039	10.24	10.28	10.30	2.125	0.750
1979–84 B2000	0.875	0.4724	0.4331	0.0039	10.24	10.28	10.30	2.125	0.875
1982–84 B2200	0.813	0.7874	0.7480	0.0039	10.24	10.28	10.30	2.125	0.875
1986 B2000	0.875	0.7874	0.7086	0.0016	10.24	10.31	—	2.125	0.750

ing clip and pull the upper cable and housing from the slotted bracket on the firewall.

8. Push the upper cable, cable housing and dust shield grommet through the firewall opening and into the engine compartment.

9. Remove the cable and housing.

10. Installation is the reverse of removal.

Rear Cable

1. Raise and support the rear end on jackstands.

2. Remove the pin and disconnect the equalizer from the clevis.

3. Disconnect the right hand cable from the left.

4. Remove the rear brake shoes.

5. Disengage the cables from the brake shoe levers.

6. Remove the cable housing retainer from the backing plate.

7. Pull the return spring to release the retainer plate from the end of the housing.

8. Loosen the cable housing-to-frame bracket locknut and remove the forward end of the cable housing from the frame bracket.

9. Remove the cable housing retaining clip bolts.

10. Disengage the cable housing-to-frame tension springs and pull the cable out of the backing plate.

11. Installation is the reverse of removal.

Parking Brake Warning Light Switch

REMOVAL AND INSTALLATION

1. Apply the parking brake to provide clearance between the switch assembly and the switch stop tab on the parking brake lever shaft.

2. Disconnect the switch wiring connector.

3. Remove the switch from its mounting bracket.

5. Install the attaching screws.

6. Connect the switch wire connector.

7. Turn the ignition switch ON and check the operation of the switch. No adjustment to the switch is possible. If it is defective, replace the switch.

Body and Trim

9

EXTERIOR

Doors

REMOVAL AND INSTALLATION

NOTE: *If the door being removed is to be reinstalled, matchmark the hinge position.*

1. If the door is to be replaced with a new one, remove the trim panels weathersheets and all molding.

2. If the door is to be replaced with a new one, remove the glass, locks and latches.

3. Support the door and remove the hinge-to-body attaching bolts. Lift the door from the truck.

4. Installation is the reverse of removal. Perform the alignment procedures indicated below.

ALIGNMENT

NOTE: *The holes for the hinges are oversized to provide for latitude in alignment. Align the door hinges first, then the striker.*

Hinges

1. If a door is being installed, first mount the door and tighten the hinge bolts lightly. If the door has not been removed, determine which hinge bolts must be loosed to effect alignment.

2. Loosen the necessary bolts just enough to allow the door to be moved with a padded prybar.

3. Move the door in small movements and check the fit after each movement. Be sure that there is no binding or interference with adjacent panels. Keep repeating this procedure until the door is properly aligned. Tighten all the bolts. Shims may be either fabricated or purchased to install behind the hinges as an aid in alignment.

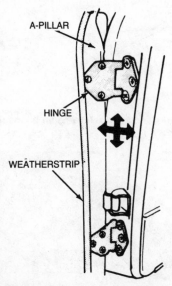

Door hinge adjustments for 1972–84 trucks

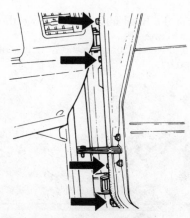

Door hinge adjustments for 1986 trucks

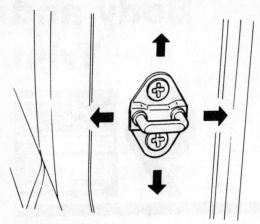

Striker adjustments for 1986 trucks

Striker adjustments for 1972–84 trucks

Striker Plate

Striker adjustment is made by loosening the bolts and moving the striker plate in the desired direction or adding or deleting shims behind the plate, or both. The striker is properly adjusted when the locking latch enters the striker without rubbing and the door closes fully and solidly, with no play when closed.

NOTE: *The striker is attached to the pillar using oversized holes, providing latitude in movement.*

Hood

REMOVAL AND INSTALLATION

NOTE: *You are going to need an assistant for this job.*

Models with Self-Supporting Hood

1. Open the hood and trace the outline of the hinges on the body.
2. While an assistant holds the hood, remove the cotter pin from the right side hood stop retaining pin.
3. Remove the retaining pin and the hood stop.
4. Tilt the hood forward and move the torsion bar to one side.
5. Remove the hinge-to-body bolts and lift the hood off.

6. Installation is the reverse of removal. Align the outlines previously made. Check that the hood closes properly. Adjust hood alignment, if necessary.

Models with Hood Prop

1. Outline the hinge position on the hood.
2. Support the hood and remove the hinge-to-hood bolts. Lift off the hood.
3. Installation of the hood is the reverse of removal. Check the hood for fit and closure. Adjust the hood alignment, if necessary.

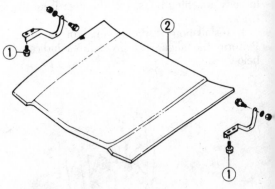

1. Hood
2. Hinges

Hood hinges and hood reference on hoods using a prop support

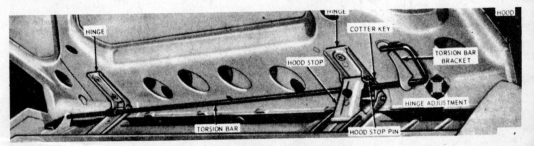

Hood removal points for self-supporting hoods

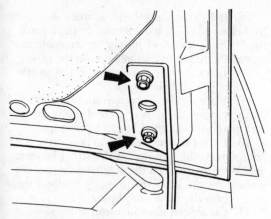

Hood-to-hinge attachment nuts on hoods using a prop support

ALIGNMENT

On self-supporting hoods, alignment can be adjusted front-to-rear or side-to-side by loosening the hood-to-hinge or hinge-to-body bolts. The front edge of the hood can be adjusted for closing height by adding or deleting shims under the hinges. The rear edge of the hood can be adjusted for closing height by raising or lowering the rear hood bumpers.

On hoods supported with a prop, alignment is accomplished by loosening the lockplate bolts and moving the lockplate up or down; side-to-side.

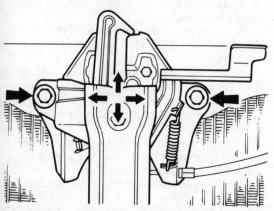

Hood latch adjustment point for hoods using a prop support

Tailgate
REMOVAL AND INSTALLATION

1. Open and support the tailgate.
2. Remove the hinge pins by removing the cotter pins and washers, then driving the hinge pins out.
3. Lift off the tailgate.
4. Installation is the reverse of removal.

Windshield or Rear Window Glass
REMOVAL AND INSTALLATION

NOTE: *You'll need an assistant for this job.*

1972–84 Windshield
1972–86 Rear Window

1. Remove the wiper arms.
2. Carefully snap the windshield molding from the weatherstripping.
3. Using a wood spatula, break the adhesive bond between the weatherstripping and the body flange.
4. Push out the inner lip of the weatherstripping, from inside the truck, while pushing out on the glass.
5. With the aid of an assistant, remove the glass and weatherstripping.

Cutting the sealer at points 1, 2, 3 from molding A

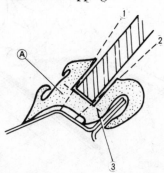

Applying primer

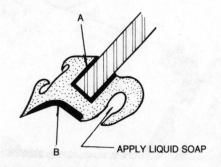

Applying soap and bonding agent. Bonding agent is applied at A and B

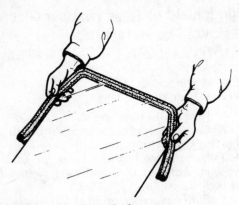

Installing the weatherstripping

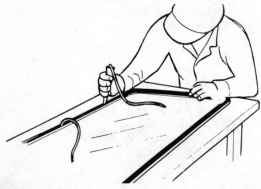

Fitting the string

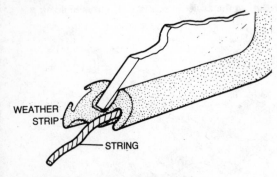

WEATHER
STRIP

STRING

String installed in the weatherstripping

6. Before installing the glass, make sure that you clean all of the old adhesive from all parts.

7. Place a coat of primer in the molding. Install the weatherstripping around the glass.

8. Liberally wet the groove in the weatherstripping with liquid soap.

9. Place a string, about 4mm in diameter, in the groove all the way around the weatherstripping. Allow a good length to hang free.

10. Place the windshield into position in the frame, with the free end of the string hanging inside the truck. Pull the string while pushing inward on the glass, to properly position the inner lip of the weatherstripping.

11. Go around the inner and outer sides of the weatherstripping with a thin tool to make sure that the weatherstripping is flat against the frame.

12. Using a thin coat of rubber sealer, seal the outer edge of the weatherstripping against the frame.

13. Snap the molding into place.

1986 Windshield

NOTE: *A special kit, Mazda #49 0305 870A, is available for replacing glass. The references to adhesives and bonding agents contained in this procedure are taking for granted that this kit is being used. Aftermarket kits are also available which contain all the necessary equipment.*

1. Remove the wiper arms.

2. Remove the rear view mirror and front pillar trim molding.

3. Cover the sheet metal around the windshield with masking tape to protect it from scratches.

4. Remove the windshield trim molding. It's best to use a tool made for that purpose, although it can be pried off. If a special tool is not used, it's very easy to damage the molding, so be careful!

5. Drill a small hole through the rubber weatherstripping at its base. Pass a length of piano wire through the hole. Wrap each end of the wire around a wood dowel. Grip one dowel

Pulling the string to position the weatherstripping inner lip

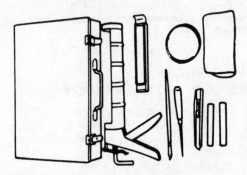

Typical installation kit for 1986 trucks

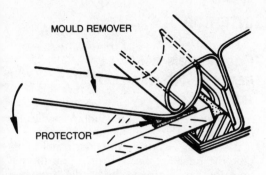

Typical moldong removal tool

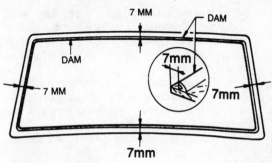

Installing the dam

Using the piano wire to cut the sealer

Applying the primer

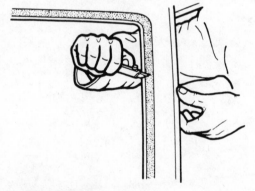

Trimming the sealer

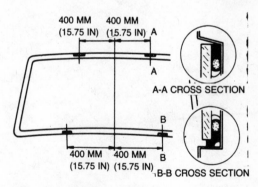

Installing the spacers

in each hand, or have your assistant take one dowel, and, using a sawing motion, pass the wire all the way around the perimeter of the weatherstripping to cut through the sealer.

6. Remove the glass.

7. Using a sharp knife, cut away the old sealer so that a 1–2mm thickness of old sealer remains around the circumference of the frame. If the old sealer comes completely off in any spot, rebuild that spot to the 1–2mm thickness with new sealer.

8. Secure a new windshield trim dam to the glass with a glass cement. The new dam should be positioned so that its outer edge is 7mm from the edge of the glass, with the lip facing outward.

9. Apply a thin coat of primer to the bond-

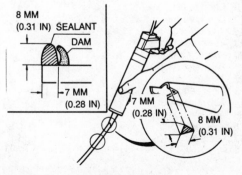

Proper use of the sealant dispenser

ing areas of the frame and glass. Allow the primer to dry for 30 minutes. Do not allow any dirt or dust to contact the primer while it's drying. If primer gets on your hands, wash it off immediately.

10. Cement the spacers to the frame as shown in the accompanying illustration.

NOTE: *The upper and lower spacers are different. Don't get them mixed up.*

11. Install the molding clips. If any are defective, replace them.

12. Cut the nozzle of the sealer tube as illustrated, so that it will run along the edge of the glass.

13. Apply sealer around the whole circumference so that it will fill the gap between the dam and the edge of the glass, with a bead of sealer about 8mm high. Keep the bead smooth and even, shaping it with the spatula where necessary.

14. Open the door windows. Position the glass in the frame, pushing inward lightly to compress the sealer.

15. Trim away excess sealer and fill any gaps which may have appeared. Give the sealer at least 5 hours to dry at 68°F; 24 hours at 41°F.

16. Leak test the glass.

INTERIOR

Door Panels
REMOVAL AND INSTALLATION
1972-84

1. Invert the door and window handles for easy access to the retaining pins.

2. Push in slightly on the door panel to expose the retaining pin, and drive out the pin from the window regulator handle, from the bottom side, using a small punch.

3. Drive the tapered pin from the door handle in the same manner.

4. Remove the plastic molding from the armrest, revealing the arm rest attaching screws.

5. Remove the arm rest.

6. Carefully slip a thin prying instrument behind the door panel and slide it along until you hit one of the eight retaining clips. Pry as close as possible to the clip to snap the clip from the door. Be very careful to avoid tearing the clip from the panel.

7. Once all eight clips have been pried loose, lift the door from the bottom channel.

8. Installation is the reverse of removal.

1. Striker seat
2. Door lock striker
3. Door lock rack
4. Door lock
5. Seat No. 1
6. Outer handle
7. Seat No. 2
8. Door hinge
9. Bush
10. Hinge pin
11. Spacer
12. Door checker set plate
13. Check sub spring
14. Check spring
15. Checker washer
16. Checker pin
17. Checker roller
18. Window regulator
19. Escutcheon crown
20. Handle escutcheon
21. Regulator handle
22. Tapered pin
23. Inner handle
24. Anti-burst block
25. Anti-burst block shim
26. Arm rest
27. Garnish

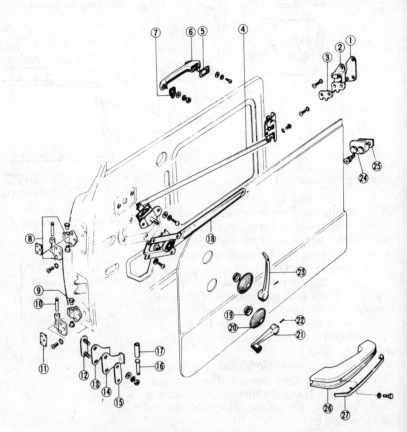

Exploded view of the door on 1972–76 trucks

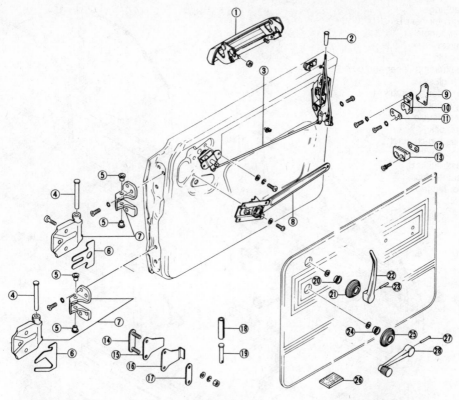

1. Outer handle
2. Door lock knob
3. Door lock
4. Hinge pin
5. Bush
6. Hinge spacer
7. Door hinge
8. Window regulator
9. Striker seat
10. Door lock striker
11. Door lock
12. Anti-burst block shim
13. Anti-burst block
14. Door checker set plate
15. Check sub spring
16. Check spring
17. Checker washer
18. Checker roller
19. Checker pin
20. Escutcheon crown
21. Handle escutcheon
22. Inner handle
23. Tapered pin
24. Escutcheon crown
25. Handle escutcheon
26. Cushion
27. Tapered pin
28. Regulator handle

Exploded view of the door on 1977–84 trucks

When snapping the clips into place, make sure that they are squarely over the holes to avoid bending them.

1986

1. Remove the attaching screw and door handle.
2. Remove the armrest.
3. Push in on the door panel, slightly, at the window handle and pry off the snapring retaining the handle to the regulator stem. Remove the handle.
4. Carefully slip a thin prying instrument behind the door panel and slide it along until you hit one of the retaining clips. Pry as close as possible to the clip to snap the clip from the door. Be very careful to avoid tearing the clip from the panel.
5. Pry out each clip, in turn, and lift off the door panel.

6. Installation is the reverse of removal. When snapping the clips into place, make sure that they are squarely over the holes to avoid bending them.

Door Glass and Regulator
REMOVAL AND INSTALLATION
1972–84

1. Remove the trim panel from the door.
2. Remove the window frame assembly from the door by removing the seven attaching screws.
3. Lower the door glass.
4. Disengage the regulator roller and arm from the glass.
5. Tilt the glass slightly and slide it up and out of the door.

1. Snap ring
2. Regulator handle
3. Inner handle
4. Armrest
5. Door trim
6. Weatherstrip (inner and outer)
7. Door glass
8. Regulator assembly
9. Key cylinder
10. Outer handle
11. Door lock
12. Glass run-channel
13. Glass guide A
14. Glass guide B
15. Weatherstrip
16. Door hinge
17. Door

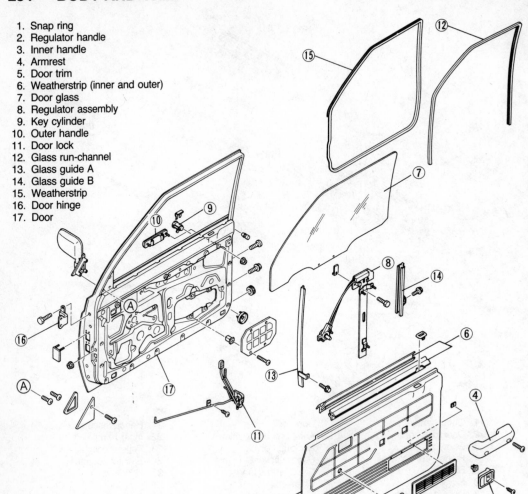

Exploded view of the door on 1986 trucks

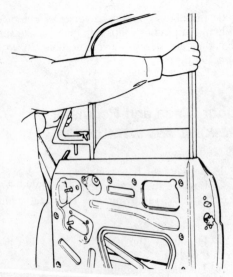

Removing the window frame

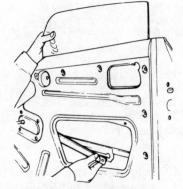

Disengaging the regulator roller and arm

6. Remove and discard the tape from the door glass channel.

7. Unbolt and remove the regulator.

8. Installation is the reverse of removal. Use

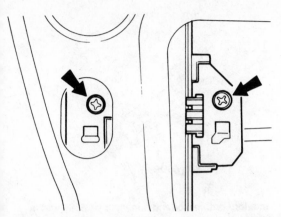

Door glass mounting screw, left; door glass guide bolt, right

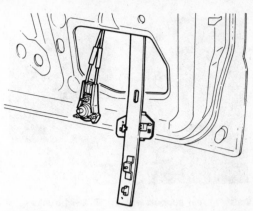

Removing regulator assembly through the access hole

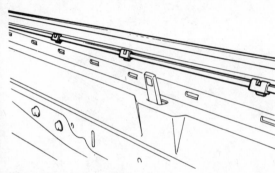

Weatherstripping clips

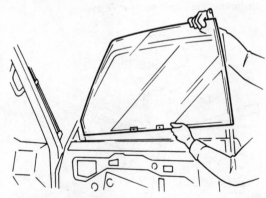

Removing door glass

new tape in the channel. Use waterproof sealer on the window frame screws.

1986

1. Remove the door panel.
2. Remove the weatherscreening carefully, so that it can be reused.
3. Remove the door glass mounting screws.
4. Remove the inner and outer weatherstripping around the frame.
5. Remove the glass guide mounting bolt.
6. Pull the glass up and out of the door.

7. Remove the mounting bolts and pull the regulator assembly from the access hole.
8. Installation is the reverse of removal. Adjust the door glass so that it closes properly.

Door Locks

REMOVAL AND INSTALLATION

NOTE: *A key code is stamped on the lock cylinder to aid in replacing lost keys.*
1. Remove the door trim panel.
2. Pull the weathersheet, gently, away from the door lock access holes.
3. Using a screwdriver, push the lock cylinder retaining clip upward, noting the position of the lock cylinder.
4. Remove the lock cylinder from the door.
5. Install the lock cylinder in reverse of removal. It's a good idea to open the window before checking the lock operation, just in case it doesn't work properly.

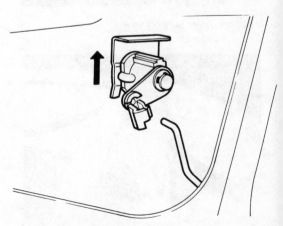

Removing door lock clip

Installing rear support wire on 1972–84 trucks

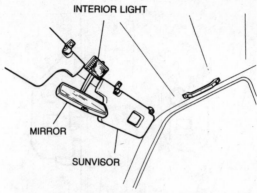

Interior light, mirror and sun visor on 1986 trucks

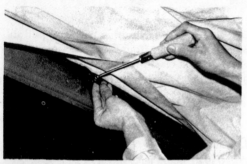

Installing support wire bracket

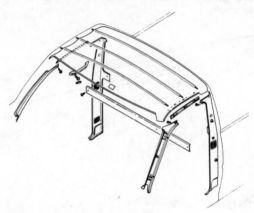

Removing the upper seam welt

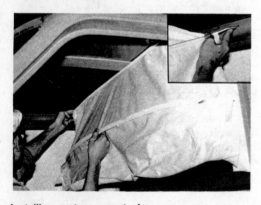

Installing center support wire

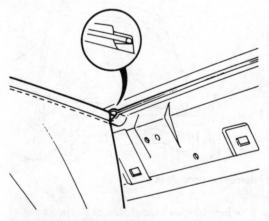

Inserting front support wire

Gluing headliner

Headliner

REMOVAL AND INSTALLATION

1972–84

1. Remove the windshield and rear window glass.

2. Remove the rear view mirror and sun visors.

3. Pull the headliner loose from the ce-

FRONT   REAR

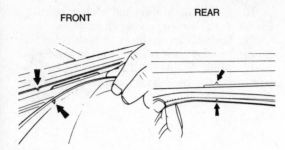

Front and rear centering marks

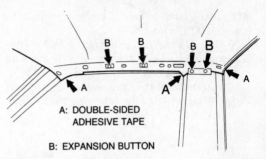

A: DOUBLE-SIDED
ADHESIVE TAPE

B: EXPANSION BUTTON

Applying double sided tape and expansion buttons

WINDSHIELD GLASS

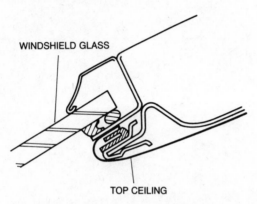

TOP CEILING

Inserting the front edge of the headliner

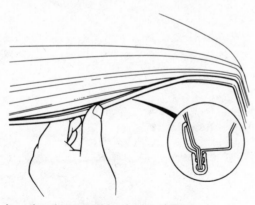

Inserting the rear edge of the headliner

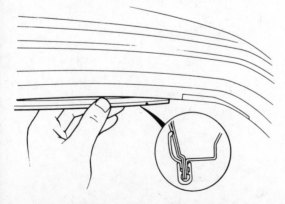

Inserting the sides of the headliner

mented areas of the windshield frame and door openings.

4. Disengage the front and center support wires from the holes in the roof rails.

5. Remove the dome light.

6. Remove the rear support wire brackets from the backing plate.

7. Pull the rear support wire upward and remove the headliner.

NOTE: *When installing new headlining material, access holes will have to be cut and the material will have to be trimmed after installation.*

8. Start at the rear and insert both ends of the rear support wire into the backing plate. Tighten the rear support wire bracket screws.

9. Unfold the headliner against the roof to make sure it's straight, and, in the case of new material, cut a hole for the dome light.

10. Install the two remaining support wires, making sure that the material is stretched evenly.

11. Apply cement to the windshield and door pillar areas; wait until the cement becomes tacky, then stretch the material into place.

12. When the cement is dry, trim the material as necessary and install the dome light, windshield and rear window.

13. Install the rear view mirror and sun visors.

1986

1. Remove the rear window.

2. Remove the rear view mirror and sun visors.

3. Remove the dome light.

4. Remove the seat belt anchors.

5. Remove the upper seam welt from the headliner.

6. Remove the front pillar trims, the top side moldings and the rear pillar trims.

7. Unhook the support wires and remove the headliner.

8. Unless the ambient temperature is above

90°F, you'll have to heat the new headliner to between 90°F a nd 120°F.

NOTE: *On the headliner you'll find a centering mark which corresponds to a mark on the roof of the cab.*

9. Beginning at the front, install the support wires. Make sure that the centering marks align.

10. Install the leading and trailing edges as shown in the accompanying illustrations.

11. Stretch the headliner to both sides and insert it as shown, leaving no sags or looseness.

12. Apply double sided adhesive tape to the outside of the body flange and push in the expansion buttons.

Troubleshooting
10

This section is designed to aid in the quick, accurate diagnosis of automotive problems. While automotive repairs can be made by many people, accurate troubleshooting is a rare skill for the amateur and professional alike.

In its simplest state, troubleshooting is an exercise in logic. It is essential to realize that an automobile is really composed of a series of systems. Some of these systems are interrelated; others are not. Automobiles operate within a framework of logical rules and physical laws, and the key to troubleshooting is a good understanding of all the automotive systems.

This section breaks the car or truck down into its component systems, allowing the problem to be isolated. The charts and diagnostic road maps list the most common problems and the most probable causes of trouble. Obviously it would be impossible to list every possible problem that could happen along with every possible cause, but it will locate MOST problems and eliminate a lot of unnecessary guesswork. The systematic format will locate problems within a given system, but, because many automotive systems are interrelated, the solution to your particular problem may be found in a number of systems on the car or truck.

USING THE TROUBLESHOOTING CHARTS

This book contains all of the specific information that the average do-it-yourself mechanic needs to repair and maintain his or her car or truck. The troubleshooting charts are designed to be used in conjunction with the specific procedures and information in the text. For instance, troubleshooting a point-type ignition system is fairly standard for all models, but you may be directed to the text to find procedures for troubleshooting an individual type of electronic ignition. You will also have to refer to the specification charts throughout the book for specifications applicable to your car or truck.

TOOLS AND EQUIPMENT

The tools illustrated in Chapter 1 (plus two more diagnostic pieces) will be adequate to troubleshoot most problems. The two other tools needed are a voltmeter and an ohmmeter. These can be purchased separately or in combination, known as a VOM meter.

In the event that other tools are required, they will be noted in the procedures.

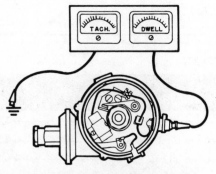

Tach-dwell hooked-up to distributor

Troubleshooting Engine Problems

See Chapters 2, 3, 4 for more information and service procedures.

Index to Systems

System	To Test	Group
Battery	Engine need not be running	1
Starting system	Engine need not be running	2
Primary electrical system	Engine need not be running	3
Secondary electrical system	Engine need not be running	4
Fuel system	Engine need not be running	5
Engine compression	Engine need not be running	6
Engine vacuum	Engine must be running	7
Secondary electrical system	Engine must be running	8
Valve train	Engine must be running	9
Exhaust system	Engine must be running	10
Cooling system	Engine must be running	11
Engine lubrication	Engine must be running	12

Index to Problems

Problem: Symptom	Begin at Specific Diagnosis, Number ___
Engine Won't Start:	
Starter doesn't turn	1.1, 2.1
Starter turns, engine doesn't	2.1
Starter turns engine very slowly	1.1, 2.4
Starter turns engine normally	3.1, 4.1
Starter turns engine very quickly	6.1
Engine fires intermittently	4.1
Engine fires consistently	5.1, 6.1
Engine Runs Poorly:	
Hard starting	3.1, 4.1, 5.1, 8.1
Rough idle	4.1, 5.1, 8.1
Stalling	3.1, 4.1, 5.1, 8.1
Engine dies at high speeds	4.1, 5.1
Hesitation (on acceleration from standing stop)	5.1, 8.1
Poor pickup	4.1, 5.1, 8.1
Lack of power	3.1, 4.1, 5.1, 8.1
Backfire through the carburetor	4.1, 8.1, 9.1
Backfire through the exhaust	4.1, 8.1, 9.1
Blue exhaust gases	6.1, 7.1
Black exhaust gases	5.1
Running on (after the ignition is shut off)	3.1, 8.1
Susceptible to moisture	4.1
Engine misfires under load	4.1, 7.1, 8.4, 9.1
Engine misfires at speed	4.1, 8.4
Engine misfires at idle	3.1, 4.1, 5.1, 7.1, 8.4

Sample Section

Test and Procedure	Results and Indications	Proceed to
4.1—Check for spark: Hold each spark plug wire approximately ¼" from ground with gloves or a heavy, dry rag. Crank the engine and observe the spark.	→ If no spark is evident:	→4.2
	→ If spark is good in some cases:	→4.3
	→ If spark is good in all cases:	→4.6

Specific Diagnosis

This section is arranged so that following each test, instructions are given to proceed to another, until a problem is diagnosed.

Section 1—Battery

Test and Procedure	Results and Indications	Proceed to
1.1—Inspect the battery visually for case condition (corrosion, cracks) and water level.	If case is cracked, replace battery:	**1.4**
	If the case is intact, remove corrosion with a solution of baking soda and water (**CAUTION**: *do not get the solution into the battery*), and fill with water:	**1.2**

DIRT ON TOP OF BATTERY   PLUGGED VENT
CORROSION
LOOSE CABLE OR POSTS
CRACKS
LOW WATER LEVEL

Inspect the battery case

Test and Procedure	Results and Indications	Proceed to
1.2—Check the battery cable connections: Insert a screwdriver between the battery post and the cable clamp. Turn the headlights on high beam, and observe them as the screwdriver is gently twisted to ensure good metal to metal contact.	If the lights brighten, remove and clean the clamp and post; coat the post with petroleum jelly, install and tighten the clamp:	**1.4**
	If no improvement is noted:	**1.3**

TESTING BATTERY CABLE CONNECTIONS USING A SCREWDRIVER

Test and Procedure	Results and Indications	Proceed to
1.3—Test the state of charge of the battery using an individual cell tester or hydrometer.	If indicated, charge the battery. **NOTE:** *If no obvious reason exists for the low state of charge (i.e., battery age, prolonged storage), proceed to:*	**1.4**

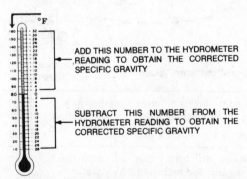

ADD THIS NUMBER TO THE HYDROMETER READING TO OBTAIN THE CORRECTED SPECIFIC GRAVITY

SUBTRACT THIS NUMBER FROM THE HYDROMETER READING TO OBTAIN THE CORRECTED SPECIFIC GRAVITY

Specific Gravity (@ 80° F.)

Minimum	Battery Charge
1.260	100% Charged
1.230	75% Charged
1.200	50% Charged
1.170	25% Charged
1.140	Very Little Power Left
1.110	Completely Discharged

The effects of temperature on battery specific gravity (left) and amount of battery charge in relation to specific gravity (right)

Test and Procedure	Results and Indications	Proceed to
1.4—Visually inspect battery cables for cracking, bad connection to ground, or bad connection to starter.	If necessary, tighten connections or replace the cables:	**2.1**

Section 2—Starting System
See Chapter 3 for service procedures

Test and Procedure	Results and Indications	Proceed to
Note: Tests in Group 2 are performed with coil high tension lead disconnected to prevent accidental starting.		
2.1—Test the starter motor and solenoid: Connect a jumper from the battery post of the solenoid (or relay) to the starter post of the solenoid (or relay).	If starter turns the engine normally:	**2.2**
	If the starter buzzes, or turns the engine very slowly:	**2.4**
	If no response, replace the solenoid (or relay).	**3.1**
	If the starter turns, but the engine doesn't, ensure that the flywheel ring gear is intact. If the gear is undamaged, replace the starter drive.	**3.1**
2.2—Determine whether ignition override switches are functioning properly (clutch start switch, neutral safety switch), by connecting a jumper across the switch(es), and turning the ignition switch to "start".	If starter operates, adjust or replace switch:	**3.1**
	If the starter doesn't operate:	**2.3**
2.3—Check the ignition switch "start" position: Connect a 12V test lamp or voltmeter between the starter post of the solenoid (or relay) and ground. Turn the ignition switch to the "start" position, and jiggle the key.	If the lamp doesn't light or the meter needle doesn't move when the switch is turned, check the ignition switch for loose connections, cracked insulation, or broken wires. Repair or replace as necessary:	**3.1**
	If the lamp flickers or needle moves when the key is jiggled, replace the ignition switch.	**3.3**

Checking the ignition switch "start" position

STARTER RELAY (IF EQUIPPED)

2.4—Remove and bench test the starter, according to specifications in the engine electrical section.	If the starter does not meet specifications, repair or replace as needed:	**3.1**
	If the starter is operating properly:	**2.5**
2.5—Determine whether the engine can turn freely: Remove the spark plugs, and check for water in the cylinders. Check for water on the dipstick, or oil in the radiator. Attempt to turn the engine using an 18″ flex drive and socket on the crankshaft pulley nut or bolt.	If the engine will turn freely only with the spark plugs out, and hydrostatic lock (water in the cylinders) is ruled out, check valve timing:	**9.2**
	If engine will not turn freely, and it is known that the clutch and transmission are free, the engine must be disassembled for further evaluation:	**Chapter 3**

Section 3—Primary Electrical System

Test and Procedure	Results and Indications	Proceed to
3.1—Check the ignition switch "on" position: Connect a jumper wire between the distributor side of the coil and ground, and a 12V test lamp between the switch side of the coil and ground. Remove the high tension lead from the coil. Turn the ignition switch on and jiggle the key.	If the lamp lights:	3.2
	If the lamp flickers when the key is jiggled, replace the ignition switch:	3.3
	If the lamp doesn't light, check for loose or open connections. If none are found, remove the ignition switch and check for continuity. If the switch is faulty, replace it:	3.3

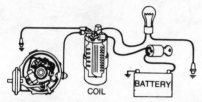

Checking the ignition switch "on" position

3.2—Check the ballast resistor or resistance wire for an open circuit, using an ohmmeter. See Chapter 3 for specific tests.	Replace the resistor or resistance wire if the resistance is zero. **NOTE:** *Some ignition systems have no ballast resistor.*	3.3

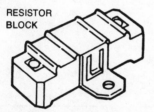

Two types of resistors

3.3—On point-type ignition systems, visually inspect the breaker points for burning, pitting or excessive wear. Gray coloring of the point contact surfaces is normal. Rotate the crankshaft until the contact heel rests on a high point of the distributor cam and adjust the point gap to specifications. On electronic ignition models, remove the distributor cap and visually inspect the armature. Ensure that the armature pin is in place, and that the armature is on tight and rotates when the engine is cranked. Make sure there are no cracks, chips or rounded edges on the armature.	If the breaker points are intact, clean the contact surfaces with fine emery cloth, and adjust the point gap to specifications. If the points are worn, replace them. On electronic systems, replace any parts which appear defective. If condition persists:	3.4

Test and Procedure	Results and Indications	Proceed to
3.4—On point-type ignition systems, connect a dwell-meter between the distributor primary lead and ground. Crank the engine and observe the point dwell angle. On electronic ignition systems, conduct a stator (magnetic pickup assembly) test. See Chapter 3.	On point-type systems, adjust the dwell angle if necessary. **NOTE:** *Increasing the point gap decreases the dwell angle and vice-versa.*	**3.6**
	If the dwell meter shows little or no reading;	**3.5**
	On electronic ignition systems, if the stator is bad, replace the stator. If the stator is good, proceed to the other tests in Chapter 3.	

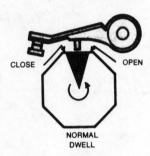
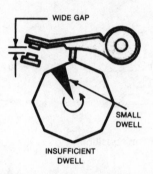
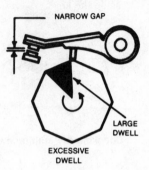

Dwell is a function of point gap

3.5—On the point-type ignition systems, check the condenser for short: connect an ohmeter across the condenser body and the pigtail lead.	If any reading other than infinite is noted, replace the condenser	**3.6**

Checking the condenser for short

3.6—Test the coil primary resistance: On point-type ignition systems, connect an ohmmeter across the coil primary terminals, and read the resistance on the low scale. Note whether an external ballast resistor or resistance wire is used. On electronic ignition systems, test the coil primary resistance as in Chapter 3.	Point-type ignition coils utilizing ballast resistors or resistance wires should have approximately 1.0 ohms resistance. Coils with internal resistors should have approximately 4.0 ohms resistance. If values far from the above are noted, replace the coil.	**4.1**

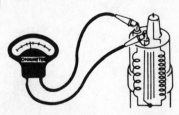

Check the coil primary resistance

Section 4—Secondary Electrical System

See Chapters 2–3 for service procedures

Test and Procedure	Results and Indications	Proceed to
4.1—Check for spark: Hold each spark plug wire approximately ¼″ from ground with gloves or a heavy, dry rag. Crank the engine, and observe the spark.	If no spark is evident:	**4.2**
	If spark is good in some cylinders:	**4.3**
	If spark is good in all cylinders:	**4.6**

Check for spark at the plugs

Test and Procedure	Results and Indications	Proceed to
4.2—Check for spark at the coil high tension lead: Remove the coil high tension lead from the distributor and position it approximately ¼″ from ground. Crank the engine and observe spark. **CAUTION: *This test should not be performed on engines equipped with electronic ignition.***	If the spark is good and consistent:	**4.3**
	If the spark is good but intermittent, test the primary electrical system starting at 3.3:	**3.3**
	If the spark is weak or non-existent, replace the coil high tension lead, clean and tighten all connections and retest. If no improvement is noted:	**4.4**
4.3—Visually inspect the distributor cap and rotor for burned or corroded contacts, cracks, carbon tracks, or moisture. Also check the fit of the rotor on the distributor shaft (where applicable).	If moisture is present, dry thoroughly, and retest per 4.1:	**4.1**
	If burned or excessively corroded contacts, cracks, or carbon tracks are noted, replace the defective part(s) and retest per 4.1:	**4.1**
	If the rotor and cap appear intact, or are only slightly corroded, clean the contacts thoroughly (including the cap towers and spark plug wire ends) and retest per 4.1:	
	If the spark is good in all cases:	**4.6**
	If the spark is poor in all cases:	**4.5**

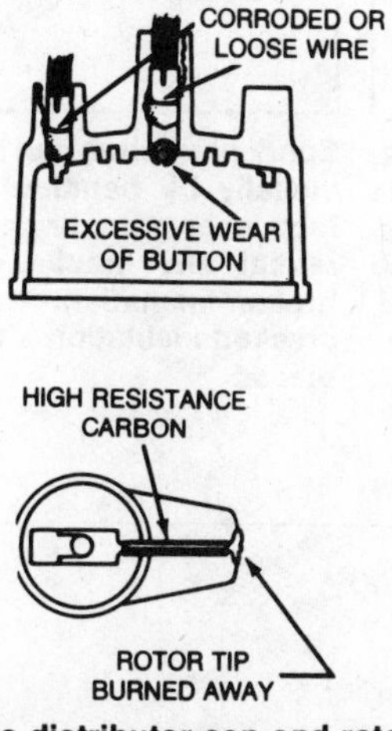

CORRODED OR LOOSE WIRE

EXCESSIVE WEAR OF BUTTON

HIGH RESISTANCE CARBON

ROTOR TIP BURNED AWAY

Inspect the distributor cap and rotor

Test and Procedure	Results and Indications	Proceed to
4.4—Check the coil secondary resistance: On point-type systems connect an ohmmeter across the distributor side of the coil and the coil tower. Read the resistance on the high scale of the ohmmeter. On electronic ignition systems, see Chapter 3 for specific tests.	The resistance of a satisfactory coil should be between 4,000 and 10,000 ohms. If resistance is considerably higher (i.e., 40,000 ohms) replace the coil and retest per 4.1. **NOTE:** *This does not apply to high performance coils.*	

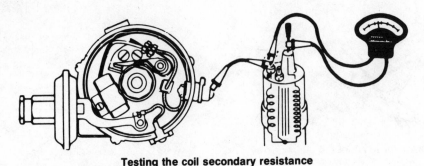

Testing the coil secondary resistance

| 4.5—Visually inspect the spark plug wires for cracking or brittleness. Ensure that no two wires are positioned so as to cause induction firing (adjacent and parallel). Remove each wire, one by one, and check resistance with an ohmmeter. | Replace any cracked or brittle wires. If any of the wires are defective, replace the entire set. Replace any wires with excessive resistance (over $8000\,\Omega$ per foot for suppression wire), and separate any wires that might cause induction firing. | 4.6 |

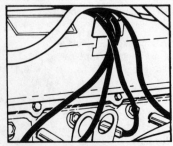

Misfiring can be the result of spark plug leads to adjacent, consecutively firing cylinders running parallel and too close together

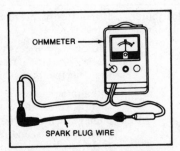

On point-type ignition systems, check the spark plug wires as shown. On electronic ignitions, do not remove the wire from the distributor cap terminal; instead, test through the cap

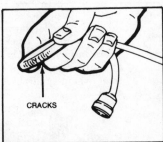

Spark plug wires can be checked visually by bending them in a loop over your finger. This will reveal any cracks, burned or broken insulation. Any wire with cracked insulation should be replaced

| 4.6—Remove the spark plugs, noting the cylinders from which they were removed, and evaluate according to the color photos in the middle of this book. | See following. | **See following.** |

Test and Procedure	Results and Indications	Proceed to
4.7—Examine the location of all the plugs.	The following diagrams illustrate some of the conditions that the location of plugs will reveal.	4.8

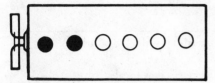

Two adjacent plugs are fouled in a 6-cylinder engine, 4-cylinder engine or either bank of a V-8. This is probably due to a blown head gasket between the two cylinders

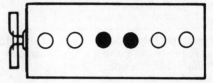

The two center plugs in a 6-cylinder engine are fouled. Raw fuel may be "boiled" out of the carburetor into the intake manifold after the engine is shut-off. Stop-start driving can also foul the center plugs, due to overly rich mixture. Proper float level, a new float needle and seat or use of an insulating spacer may help this problem

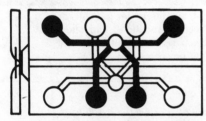

An unbalanced carburetor is indicated. Following the fuel flow on this particular design shows that the cylinders fed by the right-hand barrel are fouled from overly rich mixture, while the cylinders fed by the left-hand barrel are normal

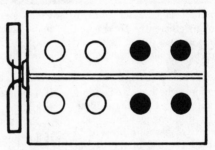

If the four rear plugs are overheated, a cooling system problem is suggested. A thorough cleaning of the cooling system may restore coolant circulation and cure the problem

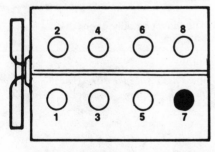

Finding one plug overheated may indicate an intake manifold leak near the affected cylinder. If the overheated plug is the second of two adjacent, consecutively firing plugs, it could be the result of ignition cross-firing. Separating the leads to these two plugs will eliminate cross-fire

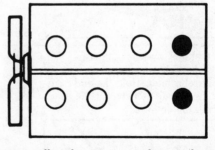

Occasionally, the two rear plugs in large, lightly used V-8's will become oil fouled. High oil consumption and smoky exhaust may also be noticed. It is probably due to plugged oil drain holes in the rear of the cylinder head, causing oil to be sucked in around the valve stems. This usually occurs in the rear cylinders first, because the engine slants that way

Test and Procedure	Results and Indications	Proceed to
4.8—Determine the static ignition timing. Using the crankshaft pulley timing marks as a guide, locate top dead center on the compression stroke of the number one cylinder.	The rotor should be pointing toward the No. 1 tower in the distributor cap, and, on electronic ignitions, the armature spoke for that cylinder should be lined up with the stator.	**4.8**
4.9—Check coil polarity: Connect a voltmeter negative lead to the coil high tension lead, and the positive lead to ground (**NOTE:** *Reverse the hook-up for positive ground systems*). Crank the engine momentarily. **Checking coil polarity**	If the voltmeter reads up-scale, the polarity is correct: If the voltmeter reads down-scale, reverse the coil polarity (switch the primary leads):	**5.1** **5.1**

Section 5—Fuel System
See Chapter 4 for service procedures

Test and Procedure	Results and Indications	Proceed to
5.1—Determine that the air filter is functioning efficiently: Hold paper elements up to a strong light, and attempt to see light through the filter.	Clean permanent air filters in solvent (or manufacturer's recommendation), and allow to dry. Replace paper elements through which light cannot be seen:	**5.2**
5.2—Determine whether a flooding condition exists: Flooding is identified by a strong gasoline odor, and excessive gasoline present in the throttle bore(s) of the carburetor. **If the engine floods repeatedly, check the choke butterfly flap**	If flooding is not evident: If flooding is evident, permit the gasoline to dry for a few moments and restart. If flooding doesn't recur: If flooding is persistent:	**5.3** **5.7** **5.5**
5.3—Check that fuel is reaching the carburetor: Detach the fuel line at the carburetor inlet. Hold the end of the line in a cup (not styrofoam), and crank the engine. **Check the fuel pump by disconnecting the output line (fuel pump-to-carburetor) at the carburetor and operating the starter briefly**	If fuel flows smoothly: If fuel doesn't flow (**NOTE:** *Make sure that there is fuel in the tank*), or flows erratically:	**5.7** **5.4**

Test and Procedure	Results and Indications	Proceed to
5.4—Test the fuel pump: Disconnect all fuel lines from the fuel pump. Hold a finger over the input fitting, crank the engine (with electric pump, turn the ignition or pump on); and feel for suction.	If suction is evident, blow out the fuel line to the tank with low pressure compressed air until bubbling is heard from the fuel filler neck. Also blow out the carburetor fuel line (both ends disconnected):	5.7
	If no suction is evident, replace or repair the fuel pump: NOTE: *Repeated oil fouling of the spark plugs, or a no-start condition, could be the result of a ruptured vacuum booster pump diaphragm, through which oil or gasoline is being drawn into the intake manifold (where applicable).*	5.7
5.5—Occasionally, small specks of dirt will clog the small jets and orifices in the carburetor. With the engine cold, hold a flat piece of wood or similar material over the carburetor, where possible, and crank the engine.	If the engine starts, but runs roughly the engine is probably not run enough. If the engine won't start:	5.9
5.6—Check the needle and seat: Tap the carburetor in the area of the needle and seat.	If flooding stops, a gasoline additive (e.g., Gumout) will often cure the problem:	5.7
	If flooding continues, check the fuel pump for excessive pressure at the carburetor (according to specifications). If the pressure is normal, the needle and seat must be removed and checked, and/or the float level adjusted:	5.7
5.7—Test the accelerator pump by looking into the throttle bores while operating the throttle.	If the accelerator pump appears to be operating normally:	5.8
	If the accelerator pump is not operating, the pump must be reconditioned. Where possible, service the pump with the carburetor(s) installed on the engine. If necessary, remove the carburetor. Prior to removal:	5.8

Check for gas at the carburetor by looking down the carburetor throat while someone moves the accelerator

Test and Procedure	Results and Indications	Proceed to
5.8—Determine whether the carburetor main fuel system is functioning: Spray a commercial starting fluid into the carburetor while attempting to start the engine.	If the engine starts, runs for a few seconds, and dies:	5.9
	If the engine doesn't start:	6.1

Test and Procedure	Results and Indications	Proceed to
5.9—Uncommon fuel system malfunctions: See below:	If the problem is solved: If the problem remains, remove and recondition the carburetor.	**6.1**

Condition	Indication	Test	Prevailing Weather Conditions	Remedy
Vapor lock	Engine will not restart shortly after running.	Cool the components of the fuel system until the engine starts. Vapor lock can be cured faster by draping a wet cloth over a mechanical fuel pump.	Hot to very hot	Ensure that the exhaust manifold heat control valve is operating. Check with the vehicle manufacturer for the recommended solution to vapor lock on the model in question.
Carburetor icing	Engine will not idle, stalls at low speeds.	Visually inspect the throttle plate area of the throttle bores for frost.	High humidity, 32–40° F.	Ensure that the exhaust manifold heat control valve is operating, and that the intake manifold heat riser is not blocked.
Water in the fuel	Engine sputters and stalls; may not start.	Pump a small amount of fuel into a glass jar. Allow to stand, and inspect for droplets or a layer of water.	High humidity, extreme temperature changes.	For droplets, use one or two cans of commercial gas line anti-freeze. For a layer of water, the tank must be drained, and the fuel lines blown out with compressed air.

Section 6—Engine Compression
See Chapter 3 for service procedures

6.1—Test engine compression: Remove all spark plugs. Block the throttle wide open. Insert a compression gauge into a spark plug port, crank the engine to obtain the maximum reading, and record.	If compression is within limits on all cylinders:	**7.1**
	If gauge reading is extremely low on all cylinders:	**6.2**
	If gauge reading is low on one or two cylinders: (If gauge readings are identical and low on two or more adjacent cylinders, the head gasket must be replaced.)	**6.2**

Checking compression

6.2—Test engine compression (wet): Squirt approximately 30 cc. of engine oil into each cylinder, and retest per 6.1.	If the readings improve, worn or cracked rings or broken pistons are indicated:	**See Chapter 3**
	If the readings do not improve, burned or excessively carboned valves or a jumped timing chain are indicated: **NOTE: A jumped timing chain is often indicated by difficult cranking.**	**7.1**

CHILTON'S
AUTO BODY
REPAIR TIPS

Tools and Materials • Step-by-Step Illustrated Procedures
How To Repair Dents, Scratches and Rust Holes
Spray Painting and Refinishing Tips

EASY
STEP-BY-STEP
TIPS FROM PROS

With a little practice, basic body repair procedures can be mastered by any do-it-yourself mechanic. The step-by-step repairs shown here can be applied to almost any type of auto body repair.

TOOLS & MATERIALS

You may already have basic tools, such as hammers and electric drills. Other tools unique to body repair — body hammers, grinding attachments, sanding blocks, dent puller, half-round plastic file and plastic spreaders — are relatively inexpensive and can be obtained wherever auto parts or auto body repair parts are sold. Portable air compressors and paint spray guns can be purchased or rented.

Auto Body Repair Kits

The best and most often used products are available to the do-it-yourselfer in kit form, from major manufacturers of auto body repair products. The same manufacturers also merchandise the individual products for use by pros.

Kits are available to make a wide variety of repairs, including holes, dents and scratches and fiberglass, and offer the advantage of buying the materials you'll need for the job. There is little waste or chance of materials going bad from not being used. Many kits may also contain basic body-working tools such as body files, sanding blocks and spreaders. Check the contents of the kit before buying your tools.

BODY REPAIR TIPS

Safety

Many of the products associated with auto body repair and refinishing contain toxic chemicals. Read all labels before opening containers and store them in a safe place and manner.

• Wear eye protection (safety goggles) when using power tools or when performing any operation that involves

the removal of any type of material.

• Wear lung protection (disposable mask or respirator) when grinding, sanding or painting.

Sanding

1 Sand off paint before using a dent puller. When using a non-adhesive sanding disc, cover the back of the disc with an overlapping layer or two of masking tape and trim the edges. The disc will last considerably longer.

2 Use the circular motion of the sanding disc to grind *into* the edge of the repair. Grinding or sanding away from the jagged edge will only tear the sandpaper.

3 Use the palm of your hand flat on the panel to detect high and low spots. Do not use your fingertips. Slide your hand slowly back and forth.

WORKING WITH BODY FILLER

Mixing The Filler

Cleanliness and proper mixing and application are extremely important. Use a clean piece of plastic or glass or a disposable artist's palette to mix body filler.

1 Allow plenty of time and follow directions. No useful purpose will be served by adding more hardener to make it cure (set-up) faster. Less hardener means more curing time, but the mixture dries harder; more hardener means less curing time but a softer mixture.

2 Both the hardener and the filler should be thoroughly kneaded or stirred before mixing. Hardener should be a solid paste and dispense like thin toothpaste. Body filler should be smooth, and free of lumps or thick spots.

Getting the proper amount of hardener in the filler is the trickiest part of preparing the filler. Use the same amount of hardener in cold or warm weather. For contour filler (thick coats), a bead of hardener twice the diameter of the filler is about right. There's about a 15% margin on either side, but, if in doubt use less hardener.

3 Mix the body filler and hardener by wiping across the mixing surface, picking the mixture up and wiping it again. Colder weather requires longer mixing times. Do not mix in a circular motion; this will trap air bubbles which will become holes in the cured filler.

Applying The Filler

1 For best results, filler should not be applied over ¼″ thick.

Apply the filler in several coats. Build it up to above the level of the repair surface so that it can be sanded or grated down.

The first coat of filler must be pressed on with a firm wiping motion.

Apply the filler in one direction only. Working the filler back and forth will either pull it off the metal or trap air bubbles.

REPAIRING DENTS

Before you start, take a few minutes to study the damaged area. Try to visualize the shape of the panel before it was damaged. If the damage is on the left fender, look at the right fender and use it as a guide. If there is access to the panel from behind, you can reshape it with a body hammer. If not, you'll have to use a dent puller. Go slowly and work the metal a little at a time. Get the panel as straight as possible before applying filler.

1 This dent is typical of one that can be pulled out or hammered out from behind. Remove the headlight cover, headlight assembly and turn signal housing.

2 Drill a series of holes 1/2 the size of the end of the dent puller along the stress line. Make some trial pulls and assess the results. If necessary, drill more holes and try again. Do not hurry.

3 If possible, use a body hammer and block to shape the metal back to its original contours. Get the metal back as close to its original shape as possible. Don't depend on body filler to fill dents.

4 Using an 80-grit grinding disc on an electric drill, grind the paint from the surrounding area down to bare metal. Use a new grinding pad to prevent heat buildup that will warp metal.

5 The area should look like this when you're finished grinding. Knock the drill holes in and tape over small openings to keep plastic filler out.

6 Mix the body filler (see Body Repair Tips). Spread the body filler evenly over the entire area (see Body Repair Tips). Be sure to cover the area completely.

7 Let the body filler dry until the surface can just be scratched with your fingernail. Knock the high spots from the body filler with a body file ("Cheesegrater"). Check frequently with the palm of your hand for high and low spots.

8 Check to be sure that trim pieces that will be installed later will fit exactly. Sand the area with 40-grit paper.

9 If you wind up with low spots, you may have to apply another layer of filler.

10 Knock the high spots off with 40-grit paper. When you are satisfied with the contours of the repair, apply a thin coat of filler to cover pin holes and scratches.

11 Block sand the area with 40-grit paper to a smooth finish. Pay particular attention to body lines and ridges that must be well-defined.

12 Sand the area with 400 paper and then finish with a scuff pad. The finished repair is ready for priming and painting (see Painting Tips).

Materials and photos courtesy of Ritt Jones Auto Body, Prospect Park, PA.

REPAIRING RUST HOLES

There are many ways to repair rust holes. The fiberglass cloth kit shown here is one of the most cost efficient for the owner because it provides a strong repair that resists cracking and moisture and is relatively easy to use. It can be used on large and small holes (with or without backing) and can be applied over contoured areas. Remember, however, that short of replacing an entire panel, no repair is a guarantee that the rust will not return.

1 Remove any trim that will be in the way. Clean away all loose debris. Cut away all the rusted metal. But be sure to leave enough metal to retain the contour or body shape.

2 Grind away all traces of rust with a 24-grit grinding disc. Be sure to grind back 3-4 inches from the edge of the hole down to bare metal and be sure all traces of paint, primer and rust are removed.

3 Block sand the area with 80 or 100 grit sandpaper to get a clear, shiny surface and feathered paint edge. Tap the edges of the hole inward with a ball peen hammer.

4 If you are going to use release film, cut a piece about 2-3″ larger than the area you have sanded. Place the film over the repair and mark the sanded area on the film. Avoid any unnecessary wrinkling of the film.

5 Cut 2 pieces of fiberglass matte to match the shape of the repair. One piece should be about 1″ smaller than the sanded area and the second piece should be 1″ smaller than the first. Mix enough filler and hardener to saturate the fiberglass material (see Body Repair Tips).

6 Lay the release sheet on a flat surface and spread an even layer of filler, large enough to cover the repair. Lay the smaller piece of fiberglass cloth in the center of the sheet and spread another layer of filler over the fiberglass cloth. Repeat the operation for the larger piece of cloth.

7 Place the repair material over the repair area, with the release film facing outward. Use a spreader and work from the center outward to smooth the material, following the body contours. Be sure to remove all air bubbles.

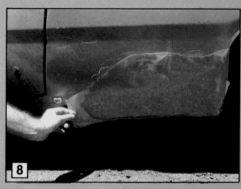

8 Wait until the repair has dried tack-free and peel off the release sheet. The ideal working temperature is 60°-90° F. Cooler or warmer temperatures or high humidity may require additional curing time. Wait longer, if in doubt.

9 Sand and feather-edge the entire area. The initial sanding can be done with a sanding disc on an electric drill if care is used. Finish the sanding with a block sander. Low spots can be filled with body filler; this may require several applications.

10 When the filler can just be scratched with a fingernail, knock the high spots down with a body file and smooth the entire area with 80-grit. Feather the filled areas into the surrounding areas.

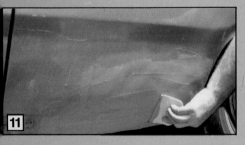

11 When the area is sanded smooth, mix some topcoat and hardener and apply it directly with a spreader. This will give a smooth finish and prevent the glass matte from showing through the paint.

12 Block sand the topcoat smooth with finishing sandpaper (200 grit), and 400 grit. The repair is ready for masking, priming and painting (see Painting Tips).

Materials and photos courtesy Marson Corporation, Chelsea, Massachusetts

PAINTING TIPS

Preparation

1 SANDING — Use a 400 or 600 grit wet or dry sandpaper. Wet-sand the area with a 1/4 sheet of sandpaper soaked in clean water. Keep the paper wet while sanding. Sand the area until the repaired area tapers into the original finish.

2 CLEANING — Wash the area to be painted thoroughly with water and a clean rag. Rinse it thoroughly and wipe the surface dry until you're sure it's completely free of dirt, dust, fingerprints, wax, detergent or other foreign matter.

3 MASKING — Protect any areas you don't want to overspray by covering them with masking tape and newspaper. Be careful not get fingerprints on the area to be painted.

4 PRIMING — All exposed metal should be primed before painting. Primer protects the metal and provides an excellent surface for paint adhesion. When the primer is dry, wet-sand the area again with 600 grit wet-sandpaper. Clean the area again after sanding.

Painting Techniques

P aint applied from either a spray gun or a spray can (for small areas) will provide good results. Experiment on an old piece of metal to get the right combination before you begin painting.

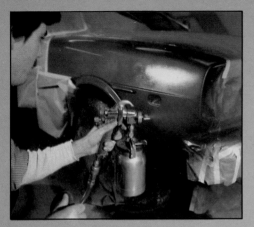

SPRAYING VISCOSITY (SPRAY GUN ONLY) — Paint should be thinned to spraying viscosity according to the directions on the can. Use only the recommended thinner or reducer and the same amount of reduction regardless of temperature.

AIR PRESSURE (SPRAY GUN ONLY) — This is extremely important. Be sure you are using the proper recommended pressure.

TEMPERATURE — The surface to be painted should be approximately the same temperature as the surrounding air. Applying warm paint to a cold surface, or vice versa, will completely upset the paint characteristics.

THICKNESS — Spray with smooth strokes. In general, the thicker the coat of paint, the longer the drying time. Apply several thin coats about 30 seconds apart. The paint should remain wet long enough to flow out and no longer; heavier coats will only produce sags or wrinkles. Spray a light (fog) coat, followed by heavier color coats.

DISTANCE — The ideal spraying distance is 8″-12″ from the gun or can to the surface. Shorter distances will produce ripples, while greater distances will result in orange peel, dry film and poor color match and loss of material due to overspray.

OVERLAPPING — The gun or can should be kept at right angles to the surface at all times. Work to a wet edge at an even speed, using a 50% overlap and direct the center of the spray at the lower or nearest edge of the previous stroke.

RUBBING OUT (BLENDING) FRESH PAINT — Let the paint dry thoroughly. Runs or imperfections can be sanded out, primed and repainted.

Don't be in too big a hurry to remove the masking. This only produces paint ridges. When the finish has dried for at least a week, apply a small amount of fine grade rubbing compound with a clean, wet cloth. Use lots of water and blend the new paint with the surrounding area.

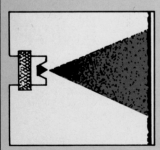

WRONG

Thin coat. Stroke too fast, not enough overlap, gun too far away.

CORRECT

Medium coat. Proper distance, good stroke, proper overlap.

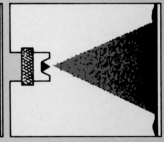

WRONG

Heavy coat. Stroke too slow, too much overlap, gun too close.

Section 7—Engine Vacuum
See Chapter 3 for service procedures

Test and Procedure	Results and Indications	Proceed to
7.1—Attach a vacuum gauge to the intake manifold beyond the throttle plate. Start the engine, and observe the action of the needle over the range of engine speeds.	See below.	**See below**

Normal engine
Gauge reading: steady, from 17–22 in./Hg.

INDICATION: normal engine in good condition

Proceed to: 8.1

Sticking valves
Gauge reading: intermittent fluctuation at idle

INDICATION: sticking valves or ignition miss

Proceed to: 9.1, 8.3

Incorrect valve timing
Gauge reading: low (10–15 in./Hg) but steady

INDICATION: late ignition or valve timing, low compression, stuck throttle valve, leaking carburetor or manifold gasket

Proceed to: 6.1

Carburetor requires adjustment
Gauge reading: drifting needle

INDICATION: improper carburetor adjustment or minor intake leak.

Proceed to: 7.2

Blown head gasket
Gauge reading: needle fluctuates as engine speed increases

INDICATION: ignition miss, blown cylinder head gasket, leaking valve or weak valve spring

Proceed to: 8.3, 6.1

Burnt or leaking valves
Gauge reading: steady needle, but drops regularly

INDICATION: burnt valve or faulty valve clearance. Needle will fall when defective valve operates

Proceed to: 9.1

Clogged exhaust system
Gauge reading: gradual drop in reading at idle

INDICATION: choked muffler, excessive back pressure in system

Proceed to: 10.1

Worn valve guides
Gauge reading: needle vibrates excessively at idle, but steadies as engine speed increases

INDICATION: worn valve guides

Proceed to: 9.1

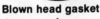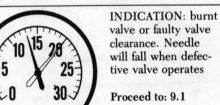

White pointer = steady gauge hand   Black pointer = fluctuating gauge hand

Test and Procedure	Results and Indications	Proceed to
7.2—Attach a vacuum gauge per 7.1, and test for an intake manifold leak. Squirt a small amount of oil around the intake manifold gaskets, carburetor gaskets, plugs and fittings. Observe the action of the vacuum gauge.	If the reading improves, replace the indicated gasket, or seal the indicated fitting or plug:	**8.1**
	If the reading remains low:	**7.3**
7.3—Test all vacuum hoses and accessories for leaks as described in 7.2. Also check the carburetor body (dashpots, automatic choke mechanism, throttle shafts) for leaks in the same manner.	If the reading improves, service or replace the offending part(s):	**8.1**
	If the reading remains low:	**6.1**

Section 8—Secondary Electrical System
See Chapter 2 for service procedures

Test and Procedure	Results and Indications	Proceed to
8.1—Remove the distributor cap and check to make sure that the rotor turns when the engine is cranked. Visually inspect the distributor components.	Clean, tighten or replace any components which appear defective.	**8.2**
8.2—Connect a timing light (per manufacturer's recommendation) and check the dynamic ignition timing. Disconnect and plug the vacuum hose(s) to the distributor if specified, start the engine, and observe the timing marks at the specified engine speed.	If the timing is not correct, adjust to specifications by rotating the distributor in the engine: (Advance timing by rotating distributor opposite normal direction of rotor rotation, retard timing by rotating distributor in same direction as rotor rotation.)	**8.3**
8.3—Check the operation of the distributor advance mechanism(s): To test the mechanical advance, disconnect the vacuum lines from the distributor advance unit and observe the timing marks with a timing light as the engine speed is increased from idle. If the mark moves smoothly, without hesitation, it may be assumed that the mechanical advance is functioning properly. To test vacuum advance and/or retard systems, alternately crimp and release the vacuum line, and observe the timing mark for movement. If movement is noted, the system is operating.	If the systems are functioning:	**8.4**
	If the systems are not functioning, remove the distributor, and test on a distributor tester:	**8.4**
8.4—Locate an ignition miss: With the engine running, remove each spark plug wire, one at a time, until one is found that doesn't cause the engine to roughen and slow down.	When the missing cylinder is identified:	**4.1**

Section 9—Valve Train
See Chapter 3 for service procedures

Test and Procedure	Results and Indications	Proceed to
9.1—Evaluate the valve train: Remove the valve cover, and ensure that the valves are adjusted to specifications. A mechanic's stethoscope may be used to aid in the diagnosis of the valve train. By pushing the probe on or near push rods or rockers, valve noise often can be isolated. A timing light also may be used to diagnose valve problems. Connect the light according to manufacturer's recommendations, and start the engine. Vary the firing moment of the light by increasing the engine speed (and therefore the ignition advance), and moving the trigger from cylinder to cylinder. Observe the movement of each valve.	Sticking valves or erratic valve train motion can be observed with the timing light. The cylinder head must be disassembled for repairs.	**See Chapter 3**
9.2—Check the valve timing: Locate top dead center of the No. 1 piston, and install a degree wheel or tape on the crankshaft pulley or damper with zero corresponding to an index mark on the engine. Rotate the crankshaft in its direction of rotation, and observe the opening of the No. 1 cylinder intake valve. The opening should correspond with the correct mark on the degree wheel according to specifications.	If the timing is not correct, the timing cover must be removed for further investigation.	**See Chapter 3**

Section 10—Exhaust System

Test and Procedure	Results and Indications	Proceed to
10.1—Determine whether the exhaust manifold heat control valve is operating: Operate the valve by hand to determine whether it is free to move. If the valve is free, run the engine to operating temperature and observe the action of the valve, to ensure that it is opening.	If the valve sticks, spray it with a suitable solvent, open and close the valve to free it, and retest. If the valve functions properly:	**10.2**
	If the valve does not free, or does not operate, replace the valve:	**10.2**
10.2—Ensure that there are no exhaust restrictions: Visually inspect the exhaust system for kinks, dents, or crushing. Also note that gases are flowing freely from the tailpipe at all engine speeds, indicating no restriction in the muffler or resonator.	Replace any damaged portion of the system:	**11.1**

Section 11—Cooling System
See Chapter 3 for service procedures

Test and Procedure	Results and Indications	Proceed to
11.1—Visually inspect the fan belt for glazing, cracks, and fraying, and replace if necessary. Tighten the belt so that the longest span has approximately ½″ play at its midpoint under thumb pressure (see Chapter 1).	Replace or tighten the fan belt as necessary:	**11.2**

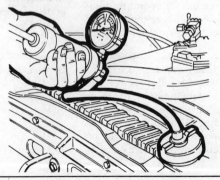

Checking belt tension

Test and Procedure	Results and Indications	Proceed to
11.2—Check the fluid level of the cooling system.	If full or slightly low, fill as necessary:	**11.5**
	If extremely low:	**11.3**
11.3—Visually inspect the external portions of the cooling system (radiator, radiator hoses, thermostat elbow, water pump seals, heater hoses, etc.) for leaks. If none are found, pressurize the cooling system to 14–15 psi.	If cooling system holds the pressure:	**11.5**
	If cooling system loses pressure rapidly, reinspect external parts of the system for leaks under pressure. If none are found, check dipstick for coolant in crankcase. If no coolant is present, but pressure loss continues:	**11.4**
	If coolant is evident in crankcase, remove cylinder head(s), and check gasket(s). If gaskets are intact, block and cylinder head(s) should be checked for cracks or holes.	
	If the gasket(s) is blown, replace, and purge the crankcase of coolant: **NOTE:** *Occasionally, due to atmospheric and driving conditions, condensation of water can occur in the crankcase. This causes the oil to appear milky white. To remedy, run the engine until hot, and change the oil and oil filter.*	**12.6**
11.4—Check for combustion leaks into the cooling system: Pressurize the cooling system as above. Start the engine, and observe the pressure gauge. If the needle fluctuates, remove each spark plug wire, one at a time, noting which cylinder(s) reduce or eliminate the fluctuation.	Cylinders which reduce or eliminate the fluctuation, when the spark plug wire is removed, are leaking into the cooling system. Replace the head gasket on the affected cylinder bank(s).	

Pressurizing the cooling system

Test and Procedure	Results and Indications	Proceed to
11.5—Check the radiator pressure cap: Attach a radiator pressure tester to the radiator cap (wet the seal prior to installation). Quickly pump up the pressure, noting the point at which the cap releases.	If the cap releases within ± 1 psi of the specified rating, it is operating properly:	**11.6**
	If the cap releases at more than ± 1 psi of the specified rating, it should be replaced:	**11.6**

Checking radiator pressure cap

Test and Procedure	Results and Indications	Proceed to
11.6—Test the thermostat: Start the engine cold, remove the radiator cap, and insert a thermometer into the radiator. Allow the engine to idle. After a short while, there will be a sudden, rapid increase in coolant temperature. The temperature at which this sharp rise stops is the thermostat opening temperature.	If the thermostat opens at or about the specified temperature:	**11.7**
	If the temperature doesn't increase: (If the temperature increases slowly and gradually, replace the thermostat.)	**11.7**
11.7—Check the water pump: Remove the thermostat elbow and the thermostat, disconnect the coil high tension lead (to prevent starting), and crank the engine momentarily.	If coolant flows, replace the thermostat and retest per 11.6:	**11.6**
	If coolant doesn't flow, reverse flush the cooling system to alleviate any blockage that might exist. If system is not blocked, and coolant will not flow, replace the water pump.	

Section 12—Lubrication
See Chapter 3 for service procedures

Test and Procedure	Results and Indications	Proceed to
12.1—Check the oil pressure gauge or warning light: If the gauge shows low pressure, or the light is on for no obvious reason, remove the oil pressure sender. Install an accurate oil pressure gauge and run the engine momentarily.	If oil pressure builds normally, run engine for a few moments to determine that it is functioning normally, and replace the sender.	—
	If the pressure remains low:	**12.2**
	If the pressure surges:	**12.3**
	If the oil pressure is zero:	**12.3**
12.2—Visually inspect the oil: If the oil is watery or very thin, milky, or foamy, replace the oil and oil filter.	If the oil is normal:	**12.3**
	If after replacing oil the pressure remains low:	**12.3**
	If after replacing oil the pressure becomes normal:	—

Test and Procedure	Results and Indications	Proceed to
12.3—Inspect the oil pressure relief valve and spring, to ensure that it is not sticking or stuck. Remove and thoroughly clean the valve, spring, and the valve body.	If the oil pressure improves: If no improvement is noted:	— **12.4**
12.4—Check to ensure that the oil pump is not cavitating (sucking air instead of oil): See that the crankcase is neither over nor underfull, and that the pickup in the sump is in the proper position and free from sludge.	Fill or drain the crankcase to the proper capacity, and clean the pickup screen in solvent if necessary. If no improvement is noted:	**12.5**
12.5—Inspect the oil pump drive and the oil pump:	If the pump drive or the oil pump appear to be defective, service as necessary and retest per 12.1: If the pump drive and pump appear to be operating normally, the engine should be disassembled to determine where blockage exists:	**12.1** **See Chapter 3**
12.6—Purge the engine of ethylene glycol coolant: Completely drain the crankcase and the oil filter. Obtain a commercial butyl cellosolve base solvent, designated for this purpose, and follow the instructions precisely. Following this, install a new oil filter and refill the crankcase with the proper weight oil. The next oil and filter change should follow shortly thereafter (1000 miles).		

TROUBLESHOOTING EMISSION CONTROL SYSTEMS

See Chapter 4 for procedures applicable to individual emission control systems used on specific combinations of engine/transmission/model.

TROUBLESHOOTING THE CARBURETOR
See Chapter 4 for service procedures

Carburetor problems cannot be effectively isolated unless all other engine systems (particularly ignition and emission) are functioning properly and the engine is properly tuned.

Condition	Possible Cause
Engine cranks, but does not start	1. Improper starting procedure 2. No fuel in tank 3. Clogged fuel line or filter 4. Defective fuel pump 5. Choke valve not closing properly 6. Engine flooded 7. Choke valve not unloading 8. Throttle linkage not making full travel 9. Stuck needle or float 10. Leaking float needle or seat 11. Improper float adjustment
Engine stalls	1. Improperly adjusted idle speed or mixture **Engine hot** 2. Improperly adjusted dashpot 3. Defective or improperly adjusted solenoid 4. Incorrect fuel level in fuel bowl 5. Fuel pump pressure too high 6. Leaking float needle seat 7. Secondary throttle valve stuck open 8. Air or fuel leaks 9. Idle air bleeds plugged or missing 10. Idle passages plugged **Engine Cold** 11. Incorrectly adjusted choke 12. Improperly adjusted fast idle speed 13. Air leaks 14. Plugged idle or idle air passages 15. Stuck choke valve or binding linkage 16. Stuck secondary throttle valves 17. Engine flooding—high fuel level 18. Leaking or misaligned float
Engine hesitates on acceleration	1. Clogged fuel filter 2. Leaking fuel pump diaphragm 3. Low fuel pump pressure 4. Secondary throttle valves stuck, bent or misadjusted 5. Sticking or binding air valve 6. Defective accelerator pump 7. Vacuum leaks 8. Clogged air filter 9. Incorrect choke adjustment (engine cold)
Engine feels sluggish or flat on acceleration	1. Improperly adjusted idle speed or mixture 2. Clogged fuel filter 3. Defective accelerator pump 4. Dirty, plugged or incorrect main metering jets 5. Bent or sticking main metering rods 6. Sticking throttle valves 7. Stuck heat riser 8. Binding or stuck air valve 9. Dirty, plugged or incorrect secondary jets 10. Bent or sticking secondary metering rods. 11. Throttle body or manifold heat passages plugged 12. Improperly adjusted choke or choke vacuum break.
Carburetor floods	1. Defective fuel pump. Pressure too high. 2. Stuck choke valve 3. Dirty, worn or damaged float or needle valve/seat 4. Incorrect float/fuel level 5. Leaking float bowl

Condition	Possible Cause
Engine idles roughly and stalls	1. Incorrect idle speed 2. Clogged fuel filter 3. Dirt in fuel system or carburetor 4. Loose carburetor screws or attaching bolts 5. Broken carburetor gaskets 6. Air leaks 7. Dirty carburetor 8. Worn idle mixture needles 9. Throttle valves stuck open 10. Incorrectly adjusted float or fuel level 11. Clogged air filter
Engine runs unevenly or surges	1. Defective fuel pump 2. Dirty or clogged fuel filter 3. Plugged, loose or incorrect main metering jets or rods 4. Air leaks 5. Bent or sticking main metering rods 6. Stuck power piston 7. Incorrect float adjustment 8. Incorrect idle speed or mixture 9. Dirty or plugged idle system passages 10. Hard, brittle or broken gaskets 11. Loose attaching or mounting screws 12. Stuck or misaligned secondary throttle valves
Poor fuel economy	1. Poor driving habits 2. Stuck choke valve 3. Binding choke linkage 4. Stuck heat riser 5. Incorrect idle mixture 6. Defective accelerator pump 7. Air leaks 8. Plugged, loose or incorrect main metering jets 9. Improperly adjusted float or fuel level 10. Bent, misaligned or fuel-clogged float 11. Leaking float needle seat 12. Fuel leak 13. Accelerator pump discharge ball not seating properly 14. Incorrect main jets
Engine lacks high speed performance or power	1. Incorrect throttle linkage adjustment 2. Stuck or binding power piston 3. Defective accelerator pump 4. Air leaks 5. Incorrect float setting or fuel level 6. Dirty, plugged, worn or incorrect main metering jets or rods 7. Binding or sticking air valve 8. Brittle or cracked gaskets 9. Bent, incorrect or improperly adjusted secondary metering rods 10. Clogged fuel filter 11. Clogged air filter 12. Defective fuel pump

TROUBLESHOOTING FUEL INJECTION PROBLEMS

Each fuel injection system has its own unique components and test procedures, for which it is impossible to generalize. Refer to Chapter 4 of this Repair & Tune-Up Guide for specific test and repair procedures, if the vehicle is equipped with fuel injection.

TROUBLESHOOTING ELECTRICAL PROBLEMS

See Chapter 5 for service procedures

For any electrical system to operate, it must make a complete circuit. This simply means that the power flow from the battery must make a complete circle. When an electrical component is operating, power flows from the battery to the component, passes through the component causing it to perform its function (lighting a light bulb), and then returns to the battery through the ground of the circuit. This ground is usually (but not always) the metal part of the car or truck on which the electrical component is mounted.

Perhaps the easiest way to visualize this is to think of connecting a light bulb with two wires attached to it to the battery. If one of the two wires attached to the light bulb were attached to the negative post of the battery and the other were attached to the positive post of the battery, you would have a complete circuit. Current from the battery would flow to the light bulb, causing it to light, and return to the negative post of the battery.

The normal automotive circuit differs from this simple example in two ways. First, instead of having a return wire from the bulb to the battery, the light bulb returns the current to the battery through the chassis of the vehicle. Since the negative battery cable is attached to the chassis and the chassis is made of electrically conductive metal, the chassis of the vehicle can serve as a ground wire to complete the circuit. Secondly, most automotive circuits contain switches to turn components on and off as required.

Every complete circuit from a power source must include a component which is using the power from the power source. If you were to disconnect the light bulb from the wires and touch the two wires together (don't do this) the power supply wire to the component would be grounded before the normal ground connection for the circuit.

Because grounding a wire from a power source makes a complete circuit—less the required component to use the power—this phenomenon is called a short circuit. Common causes are: broken insulation (exposing the metal wire to a metal part of the car or truck), or a shorted switch.

Some electrical components which require a large amount of current to operate also have a relay in their circuit. Since these circuits carry a large amount of current, the thickness of the wire in the circuit (gauge size) is also greater. If this large wire were connected from the component to the control switch on the instrument panel, and then back to the component, a voltage drop would occur in the circuit. To prevent this potential drop in voltage, an electromagnetic switch (relay) is used. The large wires in the circuit are connected from the battery to one side of the relay, and from the opposite side of the relay to the component. The relay is normally open, preventing current from passing through the circuit. An additional, smaller, wire is connected from the relay to the control switch for the circuit. When the control switch is turned on, it grounds the smaller wire from the relay and completes the circuit. This closes the relay and allows current to flow from the battery to the component. The horn, headlight, and starter circuits are three which use relays.

It is possible for larger surges of current to pass through the electrical system of your car or truck. If this surge of current were to reach an electrical component, it could burn it out. To prevent this, fuses, circuit breakers or fusible links are connected into the current supply wires of most of the major electrical systems. When an electrical current of excessive power passes through the component's fuse, the fuse blows out and breaks the circuit, saving the component from destruction.

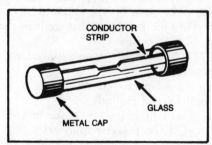

Typical automotive fuse

A circuit breaker is basically a self-repairing fuse. The circuit breaker opens the circuit the same way a fuse does. However, when either the short is removed from the circuit or the surge subsides, the circuit breaker resets itself and does not have to be replaced as a fuse does.

A fuse link is a wire that acts as a fuse. It is normally connected between the starter relay and the main wiring harness. This connection is usually under the hood. The fuse link (if installed) protects all the

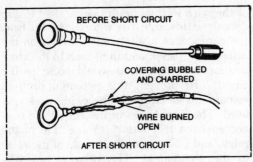

Most fusible links show a charred, melted insulation when they burn out

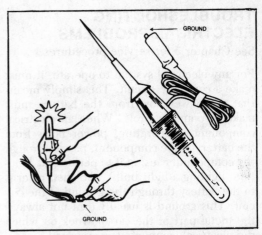

The test light will show the presence of current when touched to a hot wire and grounded at the other end

chassis electrical components, and is the probable cause of trouble when none of the electrical components function, unless the battery is disconnected or dead.

Electrical problems generally fall into one of three areas:

1. The component that is not functioning is not receiving current.

2. The component itself is not functioning.

3. The component is not properly grounded.

The electrical system can be checked with a test light and a jumper wire. A test light is a device that looks like a pointed screwdriver with a wire attached to it and has a light bulb in its handle. A jumper wire is a piece of insulated wire with an alligator clip attached to each end.

If a component is not working, you must follow a systematic plan to determine which of the three causes is the villain.

1. Turn on the switch that controls the inoperable component.

2. Disconnect the power supply wire from the component.

3. Attach the ground wire on the test light to a good metal ground.

4. Touch the probe end of the test light to the end of the power supply wire that was disconnected from the component. If the component is receiving current, the test light will go on.

NOTE: *Some components work only when the ignition switch is turned on.*

If the test light does not go on, then the problem is in the circuit between the battery and the component. This includes all the switches, fuses, and relays in the system. Follow the wire that runs back to the battery. The problem is an open circuit between the

battery and the component. If the fuse is blown and, when replaced, immediately blows again, there is a short circuit in the system which must be located and repaired. If there is a switch in the system, bypass it with a jumper wire. This is done by connecting one end of the jumper wire to the power supply wire into the switch and the other end of the jumper wire to the wire coming out of the switch. If the test light lights with the jumper wire installed, the switch or whatever was bypassed is defective.

NOTE: *Never substitute the jumper wire for the component, since it is required to use the power from the power source.*

5. If the bulb in the test light goes on, then the current is getting to the component that is not working. This eliminates the first of the three possible causes. Connect the power supply wire and connect a jumper wire from the component to a good metal ground. Do this with the switch which controls the component turned on, and also the ignition switch turned on if it is required for the component to work. If the component works with the jumper wire installed, then it has a bad ground. This is usually caused by the metal area on which the component mounts to the chassis being coated with some type of foreign matter.

6. If neither test located the source of the trouble, then the component itself is defective. Remember that for any electrical system to work, all connections must be clean and tight.

Troubleshooting Basic Turn Signal and Flasher Problems
See Chapter 5 for service procedures

Most problems in the turn signals or flasher system can be reduced to defective flashers or bulbs, which are easily replaced. Occasionally, the turn signal switch will prove defective.

F = Front   R = Rear   ● = Lights off   ○ = Lights on

Condition	Possible Cause
Turn signals light, but do not flash 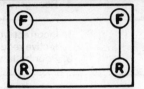	Defective flasher
No turn signals light on either side 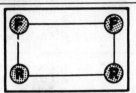	Blown fuse. Replace if defective. Defective flasher. Check by substitution. Open circuit, short circuit or poor ground.
Both turn signals on one side don't work 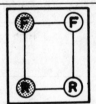	Bad bulbs. Bad ground in both (or either) housings.
One turn signal light on one side doesn't work 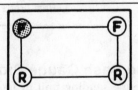	Defective bulb. Corrosion in socket. Clean contacts. Poor ground at socket.
Turn signal flashes too fast or too slowly 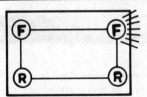	Check any bulb on the side flashing too fast. A heavy-duty bulb is probably installed in place of a regular bulb. Check the bulb flashing too slowly. A standard bulb was probably installed in place of a heavy-duty bulb. Loose connections or corrosion at the bulb socket.
Indicator lights don't work in either direction 	Check if the turn signals are working. Check the dash indicator lights. Check the flasher by substitution.
One indicator light doesn't light 	On systems with one dash indicator: See if the lights work on the same side. Often the filaments have been reversed in systems combining stoplights with taillights and turn signals. Check the flasher by substitution. On systems with two indicators: Check the bulbs on the same side. Check the indicator light bulb. Check the flasher by substitution.

Troubleshooting Lighting Problems
See Chapter 5 for service procedures

Condition	Possible Cause
One or more lights don't work, but others do	1. Defective bulb(s) 2. Blown fuse(s) 3. Dirty fuse clips or light sockets 4. Poor ground circuit
Lights burn out quickly	1. Incorrect voltage regulator setting or defective regulator 2. Poor battery/alternator connections
Lights go dim	1. Low/discharged battery 2. Alternator not charging 3. Corroded sockets or connections 4. Low voltage output
Lights flicker	1. Loose connection 2. Poor ground. (Run ground wire from light housing to frame) 3. Circuit breaker operating (short circuit)
Lights "flare"—Some flare is normal on acceleration—If excessive, see "Lights Burn Out Quickly"	High voltage setting
Lights glare—approaching drivers are blinded	1. Lights adjusted too high 2. Rear springs or shocks sagging 3. Rear tires soft

Troubleshooting Dash Gauge Problems
Most problems can be traced to a defective sending unit or faulty wiring. Occasionally, the gauge itself is at fault. See Chapter 5 for service procedures.

Condition	Possible Cause
COOLANT TEMPERATURE GAUGE	
Gauge reads erratically or not at all	1. Loose or dirty connections 2. Defective sending unit. 3. Defective gauge. To test a bi-metal gauge, remove the wire from the sending unit. Ground the wire for an instant. If the gauge registers, replace the sending unit. To test a magnetic gauge, disconnect the wire at the sending unit. With ignition ON gauge should register COLD. Ground the wire; gauge should register HOT.
AMMETER GAUGE—TURN HEADLIGHTS ON (DO NOT START ENGINE). NOTE REACTION	
Ammeter shows charge Ammeter shows discharge Ammeter does not move	1. Connections reversed on gauge 2. Ammeter is OK 3. Loose connections or faulty wiring 4. Defective gauge

Condition	Possible Cause

OIL PRESSURE GAUGE

Condition	Possible Cause
Gauge does not register or is inaccurate	1. On mechanical gauge, Bourdon tube may be bent or kinked. 2. Low oil pressure. Remove sending unit. Idle the engine briefly. If no oil flows from sending unit hole, problem is in engine. 3. Defective gauge. Remove the wire from the sending unit and ground it for an instant with the ignition ON. A good gauge will go to the top of the scale. 4. Defective wiring. Check the wiring to the gauge. If it's OK and the gauge doesn't register when grounded, replace the gauge. 5. Defective sending unit.

ALL GAUGES

Condition	Possible Cause
All gauges do not operate All gauges read low or erratically All gauges pegged	1. Blown fuse 2. Defective instrument regulator 3. Defective or dirty instrument voltage regulator 4. Loss of ground between instrument voltage regulator and frame 5. Defective instrument regulator

WARNING LIGHTS

Condition	Possible Cause
Light(s) do not come on when ignition is ON, but engine is not started Light comes on with engine running	1. Defective bulb 2. Defective wire 3. Defective sending unit. Disconnect the wire from the sending unit and ground it. Replace the sending unit if the light comes on with the ignition ON. 4. Problem in individual system 5. Defective sending unit

Troubleshooting Clutch Problems

It is false economy to replace individual clutch components. The pressure plate, clutch plate and throwout bearing should be replaced as a set, and the flywheel face inspected, whenever the clutch is overhauled. See Chapter 6 for service procedures.

Condition	Possible Cause
Clutch chatter	1. Grease on driven plate (disc) facing 2. Binding clutch linkage or cable 3. Loose, damaged facings on driven plate (disc) 4. Engine mounts loose 5. Incorrect height adjustment of pressure plate release levers 6. Clutch housing or housing to transmission adapter misalignment 7. Loose driven plate hub
Clutch grabbing	1. Oil, grease on driven plate (disc) facing 2. Broken pressure plate 3. Warped or binding driven plate. Driven plate binding on clutch shaft
Clutch slips	1. Lack of lubrication in clutch linkage or cable (linkage or cable binds, causes incomplete engagement) 2. Incorrect pedal, or linkage adjustment 3. Broken pressure plate springs 4. Weak pressure plate springs 5. Grease on driven plate facings (disc)

Troubleshooting Clutch Problems (cont.)

Condition	Possible Cause
Incomplete clutch release	1. Incorrect pedal or linkage adjustment or linkage or cable binding 2. Incorrect height adjustment on pressure plate release levers 3. Loose, broken facings on driven plate (disc) 4. Bent, dished, warped driven plate caused by overheating
Grinding, whirring grating noise when pedal is depressed	1. Worn or defective throwout bearing 2. Starter drive teeth contacting flywheel ring gear teeth. Look for milled or polished teeth on ring gear.
Squeal, howl, trumpeting noise when pedal is being released (occurs during first inch to inch and one-half of pedal travel)	Pilot bushing worn or lack of lubricant. If bushing appears OK, polish bushing with emery cloth, soak lube wick in oil, lube bushing with oil, apply film of chassis grease to clutch shaft pilot hub, reassemble. NOTE: Bushing wear may be due to misalignment of clutch housing or housing to transmission adapter
Vibration or clutch pedal pulsation with clutch disengaged (pedal fully depressed)	1. Worn or defective engine transmission mounts 2. Flywheel run out. (Flywheel run out at face not to exceed 0.005") 3. Damaged or defective clutch components

Troubleshooting Manual Transmission Problems
See Chapter 6 for service procedures

Condition	Possible Cause
Transmission jumps out of gear	1. Misalignment of transmission case or clutch housing. 2. Worn pilot bearing in crankshaft. 3. Bent transmission shaft. 4. Worn high speed sliding gear. 5. Worn teeth or end-play in clutch shaft. 6. Insufficient spring tension on shifter rail plunger. 7. Bent or loose shifter fork. 8. Gears not engaging completely. 9. Loose or worn bearings on clutch shaft or mainshaft. 10. Worn gear teeth. 11. Worn or damaged detent balls.
Transmission sticks in gear	1. Clutch not releasing fully. 2. Burred or battered teeth on clutch shaft, or sliding sleeve. 3. Burred or battered transmission mainshaft. 4. Frozen synchronizing clutch. 5. Stuck shifter rail plunger. 6. Gearshift lever twisting and binding shifter rail. 7. Battered teeth on high speed sliding gear or on sleeve. 8. Improper lubrication, or lack of lubrication. 9. Corroded transmission parts. 10. Defective mainshaft pilot bearing. 11. Locked gear bearings will give same effect as stuck in gear.
Transmission gears will not synchronize	1. Binding pilot bearing on mainshaft, will synchronize in high gear only. 2. Clutch not releasing fully. 3. Detent spring weak or broken. 4. Weak or broken springs under balls in sliding gear sleeve. 5. Binding bearing on clutch shaft, or binding countershaft. 6. Binding pilot bearing in crankshaft. 7. Badly worn gear teeth. 8. Improper lubrication. 9. Constant mesh gear not turning freely on transmission mainshaft. Will synchronize in that gear only.

Condition	Possible Cause
Gears spinning when shifting into gear from neutral	1. Clutch not releasing fully. 2. In some cases an extremely light lubricant in transmission will cause gears to continue to spin for a short time after clutch is released. 3. Binding pilot bearing in crankshaft.
Transmission noisy in all gears	1. Insufficient lubricant, or improper lubricant. 2. Worn countergear bearings. 3. Worn or damaged main drive gear or countergear. 4. Damaged main drive gear or mainshaft bearings. 5. Worn or damaged countergear anti-lash plate.
Transmission noisy in neutral only	1. Damaged main drive gear bearing. 2. Damaged or loose mainshaft pilot bearing. 3. Worn or damaged countergear anti-lash plate. 4. Worn countergear bearings.
Transmission noisy in one gear only	1. Damaged or worn constant mesh gears. 2. Worn or damaged countergear bearings. 3. Damaged or worn synchronizer.
Transmission noisy in reverse only	1. Worn or damaged reverse idler gear or idler bushing. 2. Worn or damaged mainshaft reverse gear. 3. Worn or damaged reverse countergear. 4. Damaged shift mechanism.

TROUBLESHOOTING AUTOMATIC TRANSMISSION PROBLEMS

Keeping alert to changes in the operating characteristics of the transmission (changing shift points, noises, etc.) can prevent small problems from becoming large ones. If the problem cannot be traced to loose bolts, fluid level, misadjusted linkage, clogged filters or similar problems, you should probably seek professional service.

Transmission Fluid Indications

The appearance and odor of the transmission fluid can give valuable clues to the overall condition of the transmission. Always note the appearance of the fluid when you check the fluid level or change the fluid. Rub a small amount of fluid between your fingers to feel for grit and smell the fluid on the dipstick.

If the fluid appears:	It indicates:
Clear and red colored	Normal operation
Discolored (extremely dark red or brownish) or smells burned	Band or clutch pack failure, usually caused by an overheated transmission. Hauling very heavy loads with insufficient power or failure to change the fluid often result in overheating. Do not confuse this appearance with newer fluids that have a darker red color and a strong odor (though not a burned odor).
Foamy or aerated (light in color and full of bubbles)	1. The level is too high (gear train is churning oil) 2. An internal air leak (air is mixing with the fluid). Have the transmission checked professionally.
Solid residue in the fluid	Defective bands, clutch pack or bearings. Bits of band material or metal abrasives are clinging to the dipstick. Have the transmission checked professionally.
Varnish coating on the dipstick	The transmission fluid is overheating

TROUBLESHOOTING DRIVE AXLE PROBLEMS

First, determine when the noise is most noticeable.

Drive Noise: Produced under vehicle acceleration.

Coast Noise: Produced while coasting with a closed throttle.

Float Noise: Occurs while maintaining constant speed (just enough to keep speed constant) on a level road.

External Noise Elimination

It is advisable to make a thorough road test to determine whether the noise originates in the rear axle or whether it originates from the tires, engine, transmission, wheel bearings or road surface. Noise originating from other places cannot be corrected by servicing the rear axle.

ROAD NOISE

Brick or rough surfaced concrete roads produce noises that seem to come from the rear axle. Road noise is usually identical in Drive or Coast and driving on a different type of road will tell whether the road is the problem.

TIRE NOISE

Tire noise can be mistaken as rear axle noise, even though the tires on the front are at fault. Snow tread and mud tread tires or tires worn unevenly will frequently cause vibrations which seem to originate elsewhere; *temporarily, and for test purposes only,* inflate the tires to 40–50 lbs. This will significantly alter the noise produced by the tires, but will not alter noise from the rear axle. Noises from the rear axle will normally cease at speeds below 30 mph on coast, while tire noise will continue at lower tone as speed is decreased. The rear axle noise will usually change from drive conditions to coast conditions, while tire noise will not. Do not forget to lower the tire pressure to normal after the test is complete.

ENGINE/TRANSMISSION NOISE

Determine at what speed the noise is most pronounced, then stop in a quiet place. With the transmission in Neutral, run the engine through speeds corresponding to road speeds where the noise was noticed. Noises produced with the vehicle standing still are coming from the engine or transmission.

FRONT WHEEL BEARINGS

Front wheel bearing noises, sometimes confused with rear axle noises, will not change when comparing drive and coast conditions. While holding the speed steady, lightly apply the footbrake. This will often cause wheel bearing noise to lessen, as some of the weight is taken off the bearing. Front wheel bearings are easily checked by jacking up the wheels and spinning the wheels. Shaking the wheels will also determine if the wheel bearings are excessively loose.

REAR AXLE NOISES

Eliminating other possible sources can narrow the cause to the rear axle, which normally produces noise from worn gears or bearings. Gear noises tend to peak in a narrow speed range, while bearing noises will usually vary in pitch with engine speeds.

Noise Diagnosis

The Noise Is:	Most Probably Produced By:
1. Identical under Drive or Coast	Road surface, tires or front wheel bearings
2. Different depending on road surface	Road surface or tires
3. Lower as speed is lowered	Tires
4. Similar when standing or moving	Engine or transmission
5. A vibration	Unbalanced tires, rear wheel bearing, unbalanced driveshaft or worn U-joint
6. A knock or click about every two tire revolutions	Rear wheel bearing
7. Most pronounced on turns	Damaged differential gears
8. A steady low-pitched whirring or scraping, starting at low speeds	Damaged or worn pinion bearing
9. A chattering vibration on turns	Wrong differential lubricant or worn clutch plates (limited slip rear axle)
10. Noticed only in Drive, Coast or Float conditions	Worn ring gear and/or pinion gear

Troubleshooting Steering & Suspension Problems

Condition	Possible Cause
Hard steering (wheel is hard to turn)	1. Improper tire pressure 2. Loose or glazed pump drive belt 3. Low or incorrect fluid 4. Loose, bent or poorly lubricated front end parts 5. Improper front end alignment (excessive caster) 6. Bind in steering column or linkage 7. Kinked hydraulic hose 8. Air in hydraulic system 9. Low pump output or leaks in system 10. Obstruction in lines 11. Pump valves sticking or out of adjustment 12. Incorrect wheel alignment
Loose steering (too much play in steering wheel)	1. Loose wheel bearings 2. Faulty shocks 3. Worn linkage or suspension components 4. Loose steering gear mounting or linkage points 5. Steering mechanism worn or improperly adjusted 6. Valve spool improperly adjusted 7. Worn ball joints, tie-rod ends, etc.
Veers or wanders (pulls to one side with hands off steering wheel)	1. Improper tire pressure 2. Improper front end alignment 3. Dragging or improperly adjusted brakes 4. Bent frame 5. Improper rear end alignment 6. Faulty shocks or springs 7. Loose or bent front end components 8. Play in Pitman arm 9. Steering gear mountings loose 10. Loose wheel bearings 11. Binding Pitman arm 12. Spool valve sticking or improperly adjusted 13. Worn ball joints
Wheel oscillation or vibration transmitted through steering wheel	1. Low or uneven tire pressure 2. Loose wheel bearings 3. Improper front end alignment 4. Bent spindle 5. Worn, bent or broken front end components 6. Tires out of round or out of balance 7. Excessive lateral runout in disc brake rotor 8. Loose or bent shock absorber or strut
Noises (see also "Troubleshooting Drive Axle Problems")	1. Loose belts 2. Low fluid, air in system 3. Foreign matter in system 4. Improper lubrication 5. Interference or chafing in linkage 6. Steering gear mountings loose 7. Incorrect adjustment or wear in gear box 8. Faulty valves or wear in pump 9. Kinked hydraulic lines 10. Worn wheel bearings
Poor return of steering	1. Over-inflated tires 2. Improperly aligned front end (excessive caster) 3. Binding in steering column 4. No lubrication in front end 5. Steering gear adjusted too tight
Uneven tire wear (see "How To Read Tire Wear")	1. Incorrect tire pressure 2. Improperly aligned front end 3. Tires out-of-balance 4. Bent or worn suspension parts

HOW TO READ TIRE WEAR

The way your tires wear is a good indicator of other parts of the suspension. Abnormal wear patterns are often caused by the need for simple tire maintenance, or for front end alignment.

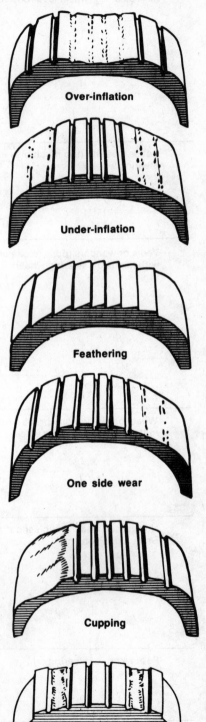

Excessive wear at the center of the tread indicates that the air pressure in the tire is consistently too high. The tire is riding on the center of the tread and wearing it prematurely. Occasionally, this wear pattern can result from outrageously wide tires on narrow rims. The cure for this is to replace either the tires or the wheels.

Over-inflation

This type of wear usually results from consistent under-inflation. When a tire is under-inflated, there is too much contact with the road by the outer treads, which wear prematurely. When this type of wear occurs, and the tire pressure is known to be consistently correct, a bent or worn steering component or the need for wheel alignment could be indicated.

Under-inflation

Feathering is a condition when the edge of each tread rib develops a slightly rounded edge on one side and a sharp edge on the other. By running your hand over the tire, you can usually feel the sharper edges before you'll be able to see them. The most common causes of feathering are incorrect toe-in setting or deteriorated bushings in the front suspension.

Feathering

When an inner or outer rib wears faster than the rest of the tire, the need for wheel alignment is indicated. There is excessive camber in the front suspension, causing the wheel to lean too much putting excessive load on one side of the tire. Misalignment could also be due to sagging springs, worn ball joints, or worn control arm bushings. Be sure the vehicle is loaded the way it's normally driven when you have the wheels aligned.

One side wear

Cups or scalloped dips appearing around the edge of the tread almost always indicate worn (sometimes bent) suspension parts. Adjustment of wheel alignment alone will seldom cure the problem. Any worn component that connects the wheel to the suspension can cause this type of wear. Occasionally, wheels that are out of balance will wear like this, but wheel imbalance usually shows up as bald spots between the outside edges and center of the tread.

Cupping

Second-rib wear is usually found only in radial tires, and appears where the steel belts end in relation to the tread. It can be kept to a minimum by paying careful attention to tire pressure and frequently rotating the tires. This is often considered normal wear but excessive amounts indicate that the tires are too wide for the wheels.

Second-rib wear

Troubleshooting Disc Brake Problems

Condition	Possible Cause
Noise—groan—brake noise emanating when slowly releasing brakes (creep-groan)	Not detrimental to function of disc brakes—no corrective action required. (This noise may be eliminated by slightly increasing or decreasing brake pedal efforts.)
Rattle—brake noise or rattle emanating at low speeds on rough roads, (front wheels only).	1. Shoe anti-rattle spring missing or not properly positioned. 2. Excessive clearance between shoe and caliper. 3. Soft or broken caliper seals. 4. Deformed or misaligned disc. 5. Loose caliper.
Scraping	1. Mounting bolts too long. 2. Loose wheel bearings. 3. Bent, loose, or misaligned splash shield.
Front brakes heat up during driving and fail to release	1. Operator riding brake pedal. 2. Stop light switch improperly adjusted. 3. Sticking pedal linkage. 4. Frozen or seized piston. 5. Residual pressure valve in master cylinder. 6. Power brake malfunction. 7. Proportioning valve malfunction.
Leaky brake caliper	1. Damaged or worn caliper piston seal. 2. Scores or corrosion on surface of cylinder bore.
Grabbing or uneven brake action—Brakes pull to one side	1. Causes listed under "Brakes Pull". 2. Power brake malfunction. 3. Low fluid level in master cylinder. 4. Air in hydraulic system. 5. Brake fluid, oil or grease on linings. 6. Unmatched linings. 7. Distorted brake pads. 8. Frozen or seized pistons. 9. Incorrect tire pressure. 10. Front end out of alignment. 11. Broken rear spring. 12. Brake caliper pistons sticking. 13. Restricted hose or line. 14. Caliper not in proper alignment to braking disc. 15. Stuck or malfunctioning metering valve. 16. Soft or broken caliper seals. 17. Loose caliper.
Brake pedal can be depressed without braking effect	1. Air in hydraulic system or improper bleeding procedure. 2. Leak past primary cup in master cylinder. 3. Leak in system. 4. Rear brakes out of adjustment. 5. Bleeder screw open.
Excessive pedal travel	1. Air, leak, or insufficient fluid in system or caliper. 2. Warped or excessively tapered shoe and lining assembly. 3. Excessive disc runout. 4. Rear brake adjustment required. 5. Loose wheel bearing adjustment. 6. Damaged caliper piston seal. 7. Improper brake fluid (boil). 8. Power brake malfunction. 9. Weak or soft hoses.

Troubleshooting Disc Brake Problems (cont.)

Condition	Possible Cause
Brake roughness or chatter (pedal pumping)	1. Excessive thickness variation of braking disc. 2. Excessive lateral runout of braking disc. 3. Rear brake drums out-of-round. 4. Excessive front bearing clearance.
Excessive pedal effort	1. Brake fluid, oil or grease on linings. 2. Incorrect lining. 3. Frozen or seized pistons. 4. Power brake malfunction. 5. Kinked or collapsed hose or line. 6. Stuck metering valve. 7. Scored caliper or master cylinder bore. 8. Seized caliper pistons.
Brake pedal fades (pedal travel increases with foot on brake)	1. Rough master cylinder or caliper bore. 2. Loose or broken hydraulic lines/connections. 3. Air in hydraulic system. 4. Fluid level low. 5. Weak or soft hoses. 6. Inferior quality brake shoes or fluid. 7. Worn master cylinder piston cups or seals.

Troubleshooting Drum Brakes

Condition	Possible Cause
Pedal goes to floor	1. Fluid low in reservoir. 2. Air in hydraulic system. 3. Improperly adjusted brake. 4. Leaking wheel cylinders. 5. Loose or broken brake lines. 6. Leaking or worn master cylinder. 7. Excessively worn brake lining.
Spongy brake pedal	1. Air in hydraulic system. 2. Improper brake fluid (low boiling point). 3. Excessively worn or cracked brake drums. 4. Broken pedal pivot bushing.
Brakes pulling	1. Contaminated lining. 2. Front end out of alignment. 3. Incorrect brake adjustment. 4. Unmatched brake lining. 5. Brake drums out of round. 6. Brake shoes distorted. 7. Restricted brake hose or line. 8. Broken rear spring. 9. Worn brake linings. 10. Uneven lining wear. 11. Glazed brake lining. 12. Excessive brake lining dust. 13. Heat spotted brake drums. 14. Weak brake return springs. 15. Faulty automatic adjusters. 16. Low or incorrect tire pressure.

Condition	Possible Cause
Squealing brakes	1. Glazed brake lining. 2. Saturated brake lining. 3. Weak or broken brake shoe retaining spring. 4. Broken or weak brake shoe return spring. 5. Incorrect brake lining. 6. Distorted brake shoes. 7. Bent support plate. 8. Dust in brakes or scored brake drums. 9. Linings worn below limit. 10. Uneven brake lining wear. 11. Heat spotted brake drums.
Chirping brakes	1. Out of round drum or eccentric axle flange pilot.
Dragging brakes	1. Incorrect wheel or parking brake adjustment. 2. Parking brakes engaged or improperly adjusted. 3. Weak or broken brake shoe return spring. 4. Brake pedal binding. 5. Master cylinder cup sticking. 6. Obstructed master cylinder relief port. 7. Saturated brake lining. 8. Bent or out of round brake drum. 9. Contaminated or improper brake fluid. 10. Sticking wheel cylinder pistons. 11. Driver riding brake pedal. 12. Defective proportioning valve. 13. Insufficient brake shoe lubricant.
Hard pedal	1. Brake booster inoperative. 2. Incorrect brake lining. 3. Restricted brake line or hose. 4. Frozen brake pedal linkage. 5. Stuck wheel cylinder. 6. Binding pedal linkage. 7. Faulty proportioning valve.
Wheel locks	1. Contaminated brake lining. 2. Loose or torn brake lining. 3. Wheel cylinder cups sticking. 4. Incorrect wheel bearing adjustment. 5. Faulty proportioning valve.
Brakes fade (high speed)	1. Incorrect lining. 2. Overheated brake drums. 3. Incorrect brake fluid (low boiling temperature). 4. Saturated brake lining. 5. Leak in hydraulic system. 6. Faulty automatic adjusters.
Pedal pulsates	1. Bent or out of round brake drum.
Brake chatter and shoe knock	1. Out of round brake drum. 2. Loose support plate. 3. Bent support plate. 4. Distorted brake shoes. 5. Machine grooves in contact face of brake drum (Shoe Knock). 6. Contaminated brake lining. 7. Missing or loose components. 8. Incorrect lining material. 9. Out-of-round brake drums. 10. Heat spotted or scored brake drums. 11. Out-of-balance wheels.

Troubleshooting Drum Brakes (cont.)

Condition	Possible Cause
Brakes do not self adjust	1. Adjuster screw frozen in thread. 2. Adjuster screw corroded at thrust washer. 3. Adjuster lever does not engage star wheel. 4. Adjuster installed on wrong wheel.
Brake light glows	1. Leak in the hydraulic system. 2. Air in the system. 3. Improperly adjusted master cylinder pushrod. 4. Uneven lining wear. 5. Failure to center combination valve or proportioning valve.

Mechanic's Data

General Conversion Table

Multiply By	To Convert	To	
	LENGTH		
2.54	Inches	Centimeters	.3937
25.4	Inches	Millimeters	.03937
30.48	Feet	Centimeters	.0328
.304	Feet	Meters	3.28
.914	Yards	Meters	1.094
1.609	Miles	Kilometers	.621
	VOLUME		
.473	Pints	Liters	2.11
.946	Quarts	Liters	1.06
3.785	Gallons	Liters	.264
.016	Cubic inches	Liters	61.02
16.39	Cubic inches	Cubic cms.	.061
28.3	Cubic feet	Liters	.0353
	MASS (Weight)		
28.35	Ounces	Grams	.035
.4536	Pounds	Kilograms	2.20
—	To obtain	From	Multiply by

Multiply By	To Convert	To	
	AREA		
.645	Square inches	Square cms.	.155
.836	Square yds.	Square meters	1.196
	FORCE		
4.448	Pounds	Newtons	.225
.138	Ft./lbs.	Kilogram/meters	7.23
1.36	Ft./lbs.	Newton-meters	.737
.112	In./lbs.	Newton-meters	8.844
	PRESSURE		
.068	Psi	Atmospheres	14.7
6.89	Psi	Kilopascals	.145
	OTHER		
1.104	Horsepower (DIN)	Horsepower (SAE)	.9861
.746	Horsepower (SAE)	Kilowatts (KW)	1.34
1.60	Mph	Km/h	.625
.425	Mpg	Km/1	2.35
—	To obtain	From	Multiply by

Tap Drill Sizes

National Coarse or U.S.S.

Screw & Tap Size	Threads Per Inch	Use Drill Number
No. 5	40	39
No. 6	32	36
No. 8	32	29
No. 10	24	25
No. 12	24	17
1/4	20	8
5/16	18	F
3/8	16	5/16
7/16	14	U
1/2	13	27/64
9/16	12	31/64
5/8	11	17/32
3/4	10	21/32
7/8	9	49/64

National Coarse or U.S.S.

Screw & Tap Size	Threads Per Inch	Use Drill Number
1	8	7/8
1 1/8	7	63/64
1 1/4	7	1 7/64
1 1/2	6	1 11/32

National Fine or S.A.E.

Screw & Tap Size	Threads Per Inch	Use Drill Number
No. 5	44	37
No. 6	40	33
No. 8	36	29
No. 10	32	21

National Fine or S.A.E.

Screw & Tap Size	Threads Per Inch	Use Drill Number
No. 12	28	15
1/4	28	3
6/16	24	1
3/8	24	Q
7/16	20	W
1/2	20	29/64
9/16	18	33/64
5/8	18	37/64
3/4	16	11/16
7/8	14	13/16
1 1/8	12	1 3/64
1 1/4	12	1 11/64
1 1/2	12	1 27/64

Drill Sizes In Decimal Equivalents

Inch	Decimal	Wire	mm	Inch	Decimal	Wire	mm	Inch	Decimal	Wire & Letter	mm	Inch	Decimal	Letter	mm	Inch	Decimal	mm
1/64	.0156		.39		.0730	49			.1614		4.1		.2717		6.9		.4331	11.0
	.0157		.4		.0748		1.9		.1654		4.2		.2720	I		7/16	.4375	11.11
	.0160	78			.0760	48			.1660	19			.2756		7.0		.4528	11.5
	.0165		.42		.0768		1.95		.1673		4.25		.2770	J		29/64	.4531	11.51
	.0173		.44	5/64	.0781		1.98		.1693		4.3		.2795		7.1	15/32	.4688	11.90
	.0177		.45		.0785	47			.1695	18			.2810	K			.4724	12.0
	.0180	77			.0787		2.0	11/64	.1719		4.36	9/32	.2812		7.14	31/64	.4844	12.30
	.0181		.46		.0807		2.05		.1730	17			.2835		7.2		.4921	12.5
	.0189		.48		.0810	46			.1732		4.4		.2854		7.25	1/2	.5000	12.70
	.0197		.5		.0820	45			.1770	16			.2874		7.3		.5118	13.0
	.0200	76			.0827		2.1		.1772		4.5		.2900	L		33/64	.5156	13.09
	.0210	75			.0846		2.15		.1800	15			.2913		7.4	17/32	.5312	13.49
	.0217		.55		.0860	44			.1811		4.6		.2950	M			.5315	13.5
	.0225	74			.0866		2.2		.1820	14			.2953		7.5	35/64	.5469	13.89
	.0236		.6		.0886		2.25		.1850	13		19/64	.2969		7.54		.5512	14.0
	.0240	73			.0890	43			.1850		4.7		.2992		7.6	9/16	.5625	14.28
	.0250	72			.0906		2.3		.1870		4.75		.3020	N			.5709	14.5
	.0256		.65		.0925		2.35	3/16	.1875		4.76		.3031		7.7	37/64	.5781	14.68
	.0260	71			.0935	42			.1890		4.8		.3051		7.75		.5906	15.0
	.0276		.7	3/32	.0938		2.38		.1890	12			.3071		7.8	19/32	.5938	15.08
	.0280	70			.0945		2.4		.1910	11			.3110		7.9	39/64	.6094	15.47
	.0292	69			.0960	41			.1929		4.9	5/16	.3125		7.93		.6102	15.5
	.0295		.75		.0965		2.45		.1935	10			.3150		8.0	5/8	.6250	15.87
	.0310	68			.0980	40			.1960	9			.3160	O			.6299	16.0
1/32	.0312		.79		.0981		2.5		.1969		5.0		.3189		8.1	41/64	.6406	16.27
	.0315		.8		.0995	39			.1990	8			.3228		8.2		.6496	16.5
	.0320	67			.1015	38			.2008		5.1		.3230	P		21/32	.6562	16.66
	.0330	66			.1024		2.6		.2010	7			.3248		8.25		.6693	17.0
	.0335		.85		.1040	37		13/64	.2031		5.16		.3268		8.3	43/64	.6719	17.06
	.0350	65			.1063		2.7		.2040	6		21/64	.3281		8.33	11/16	.6875	17.46
	.0354		.9		.1065	36			.2047		5.2		.3307		8.4		.6890	17.5
	.0360	64			.1083		2.75		.2055	5			.3320	Q		45/64	.7031	17.85
	.0370	63		7/64	.1094		2.77		.2067		5.25		.3346		8.5		.7087	18.0
	.0374		.95		.1100	35			.2087		5.3		.3386		8.6	23/32	.7188	18.25
	.0380	62			.1102		2.8		.2090	4			.3390	R			.7283	18.5
	.0390	61			.1110	34			.2126		5.4		.3425		8.7	47/64	.7344	18.65
	.0394		1.0		.1130	33			.2130	3		11/32	.3438		8.73		.7480	19.0
	.0400	60			.1142		2.9		.2165		5.5		.3445		8.75	3/4	.7500	19.05
	.0410	59			.1160	32		7/32	2188		5.55		.3465		8.8	49/64	.7656	19.44
	.0413		1.05		.1181		3.0		.2205		5.6		.3480	S			.7677	19.5
	.0420	58			.1200	31			.2210	2			.3504		8.9	25/32	.7812	19.84
	.0430	57			.1220		3.1		.2244		5.7		.3543		9.0		.7874	20.0
	.0433		1.1	1/8	.1250		3.17		.2264		5.75		.3580	T		51/64	.7969	20.24
	.0453		1.15		.1260		3.2		.2280	1			.3583		9.1		.8071	20.5
	.0465	56			.1280		3.25		.2283		5.8	23/64	.3594		9.12	13/16	.8125	20.63
3/64	.0469		1.19		.1285	30			.2323		5.9		.3622		9.2		.8268	21.0
	.0472		1.2		.1299		3.3		.2340	A			.3642		9.25	53/64	.8281	21.03
	.0492		1.25		.1339		3.4	15/64	.2344		5.95		.3661		9.3	27/32	.8438	21.43
	.0512		1.3		.1360	29			.2362		6.0		.3680	U			.8465	21.5
	.0520	55			.1378		3.5		.2380	B			.3701		9.4	55/64	.8594	21.82
	.0531		1.35		.1405	28			.2402		6.1		.3740		9.5		.8661	22.0
	.0550	54		9/64	.1406		3.57		.2420	C		3/8	.3750		9.52	7/8	.8750	22.22
	.0551		1.4		.1417		3.6		.2441		6.2		.3770	V			.8858	22.5
	.0571		1.45		.1440	27			.2460	D			.3780		9.6	57/64	.8906	22.62
	.0591		1.5		.1457		3.7		.2461		6.25		.3819		9.7		.9055	23.0
	.0595	53			.1470	26			.2480		6.3		.3839		9.75	29/32	.9062	23.01
	.0610		1.55		.1476		3.75	1/4	.2500	E	6.35		.3858		9.8		.9219	23.41
1/16	.0625		1.59		.1495	25			.2520		6.		.3860	W		59/64	.9252	23.5
	.0630		1.6		.1496		3.8		.2559		6.5		.3898		9.9	15/16	.9375	23.81
	.0635	52			.1520	24			.2570	F		25/64	.3906		9.92		.9449	24.0
	.0650		1.65		.1535		3.9		.2598		6.6		.3937		10.0	61/64	.9531	24.2
	.0669		1.7		.1540	23			.2610	G			.3970	X			.9646	24.5
	.0670	51		5/32	.1562		3.96		.2638		6.7		.4040	Y		31/32	.9688	24.6
	.0689		1.75		.1570	22		17/64	.2656		6.74	13/32	.4062		10.31		.9843	25.0
	.0700	50			.1575		4.0		.2657		6.75		.4130	Z		63/64	.9844	25.0
	.0709		1.8		.1590	21			.2660	H			.4134		10.5	1	1.0000	25.4
	.0728		1.85		.1610	20			.2677		6.8	27/64	.4219		10.71			

Index

Chilton's Repair & Tune-Up Guides

The Complete line covers domestic cars, imports, trucks, vans, RV's and 4-wheel drive vehicles.

RTUG Title	Part No.	RTUG Title	Part No.
AMC 1975-82 Covers all U.S. and Canadian models	7199	**Corvair 1960-69** Covers all U.S. and Canadian models	6691
Aspen/Volare 1976-80 Covers all U.S. and Canadian models	6637	**Corvette 1953-62** Covers all U.S. and Canadian models	6576
Audi 1970-73 Covers all U.S. and Canadian models.	5902	**Corvette 1963-84** Covers all U.S. and Canadian models	6843
Audi 4000/5000 1978-81 Covers all U.S. and Canadian models including turbocharged and diesel engines	7028	**Cutlass 1970-85** Covers all U.S. and Canadian models	6933
Barracuda/Challenger 1965-72 Covers all U.S. and Canadian models	5807	**Dart/Demon 1968-76** Covers all U.S. and Canadian models	6324
Blazer/Jimmy 1969-82 Covers all U.S. and Canadian 2- and 4-wheel drive models, including diesel engines	6931	**Datsun 1961-72** Covers all U.S. and Canadian models of Nissan Patrol; 1500, 1600 and 2000 sports cars; Pick-Ups; 410, 411, 510, 1200 and 240Z	5790
BMW 1970-82 Covers U.S. and Canadian models	6844	**Datsun 1973-80 Spanish**	7083
Buick/Olds/Pontiac 1975-85 Covers all U.S. and Canadian full size rear wheel drive models	7308	**Datsun/Nissan F-10, 310, Stanza, Pulsar 1977-86** Covers all U.S. and Canadian models	7196
Cadillac 1967-84 Covers all U.S. and Canadian rear wheel drive models	7462	**Datsun/Nissan Pick-Ups 1970-84** Covers all U.S. and Canadian models	6816
Camaro 1967-81 Covers all U.S. and Canadian models	6735	**Datsun/Nissan Z & ZX 1970-86** Covers all U.S. and Canadian models	6932
Camaro 1982-85 Covers all U.S. and Canadian models	7317	**Datsun/Nissan 1200, 210, Sentra 1973-86** Covers all U.S. and Canadian models	7197
Capri 1970-77 Covers all U.S. and Canadian models	6695	**Datsun/Nissan 200SX, 510, 610, 710, 810, Maxima 1973-84** Covers all U.S. and Canadian models	7170
Caravan/Voyager 1984-85 Covers all U.S. and Canadian models	7482	**Dodge 1968-77** Covers all U.S. and Canadian models	6554
Century/Regal 1975-85 Covers all U.S. and Canadian rear wheel drive models, including turbocharged engines	7307	**Dodge Charger 1967-70** Covers all U.S. and Canadian models	6486
Champ/Arrow/Sapporo 1978-83 Covers all U.S. and Canadian models	7041	**Dodge/Plymouth Trucks 1967-84** Covers all $1/2$, $3/4$, and 1 ton 2- and 4-wheel drive U.S. and Canadian models, including diesel engines	7459
Chevette/1000 1976-86 Covers all U.S. and Canadian models	6836	**Dodge/Plymouth Vans 1967-84** Covers all $1/2$, $3/4$, and 1 ton U.S. and Canadian models of vans, cutaways and motor home chassis	6934
Chevrolet 1968-85 Covers all U.S. and Canadian models	7135	**D-50/Arrow Pick-Up 1979-81** Covers all U.S. and Canadian models	7032
Chevrolet 1968-79 Spanish	7082	**Fairlane/Torino 1962-75** Covers all U.S. and Canadian models	6320
Chevrolet/GMC Pick-Ups 1970-82 Spanish	7468	**Fairmont/Zephyr 1978-83** Covers all U.S. and Canadian models	6965
Chevrolet/GMC Pick-Ups and Suburban 1970-86 Covers all U.S. and Canadian $1/2$, $3/4$ and 1 ton models, including 4-wheel drive and diesel engines	6936	**Fiat 1969-81** Covers all U.S. and Canadian models	7042
Chevrolet LUV 1972-81 Covers all U.S. and Canadian models	6815	**Fiesta 1978-80** Covers all U.S. and Canadian models	6846
Chevrolet Mid-Size 1964-86 Covers all U.S. and Canadian models of 1964-77 Chevelle, Malibu and Malibu SS; 1974-77 Laguna; 1978-85 Malibu; 1970-86 Monte Carlo; 1964-84 El Camino, including diesel engines	6840	**Firebird 1967-81** Covers all U.S. and Canadian models	5996
Chevrolet Nova 1986 Covers all U.S. and Canadian models	7658	**Firebird 1982-85** Covers all U.S. and Canadian models	7345
Chevy/GMC Vans 1967-84 Covers all U.S. and Canadian models of $1/2$, $3/4$, and 1 ton vans, cutaways, and motor home chassis, including diesel engines	6930	**Ford 1968-79 Spanish**	7084
Chevy S-10 Blazer/GMC S-15 Jimmy 1982-85 Covers all U.S. and Canadian models	7383	**Ford Bronco 1966-83** Covers all U.S. and Canadian models	7140
Chevy S-10/GMC S-15 Pick-Ups 1982-85 Covers all U.S. and Canadian models	7310	**Ford Bronco II 1984** Covers all U.S. and Canadian models	7408
Chevy II/Nova 1962-79 Covers all U.S. and Canadian models	6841	**Ford Courier 1972-82** Covers all U.S. and Canadian models	6983
Chrysler K- and E-Car 1981-85 Covers all U.S. and Canadian front wheel drive models	7163	**Ford/Mercury Front Wheel Drive 1981-85** Covers all U.S. and Canadian models Escort, EXP, Tempo, Lynx, LN-7 and Topaz	7055
Colt/Challenger/Vista/Conquest 1971-85 Covers all U.S. and Canadian models	7037	**Ford/Mercury/Lincoln 1968-85** Covers all U.S. and Canadian models of FORD Country Sedan, Country Squire, Crown Victoria, Custom, Custom 500, Galaxie 500, LTD through 1982, Ranch Wagon, and XL; MERCURY Colony Park, Commuter, Marquis through 1982, Gran Marquis, Monterey and Park Lane; LINCOLN Continental and Towne Car	6842
Corolla/Carina/Tercel/Starlet 1970-85 Covers all U.S. and Canadian models	7036	**Ford/Mercury/Lincoln Mid-Size 1971-85** Covers all U.S. and Canadian models of FORD Elite, 1983-85 LTD, 1977-79 LTD II, Ranchero, Torino, Gran Torino, 1977-85 Thunderbird; MERCURY 1972-85 Cougar,	6696
Corona/Cressida/Crown/Mk.II/Camry/Van 1970-84 Covers all U.S. and Canadian models	7044		

continued on next page

RTUG Title	Part No.
1983-85 Marquis, Montego, 1980-85 XR-7; LINCOLN 1982-85 Continental, 1984-85 Mark VII, 1978-80 Versailles	
Ford Pick-Ups 1965-86	6913
Covers all $1/2$, $3/4$ and 1 ton, 2- and 4-wheel drive U.S. and Canadian pick-up, chassis cab and camper models, including diesel engines	
Ford Pick-Ups 1965-82 Spanish	7469
Ford Ranger 1983-84	7338
Covers all U.S. and Canadian models	
Ford Vans 1961-86	6849
Covers all U.S. and Canadian $1/2$, $3/4$ and 1 ton van and cutaway chassis models, including diesel engines	
GM A-Body 1982-85	7309
Covers all front wheel drive U.S. and Canadian models of BUICK Century, CHEVROLET Celebrity, OLDSMOBILE Cutlass Ciera and PONTIAC 6000	
GM C-Body 1985	7587
Covers all front wheel drive U.S. and Canadian models of BUICK Electra Park Avenue and Electra T-Type, CADILLAC Fleetwood and deVille, OLDSMOBILE 98 Regency and Regency Brougham	
GM J-Car 1982-85	7059
Covers all U.S. and Canadian models of BUICK Skyhawk, CHEVROLET Cavalier, CADILLAC Cimarron, OLDSMOBILE Firenza and PONTIAC 2000 and Sunbird	
GM N-Body 1985-86	7657
Covers all U.S. and Canadian models of front wheel drive BUICK Somerset and Skylark, OLDSMOBILE Calais, and PONTIAC Grand Am	
GM X-Body 1980-85	7049
Covers all U.S. and Canadian models of BUICK Skylark, CHEVROLET Citation, OLDSMOBILE Omega and PONTIAC Phoenix	
GM Subcompact 1971-80	6935
Covers all U.S. and Canadian models of BUICK Skyhawk (1975-80), CHEVROLET Vega and Monza, OLDSMOBILE Starfire, and PONTIAC Astre and 1975-80 Sunbird	
Granada/Monarch 1975-82	6937
Covers all U.S. and Canadian models	
Honda 1973-84	6980
Covers all U.S. and Canadian models	
International Scout 1967-73	5912
Covers all U.S. and Canadian models	
Jeep 1945-87	6817
Covers all U.S. and Canadian CJ-2A, CJ-3A, CJ-3B, CJ-5, CJ-6, CJ-7, Scrambler and Wrangler models	
Jeep Wagoneer, Commando, Cherokee, Truck 1957-86	6739
Covers all U.S. and Canadian models of Wagoneer, Cherokee, Grand Wagoneer, Jeepster, Jeepster Commando, J-100, J-200, J-300, J-10, J20, FC-150 and FC-170	
Laser/Daytona 1984-85	7563
Covers all U.S. and Canadian models	
Maverick/Comet 1970-77	6634
Covers all U.S. and Canadian models	
Mazda 1971-84	6981
Covers all U.S. and Canadian models of RX-2, RX-3, RX-4, 808, 1300, 1600, Cosmo, GLC and 626	
Mazda Pick-Ups 1972-86	7659
Covers all U.S. and Canadian models	
Mercedes-Benz 1959-70	6065
Covers all U.S. and Canadian models	
Mereceds-Benz 1968-73	5907
Covers all U.S. and Canadian models	

RTUG Title	Part No.
Mercedes-Benz 1974-84	6809
Covers all U.S. and Canadian models	
Mitsubishi, Cordia, Tredia, Starion, Galant 1983-85	7583
Covers all U.S. and Canadian models	
MG 1961-81	6780
Covers all U.S. and Canadian models	
Mustang/Capri/Merkur 1979-85	6963
Covers all U.S. and Canadian models	
Mustang/Cougar 1965-73	6542
Covers all U.S. and Canadian models	
Mustang II 1974-78	6812
Covers all U.S. and Canadian models	
Omni/Horizon/Rampage 1978-84	6845
Covers all U.S. and Canadian models of DODGE omni, Miser, 024, Charger 2.2; PLYMOUTH Horizon, Miser, TC3, TC3 Tourismo; Rampage	
Opel 1971-75	6575
Covers all U.S. and Canadian models	
Peugeot 1970-74	5982
Covers all U.S. and Canadian models	
Pinto/Bobcat 1971-80	7027
Covers all U.S. and Canadian models	
Plymouth 1968-76	6552
Covers all U.S. and Canadian models	
Pontiac Fiero 1984-85	7571
Covers all U.S. and Canadian models	
Pontiac Mid-Size 1974-83	7346
Covers all U.S. and Canadian models of Ventura, Grand Am, LeMans, Grand LeMans, GTO, Phoenix, and Grand Prix	
Porsche 924/928 1976-81	7048
Covers all U.S. and Canadian models	
Renault 1975-85	7165
Covers all U.S. and Canadian models	
Roadrunner/Satellite/Belvedere/GTX 1968-73	5821
Covers all U.S. and Canadian models	
RX-7 1979-81	7031
Covers all U.S. and Canadian models	
SAAB 99 1969-75	5988
Covers all U.S. and Canadian models	
SAAB 900 1979-85	7572
Covers all U.S. and Canadian models	
Snowmobiles 1976-80	6978
Covers Arctic Cat, John Deere, Kawasaki, Polaris, Ski-Doo and Yamaha	
Subaru 1970-84	6982
Covers all U.S. and Canadian models	
Tempest/GTO/LeMans 1968-73	5905
Covers all U.S. and Canadian models	
Toyota 1966-70	5795
Covers all U.S. and Canadian models of Corona, MkII, Corolla, Crown, Land Cruiser, Stout and Hi-Lux	
Toyota 1970-79 Spanish	7467
Toyota Celica/Supra 1971-85	7043
Covers all U.S. and Canadian models	
Toyota Trucks 1970-85	7035
Covers all U.S. and Canadian models of pickups, Land Cruiser and 4Runner	
Valiant/Duster 1968-76	6326
Covers all U.S. and Canadian models	
Volvo 1956-69	6529
Covers all U.S. and Canadian models	
Volvo 1970-83	7040
Covers all U.S. and Canadian models	
VW Front Wheel Drive 1974-85	6962
Covers all U.S. and Canadian models	
VW 1949-71	5796
Covers all U.S. and Canadian models	
VW 1970-79 Spanish	7081
VW 1970-81	6837
Covers all U.S. and Canadian Beetles, Karmann Ghia, Fastback, Squareback, Vans, 411 and 412	

Chilton's Repair & Tune-Up Guides are available at your local retailer or by mailing a check or money order for **$13.95** plus **$3.25** to cover postage and handling to:

Chilton Book Company
Dept. DM
Radnor, PA 19089

NOTE: When ordering be sure to include your name & address, book part No. & title.